THE RISE
OF THE
WEHRMACHT

THE RISE
OF THE
WEHRMACHT

The German Armed Forces and World War II

Volume 2

Samuel W. Mitcham Jr.

PRAEGER SECURITY INTERNATIONAL
Westport, Connecticut • London

Library of Congress Cataloging-in-Publication Data

Mitcham, Samuel W.
  The rise of the Wehrmacht : the German armed forces and World War II /
Samuel W. Mitcham Jr.
      p. cm.
  Includes bibliographical references and index.
  ISBN 978-0-275-99641-3 (set : alk. paper) — ISBN 978-0-275-99659-8
(v. 1 : alk. paper) — ISBN 978-0-275-99661-1 (v. 2 : alk. paper)
  1. Germany—Armed Forces—History—World War, 1939–1945. 2. World
War, 1939–1945—Campaigns—Europe. 3. World War, 1939–1945—
Germany. I. Title.
  D757.M575 2008
  940.54′1343—dc22   2008000667

British Library Cataloguing in Publication Data is available.

Library of Congress Catalog Card Number: 2008000667

ISBN: 978-0-275-99641-3 (set)
        978-0-275-99659-8 (vol. 1)
        978-0-275-99661-1 (vol. 2)

First published in 2008

Praeger Security International, 88 Post Road West, Westport, CT 06881
An imprint of Greenwood Publishing Group, Inc.
www.praeger.com

Printed in the United States of America

The paper used in this book complies with the
Permanent Paper Standard issued by the National
Information Standards Organization (Z39.48–1984).

10   9   8   7   6   5   4   3   2   1

CONTENTS

Tables and Figures   ix

VOLUME 1

Preface   xiii

I	The Reichsheer	1
II	Enter Adolf Hitler	21
III	The Secret Rearmament	31
IV	Diplomatic Successes and Panzer Divisions	47
V	The Rhineland Crisis	59
VI	Expansion and Training	69
VII	The Luftwaffe Takes the Wrong Path	81
VIII	Expansion and Purges	101
IX	The Anschluss	117
X	The Sudetenland Crisis	127
XI	The Wehrmacht Expands Too Rapidly	155

Contents

XII	The Fall of Czechoslovakia	165
XIII	Over the Edge	171
XIV	Mobilization and Deployment	183
XV	First Blood: Poland, 1939	197
XVI	Sitzkrieg	219
XVII	Denmark and Norway	245
XVIII	The Manstein Plan	273
XIX	The Conquest of Holland	291
XX	The Drive to the Channel	303
XXI	The Battle of the Dunkirk Pocket	323
XXII	The Fall of France	333
XXIII	The Battle of Britain	349

VOLUME 2

XXIV	The Winter of Frustration, 1940–41	371
XXV	Hitler Comes to the Aid of His Ally	381
XXVI	The Balkans Campaign	387
XXVII	The Invasion of Crete	405
XXVIII	The Siege of Britain, Late 1940 to May 1941	421
XXIX	The North African Sideshow	431
XXX	Prelude to Barbarossa	439
XXXI	Operation Barbarossa: The Invasion of the Soviet Union	459
XXXII	Stalin's Winter Offensive, 1941–42	497

XXXIII	The Holocaust Begins	527
XXXIV	The Desert War	543
XXXV	Crisis in the Desert	557
XXXVI	The Battles of El Alamein	569
XXXVII	The Holocaust Continues	583
XXXVIII	The Battle of the North Atlantic, 1941–42	613
XXXIX	The Bombings Begin, 1942	623
XL	Hitler's Summer Offensive, 1942	631
XLI	The Battle of Stalingrad	651

Appendix 1. Table of Comparative Ranks 671

Appendix 2. German Staff Positions 674

Appendix 3. German Army Chain of Command: German Units, Ranks, and Strengths 675

Appendix 4. Characteristics of Selected Tanks 676

Appendix 5. Luftwaffe Aviation Units, Strengths and Ranks of Commanders 677

Bibliography 679

Index of German Military Units 695

General Index 705

Photo essays follow pages 182 (volume 1) and 542 (volume 2).

TABLES AND FIGURES

TABLES

3.1 The German Army Divisions, October 1934   34

3.2 German Naval Budgets, 1932–39   38

6.1 Organization of the German Army, End of 1935   70

7.1 Luftwaffe Territorial Organization, 1935   82

10.1 Order of Battle of the German Army, September 1938   145

10.2 Order of Battle of the Luftwaffe, September 1938   146

14.1 Panzer Formations in the Polish Campaign, 1939   187

14.2 German Army Order of Battle, September 1, 1939   190

14.3 Polish Army Order of Battle, September 1, 1939   193

16.1 Order of Battle of the Home Army, Spring 1940   221

16.2 Corps-Level Headquarters Established Between October 1939 and June 1940   224

16.3 Quarterly Allocation of Finished Steel, 1939–40   242

Tables and Figures

17.1 Order of Battle, German Forces Employed in the
Invasion of Denmark and Norway, April–June 1940 250

17.2 Naval Echelons Employed in Operation Wereruebung 253

23.1 Panzer Divisions Created in the Winter of 1940–41 351

23.2 Luftwaffe Order of Battle, Eagle Day, August 13, 1940 360

26.1 Order of Battle, Axis Forces Involved in the Invasions
of Yugoslavia and Greece, April 6, 1941 392

30.1 Order of Battle, OKH German Forces, Eastern
Front, June 22, 1941 445

30.2 Strength of the Luftwaffe by Aircraft Type, May 10,
1940, and June 21, 1941 448

34.1 Order of Battle of Opposing Forces, Operation
Crusader, November 1941 549

35.1 Opposing Tank Strength, North Africa, May 1942 558

35.2 Opposing Forces, Battle of the Gazala Line, May 1942 559

36.1 Strengths of Opposing Forces, Second Battle of
El Alamein, October 1942 576

37.1 Weekly Rations for Inmates in Class II Concentration Camps 593

40.1 The Odds on the Eastern Front, September 20, 1942 637

FIGURES

1.1 Europe, 1920–38 2

1.2 General Regions of the Third Reich 3

1.3 Austria, 1938 4

1.4 The Western Front 5

1.5 The North African Theater of Operations 6

1.6   The Eastern Front   7

1.7   The Major Cities of Germany   8

5.1   The Rhineland Demilitarized Zone   60

10.1 The Deployment Against Czechoslovakia   149

14.1 The Wehrkreise, 1939   184

14.2 Poland, 1939   189

15.1 The Invasion of Poland, 1939   202

17.1 The Conquest of Denmark   251

17.2 The Conquest of Norway   252

18.1 The Manstein Plan   275

18.2 German Dispositions, May 10, 1940   287

19.1 The Conquest of Holland   295

20.1 The Battle of Sedan   309

20.2 The Manstein Plan Completed   314

23.1 Great Britain, August 1940   361

26.1 The Conquest of Yugoslavia   395

26.2 The Greek Campaign   399

27.1 The Conquest of Crete   409

31.1 The Battles of Encirclement on the Eastern Front, 1941   472

31.2 The Battle of Kiev   485

31.3 The Vyazma-Bryansk Encirclement   488

31.4 Army Group Center, November 15 to December 5, 1941   493

Tables and Figures

32.1 The Battle of Moscow, January 1–14, 1942   511

32.2 Army Group South, November 28 to December 3, 1941   516

32.3 The Soviet Kerch Offensive, December 26, 1941
to January 18, 1942   518

32.4 Army Group North, January to March 1942   522

34.1 Operation Crusader, Phase 1   551

34.2 British Dispositions, January 1942   554

35.1 The Gazala Line, Phase 1   560

35.2 Rommel's Plan of Attack on Tobruk, June 17, 1942   565

36.1 El Alamein, July 1, 1942   570

36.2 The Battle of Alam Halfa Ridge   574

39.1 German Cities, 1942   624

40.1 Operation Blue: The Plan for the Summer Campaign of 1942   640

41.1 The Eastern Front, November 15, 1942   656

41.2 The Stalingrad Encirclement   659

CHAPTER XXIV

THE WINTER OF
FRUSTRATION, 1940–41

THE AIR WAR

Hitler's order to cancel Operation Sea Lion did not end the air war over Great Britain; in fact, he had little choice but to continue it. During the period September 7–15, 1940, British fighters had shot down 321 German warplanes (as opposed to British losses of 174 airplanes). By October 20, in a period of less than seven weeks, the Luftwaffe bomber wings had lost 30 to 35 percent of their strength and the fighter squadrons had lost 20 to 25 percent. General Moelders called it a "Verdun of the air."[1] For the first time, Luftwaffe morale began to deteriorate.

After commenting that "the fighters have let us down," Hermann Goering lost interest in the war once more.[2] He withdrew to the luxurious Ritz Hotel in Paris, where his signal officer caught him telling his wife on the telephone that he was at that very moment on the cliffs of Calais, watching his squadrons crossing the English Channel for Britain.

The raids on London continued, however. In the 57 days between September 7 and November 3, an average of 200 bombers per night attacked London.[3] Losses were heavy—55 airplanes on September 27 alone, and the Luftwaffe was not receiving enough replacement aircraft. In fact, in 1940 alone, aircraft factories in Great Britain outproduced those in Germany by 9,924 to 8,070 airplanes. On September 30, the Luftwaffe nevertheless launched another daylight raid over London and lost another 47 airplanes, as opposed to only 20 for Fighter Command. This brought German Air Force losses since June to 1,650—more than the Luftwaffe could afford. Accordingly, Goering finally changed tactics. The around-the-clock raids were to be abandoned, he ordered;

daylight bombing had proven too costly. Henceforth, the Luftwaffe was to attack only at night.

For a time, these tactics were quite effective. Night aerial warfare was in its infancy and the British, as of yet, had no effective countermeasures for nighttime bombers. Hitler continued this nighttime blitz against Britain, because he had publicly committed himself to heavy bombing raids; besides, they were damaging the economic infrastructure of the United Kingdom, and the raids were a safe way to continue the war without significant loss to the Luftwaffe. London was hit frequently, as were Manchester, Liverpool, Birmingham, Bristol, Glasgow, and other cities.

One of the most highly publicized raids occurred on the night of November 14, 1940, when Coventry was demolished. Coventry was a medieval city that boasted a beautiful fourteenth-century cathedral; it was perhaps even more famous for the legendary ride of Lady Godiva in the eleventh century; however, it was made mostly of wooden buildings and was burned almost totally to the ground when 437 He-111s dropped 450 tons of HE and incendiary bombs on it. More than 50,000 buildings were destroyed (including the cathedral), and 380 people were killed. One hundred and sixty-five of these people were so badly burned that identification was impossible and they had to be buried in a common grave.

Since the raid, the myth has grown that Coventry was not a military target, and Hitler devastated it solely for the purpose of striking a blow at British morale; furthermore, the story goes, Churchill and his government knew about the raid three days in advance, because his electronic warfare experts had cracked the German code. If he had evacuated the city, or so the tale continues, the Germans would have known that their code was broken, so Churchill deliberately withheld the news of the upcoming raid from the civil defense authorities, for the greater good of the war effort. None of this is true. First of all, Coventry *was* a military target; in fact, it housed one of the largest concentrations of armaments factories in Great Britain. Second, Churchill did not receive advanced warning; in fact, he expected a raid on London that night.

Fighter Command flew 165 sorties that night, but, since their planes were still not equipped with radar, they only managed to engage seven bombers and did not shoot down any of them. The only bomber Goering lost that night was a victim of ground fire.

The air campaign against Britain did not end with a bang; it merely petered out. The Luftwaffe flew 3,884 sorties in December 1940. The number gradually declined to 2,465 in January 1941, and to only 1,400 in February.[4] Meanwhile, the British began to receive huge amounts of aid from the United States, where President Franklin Roosevelt adopted a policy of "all aid short of war." On September 2, 1940, the Anglo-Americans signed an agreement by which London got 50 World War I destroyers (for use against the Wolf Packs), in exchange for 99-year leases on Great Exuma Island in the Bahamas, and on bases in Jamaica, Antigua, St. Lucia, Trinidad, and British Guiana. The British also turned over bases in Bermuda and Newfoundland—which freed more British forces for employment against Germany. The 50 destroyers—most of which had been in mothballs in the Philadelphia Naval Yard—were refitted and steamed to Halifax, Nova Scotia, where the Royal Navy took them over.

On November 5, 1940, Roosevelt was reelected for an unprecedented third term, but it was the closest election of his presidential career. Even so, in early December, he proposed what was soon introduced in Congress as the Lend-Lease Bill. It called for the United States to loan the United Kingdom $7 billion worth of American military equipment by June 30, 1942. According to the bill, London would have to return the guns, ships, and other equipment after the war. The Lend-Lease Act was passed by the U.S. Congress on March 11. It, in effect, placed half of the tremendous American economy and manufacturing might at the disposal of the British. A month later, the Americans quietly took control of Greenland (a Danish-owned island) and expelled the German detachments manning weather stations there.

Clearly the Americans, led by their president, were drifting closer and closer to war with the Third Reich.

THE NAVAL WAR

Even before the Luftwaffe became fully engaged in its life-and-struggle with the Royal Air Force, Admiral Karl Doenitz's U-boats returned to the Battle of the Atlantic. This time, they were equipped with torpedoes that worked and were in a much better geographic position. In June and July 1940, the Wehrmacht occupied the French ports on the Channel and the Bay of Biscay, giving the submarines forward bases that were much closer to the vital British shipping lanes. The convoys were now more vulnerable, because of the Royal Navy's losses in the Norwegian campaign and the evacuation of Dunkirk, coupled with the fact that the British had to keep strong naval forces in the home islands, in case Hitler did launch the threatened invasion. In addition, the French fleet was no longer available to assist in escort duties. As a result, many ships had to sail without a destroyer escort, and quite a few sailed alone. Also, few British aircraft were available to fly cover for merchant shipping.

June 1940 was the beginning of the first "Happy Time" in the history of the German submarine branch. They now had the use of French harbors and repair facilities, which were later protected by huge, concrete submarine "pins." These ports significantly reduced the U-boats' turnaround time to the shipping lanes and greatly increased the amount of time the submarine could remain in the battle zone. In June, U-boat aces sank 64 ships, totaling 260,500 tons—their highest total in any month to date. Only eight of these ships were sunk in convoy; all of the rest were unescorted vessels. Nazi Germany also had a new list of war heroes. Lieutenant Englebert Endrass in *U-46* sank six ships, and Lieutenant Hans Jenisch in *U-32* sank five, bringing his personal total to 10 ships and one destroyer. The big hero, however, was once again Guenther Prien, who sank 10 ships on one patrol.

July was another good month for the U-boats—they sank 267,000 tons of Allied and neutral shipping. This figure fell to 214,000 tons in August, but the British losses were still devastating. The effectiveness of the U-boats was enhanced by the Focke-Wulf 200, which began operating in July and August. The Condor, as it was called, was a four-engine transport developed by Lufthansa solely for long-range commercial fights. It was adapted to military purposes by the 40th Bomber Wing, operating out of Bordeaux-Merignac, and it was used as a long-range reconnaissance bomber. It still had all of the characteristics of a civilian airplane, however, and could easily be defeated by any known Allied fighter, provided that fighter could engage the Condor. The FW-200, however, had a range of 2,206 miles and operated at such distances from shore that it simply could not be reached by British fighters in 1940. It sank a number of Allied merchantmen itself (a modified, C-model Condor could carry 2.3 tons of bombs) and, by September 1940, had accounted for 90,000 tons of Allied shipping. Its main value, however, lay in its ability to locate Allied convoys and to relay that information to Admiral Doenitz. For this reason, Churchill called it "the scourge of the Atlantic." It would take the Allies years to completely solve the problem presented by the Condor, but they fought back by providing the convoys with CAMs (Catapult-Armed Merchantmen), which could launch fighter aircraft against the Condors. CAM-launched fighters had a major disadvantage, however; they could not be recovered and had to ditch into the ocean—an act that often had fatal consequences for the pilot.[5]

By now, Doenitz was working on his Wolf Pack tactics. The focus of the Battle of the Atlantic now shifted to the area the British called the Western Approaches: the route around Northern Ireland, through the North Channel, and across the Irish Sea to Britain's west-coast ports, Liverpool and Glasgow. Doenitz, therefore, deployed his U-boats in the waters of the Western Approaches north of the British Isles. When a convoy was spotted, a message was immediately dispatched to Doenitz's headquarters at Kerneval, near Lorient. Doenitz would then order all available U-boats to converge on the convoy. The first victim was SC 2, a convoy of 51 merchant ships. It was escorted part of the way by the Canadian Navy, and the Royal Navy was to escort it on its last leg; in the middle, however, it was on its own. Doenitz ordered four U-boats to intercept it. The head of this reception committee was Guenther Prien, who attacked the convoy at 11:30 P.M. on September 7 and was soon joined by Guenter Kuhnke in *U-28*. Between them, they sank five ships, and SC 2 was only saved from horrendous losses by the abysmal weather.

The next convoy, HX 72, was not so fortunate. On the night of September 21–22, a Wolf Pack attacked the 37 ship convoy and sank 14 of them. Lieutenant Joachim Schepke in *U-100* accounted for eight vessels, and Otto Krestschmer in *U-99* sank three. And so it went. By the end of September, the U-boat captains had sunk 59 ships, totaling 295,000 tons—a tremendous total, especially when one considers that Doenitz rarely had more than 30 operational submarines at any one time. The Wolf Pack's tactics had been proven effective, and undersea warfare had been revolutionized.

October was another disastrous month for the Allied convoys. On the 9th, Convoy SC 6 was attacked by two U-boats (*U-103* and *U-123*), and lost three ships. In the next six days, three more convoys lost 10 more ships. Then, for four horrifying days, SC 7 (35 ships) was brought under attack by Heinrich Bleichrodt's *U-48*, Georg Wilhelm Schulz's *U-124*, Heinrich Liebe's *U-38*, Karl-Heinz Mohle's *U-123*, Endrass's *U-46*, Fritz Frauenheim's *U-101*, Kretschmer's *U-99*, and Schepke's *U-100*. The German submariners scattered the convoy and sank 27 ships in all—a total of 105,000 tons. On board the downed ships were 200 tanks (enough to equip an entire armored division), 670 guns, 120 armored cars, 250 Bren carriers, 26,000 tons of ammunition, 3,000 rifles, 10,000 tons of rations, several tons of food, 2,100 tons of tank supplies and repair parts, and tens of thousands of gallons of gasoline.[6] The German propaganda ministry jubilantly dubbed this battle "The Night of the Long Knives." Total Allied losses to submarines for the month of October stood at 78 ships (60 lost in convoys, 15 unescorted vessels sunk, and three sunk by Italian submarines). Only the advent of winter weather (the winter of 1940–41 was one of the worst on record in the North Atlantic) brought the first "Happy Time" of the U-boats to an end.

By the end of 1940, only 22 German U-boats had been sunk. The number of operational U-boats, however, had dropped to 22, less than the total available at the beginning of the war. But, at last, the U-boat construction program—long delayed by Hermann Goering—was more than catching up with the losses, and the future looked grim for the United Kingdom. In 1940, almost 4 million tons of Allied and neutral shipping (1,059 ships) had been sunk—2,186,158 tons of it by U-boats.[7] Great Britain was slowly strangling under the effects of Hitler's blockade. Her imports had fallen drastically, as had her per capita calorie consumption. When 1941 began, it was by no means certain that Britain would be able to survive another year, even if Hitler did not invade the island.

THE GREAT DECISION

Hardly a month before his armies completed the conquest of France, Hitler made perhaps the greatest and most fateful decision of his career. He decided to invade the Soviet Union. As early as June 2, during a visit to Army Group A's headquarters in Charleville, he informed some of his officers (General of Infantry Georg von Sodenstern among them) that, after the anticipated peace with Great Britain, he would at last "be able to concentrate on [his] major and real task: the conflict with Bolshevism."[8]

Hitler had always looked on Russia as part of Germany's natural Lebensraum and had never been comfortable with the Soviet alliance, which was so dear to the heart of his foreign minister, Joachim von Ribbentrop. Hitler was quite upset by the aggressive tendencies Stalin exhibited when he was busy in the West. In 1939, the Reds invaded Finland and made territorial demands on Turkey. On June 15, the after day Hitler's divisions entered Paris, the Soviet Union occupied Lithuania. Shortly thereafter, Stalin annexed Latvia and Estonia as well.

Hitler and von Ribbentrop were completely taken aback by Stalin's actions in the Baltic area. It is true that, under the terms of the Moscow Pact, Estonia, Latvia, and most of Lithuania were in the Soviet sphere of interest, but, to the Germans, "sphere of interest" meant just that. They had no idea that Stalin intended to use the pact to annex the Baltic States—even the Mariampul area of southern Lithuania, which, according to the pact, was in the German sphere of interest.

The loss of the Baltic States was certainly economically damaging to the Third Reich, but Stalin was by no means through. On June 23, the day after the French signed the armistice at Compiegne, Molotov summoned Count Werner von der Schulenburg, the German ambassador, and told him that the Bessarabian question must be settled at once. Moscow, he said, was determined to use force if Romania did not peacefully accept Stalin's dictates. In addition, Molotov said, the Soviets were demanding that the Romanians hand over Bucovina, and he expected Berlin to support the Soviet claims. Bessarabia had belonged to Imperial Russia until the end of World War I, but the Soviets had absolutely no claim to Bucovina, nor was it in the Soviet sphere of influence as spelled out in the Ribbentrop-Molotov agreement of 1939.

The Soviet demand caused a great deal of alarm in Berlin, especially at OKW, because the German armed forces could not function without

Romanian oil. The Reich also imported large amounts of food and fodder from that country; however, the Wehrmacht was still too involved in the West to interfere with Stalin's aggression. The Romanians received the Soviet ultimatum on June 26, and it gave Bucharest less than 24 hours to cede Bessarabia and northern Bucovina or face the threat of Soviet invasion. Ribbentrop hastily sent instructions to his ambassador in Bucharest, telling him to advise the Romanians to accept the ultimatum. Obediently, Romania agreed the next day, and the Red Army marched into the territories the day after that. Berlin was relieved, because it would have lost almost all of its oil had the Soviets been given an excuse to seize all of Romania; nevertheless, the entire incident pointed out how vulnerable the economy of Nazi Germany was to Soviet aggression and how dangerous it was to have Joseph Stalin as a neighbor. In fact, since September 1939, the Soviet Union had annexed more than 286,000 square miles—an area containing 20 million people.

The Soviet annexation of Bessarabia and northern Bucovina, coupled with its annexation of Latvia, Lithuania, and Estonia, spurred Hitler to a decision. He told Jodl that he intended to invade Russia that fall, and on July 21, he instructed Brauchitsch to plan an autumn invasion of Soviet Russia. The army commander-in-chief was now completely cowed by the domineering Fuehrer, but, for once, the normally wooden-headed Field Marshal Keitel opposed Adolf Hitler's plans and sent him a detailed written memorandum, enumerating the reasons why this plan was impossible to execute.[9] The bulk of the armed forces were in the West and the transportation difficulties would be insurmountable, even if it were not too late in the season to begin a campaign in Russia, which it was. On this occasion, Hitler listened to military reason and moved the date of the invasion back to the spring of 1941.

Was the plan to invade the Soviet Union in 1941 meant to be a preventive stroke, or was it an act of aggression? Actually, it was both. In view of the Soviet actions and attitudes since August 1939, Hitler was convinced that Stalin would not keep to the letter of any agreement any longer than it was in his interest to do so. Russia's entire policy in 1940 had been aimed at Soviet domination of southeastern and northeastern Europe. "Hitler was not prepared to accept the risk of conducting [a] war in which he was dependent on the goodwill of Stalin, whose ambitions he assessed rather more realistically than either Churchill or Roosevelt," Wolfgang Koch wrote.[10]

On July 29, Hitler told his staff generals that Britain's only remaining hopes were the United States and the Soviet Union. If Russia were destroyed, the United States would also be effectively eliminated from the European geopolitical calculations, because it would be too busy with Japan in the Pacific. If Russia were overwhelmed, Britain's last chance would be gone. Germany would then be the master of Europe and the Balkans.[11]

Foerster pointed out that, between 1935 and 1940, Hitler and his generals refused to recognize one of the lessons of the 1914–18 war: that a Continental War could not remain limited to Europe. In the summer of 1940, according to Foerster, Hitler recognized the basic facts of Germany's position more fully than his strategic advisers. He understood that Germany was not capable of winning a worldwide war. To him, the conquest of Russia was looked on as a panacea for both the strategic dilemma facing the Reich and for Germany's inferior capabilities for sustaining a war of attrition.[12] Despite his later claims that he opposed the entire venture, Halder enthusiastically went to work on the detailed planning for the invasion. In fact, he had preceded the dictator. Quite independently, Halder had begun to plan a preventive military blow against the Soviet Union in mid-June, and, by July 3, the General Staff was already engaged in a detailed study of the "Eastern Question," almost four weeks before the Fuehrer gave them the go-ahead.[13]

Hitler, at this time, was pursuing a multifaceted policy of waging a delusitory war against England while simultaneously maintaining peace in the Balkans and preparing to invade the Soviet Union. Grand Admiral Raeder, meanwhile, was looking for another way to attack Great Britain, now that the idea of a direct assault (Operation Sea Lion) had been ruled out. He felt strongly that the United Kingdom should be defeated before the invasion of the Soviet Union took place. On September 26, he met with the Fuehrer and tried to divert his attention to the Mediterranean, where the Italians had become the main focus of the British offensive war effort. Rome did not yet realize this, Raeder said, which is why it turned down German offers of military aid; however, he added, it was of vital importance that Germany clear up the situation in the Mediterranean during the winter (that is, before the invasion of the Soviet Union).

Hitler asked how the grand admiral thought the situation in the Mediterranean could be settled. Raeder had a ready answer: seize Gibraltar, the Suez Canal, and the Canary Islands. Once the Suez was captured, German forces could advance through Palestine and Syria as far as the Turkish border. He also stated (correctly) that the United States would eventually enter the war on the side of the United Kingdom, and the Anglo-American and Gaullist forces would try to take advantage of the weakness of Vichy France to seize French North Africa. Germany, he declared, should preempt them by taking this strategically important region themselves. The Grand Admiral was, in fact, trying to convince Hitler to adopt a peripheral strategy against the

British Empire by striking it in what he considered to be vulnerable areas: the Near and Middle East, the Iberian peninsula, and Africa.

Erich Raeder certainly gave Hitler enough to think about. The dictator ordered the National Defense Department of OKW (General Warlimont and his staff) to study the proposed operations, while he discussed them with Mussolini, Franco, and Petain. He arranged to meet with Franco at Hendaye, a small town on the French-Spanish border, on October 23—beginning one of the most frustrating weeks of Adolf Hitler's life.

Franco refused to enter the war on the side of the Third Reich and would not cooperate with the plan to seize Gibraltar. In the end, he agreed to sign a treaty with Germany, but he insisted on so many restrictions and reservations that it would have amounted to little more than a mutual expression of good will, which is all Hitler could get out of the nine-hour conference. He later told Mussolini, "Rather than go through that again, I would prefer to have two or three teeth pulled out."[14]

The following day, Hitler met with Marshal Petain at Montoire, which was within the German zone of occupation. Hitler respected the 84-year-old victor of Verdun; however, he was no more successful with him than with Franco. Petain also refused to enter the war on the side of the Third Reich.

The Hendaye and Montoire conferences doomed Raeder's effort to develop a peripheral strategy against the British Empire. Predictably, Hitler was in a foul mood when he arrived in Munich on October 27, but, instead of going to Berchtesgaden or returning to Berlin, he reboarded his train and headed south, for Italy, because rumors had reached his ears that Mussolini intended to invade Greece. The Fuehrer had no territorial ambitions in the Balkans, which he rightly regarded as a powder keg. Now that Germany had succeeded in penetrating the region economically, Hitler's only desire was that peace be maintained in those troubled lands. His sole reason for going to Italy was to prevent his Axis partner from doing anything foolish in that region.

However, when Hitler dismounted his train in Florence on the morning of October 28, Mussolini greeted him with these incredible words: "Fuehrer, we are on the march! Victorious Italian troops crossed the Greco-Albanian frontier at dawn today!"

NOTES

1. Galland, pp. 46, 78.
2. Telford Taylor, *The Breaking Wave* (1967), p. 204 (hereafter cited as Taylor, *Breaking Wave*).
3. Shirer, p. 781.

4. Walter A. Musciano, *Messerschmitt Aces* (1982), p. 20.

5. Wood and Gunston, pp. 170–71.

6. Edwin P. Hoyt, *The U-Boat Wars* (1984; reprint ed., 1986), pp. 69–80 (hereafter cited as Hoyt).

7. Baldwin, *Critical Years*, pp. 162–63.

8. Gerhard Schreiber, "The Mediterranean in Hitler's Strategy in 1940. 'Programme' and Military Planning," in *The German Military in the Age of Total War*, Wilhelm Deist, ed. (1985), p. 243 (hereafter cited as Schreiber).

9. Walter Warlimont, "German Estimate of the United States, Russia, and Dakar," ETHINT 8, August 9, 1945.

10. H. W. Koch, "Hitler's 'Programme' and the Genesis of Operation 'Barbarossa'," in Koch, *Aspects*, p. 319.

11. See Halder Diaries, July 22, 1940 and subsequent entries; also see *DGFP*, vol. 10, pp. 549–50.

12. Foerster, "Volkegemeinschaft," p. 213.

13. Schreiber, p. 244.

14. Robert Payne, *The Life and Death of Adolf Hitler* (1973), p. 407 (hereafter cited as Payne).

CHAPTER XXV

HITLER COMES TO THE AID OF HIS ALLY

MUSSOLINI'S INVASION OF GREECE

Like most of Mussolini's military campaigns, his Greek adventure was a disaster. General Sebastiano Viscounti-Prasca's invasion forces (140,000 men in six divisions, plus one in reserve) attacked with two corps abreast, one on either side of the Pindus mountain range. The offensive developed into a three-prong thrust along a 140-mile front, with the northern thrust aimed at Salonika on the northern Aegean coast and the southern wing heading south, down the Adriatic coast. The middle attack was aimed at Metzovon Pass, a strategic point on the Pindus Mountains.[1] By sheer weight of numbers, the Italians (who outnumbered the Greeks six to one) made progress through the mountainous terrain, in spite of the terrible weather. The initial objective in the center was the town of Kalpaki, from which they planned to drive on to Janina, and then to the Metzovon Pass. The Italians captured Kalpaki on October 29, and by November 2 had taken the Grambala Heights, overlooking the town. Here, 15 miles from Metzovon Pass, they were checked. The Greeks counterattacked and recaptured the heights on November 3; the Italians retook the place on the 8th, but the Greeks took it back the same day. An Italian effort to retake the heights the following day was repulsed.

Mussolini responded to this defeat by sacking Visconti-Prasca on November 9 and replacing him with General Ubaldo Soddu, the undersecretary of state for war and deputy chief of the General Staff of the Army, but a poor field commander. He would last only seven weeks. On December 4, the Duce also fired Marshal Badoglio, chief of the General Staff of the Army since 1925 (described by Baldwin as "old and indecisive, a weak man"[2]) and replaced him with General Ugo

Cavallero. Count Galeazzo Ciano, the son-in-law of the dictator and a major instigator of the war, was not punished nor, of course, was Mussolini himself.

The appointment of Cavallero genuinely astonished the Italian people. He had been involved in a naval construction scandal in the 1930s and was widely regarded as a crook who had narrowly avoided prison. He owed his new position solely to his political influence with Mussolini. Naturally, the average Italian soldier had little confidence in him, and his appointment did nothing to improve sagging Italian morale. Before the campaign was over, however, the suave Cavallero would have the dual role of chief of staff and field commander in Albania.

Meanwhile, the Greeks mobilized. Ultimately, Greek President Joannis Metaxas—who had German military training—was able to reinforce his field commander, General Alexandros Papagos, to a strength of five corps: 15 infantry divisions, four infantry brigades, and a cavalry division.[3] They launched a massive counteroffensive at dawn on November 14. By November 17, the Italians were in full retreat all along the front. By the end of December, Mussolini had lost 20,000 men killed, 40,000 wounded, and 26,000 captured or missing. An additional 18,000 had been crippled with frostbite. The Greeks overran the southern quarter of Albania and did not halt until December 28, because they had outrun their supply lines. Although they had gained an impressive amount of ground and held a line running from Pogradec in the east to the Ionian Sea just north of Khimara in the west, the Greeks could not advance much further in any case; on the flatter terrain to the north, the Greek infantry would have met Italian armored units, and the Greeks had virtually no tanks and almost no anti-tank weapons. As a result, the front stabilized along the Pogradec-Khimara line, and the war was stalemated. Meanwhile, much to Hitler's chagrin, Mussolini's ill-planned invasion opened the door to British intervention in the Balkans. On October 29, the day after the Italian attack began, British troops began to land on the strategic island of Crete, and, on November 3, the first Royal Air Force units landed on the mainland of Greece.

Adolf Hitler was irritated. Contrary to all of his carefully laid plans, the Balkans had become a theater of war. The next day, he ordered the General Staff to prepare plans for the invasion of Greece.

NORTH AFRICA: THE ROUT OF THE ROMANS

And what was happening in North Africa while Mussolini was busy plotting his Greek disaster? The answer was, very little. Italy, it will be recalled, declared war on France and Great Britain on June 10. In North Africa, Italy appeared to have an overwhelming advantage over the

British in 1940. Marshal Rudolfo Graziani had 250,000 men. He was opposed by the Western Desert Force (later designated XIII Corps) under Lieutenant General Sir Richard O'Connor, which consisted of only two understrength divisions. All totaled, O'Connor could muster only about 30,000 combat effectives.

In war, numbers can be quite misleading. Nowhere is the truth of this statement better illustrated than in North Africa in 1940. The Italian Army was one of the worst in Europe. Its weapons dated from World War I, and it had few anti-tank weapons, had little modern artillery, was badly fed, was indifferently equipped, and had bad morale and low fighting spirit. Its tanks were called "self-propelled coffins" by the rank and file and were no match for even the poorest British tank. Even more seriously in the desert, its infantry was non-motorized or "marching infantry" and, as the British would soon prove, mobility in the desert was essential not for victory, but for mere survival; yet the Italian soldier walked everywhere he went. Under such a handicap, he could easily be cut off or bypassed by the fast, mobile British.

Graziani did not want to attack at all; then, on September 13, Mussolini gave him a choice: invade Egypt within two days or be relieved of his command. Graziani's strike force, General Mario Berti's 10th Army, crossed the "wire" (the Egyptian-Libyan border) on September 15. His spearheads reached the village of Sidi Barrani, 65 miles inside Egypt, on September 16. Here, to the surprise of the British, the Italians halted, rested, and began building up supplies and strong points. Despite their overwhelming numbers, they completely surrendered the initiative to their opponents.

While the Italians did nothing and the Western Desert Force prepared for an offensive of its own, Hitler made his first overture to Mussolini concerning the possibility of using panzer units in the desert. The Italian dictator turned him down flat, telling one of his generals that, if the Germans ever got a foothold in North Africa, they would never get them out.

Meanwhile, the naval war in the Mediterranean began in earnest, and the Italians suffered a shattering defeat. On November 11, 1940, the Royal Navy escorted the aircraft carrier *Illustrious* to within 170 miles of the huge Italian naval base at Taranto, on the heel of the Italian "boot." At 9 P.M., it launched 21 Swordfish airplanes—slow, lumbering, obsolete biplanes. Just before midnight, they attacked the Italian battleships, which were at anchor in the harbor. The *Cavour* was so heavily damaged that it was never used again. (It was refloated but still unrepaired at the end of the war.) The *Littorio* was knocked out of action for five months, and the *Duilio* was nonoperational for about six months. In one action, according to Admiral Andrew B. Cunningham, the commander of the British Mediterranean Fleet, 21 obsolete biplanes had inflicted more damage on the Italian Fleet than the Royal Navy had inflicted on the German High Seas Fleet in the Battle of Jutland.[4] "Half of the Italian battlefleet had been put out of action ... by the expenditure of 11 torpedoes and the loss of two aircraft."[5]

More important even than these losses was the permanent effect the Battle of Taranto had on the morale of the Italian Navy. It never did attempt to challenge the Royal Navy to a major battle on the high seas, not even in 1941, when it had every chance of winning such a battle. In fact, the Italian surface fleet became an international joke. "While the U.S. Navy drinks whiskey and the British Navy prefers rum, the Italian Navy sticks to port," the BBC quipped.[6] This they certainly did. Taranto seemed to convince the Italian Navy of its own inferiority in relation to the British, and it never recovered its morale throughout the war.

In the meantime, O'Connor and his superior, General Sir Archibald Wavell, prepared to deal a devastating blow to the Italian Army. Wavell liked to do the unexpected. "Never let yourself be trammeled by the bonds of orthodoxy," he said. "Always think for yourself ... and remember that the herd is usually wrong."[7] Under Wavell's direction, O'Connor massed a fully motorized strike force of 31,000 men and 275 tanks near Graziani's Sidi Barrani concentration and launched a surprise offensive at 7 A.M. on December 9. Before the day was over, he had captured 81,000 Italians. Astonished by his success, Wavell quickly developed his limited objective offensive into a full-scale invasion of Libya. By December 16, the Italian 10th Army was a disorganized rabble as men threw away their weapons and streamed to the rear, hoping to find safety in the coastal fortresses of Bardia and Tobruk. But there was no safety in either place.

O'Connor attacked Bardia on January 3, 1941. Two days later, it was all over. The British captured another 45,000 prisoners, along with 462 guns, 127 inferior tanks, and 700 rucks. They suffered fewer than 500 casualties.

The fall of Bardia staggered the Italians. If the Allies could not be halted at Bardia, which was generally considered the best fortress in Libya, then where could they be stopped? Suddenly, Italian resistance collapsed everywhere. Tobruk fell on January 22, after resisting for two days. It yielded 25,000 more prisoners and 87 tanks, at a cost of less than 400 Allied casualties. Sollum and Derna also quickly collapsed, and Benghazi was encircled on February 3. Finally, on February 6, 3,000 British and Australian troops, supported by only 32 tanks, cut off the remnants of the Italian 10th Army at Beda Fomm, well south of the Cyrenaican capital. They captured 20,000 Italians, who had 216 field guns and about 100 tanks. "The police in Tel Aviv gave us a better fight than this," one Australian observed.[8] Finally, Benghazi capitulated on February 7, and the British halted their offensive at El Agheila, within striking distance of Tripoli, the last major seat of resistance in what was left of Italian North Africa. In less than two months the Italians had lost 130,000 men, 1,300 guns, 380 tanks, and 241 aircraft. In the process, they had inflicted fewer than 2,000 casualties (500 killed, 1,373 wounded, and 55 missing) on the forces of the British Empire.[9] All that remained of Mussolini's previously vast North African possessions was Tripoli, which was defended by a makeshift garrison of two infantry divisions, a reinforced artillery regiment, and remnants of three other divisions, all holding a 12-mile semicircular perimeter around the city. Clearly, one more push would have wiped out the Italian Empire in North Africa.

"The Italian troops had, with good reason, lost all confidence in their arms and acquired a very serious inferiority complex, which was to remain with them throughout the war," Erwin Rommel observed.[10]

Adolf Hitler also had some observations to make. On February 6, he told his staff officers:

The loss of North Africa could be withstood in a military sense but have a strong psychological effect on Italy. Britain could hold a pistol at Italy's head.... The British would have the free use of a dozen divisions and could employ them most dangerously.... We must make every effort to prevent this.[11]

After conferring with Mussolini at the end of January, Hitler decided to send a force of two divisions to North Africa, to tie down the Western Desert Force and save the remnants of Tripoltania for his embarrassed ally, who was now definitely the junior partner in the Axis. This force, soon to become famous worldwide as the Afrika Korps (*Deutsche Afrika Korps* or DAK), consisted of the 5th Light and 15th Panzer Divisions. Initially, Major General Baron Hans von Funck, the commander of the 5th Light, was selected to command the new corps; however, he briefed Hitler on the situation in early February, and the Fuehrer was singularly unimpressed. Consequently, on February 6, Hitler named Erwin Rommel commander of the DAK and the German forces in Libya. Baron von Funck (who was held in higher esteem by OKH than by Hitler) succeeded Rommel as commander of the 7th Panzer Division, which was then on garrison duty in France. Two days later, the first German units left Naples by sea for Tripoli. The legend of the Desert Fox had begun.

NOTES

1. Jon Guttman, "Bid for Roman Empire," *World War II*, vol. 5, no. 4 (November 1990), p. 24 (hereafter cited as Guttman, "Bid").

2. Baldwin, *Critical Years*, p. 160.

3. Guttman, "Bid," p. 24.

4. Baldwin, *Critical Years*, p. 160.

5. Playfair, vol. 1, pp. 237–38.

6. Reynolds and Eleanor Packard, *Balcony Empire* (1942), p. 25 (hereafter cited as Packard).

7. John Strawson, *The Battle for North Africa* (1969), p. 10 (hereafter cited as Strawson).

8. Richard L. Collier and the editors of Time-Life Books, *War in the Desert* (1979), p. 32 (hereafter cited as Collier).

9. Goralski, p. 146.

10. Rommel Papers, p. 97.

11. Desmond Young, *Rommel: Desert Fox* (1950 edition), p. 82 (hereafter cited as Young, *Rommel*).

CHAPTER XXVI

THE BALKANS CAMPAIGN

STALEMATE

Why did the British fail to destroy the remnants of Graziani's deci-mated Italian forces and completely annihilate the Fascist empire in North Africa before the Afrika Korps could come to Mussolini's aid? The reason was Winston Churchill. He and his advisers had no doubt that every effort should be made to help the Greeks, so they sent their best forces from Libya to Greece. Both Wavell and Eden pointed out that it was bad strategy to split their efforts between these two places; the best thing to do would be to complete the conquest of North Africa and then send aid to Greece. In Churchill's view, however, the Greek situation had priority over all others. During the first week of November, without bothering to consult with Wavell, Churchill began to strip Middle East Command of its aircraft.

In the meantime, Adolf Hitler was not idle. Mussolini's blunder and the incompetence of his military commanders, coupled with increased Soviet pressure on Bulgaria, forced him to draw the conclusion that the Balkan countries must be officially brought into the Axis immediately, or they might eventually end up on the side of the Allies. On November 20, 1940, Hungary formally acceded to the Tripartite Pact between Germany, Italy, and Japan (which had been signed on September 27, 1940). Three days later Romania signed and agreed to accept a second German division (the 16th Panzer). Despite the pressure that Hitler exerted, both diplomatically and in a personal interview, King Boris of Bulgaria balked at formally allying with the Axis, but agreed to pro-vide Germany with whatever facilities she needed within her borders, mainly because he preferred Hitler's "protection" to Stalin's. Yugosla-via and Turkey remained noncommittal.

Meanwhile, Hitler tried to divert Russian expansionist ambitions into channels other than the Balkans. He wanted to interest Stalin and his colleagues in a southern drive to the Persian Gulf or the Arabian Sea. The Soviets, however, were more interested in the Dardanelles and the Danube area, which put their political and military aspirations on a collision course with the economic interests of the Third Reich. The overall deterioration in relations led to a summit conference between Molotov and Hitler and von Ribbentrop in Berlin on November 12 and 13, 1940. Hitler and Ribbentrop tried to divert Soviet territorial aspirations to the south, toward the Indian Ocean, but the Soviet foreign minister bluntly demanded, among other things, that Germany withdraw its protection from Finland (from which the Reich received 60 percent of its nickel), revoke its guarantee of Romania's frontiers, and support Moscow's claim to Southern Bukovina. These things Hitler refused to do and the meetings broke up with hard feelings all around.

If these failed negotiations did not finally convinced Hitler to invade the Soviet Union in the spring of 1941, the dispatch that Molotov handed Ambassador von der Schulenburg in Moscow on November 25 concluded the matter. As a price for joining the Tripartite Pact, Stalin demanded the withdrawal of all German forces from Finland. Russia was to receive land and naval bases and the right to station troops at the Bosphorus and the Dardanelles; should Turkey balk at this demand, Germany and the other Tripartite powers would take military action against her. The Kremlin demanded that Berlin recognize Soviet claims to the territory south of Baku and Batum, in the direction of the Persian Gulf. Also, Japan would have to cede its concessions for the exploitation of oil and coal resources in North Sakhalin to Russia, and all secret Russo-German treaties would be abrogated in Russia's favor. Stalin also in effect demanded control of the Persian Gulf and Arabian oilfields, which supplied Europe with much of its oil.[1]

Hitler read the dispatch, lay it on his desk, and did not bother to reply. "The dice had been cast," Koch wrote later.[2] He ordered Halder to bring him the General Staff's plan for the invasion of the Soviet Union. After a four-hour conference, he approved it on December 5. Among other things, the plan called for preparations to be completed by May 15, 1941, which was the target date for the invasion to begin. In the meantime, Hitler had to clear up the situation in the Balkans.

BEFORE THE STORM

The Balkan situation smoldered throughout the winter of 1940–41, as an uneasy stalemate descended on the region. On January 29, 1941, General Metaxas died after a short illness and was replaced as premier by Alexander Koryzis, a civilian who lacked Metaxas's decisiveness and ability to rally the nation. Meanwhile, the Wehrmacht prepared for the invasion of Greece and steadily infiltrated its men into Bulgaria.

Several hundred Luftwaffe personnel, dressed in civilian clothes, were already preparing landing fields for the Stukas and other airplanes and were getting ready for the arrival of the VIII Air Corps. Elsewhere, engineers and technicians studied the Bulgarian transportation system, and Hitler and the German diplomats continued to try to induce Yugoslavia and Bulgaria into joining the Tripartite Pact.

On January 23, 1940, Bulgaria secretly agreed to join the Axis, but, because of its fear of Turkey's reaction, delayed the actual signing for six weeks, until German engineers could complete the bridging of the Danube, and German troops from northern Dobruja were in a position to enter the country in strength. In exchange for the alliance, Ribbentrop and Ciano assured the Bulgarians that the postwar Balkan frontiers would give Bulgaria an outlet to the Aegean. (This alliance, incidentally, cost King Carol his life; he was poisoned by unknown assassins in 1943.)

By the end of January, the German plan for the invasion of Greece was far advanced. By that time, the headquarters of the 12th Army (Wilhelm List) and the 1st Panzer Group (Ewald von Kleist) were in Romania, as were three corps headquarters and four full-strength divisions, two of which were panzer. Bulgaria signed the Tripartite Pact in Vienna on March 1, and German troops officially entered Bulgaria at 6 A.M. on March 2. Simultaneously, Baron von Richthofen's VIII Air Corps began moving into the country and was almost completely operational by March 4.

The German entry into Bulgaria sent shock waves through Belgrade and Athens. Defeatism became widespread in Greece, as few in the government or the general population had any illusions that they could defeat the Italians *and* the Germans. Athens did, however, finally agree to accept British ground forces, leading Churchill to immediately strip Wavell and the Western Desert Force of its best ground units, some of which were already prepared for immediate shipment. The first British units arrived in Greece on March 7. Eventually, the British Expeditionary Force (under General Maitland "Jumbo" Wilson) was suppose to include three infantry divisions, the 1st Armored Brigade, and the Polish Brigade, but only 58,000 men (excluding air force personnel) had arrived when the German attack broke.

In the meantime, the Yugoslavs, now isolated by the Bulgarian decision to join the Axis, were more willing to discuss signing the Tripartite Pact, and Prince Regent Paul met with Hitler at the Berghof on March 4. In the end, however, the prince regent, who was personally pro-British, said that he wished to reserve his decision.[3]

Diplomatic haggling with Yugoslavia continued for some time, but made no progress, despite Hitler's willingness to make concessions. Finally, on March 22, the Crown Council seemed on the verge of accepting Hitler's offers, when its three Serbian ministers resigned in protest. It would take time to replace them, and Yugoslavia's decision on the pact was again postponed. This was too much for von Ribbentrop. On March 23, he gave Belgrade a deadline of March 25.[4]

Ribbentrop's deadline (it was not quite an ultimatum) did the trick, and Prince Paul decided to join the Axis. On March 25, Prime Minister Dragisha Cvetkovic and Foreign Minister Aleksander Cincar-Marcovic signed the Tripartite Pact in Vienna. Hitler, much relieved, was delighted by the prince's decision, but his diplomatic victory was destined to be short lived.

Unfortunately for the Yugoslav government, it had done nothing to prepare its people for this radical change of policy. During the night of March 26–27, a military coup overthrew the government. When Hitler awoke on March 27, he learned that 17-year-old King Peter II had acceded to the Yugoslavian throne and Prince Paul and his family had been exiled to Greece. At the same time, Cvetkovic had been replaced by General Dusan Simovic, the Pan-Slavic commander of the Yugoslav Air Force, who was known to be anti-German—and was even suspected of being a Russian agent.[5] His first act was to seal the country's frontiers. Belgrade and several other Serbian cities were rocked by anti-German demonstrations, and the Yugoslav Army mobilized on March 29, even though the new Yugoslavian foreign minister, Momcilo Nincic, immediately assured the German ambassador that his country wanted to maintain friendly relations with Germany.

Adolf Hitler did not believe Nincic's assurances of friendship and neutrality. At 1 P.M. on March 27, he met with Keitel, Jodl, Brauchitsch, Halder, Goering, Jeschonnek, and Ribbentrop and told them that, sooner or later, the Yugoslavians would join the Western Allies. Therefore, he had decided to "destroy Yugoslavia as a military power and a sovereign state with a minimum of delay." He asked Brauchitsch and Goering to submit their plans for the invasion of Yugoslavia as quickly as possible.[6]

Aware that the Germans were feverishly preparing to invade, the Simovic government did everything it could to meet the threat. Simovic even sent a delegation to Moscow, to sign a pact of mutual assistance with the Soviet Union. Stalin, however, did not want a military showdown with the Wehrmacht, so they signed a treaty of friendship and non-aggression two days later.

Working under tremendous pressure, OKH developed an outline plan for the combined invasion of Greece and Yugoslavia within 24 hours of the coup in Belgrade. List's 12th Army (which controlled the 1st Panzer Group) retained responsibility for the Greek invasion, but its area of operation was extended to include southern Yugoslavia. Colonel General Baron Maximilian von Weichs's 2nd Army (which was in Munich, while its training divisions were stationed in southern Germany) was sent to Graz, Austria, and was given the task of capturing Belgrade and overrunning northern Yugoslavia.

On the afternoon of March 29, Lieutenant General Friedrich Paulus, the deputy chief of staff for operations at OKH, presided over a special conference in Vienna, in which the final details for the invasions were worked out. Also present were Field Marshal List; Baron von Weichs; Colonel General von Kleist, commander of the 1st Panzer Group (formerly Panzer Group Kleist); and their chiefs of staff. Final dispositions for the offensive were made, movement schedules were hammered out, and the timetable for the invasion was determined.

Hitler's original plan for Operation 25 called for an air bombardment of Belgrade and air attacks against the ground installations of the Yugoslavian Air Force to take place on April 1. The invasion of Greece (Operation Marita) would begin on April 2 or 3, followed by the ground invasion of Yugoslavia between April 8 and 15. The generals, however, took the sensible step of delaying the initial air attacks so that they would coincide more closely with the ground attack on Greece. Under the revised timetable, the air attack would be launched on April 6; simultaneously, 12th Army would attack Greece, and the XXXXVI Panzer Corps of 2nd Army would attack into Yugoslavia, seize the bridges over the Drava River, and begin the drive on Belgrade on April 8. The entire 2nd Army would go over to the offensive by April 12.

Basically, the German plan envisioned concentric and converging attacks against Yugoslavia and Greece from Austria, Hungary, Romania, and Bulgaria. The German attack forces included 27 divisions (seven of them panzer), with some ancillary help from General Vittorio Ambrosio's 2nd Italian Army (attacking from the Trieste area of Italy into northwestern Yugoslavia) and the Hungarian 3rd Army, driving southward into Yugoslavia. The invasions would be supported by more than 1,000 aircraft, controlled by Colonel General Alexander Loehr's 4th Air Fleet.

Second Army assembled in Austria and Hungary within days. Its rapid concentration was almost unprecedented in its speed, flexibility, and efficiency. Three of its divisions were moved from Germany, four from France, one from Czechoslovakia, and one from the Soviet frontier. They moved by rail and road, but, despite a brilliant logistical effort, icy roads delayed several units and some divisions went into action in piecemeal fashion. Others could not arrive at their assembly areas until after the invasion began, which is why the Vienna staff conference decided to stagger the offensive of the 2nd Army. Table 26.1 shows the Order of Battle of the ground forces earmarked for the conquest of the Balkans.

Loehr's air fleet also produced a masterpiece of rapid deployment and makeshift logistical planning. On March 27, it consisted of 135 fighter and reconnaissance aircraft in Romania and 355 bombers and

Table 26.1
Order of Battle, Axis Forces Involved in the Invasions of Yugoslavia
and Greece, April 6, 1941

Supreme Commander: Adolf Hitler
OKH: Field Marshal Walter von Brauchitsch
Chief of Staff: Colonel General Franz Halder
2nd Italian Army: General Vittorio Ambrosio
2nd Army: Colonel General Baron Maximilian von Weichs
    XXXXIX Mountain Corps: General of Mountain Troops Ludwig Kuebler
      1st Mountain and 538th Frontier Guard Divisions
    LI Corps: General of Infantry Hans Reinhardt
      101st Light, 132nd Infantry, and 183rd Infantry Divisions
    LII Corps: General of Infantry Kurt von Briesen
      79th and 125th Infantry Divisions[b]
    XXXXVI Panzer Corps: General of Panzer Troops Heinrich von Vietinghoff
      8th Panzer, 14th Panzer, and 16th Motorized Divisions
3rd Hungarian Army
    XXXXI Panzer Corps: General of Panzer Troops Georg-Hans Reinhardt[c]
      2nd SS Motorized Division "Das Reich," the Gross Deutschland Motorized
      Infantry Regiment[a], and the "Hermann Goering" Panzer Regiment
1st Panzer Group: Colonel General Ewald von Kleist[d]
    XIV Panzer Corps: General of Infantry Gustav von Wietersheim
      5th Panzer, 11th Panzer, 294th Infantry, and 4th Mountain Divisions
    XI Corps: General of Infantry Joachim von Kortzfleisch
      60th Motorized Infantry Division[e]
12th Army: Field Marshal Wilhelm List
    XXXX Panzer Corps: General of Panzer Troops Georg Stumme
      9th Panzer Division, 73rd Infantry Division, 1st SS Mtz. Infantry Regiment[a]
    XVIII Mountain Corps: General of Mountain Troops Franz Boehme
      2nd Panzer Division, 5th Mountain Division, 6th Mountain Division,
      72nd Infantry Division, 125th Infantry Regiment[a]
    XXX Corps: General of Artillery Otto Hartmann
      50th Infantry and 164th Infantry Divisions
    L Corps: General of Cavalry Georg Lindemann[b]
      46th, 76th and 198th Infantry Divisions[b]
    16th Panzer Division[f]

Notes:
[a]A reinforced (or augmented) unit
[b]Did not arrive in time to participate in the campaign
[c]Initially, XXXXI Panzer Corps was directly subordinate to OKH
[d]Initially part of 12th Army; attached to 2nd Army on April 13.
[e]Several other units were attached to XI Corps, but did not arrive in time to participate in the campaign.
[f]Deployed behind Turkish-Bulgarian border, to help the Bulgarian Army in case of a Turkish attack.
Source:
United States Department of the Army, "The German Campaigns in the Balkans (Spring, 1941)," United States Department of the Army, Pamphlet 20–260 (1953).

dive-bombers in Bulgaria. Then it was given the additional task of supporting the invasion of Yugoslavia. From as far away as Sicily, Africa, and France, more than 600 bombers, dive-bombers, fighters, and reconnaissance aircraft assembled on primitive airfields in Austria, Bulgaria, and Romania, and were fully operational within 10 days.

At the beginning of April 1941, the Yugoslav Army consisted of 17 regular and 12 reserve infantry divisions, six combined-arms brigades, three regular cavalry divisions, three reserve cavalry brigades, a fortress division, a fortress brigade, 23 frontier guard battalions, and several miscellaneous units. It fully mobilized strength was more than 1 million men; however, it was never fully mobilized. North to south, it deployed as follows:

- 1st Army Group (7th and 4th Armies): responsible for defending northern Yugoslavia, including the Croatian capital of Zagreb
- 2nd Army Group (2nd and 1st Armies): defending north-central Yugoslavia, and generally deployed along the Hungarian frontier
- 6th Army: deployed opposite the Romanian frontier, defended Belgrade
- 3rd Army Group (5th and 3rd Armies): defended along the Bulgarian and Bulgarian-Albanian frontiers, respectively

Although it looked respectable on paper, the Yugoslav Army was poorly equipped and in desperate need of modernization. It had 700 airplanes, but all of them were obsolete. Its tanks were made by Czechoslovakians and lacked spare parts, because the Germans occupied the Skoda Works in early 1939. In addition, it lacked training in, and had almost no knowledge of, modern Blitzkrieg warfare, and it was badly disposed. Like the Poles in 1939, the Yugoslavs tried to defend their entire frontier (1,900 miles), ignoring Frederick the Great, who said, "He who defends everything defends nothing." The adage was even more applicable in 1940 than it was when the great king said it.

The Greek Army was badly equipped and not disposed to meet a German attack, even though it was obvious that one was coming. Most of it (14 divisions) was on the Greek left flank, in Albania, under the control of the 1st Army. It had done all it could do against the numerically superior Italians and should have pulled back to a shorter line to the south. The Greek government, however, refused to withdraw it for political reasons. Likewise, on the right flank, the government insisted on posting the 2nd Army (70,000 men in four divisions) in the so-called Metaxas Line, near the Bulgarian border, so that it could hold Eastern Macedonia and as much Greek territory as possible. Because of the Greek government's persistent refusal to withdraw to a shorter and more defensible line to the south, they were badly overextended and in a strategically unsound position.

The Greek center was weak. It was defended by Force W, which consisted of the Army of Central Macedonia (three understrength divisions), and the I Australian Corps of the B.E.F. (two divisions and the 1st Armored Brigade), all under the command of "Jumbo" Wilson. Additional troops (another Australian division and the Polish Brigade) were on the way but did not arrive in time.

Force W had the task of defending a line in the Vermion Mountains south of the Yugoslav frontier. The line was placed there because one of the most suitable areas for panzer operations in all of Greece was the Plain of Thessaly, which lay just south of Wilson's line. If the Germans could sweep through southern Yugoslavia and past the left flank of Force W, they would be in good tank country, and the Allied forces could be crushed. This is what Force W was suppose to prevent, but the Germans struck too rapidly. By D-Day, the center of the Allied line was still weak and incompletely held. If Germans attacked through southern Yugoslavia, they could outflank Force W without difficulty.

As a result of their poor deployment, the Greeks opposed the Italians with 14 divisions. They only had seven weak divisions left to oppose the German Army, which was the best in the world at that time. In addition, the Greek Air Force had been in combat for months and had suffered such heavy losses on the Albanian Front that it was virtually nonoperational by April 1941. The Royal Air Force units in Greece only had 80 serviceable aircraft when Hitler's legions struck on April 6.

THE CONQUEST OF YUGOSLAVIA

Richthofen's VIII Air Corps began the invasion with a massive terror-bombing raid on the Yugoslav capital on the morning of Sunday, April 6. The strike force included seven bomber groups, three Stuka groups, and a twin-engine fighter group. The Yugoslavian Air Force was quickly annihilated. The few Yugoslav flak guns that defended the capital were quickly knocked out, while Richthofen's bombers and dive-bombers attacked at house top level and smashed everything in sight. "The scream of Stukas [is] ... like no sound ever heard in all the universe," one survivor recalled:

Bomb after bomb exploded ... the effect almost inconceivable ... It was the perfectly appalling wind that was most terrifying. It drove like something solid through the house: every door that was latched simply burst off its hinges, every pane of glass flew into splinters, the curtains stood straight out into the room and fell back in ribbons. Everything that stood loose hit the opposite wall and was smashed. The ceilings fell with hardly a noticeable sound in the earth-shaking uproar. Then, with a weird, smooth sound like the tearing of heavy silk the neighboring houses began to collapse.[7]

The city was bombed for an hour and a half. More than 17,000 people were killed in the destruction of Belgrade, which burned for some time. In addition, the military command posts and communication centers were all knocked out, as was the palace and the government buildings. The Yugoslavs lost all central direction of their armed forces from the first hour of the campaign, and, as a result, were never able to put up effective resistance.

Baron von Richthofen lost two airplanes in the raid.

Meanwhile, the German ground units jumped off, and three separate forces converged on Belgrade from three different directions: the 1st Panzer Group from the southeast, the XXXXI Panzer Corps from the north, and the XXXXVI Panzer Corps of the 2nd Army from the northwest, as Figure 26.1 shows.

Kleist's 1st Panzer Group had the most difficult task, because the Yugoslav 5th Army was the best in the country, with a high percentage of regular troops, and it put up tough resistance initially. When the XIV Panzer Corps broke through, however, the Yugoslav commander

Figure 26.1
The Conquest of Yugoslavia

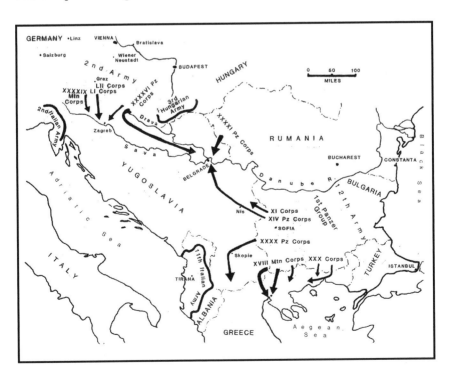

ordered his troops to withdraw behind the Morava River. The non-motorized Yugoslavs could not perform this maneuver, because the panzers moved too rapidly, and the retreating Slavs were quickly swamped. On April 9, Nis fell, the Yugoslav front collapsed, and Kleist turned northward for Belgrade. Because of his rapid success, 5th Panzer Division was diverted south and joined the XXXX Panzer Corps of the 12th Army for the Greek campaign.

In the meantime, Reinhardt's XXXXI Panzer Corps smashed the Yugoslav 6th Army near Pancevo, which fell on April 11. By April 12, Reinhardt's tanks were only 45 miles north of Belgrade and were advancing on the capital against only sporadic resistance.

To the north, XXXXVI Panzer Corps of Weichs's 2nd Army quickly broke through the Yugoslav 4th Army, which was made up mainly of Croats. Many Croat units mutinied and refused to fire on the Germans, who they hailed as liberators from Serbian oppression. By the morning of April 10, Weichs's spearhead was across the Drava and was driving southeast, between the Drava and Sava Rivers, for the Serbian capital.

All three converging forces reached Belgrade almost simultaneously. The honor of capturing the city, however, went to 28-year-old *SS-Obersturmfuehrer* (1st Lieutenant) Fritz Klingenberg, the tall, blonde, youthful looking commander of the 2nd Motorcycle Company of the 2nd SS Motorized Division. Racing ahead with his company, Klingenberg found the Danube bridges destroyed, so he led an 11-man patrol across the river in pneumatic boats. He entered the city unmolested, freed the German embassy staff (which had been interned) and at 5 P.M. hoisted the swastika flag over the German legation. At 6:45 P.M., accompanied by Colonel Rudolf Toussaint (the former German military attaché to Belgrade, whom he had freed), Klingenberg accepted the surrender of the mayor of Belgrade. For his daring actions, young Klingenberg was awarded the Knight's Cross on May 14.

With the fall of the city, 1st Panzer Group was transferred to the control of the 2nd Army, while von Vietinghoff's XXXXVI Panzer Corps was placed under Kleist's command for the next phase of the operation: the mopping up and final destruction of the remnants of the Yugoslav Army.

Northern Yugoslavia fell quickly. The German 2nd Army bypassed most of the Yugoslavian 7th Army and met only sporadic resistance from the 4th and 2nd. At one point, the Germans burst into a Yugoslav base and found an officers' party in progress. A hasty surrender was concluded, and then the party resumed, as if nothing unusual had happened. The Croatian government broke with Belgrade on April 10, and (with Hitler's blessing and the support of the Abwehr) declared itself an independent country. It called on its nationals to stop fighting the Germans. Many Croats, however, had already released themselves.

Virtually the entire Yugoslav 4th Army had mutinied by this time, and Zagreb, the capital of Croatia, was seized by Croatian rebels. When the troops of the 14th Panzer Division (LI Corps) arrived on April 10, they were greeted as liberators by a wildly cheering pro-German populace. During its drive on the city, the 14th Panzer took more than 15,000 prisoners, including 300 officers and 22 generals, among which were the commanders of the 1st Army Group and 7th Army.[8] Elsewhere, in the zone of the XXXXIX Mountain Corps, the Slovenian government followed the lead of the Croatians and declared its independence on April 11. The capital of Celje surrendered to Major General Hubert Lanz's 1st Mountain Division that same day. Meanwhile, the Italian 2nd Army advanced rapidly against the Yugoslav 7th Army and took 30,000 prisoners, while the Hungarian 3rd Army brushed aside the Yugoslav 1st Army. According to the U.S. Army's excellent study of the campaign, however, both the Italians and the Hungarians "displayed great reluctance to attack until the enemy had been soundly beaten and thoroughly disorganized by the Germans."[9]

After the collapse of the frontier defense system and the fall of Belgrade, the Yugoslav leaders tried to withdraw the remnants of their army to a mountain redoubt in the interior of Serbia. Weichs launched a rapid pursuit of the Yugoslavs, who were withdrawing in the general direction of Sarajevo. Speed was now of the essence, because OKH wanted to end the campaign as rapidly as possible, so that the panzer and motorized divisions could be refitted and made ready for the Russian campaign. Meanwhile, the Yugoslavs were surrendering by the thousands: 7,000 north of Nis, 40,000 at Uzice, 30,000 around Zvornik, and another 6,000 in Dobo.

Sarajevo fell to the 8th and 14th Panzer Divisions, which converged on the city from the east and west, respectively, on April 15. The Yugoslavian 2nd Army, which headquartered in the city, formally capitulated that same day. Meanwhile, representatives of the Yugoslav government approached General von Kleist late on the evening of April 14, and asked for an immediate cease-fire. When this request was relayed to OKH, it designed Baron von Weichs as its negotiator, although, in reality, there was little to negotiate, since the Germans were demanding an unconditional surrender. The Yugoslavs had little choice except to agree to these terms, and the armistice was concluded in Belgrade on April 17. The cease-fire went into effect at noon on April 18, just 12 days after the invasion was launched.

No one had really excepted that the Yugoslavian Army would turn back the Germans, but, even so, German losses had been surprisingly light. Its total casualty figure came to only 558 men, including 151 killed, 392 wounded, and 15 missing. Reinhardt's XXXXI Panzer Corps had suffered only one casualty: an officer who was killed by a civilian sniper.

The Germans took hundreds of thousands of prisoners, but only kept 254,000. All Croat, German, Hungarian, and Bulgarian nationals who had been inducted into the Yugoslavian Army were released after a quick screening.

The Western press and political leaders, who had been overly optimistic, were dismayed by the speed with which the Germans overran Yugoslav. They had expected too much from a poor country that was badly led, deeply divided by ethnic hatred, and had an antiquated military system.

THE FALL OF GREECE

The rapid disintegration of the Yugoslavian Army also doomed Greece to conquest.

Athens pinned its hopes of halting the Germans on the Metalax Line, a series of pillboxes and fortified positions in the steep Rhodope Mountains, extending along the Greco-Bulgarian frontier for 125 miles. Unfortunately, it was immediately outflanked by Georg Stumme's XXXX Panzer Corps, which pushed through the mountains of southern Yugoslavia on April 6, and, after some heavy fighting on the first day of the invasion, brushed aside elements of the Yugoslav 5th Army and captured Skoplje and Veles, 60 miles from Bulgaria, on April 7. This quick thrust severed the rail line between Belgrade and Salonika. Then, while Stumme pushed westward, into the rear of the 1st Greek Army and around the left flank of Force W, the 2nd Panzer Division of Franz Boehme's XVIII Mountain Corps made a shorter (inner) flanking movement through southern Yugoslavia, and outflanked the Metaxas Line to the west (see Figure 26.2). It encountered little resistance in Yugoslavia, and, on April 8, pushed through the mountains and overran the Greek 19th Motorized Infantry Division south of Lake Doiran. The Metaxas Line was turned, the 2nd Greek Army had no more reserves, and its other divisions were pinned down by the rest of the XVIII Mountain Corps, which broke through the strong but thin line on April 7 and 8. Salonika, the second most populous Greek city, fell to Lieutenant General Rudolf Veiel's 2nd Panzer Division without a struggle on the morning of April 9, and Greek resistance east of the Vardar River collapsed. At the same time, the XXX Corps overran lightly defended Thrace, and the Greek 2nd Army surrendered unconditionally the same day. The Germans captured approximately 70,000 Greek prisoners, disarmed them, and sent them home.

Also on April 9, XXXX Panzer Corps took the Monastir Gap in southern Yugoslavia—the traditional invasion route into Greece—and effectively outflanked the Vermion Mountains barrier and Force W. List was now in a position to drive a wedge between the British and

Figure 26.2
The Greek Campaign

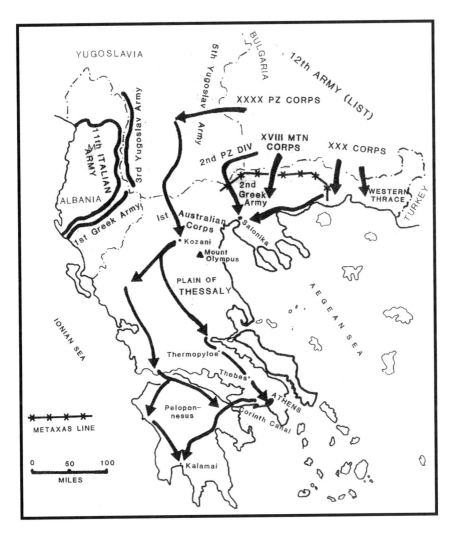

the Greek 1st Army and bring the campaign to a rapid conclusion. Realizing this, the marshal rapidly pressed his advantage. The XXXX Panzer Corps, led by the SS regiment, first clashed with the British at 11 A.M. the next morning. The speed with which the 1st SS moved surprised the British command, which gave orders for an immediate evacuation of the Vermion Mountain position. Sepp Dietrich's troops quickly set out in pursuit and captured Vevi on April 11, but they were stopped that afternoon by the Australians, who had set up on the heights that dominated a road pass that was south of the town. The SS tried to find a way to outflank this position the next day but failed. At dusk, they launched a frontal attack and broke through after heavy fighting. The British forces then continued their retreat.

On April 13, General Stumme ordered the 1st SS Motorized Regiment to drive west to Kastoria to cut off the withdrawal of the 1st Greek Army, while the 9th Panzer Division pursued the more mobile British as they fell back toward Kozani, in the hopes of cutting them off. It was unsuccessful, largely due to the fact that it was almost out of ammunition, but it did force the British rearguard to abandon 32 tanks and anti-tank guns and a number of trucks. That evening, the 9th Panzer established a bridgehead across the Aliakmon River, just north of the Plain of Thessaly. Here the British rearguards made a stand in the strong mountainous positions south of the river and held the panzer division in check for three days.

Meanwhile, the rest of the XXXX Panzer Corps, spearheaded by the 1st SS Motorized Regiment, barreled into the rear of the 1st Greek Army. At this point, Field Marshal Aleksandro Papagos, the commander-in-chief of the Greek Army, finally approved the withdrawal from Albania, but it was too late. On April 20, following a fierce battle, the SS men captured the 5,000-foot-high Metsovon Pass in the Pindus Mountains and completed the encirclement of the Greek 1st Army. Realizing that his situation was hopeless, Lieutenant General Georgias Tsolakoglu, the Greek commander, offered to surrender his army.[10]

The negotiations were brief and, on the strict orders of Adolf Hitler, were kept secret from the Italians. In recognition of their valor, Field Marshal List gave the defeated Greeks honorable terms and allowed their soldiers to go home after their units were demobilized. Officers were permitted to keep their side arms. Mussolini, however, was angry over this agreement and, for once in his life, bluntly told Hitler so. The Greeks must surrender to the Italians, too, he said, or he would continue fighting. Italy had lost 63,000 dead in her war with the Greeks, but still had 500,000 men in the field, and it was obvious that Mussolini meant what he said. Reluctantly, Hitler backed down and renounced List's terms. Much to the disgust of the field marshal and the Germans—even Ribbentrop disapproved—the Greeks were forced to sign a new surrender agreement, which included the Italians, on April 23.

For the British, the campaign became a series of difficult retreats—long, forced marches through snow, bitter cold, and icy winds, until the days ran together in the minds of the physically and mentally exhausted men. They retreated across the Thessalian Plain, where they were subjected to continuous daylight attack from the VIII Air Corps. Led by Major General Gustav Fehn, the 5th Panzer Division finally debouched on the Plain of Thessaly on April 19 and set out after

Wilson. Realizing that the end was near, Alexander Koryzis, the Greek president, committed suicide.

The decision to evacuate was made on April 21 and began three days later. Dubbed Operation Demon, it was a miniaturized Dunkirk, was just as improvised, and was almost as successful. Ports were used from as far north as Athens and Piraeus to fishing villages on the southern tip of the Peloponnesus. Most of the ships shuttled between the mainland and Crete, dropping off soldiers and heading back to Greece for another load. Some of the heavier ships, such as cruisers, carried their evacuees to Egypt.

The Luftwaffe, which lacked forward bases and was hampered by logistical problems (a result of the poor road conditions in the Balkans), was unable to halt the evacuation. As was the case at Dunkirk, however, it did hamper it. Twenty-six British vessels were sunk during Operation Demon (excluding fishing vessels) and several others were severely damaged.

The British rearguard made a last stand at Thermopylae on April 22, providing cover for the evacuation. It held off the 5th Panzer Division for two days but finally had to abandon the pass during the night of April 24–25. The difficult terrain, coupled with the poor road system and copious demolitions, allowed it to make good its escape. The mountainous roads had taken a major toll on the 12th Army. Only two weeks after the invasion began, more than one-third of List's motor vehicles were deadlined, mainly due to ruined tires. Wear and tear on tanks was also a serious problem.

List tried to cut off the British rearguards via airborne attack on the morning of April 26, when 270 Ju-52s dropped two reinforced battalions of the 2nd Parachute Regiment on the Isthmus of Corinth. The Anglo-Greek rearguard (2,300 men) was cut off and eventually captured, and the pursuit continued with little delay, but almost all of the British forces had already crossed the Isthmus, and many of them had already been evacuated. Had this operation been conducted a few days before, the B.E.F. might well have suffered disastrous losses. As events transpired, however, the Corinth drop cost the 2nd Parachute Regiment 63 men killed, 158 wounded, and 16 missing.[11]

Now the end in Greece came rapidly. On the morning of April 27, Athens fell to the motorcycle battalion of the 2nd Panzer Division. The 5th Panzer Division roared across the Corinth Canal and overran the Peloponnesus, capturing several isolated British groups that had not been able to reach their evacuation ports on time. In all, 8,000 British and Yugoslav troops were captured in this manner, and several thousand Italian prisoners were liberated. The 5th Panzer reached the southern coast of the Peloponnesus on April 29, and hostilities on the mainland ended the following day.

In all, the Germans lost 1,100 killed and 4,000 wounded or missing during the conquest of Greece. They took at least 270,000 Greek and 90,000 Yugoslavian prisoners in the Greek campaign.[12] The Royal Navy managed to evacuate 43,000 of the 58,000 men the B.E.F. committed to the mainland. Actual British casualties were somewhat higher, however, because hundreds of wounded were evacuated. Most of the British losses were prisoners of war, captured after the 5th Panzer broke into the Peloponnesus, at the very end of the campaign; many of the rest of their casualties occurred aboard evacuation ships that were sunk by the Luftwaffe.

Just as at Dunkirk, equipment losses by British forces were much heavier than personnel losses. The B.E.F. left behind some 8,000 trucks, hundreds of tanks, armored vehicles, and artillery pieces, and 209 wrecked airplanes in Greece, as well as thousands of rifles, radios, and other valuable items of military equipment. In fact, due to equipment shortages of every kind, the units that escaped were only marginally battleworthy, as we shall see.

Forming an objective conclusion concerning the relationship between the Balkans campaign and the invasion of the Soviet Union is not easy; forming a definitive one is impossible.

Many Western historians have averred that the Balkans campaign caused Hitler to postpone the start of Operation Barbarossa from May 15 to June 22: a five-week delay that proved fatal to the German Army, which was caught in the Russian winter and almost destroyed as a result. The delay caused by the invasions of Greece and Yugoslavia, these historians claim, saved Moscow and the Soviet Union and eventually led to the destruction of Nazi Germany.

Whatever the true is, it is not as simple as that. First of all, the spring rains in eastern Poland and the western sections of European Russia came late in 1941 and were much heavier than usual. Many of the Polish-Russian river valleys (including the Bug) were still flooded as late as June 1; therefore, the invasion of the Soviet Union could not have begun until after that. At the most, the Balkans campaign cost Hitler three weeks—not five or six, as some historians argue.

The truth is less simple to ascertain beyond this, because even three more weeks of good campaign weather might have been enough to allow Army Group Center to capture Moscow toward the end of 1941. The Balkans campaign was a contributing factor in Hitler's failure in Russia in 1941, but it certainly not *the* major factor. One must consider that the German armies in Russia were paralyzed for several weeks after the campaign began because of a dispute between Hitler and OKH over strategic priorities. In addition, Hitler's insistence on driving for Leningrad and capturing the Ukraine before he permitted a late season drive on Moscow also costs the Wehrmacht irreplaceable time. The delay caused by the Balkans campaign was a factor in the subsequent disaster in front of Moscow, but, when considered in light of these other unnecessary delays, the three weeks lost in the Balkans seem to be of much less significance.

On the other hand, the Balkans campaign undoubtedly resulted in another disastrous Allied defeat. Hitler secured by military force what he had not been able to secure by diplomatic means: his supply of oil, chromium, and other vital raw materials. In addition, the decision to strip Wavell's forces in Libya of its best units unquestionably cost the Allies total victory in North Africa. Finally, the equipment losses the Allied forces suffered in Greece were a major cause for their defeat in Crete, as we shall see in our next chapter.

NOTES

1. Koch, "Genesis," p. 319; *DGFP*, vol. 11, document no. 379.

2. Koch, "Genesis," p. 319.

3. Charles Cruickshank, *Greece, 1940–1941* (1976), p. 124 (hereafter cited as Cruickshank).

4. Ibid., p. 95; *DGFP*, XI, pp. 1216–217, 1236–237.

5. Irving, *Hitler's War*, p. 237; *DGFP*, XII, pp. 291–94.

6. United States Department of the Army, "The German Campaigns in the Balkans (Spring, 1941)," United States Department of the Army, Pamphlet 20–260 (1953), p. 22 (hereafter cited as DA PAM 20-260).

7. Baldwin, *Critical Years*, pp. 270–71, citing Ruth Mitchell, *The Serbs Choose War* (1941), p. 6.

8. DA PAM 20-260, p. 60.

9. Ibid., p. 65.

10. Aleksandro Papagos (born 1883) was commissioned second lieutenant in the Greek cavalry in 1906. He was a strong royalist throughout his life. In the 1930s, he served as inspector of cavalry, commander of the I Corps, minister of war, and chief of the General Staff before being named commander-in-chief of the army in 1940. After he surrendered in 1941, he was in prisoner-of-war camps until he was liberated in 1945. In 1949, he was named commander-in-chief of the Greek armed forces. He became prime minister in 1952 and died in office on October 4, 1955.

Georgios Tsolakoglu also became a prime minister of Greece—but in a collaborationist government. He took office in 1941 but was replaced in 1942. He was tried as a war criminal and was sentenced to death in 1948, but he died in prison before the sentence could be carried out.

11. Karl Gundelack, "The Battle for Crete, 1941" in *Decisive Battles of World War II: The German View*, H. A. Jacobsen and J. Rowher, eds. (1965), p. 102 (hereafter cited as Gundelack).

12. DA PAM 20-260, p. 112.

CHAPTER **XXVII**

THE INVASION OF CRETE

Crete, the largest island in the Aegean Sea, is 186 miles long (east to west) and 7 to 35 miles wide (north to south). It was not (and is not) a prosperous place. Most of the land was in rugged mountains, too barren to offer much fodder for animals or cover for military operations. There was not a single mile of railroad track on the island, and only one narrow, paved road existed in 1941. It ran approximately 160 miles along Crete's northern coast. Only one rocky dirt road to the village of Timbakion connected the paved road in the north with the southern coast. The other secondary roads deteriorated into paths or trails as they ascended into the foothills of the mountains, which reached their peaks near the southern face of the island. The mountains reached elevations of up to 10,000 feet and were often snow covered. Many of them ended in cliffs on the southern coast, as they fell into a sheer drop into the sea.

Churchill wanted Crete turned into a second Scapa Flow and said so on October 28, 1940, although Wavell, who was chronically short of troops, could not supply the men. He still had not furnished Crete with much of a garrison in April 1941. A pro-Axis government under Rashid Ali al-Gelani had seized power in Iraq, Rommel was running wild in the Western Desert, General Sir Alan G. Cunningham was fully engaged in crushing Mussolini's forces in Italian East Africa,[1] and the B.E.F. was being mauled in Greece with a speed the British had not anticipated. As a result, Wavell had almost nothing available for Crete, and he was forced to garrison the island with the men being evacuated from Greece, instead of with fresh, well-equipped troops.

As Operation Demon neared its conclusion, the defensive situation on Crete was totally inadequate. It lacked anti-aircraft and coastal defense batteries, had little transport, no telephone system, bad communications, inadequately prepared and equipped airfields, and a totally insufficient number of airplanes; in fact, there was little in the way of military equipment and hardware that the garrison of Crete did have in adequate amounts.

It is not clear whether the airborne invasion of Crete was the brain-child of Loehr or Student, but Student was certainly an early propo-nent of it. (At last recovered from the wounds he had suffered in Rotterdam, he was now the commander of the XI Air Corps—the German parachute corps. Loehr still commanded the 4th Air Fleet.) Furthermore, he knew how to manipulate Goering, who soon became an enthusiastic supporter of the operation. On April 16 and 20, the Reichsmarschall attended Fuerher conferences and tried to convert a reluctant Hitler to the idea. Finally, Hitler asked to see General Student on April 21.

The fateful conference began at 3 P.M. Hitler started by saying that he did not think that the operation was practical. Student assured him that it was not only practical, but certain. After considerable discussion, he promised him that it would not interfere with Barbarossa in the slightest. Finally, Hitler asked him why he preferred the seizure of Crete over Malta. (Field Marshal Keitel had repeatedly called for a para-chute invasion of that island and, according to Student, Jodl also favored the capture of Malta over Crete.) The slow-speaking Student pointed out that Crete would be an easier objective to seize. Malta, he said, was too small, and the British could easily transfer their reserves from one point to another. Crete, with its long northern coast, was a dif-ferent matter.

It was obvious that Hitler was at last becoming interested. "And the next step?" he asked.

"Cyprus!" Student answered, with complete self-assurance. "From there to the Suez, through the back door."

Goering, learning from Jodl, again pointed out that the airfields on Crete posed a constant threat to the Ploesti oilfields. This remark hit the target. Hitler rose, walked over to his map table, and asked Student how much time he would need for the operation. Three days, the para-trooper replied.

"That's impossible!" cried Hitler. He then gave Student five days, and warned him that he would have to move with great speed.

"Mein Fuehrer, do your words mean that you approve of the attack upon Crete?" Student asked.

"I don't know," Hitler said, bending over the map table. "I'll think it over."[2]

Four days later, however, Hitler issued Fuehrer Directive 28, order-ing the seizure of Crete. It specified that only Luftwaffe units would be involved, that it should start no later than the middle of May, and had to be completed by May 25. Hitler assigned it the codename Operation Mercury.

As early as April 18, as a result of ULTRA intercepts, Churchill first informed Wavell that an airborne attack against Crete could be expected.[3] On April 30, Wavell personally inspected the island and found its defenses in such poor condition that he replaced the island commander, British Marine Major General Eric C. Weston, with Major General Bernard C. Freyberg, the commander of the 2nd New Zealand Division. He became the seventh commander of the island since November. Freyberg was a tough and able warrior who had been a brigade commander in the last years of the Great War, even though he was still in his 20s. Despite the fact he was English, he had been selected to command the 2nd New Zealand Expeditionary Force (also known as the 2nd Division) in 1939. He immediately conducted an inspection of Crete and found, among other things, that his total air force consisted of six Hurricanes and 17 obsolete airplanes.[4] In addition, his Greek forces were largely without weapons, were undisciplined and disrespectful of authority, and showed every sign of broken morale. Those that had rifles only had an average of 20 rounds per man. The next day, he reported that he would not be able to hold the island unless he received massive amounts of equipment and strong reinforcements, especially artillery, airplanes, and naval reinforcements. Failing that, he declared, the question of holding Crete should be reconsidered.

Wavell, however, could do little to help him. With Rommel on the rampage in the desert, he had no air units to spare, could only furnish the garrison with 16 light and six infantry support tanks and could not even maintain current levels of supply. At first, it proved possible to bring in and unload 700 tons of supplies a day at Suda Bay; soon, however, the Luftwaffe was pounding the port, and the volume of supplies unloaded at Suda Bay fell to 100 tons per day. The garrison needed 20,000 to 30,000 tons per month.[5]

On May 3, Freyberg divided the island into four major sectors, each with at least one airfield and harbor. The Heraklion (Iraklion) sector was the responsibility of Brigadier Brian H. Chappel; the Rethimnon sector was held by Australian Brigadier G. A. Vasey; the Suda Bay-Canea sector was the responsibility of a composite force under Major General Weston; and the Maleme Sector was held by the 2nd New Zealand Division, temporarily under the command of Brigadier Edward Puttick. In all, Chappel had 8,024 men; Vasey, 6,730; Weston, 14,822; and Puttick, 11,859. Freyberg's total strength (including a small reserve under his personal command) totaled 42,640 men, including 10,258 Greeks. "The fighting value of the Greeks was not very high," Gundelach observed later, "they were demoralized, disorganized, and poorly equipped."[6] Freyberg used them to defend positions of secondary importance only.

Freyberg left the disposition of troops to each sector commander, but with one condition: he wanted the airfields to be defended during an attack by at least one-third of the troops allocated to each sector, with the rest available to overrun any threat to the landing strips. "You must deny the airfields to the enemy at all costs!" he told his deputies.[7]

Freyberg did as well as anyone could expect in preparing Crete for the attack. By the middle of the month, he was cautiously optimistic that the island could be held.

Meanwhile, back in Greece, Colonel General Alexander Loehr was feverishly preparing for the Battle of Crete. As commander of the 4th Air Fleet, he controlled the XI Air Corps (Student) and the VIII Air Corps (von Richthofen). For the Cretan campaign, Student controlled the Assault Regiment (three parachute battalions and one gliderborne battalion); the 7th Air Division (three parachute regiments plus divisional units and two regiments of the 5th Mountain Division); a regiment of the 6th Mountain Division; a panzer battalion and a motorcycle battalion (both from the 5th Panzer Division); and a few smaller detachments. In all, he had 13,000 men. In addition, the rest of the 6th Mountain Division (9,000 men) was on call in air fleet reserve. Some 5,000 of the men of the 5th Mountain Division were slated to be landed by sea, along with 2,000 paratroops. Student also had 10 wings of Ju-52s (502 airplanes), assembled to transport parachute and air landing troops, as well as 85 gliders. Baron von Richthofen had 650 airplanes at his disposal, including 280 bombers, 150 Stuka dive-bombers, 90 twin-engine fighters, 90 single-engine fighters, and 40 reconnaissance aircraft.

General Student planned to put down as many troops by parachute and glider as rapidly as possible. The final plan called for an airborne assault against the three airfields (Maleme, Retimo, and Heraklion). A strong force would also land at Canea, where the Allied reserves were believed to be, to keep them from being committed elsewhere. The attack would come in two waves: the western wave (against Maleme and Canea) would be dropped in the morning, and the eastern wave (against Retimo and Heraklion) would jump in the afternoon.[8] Figure 27.1 shows the final plan. D-Day was set for May 17. Because of logistical problems, however, it had to be postponed until May 20.

Meanwhile, Richthofen's forces had already "softened up" the island. On May 9, the remnants of the Royal Air Force units from the Greek campaign had to be sent back to Egypt, to save them from destruction. The last Allied airplanes left on May 19, the day before the invasion. It was now too late to crater the airfields and make them useless for the Germans.

Admiral Canaris personally took charge of the military intelligence phase of the operation. As was not unusual, he made a several serious mistakes. His estimate of the number of British troops on the island was only one-third of the actual total. He assured Student and the

Figure 27.1
The Conquest of Crete

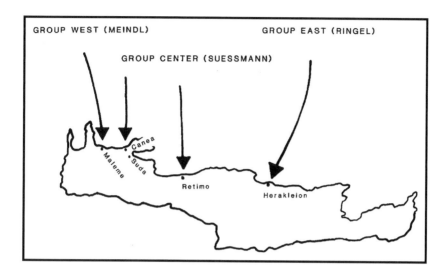

other planners that they could expect little resistance on the island, and his spies informed him that the Cretans would probably welcome the paratroopers with open arms. In fact, the Cretans actively supported the British and even killed wounded German paratroopers with axes and pitchforks. The aerial reconnaissance reports were also generally wrong. Many decoy anti-aircraft sites, armed with wooden guns, were reported as the real sites, while the real positions, which were well camouflaged, went undetected. Finally, Canaris stated that the British "Tommies" were "demoralized" and "wouldn't show much fight."[9] These mistakes would cause XI Air Corps hundreds of casualties on May 20.

On D-Day, May 20, XI Air Corps divided into three groups. Group West, led by Major General Eugen Meindl, the commander of the elite Assault Regiment, was charged with the task of seizing the Maleme Airfield in the first wave and holding it for subsequent landings. Group Center, under the direction of Lieutenant General Wilhelm Suessmann, was supposed to seize Canae and the village of Suda in the first wave to dislocate the defense, force Freyberg to commit his reserves too quickly and in the wrong place, and put the main Allied harbor out of operation. The rest of Group Center was to drop in the second wave and seize Retimo at 3:15 P.M. Finally, Group East, a second-wave operation, was to seize the town and airfield of Heraklion by parachute drops and then hold the airfield open for the subsequent landing of the mountain troops. Since the group commander, Lieutenant General Julius Ringel, was not jump qualified, the airborne spearhead was led by Colonel Bruno Braeuer, the commander of the 1st Parachute Regiment.

The first phase of the operation went like clockwork. Between 7 A.M. and 7:15 A.M., just before the paratroopers jumped, the VIII Air Corps launched a major attack against ground targets, with the objective of pinning down the enemy at and near the landing zones to protect the transports. It was extremely successful: only seven Ju-52s were lost out of the 493 that participated. Even before the gliders were released and the paratroopers dropped, however, everything began to go wrong for the first assault wave.

The glider carrying Wilhelm Suessmann, the tough and able commander of Group Center and the 7th Air Division, crashed en route and everyone aboard was killed. Many of his men were no more lucky. "Even as they dropped they were within range and the crackle of rifle fire and Bren guns rose to a crescendo," Davin wrote later.

Wildly waving their legs, some already firing their Schmeissers, the parachutists came down, in the terraced vineyards, crashing through the peaceful olive boughs, in the yards of houses, on roofs, in the open fields where the short barley hid them. Many found graves where they found earth. Others, ridding themselves of their harness, crept cautiously in search of comrades, only to meet enemies.... [Many landed] in the middle of the defenders and few were to escape. But where they landed out of range ... there was the chance to collect more weapons and ammunition from the canisters, to organize their sections, to attack. The day had indeed begun.[10]

After the death of General Suessmann, Group Center was commanded by Colonel Richard Heidrich, who also retained command of the 3rd Parachute Regiment. He inherited a disaster. "The moment we left the planes we were met with extremely heavy small arms fire," a company sergeant-major in the II Battalion of the 3rd Parachute Regiment recalled.

From my aircraft we suffered particularly heavy casualties and only three men reached the ground unhurt. Those who had jumped first, nearer to Galatas, were practically all killed, either in the air or soon after landing. The survivors rallied ... we became organized, collected equipment, and formed up for an attack up the hill to the north.... Approximately 350 men of my battalion survived the initial landing and organizing period.[11]

The Parachute Engineer Battalion, with the 3rd Parachute Machine Gun Company and a platoon of anti-tank guns in support, was put down correctly north of Alikianou. "They had to free themselves from their harness and the abundant cactus while under fire from Greek troops and civilians," the New Zealand Official History recorded. "By the time they had done so they found that the Greeks had acquired German weapons." Numerous Greek partisans, including women and children, armed themselves with shotguns and resisted fiercely. Many of the parachute engineers' weapons canisters were lost and the battalion was soon surrounded by Australians, Greek soldiers, and Greek partisans, and suffered heavy casualties. At 2 P.M., when it was low in ammunition, seven Ju-52 transports dropped it arms and ammunition, but all of the canisters landed behind Greek lines. The engineers had to struggle just to survive.[12]

The experience of Major Ludwig Heilmann's III Battalion, 3rd Parachute Regiment, was fairly typical. III/FJR 3's mission was to seize the village of Galatas, on the road to Canea. Heilmann jumped with his 9th Company, which was dropped in the wrong place and landed in the middle of a concentration of Greeks and New Zealanders. Only by violent effort, relying mainly on machine pistols and grenades, were they able to seize one of the heights southeast of Galatas. The company had lost half of its men in the process.

By midday, Heidrich signaled XI Air Corps Headquarters that the attack on Canea had been discontinued due to heavy losses. By nightfall, the largest group of survivors of Group Center was in and around a place called Prison Valley, under the personal command of Colonel Heidrich. He had fewer than 1,000 unwounded men, and his position was critical. Meanwhile, scattered and isolated groups continued to hold out to the north.

Group West initially did no better than Group Center. The III Battalion of the Assault Regiment came to ground in its assigned drop zone (DZ), south of the Maleme-Platanias Road, a sector that was supposed to be free of enemy forces. Instead, it landed on top of the 21st and 23rd New Zealand Battalions and was quickly slaughtered before it could organize or even recover its weapons containers. All of its officers and 400 of its 600 men were killed, including Major Scherber, the battalion commander. Most of the rest of the Assault Regiment (but not all of it) landed west of the Tavronitis River, in zones generally free of enemy forces, and the 15th Company of Major Braun's IV Battalion seized the bridge over the river, just west of Maleme.

General Meindl jumped at 7:30 A.M. and landed west of the Tavronitis. Quickly assessing his situation, he found that that forces he had available consisted of the 3rd Company, I Battalion; the 5th, 7th, and 8th Companies of Stentzler's II Battalion; and the 15th Company. The rest of his assault units were unaccounted for. Maleme Airfield was still in enemy hands, and the scattered troops of Major Walter Koch's I Battalion had not taken the vital Point 107, just south of the airfield, as planned. Almost as soon as he landed, Meindl concluded that his best prospect for victory lay in exploiting Braun's success at the bridge and developing it into an attack that would take Point 107 from the northwest. He reinforced Braun with the 8th Company and ordered Major Stentzler to cross the river south of the bridge with the 5th and 7th Companies and to attack Point 107 from the southwest. Meindl's forces were soon heavily engaged by New Zealanders, Greek troops, and Cretan partisans, and their initial efforts to take Point 107 by frontal assault were unsuccessful. General Meindl was shot in the chest and critically wounded during the attempt.

Meanwhile, between 9 A.M. and 10 A.M., the VIII Air Corps and Ju-52 pilots returned to the mainland from their initial missions. Perhaps because their own operations had been so successful, they had formed optimistic (and erroneous) impressions of how the ground fighting was going. Based on these reports, the second wave was sent in as planned, resulting in further errors and setbacks. The situation on the overcrowded airfields was also deteriorating. It proved impossible to get the Ju-52s ready for a second sortie by 1 P.M., and some airplanes were delayed as long as three and a half hours due to the difficulty of refueling, because airplanes that crash landed or crashed upon landing had to be removed from the runways, and because the clouds of dust on the overtaxed fields were so thick that not even fire-firing equipment helped much. As a result, the Luftwaffe squadrons started in the wrong tactical order. Instead of arriving at their destinations together, the transports arrived haphazardly between 3 P.M. and 6 P.M. Because of their short range, however, the German fighters were only able to stay over the combat zone until 4:15 P.M. As a result, a major part of the second wave was dropped without fighter protection and suffered fairly heavy losses. Also, instead of dropping all of the paratroopers at once, as originally planned, they dropped them in small units at varying times—a further advantage for the defenders.

The ill-fated second wave included the I and III Battalions of FJR 2, which landed east of Retimo, and Colonel Braeuer's Group East (the 1st Parachute Regiment and most of the II Battalion of the 2nd). By nightfall, the survivors of these units were occupying positions in the hills and mountains, tending their wounded, and wondering whether they would ever again see the lights of home.

The defense of the airfield at Maleme was the responsibility of 49-year-old Brigadier Janies Hargest, the short, plump commander of the 5th New Zealand Brigade.[13] He had assigned the defense of the airfield and Hill 107 to Lieutenant Colonel Andrew's 22nd Battalion and echeloned the 23rd and 21st Battalions east of the field. He kept the 28th (Maori) Battalion in reserve in the village of Platanias, where he set up his own headquarters.

Andrew held the airfield and Hill 107 throughout May 20, but with a growing sense of isolation. The telephone lines between his battalion headquarters and his companies had been cut by the German bombing. (Because of the lack of time, the nature of the terrain, and the lack of tools, it had been impossible to bury them.) The battalion had lost most of its communications equipment in Greece and only had one wireless set, and it worked only intermittently. At 3:30 P.M., Andrew sent a message to brigade headquarters, indicating his growing anxiety concerning his lack of contact with most of his companies. He had also been promised reinforcements; in fact, the entire 23rd Battalion was supposed to come to his aid if he were heavily attacked. Six companies of German assault troops were now putting pressure on his perimeter, and he wanted to know where his reinforcements were.

At 5 P.M., Andrew again asked Brigadier Hargest for the promised reinforcements. Shortly afterward, Hargest replied that the 23rd was too heavily engaged against the paratroopers in its own sector to aid the 22nd. At that point, Andrew committed his last reserves, the 14th Platoon and his two I tanks, and ordered them to attack the Tavronitis Bridge. One of the tanks soon withdrew because its gun would not work. The second bellied down in the rough river bed and jammed its turret, whereupon it was abandoned by its crew. Meanwhile, the 14th Platoon met a withering fire; when it at last retreated, it had only 9 or 10 men left, and most of those were wounded.

At 6 P.M., Andrew again contacted Hargest and told him that the counterattack had failed. He said that he had no further resources and could only contact two of his five companies. Without reinforcements, he said, he would have to withdraw.

"If you must, you must," Hargest replied.[14]

Apparently Hargest thought that Andrew only intended to withdraw his forward elements to a ridge near the airfield. He did not seem to grasp the full implications of Andrew's proposed move. Later he did send him two companies, but one of them got lost in the darkness. Meanwhile, Braun's forces[15] pushed the 22nd's perimeter back once again, and by nightfall the Germans held the northern (seaward) side of the airfield, but the New Zealanders continued to cling to the southern end. Finally, between 9 P.M. and 9:30 P.M., Andrew again spoke to Hargest. By now his radio was so weak that it was the last message he would be able to send, and he told the brigadier that he was withdrawing. Hargest accepted this dispatch, without thinking that it called for any action on his part.

It was the turning point of the battle.

During the night of May 20–21, in his headquarters in Athens, General Student expected to receive word that a heavy attack had been launched against the remnants of the Assault Regiment near Maleme.

When it did not materialize, he decided to concentrate all of his efforts in this sector. This decision tipped the scales of the battle in favor of the Germans. He also named the hard-charging Colonel Hermann Bernard Ramcke commander of Group West. Ramcke, a Freikorps veteran who had undergone the standard, vigorous Luftwaffe jump school course at the age of 51, parachuted into the Maleme sector early on the morning of May 21, and immediately began to try to push back the Allies, who still had the airfield under intense infantry and artillery fire.

General Freyberg still did not know that the Maleme airfield had been lost. Had he known it, he undoubtedly would have done everything possible to recapture it. But misunderstandings and communications failures paralyzed the New Zealand command. Meanwhile, several Ju-52s crash landed on the beach at Maleme, bringing in arms and ammunition that the Assault Regiment desperately needed. Beginning at 4 P.M., elements of a mountain battalion were landed on the airfield at Maleme, despite the fact that it was under continuous artillery and machine gun fire. Several Ju-52s were destroyed in the process, but Ramcke now had the resources to launch a major attack. By 5 P.M., the village of Maleme was in German hands and the German hold on the airfield had been consolidated. By nightfall, the I and II Battalions of the 100th Mountain Infantry Regiment had landed on the damaged airfield.

"Maleme was like the gate of hell," General Ringel recalled. Eighty Ju-52s—every third transport to land—was destroyed, and the single runway was cleared by pushing the damaged airplanes off with a captured British tank, which was used like a bulldozer. Bekker described the sides of the airfield as a "giant aircraft cemetery."[16] In all, 150 Ju-52s would be lost in the Battle of Crete. The cost was high, but Maleme was nevertheless secure by the next day, when Ringel took command of Group West, and three more battalions of his 5th Mountain Division landed. The next step in the land battle was to extend the bridgehead, drive the enemy out of his naval strongpoint at Suda Bay (where fast convoys were still bringing in supplies at night), and make contact with Group Center.

In the meantime, the air-sea phase of the battle of Crete began. The British Mediterranean Fleet still barred the sea lanes to the island and prevented the Germans from bringing more reinforcements, tanks, and heavy weapons to the island. On May 22, with the tide of the land battle at last turning in Germany's favor, Richthofen's VIII Air Corps finally turned its full attention to the British warships.

The first skirmish had taken place the day before, when an Italian naval flotilla (made up mostly of Greek fishing vessels) carrying heavy weapons to Crete was attacked and dispersed by a British task force, which sank 10 Italian vessels. Richthofen promptly committed his corps reserve (which he had withheld for just such an eventually), and it sank the British destroyer *Juno* and damaged the cruiser *Ajax*. On the 22nd, however, the battle became general. At 5:30 A.M., several Stukas dived from 12,000 feet and bombed the cruisers *Gloucester* and *Fiji*, damaging but not sinking them. These ships then took positions further west, nearer Cunningham's main fleet (Task Forces A, B, and D); meanwhile, Rear Admiral Edward L. S. King's Task Force C patrolled the sea north of Crete with four cruisers and three destroyers. They located and chased a German flotilla that was trying to ship heavy weapons to Crete, but, just before King could catch the small German vessels, his task force was attacked by Richthofen's Ju-88s and Do-17s. Two of the cruiser *Naiad's* gun turrets were knocked out and her side was torn open, but her bulkheads held and she limped off at half speed. The cruiser *Carlisle* suffered a direct hit and her captain was killed, but she also remained afloat.

That afternoon, Richthofen's pilots seriously damaged the battleship *Warspite* with a direct hit and sank the destroyer *Greyhound*. King ordered two destroyers to pick up survivors and recalled the cruisers *Gloucester* and *Fiji* from the west, to provide anti-aircraft covering fire for the destroyers. When he gave this order, he did not realize that they had expended virtually all of their anti-aircraft ammunition that morning. When he learned the true situation, he promptly reversed himself, but it was too late: a dozen or more Stukas and Ju-88s spotted the *Gloucester* and pounded her. Soon she was on fire and her damage control teams were unable to extinguish the blazes. At 4 P.M., the fires reached her fuel tanks or a magazine, and she was shaken by an internal explosion and sank. Admiral King made the difficult decision to leave the crew to its fate, because any ship attempting to rescue it would itself fall victim to the Luftwaffe. That night, about 500 members of the *Gloucester's* crew were rescued by the small German flotilla and by Luftwaffe sea rescue aircraft.

Meanwhile the *Fiji*, escorted by destroyers, attempted to escape to Alexandria. She was spotted by a lone Me-109, carrying a single 500-pound bomb. As luck would have it, the bomb struck the *Fiji* in the side, below the water line, and exploded, fracturing the hull. It was listing heavily when a second Me-109 (summoned by the first) finished it off with a direct hit. The *Fiji* capsized at 7:15 P.M.

During the night of May 22–23, the destroyers *Kashmir* and *Kelly* shelled the Maleme airfield. When dawn broke, they were still off the northern shore of Crete, in position to block any Axis seaborne landing attempts. The navy did not come that day, but 24 Stukas from I/StG 2 did. Both destroyers were smashed and soon sank under the weight of direct hits. This was enough for Admiral Cunningham, who signaled London that the Royal Navy would have to withdraw: the losses were becoming more than the Mediterranean Fleet could afford. Churchill, however, was not yet ready to accept defeat, so he ordered the fleet to continue daylight operations north of Crete, no matter what the cost. He also instructed Sir Andrew to reinforce and resupply Freyberg's garrison, which was still trying to check the Germans.

May 21 and 22 were desperate days for Groups Center and East. Transport planes succeeded in bringing ammunition to Heidrich's forces near Prison Valley, but yet another attempt to seize the high ground around Galatas was beaten back. The German forces in the Retimo area, on the other hand, were totally on the defensive and held their positions against Greek and Australian attacks only with difficulty. To the east, Colonel Braeuer attempted to take the Heraklion airfield but without success. The attack was hopeless without heavy weapons.

On May 23, General Ringel was at last able to launch a general offensive, and the mountain troops and paratroopers pushed back the British, Greeks, and New Zealanders. That evening, they linked up with Group Center west of Canea. The following day, however, Ringel was halted before the strongly fortified Allied position at Galatas. Here, on the plateau west of Canea, Freyberg concentrated all of his available forces for the final defense of Suda Bay, and it was here that the final battle for Crete was fought.

On May 25, the German situation at Maleme was still far from satisfactory. Airplanes were constantly crashing while attempting to land on the relatively small and damaged airfield, and the naturally confined space had been made narrower still because of wreckage. Even so, 4th Air Fleet had little choice but to continue landing planes there, at least until another airfield could be secured or Cunningham's warships could be forced to withdrawn. By the end of the day, two more battalions had off-loaded at Maleme and were rushing toward the front.

The British defense took a double blow on May 26, when the aircraft carrier *Formidable* took two direct hits from German bombs off the coast of Crete, while the destroyer *Nubian* lost her stern. Meanwhile, supported by a concentrated attack from VIII Air Corps, General Ringel penetrated Freyberg's lines west of Canea. Freyberg was now convinced that the loss of Crete was only a matter of time. That morning he signaled Wavell, stated that his men were at the limits of their endurance, and asked for permission to evacuate.

Allied resistance in the vicinity of Canea was definitely broken on May 27. Freyberg ordered preparations for evacuation from the small harbor of Sfakia on the southern coast. The following day, Canea and Suda Bay fell to the Germans, and a tug brought two lighters into Maleme, carrying four panzers for Group West. The Royal Navy had at last abandoned daylight operations in the waters north of Crete. It had prevented the Germans from bringing in reinforcements and supplies by sea during the critical days of the battle, although its losses had been prohibitively high.

During the night of May 28–29, about 4,000 British troops were evacuated from the northern coast of the island. The British task force, however, was again met by the Luftwaffe, which sank the destroyers *Hereward* and *Imperial*, with about 800 men on board. The cruisers *Ajax*, *Orion*, and *Dido* were also damaged. This action ended Royal Navy operations off northern Crete. All that was left for the defenders to do was to escape to the southern coast. Well covered by two battalions of commandos, which retreated over terrain that was favorable to the defense, most of them did just that.

Because some people feared the loss of further ships, they urged Admiral Cunningham to abandon the ground troops still on Crete to their fate. This the admiral categorically refused to do. "It takes three years to build a ship. It takes 300 years to build a tradition," he declared. The evacuation continued.

On May 29, Ringel relieved Retimo and made contact with Group East near Heraklion. That night, the evacuation of Crete was in full swing. Sfakia, the collecting point for the evacuation, was a small fishing village at the foot of an almost perpendicular rock face, which was more than 300 feet high and negotiable only by one steep goat track. During the day, the men awaiting evacuation had to hide from the Luftwaffe, while the commandos conducted a bitter series of delaying actions in the mountains behind them.

The evacuation was completed on the night of May 31–June 1. A fleet of British cruisers, destroyers, and merchant ships took off a total of 17,000 men. Half of the British forces had to be taken from open beaches during the few short hours of night—a masterly feat of seamanship. During the evacuation, a Ju-88 sank the anti-aircraft cruiser *Calcutta* 100 miles off the coast of Alexandria. The cruiser *Perth* was damaged, as were three more destroyers.

Crete at been a victory for German arms, but it had been purchased at a heavy cost on both sides. Freyberg's British forces had lost 15,314 men during the battle of Crete (1,742 killed or missing, 1,737 wounded, and 11,835 captured). The Greek military and paramilitary forces had lost 2,600 killed; the rest were captured or dispersed. The Royal Air Force lost 46 airplanes, and the Royal Navy lost 1,828 dead or missing and 183 wounded. On the other side, the Germans lost 6,116 men out of 25,000 engaged—a fourth of the total. Hitler's forces suffered more casualties in Crete than they had during the entire Balkan campaign. The elite XI Air Corps had been decimated, and the aviation component of the Luftwaffe had been severely damaged on the eve of Operation Barbarossa. In all, Goering lost 220 airplanes, with another 64 damaged. The transport branch had been especially badly mauled.

Potentially, the worse strategic damage had been done to Cunningham's Mediterranean Fleet. It had lost three cruisers and six destroyers sunk and three battleships, seven cruisers, four destroyers, and an aircraft carrier damaged. After Crete, the Royal Navy in the eastern Mediterranean had an operational strength of only two battleships, two cruisers, and 13 destroyers, making it numerically inferior to the Italian Navy. Had Mussolini's fleet ventured forth with the support of the Luftwaffe, it would have had a reasonable chance of defeating the dreaded Cunningham and might have even forced the surrender of Malta or established Italian naval dominance in the eastern Mediterranean. The Italian Navy preferred to remain in port, however, and the opportunity passed, never to present itself again.

Crete was a strategic dead end for the Germans. Hitler had at last secured his Ploesti oilfields, and he was not interested in further operations in the Mediterranean theater. Rommel's operations in the desert now became strictly a sideshow; the main event was in Russia, which he invaded the following month.

Immediately after the fall of Canae, Student flew from Athens to Crete, to see what was left of his corps. (Loehr had forbidden him to go to the island prior to this.) One of his battalion commanders, Captain Baron Friedrich-August von der Heydte, noted that, "He had visibly altered. He seemed much graver, more reserved, and older. The cost of victory had evidently proved too much for him. Some of the battalions had lost all their officers and in several companies there were only a few men left alive."[17] After the war, General Student said,

The name of Crete is for me—the man who conquered it—a bitter memory.... I made a wrong decision when I suggested this attack, since not only did it mean the loss of so many paratroopers who were my sons, but also the end of the parachute arm, which I created myself.[18]

Crete did sound the death knell of the German parachute corps as an airborne force. On July 17, Hitler told Student that "the day of the parachutist is over. The parachute arm is a surprise weapon and without the element of surprise there can be no future for airborne operations." The German parachute corps survived—indeed, grew—but as a conventional infantry force. The Germans never conducted a large-scale airborne operation again.

NOTES

1. The Duke of Aosta surrendered the last Italian forces in Ethiopia on May 19, 1941.

2. G. C. Kiriakopoulos, *Ten Days to Destiny* (1985; reprint ed., 1986), p. 30 (hereafter cited as Kiriakopoulos); Willi Frischauer, *Reichsmarschall Hermann Goering* (1951), p. 195.

3. Playfair, vol. 2, p. 126; Kiriakopoulos, p. 44.

4. Charles Whiting, *Hunters From the Sky: The German Parachute Corps, 1940–1945* (1974), pp. 49–50 (hereafter cited as Whiting, *Hunter*).

5. Gundelach, "Crete," p. 116.

6. Ibid.

7. Frischauer, *Goering*, p. 190.

8. Bekker, *Luftwaffe War Diaries*, p. 261.

9. Halder Diaries, April 24, 1941.

10. Daniel M. Davin, *Official History of New Zealand in the Second World War, 1939–1945: Crete* (1953), p. 22 (hereafter cited as Davin, *Crete*).

11. Student, *Crete*, p. 55.

12. New Zealand Official History; Kiriakopoulos, p. 30; Student, *Crete*, p. 60; Frischauer, *Goering*, p. 195.

13. Playfair, vol. 2, p. 126.

14. Whiting, *Hunters*, pp. 49–50.

15. Major Braun was killed in action during the Battle of Crete, but at what point is not clear.

16. Davin, *Crete*, p. 42.

17. Gundelach, "Crete," p. 116.

18. Student, *Crete*, p. 90.

CHAPTER **XXVIII**

THE SIEGE OF BRITAIN, LATE 1940 TO MAY 1941

Many Western observers mentally segregate the Battle of Britain and the other air operations against the British Isles from the Battle of the Atlantic and the other naval operations against the United Kingdom. This interpretation is, in a sense, proper; however, in the realm of grand strategy (insofar as Nazi Germany had a grand strategy), they were definitely interrelated, even if they were not properly coordinated. Despite the fact that they were entirely different modes of warfare, they had the same objectives: (1) bring Britain to its knees or (2) reduce London's ability to wage war. The German naval forces waged war on three different levels: those of the armed merchant raider, the submarine, and surface raids by capital ships.

The most successful commerce raider was the *Atlantis*, which was commanded by the gallant Captain Berhard Rogge, a straight-laced officer who sent one of his men to prison for stealing a pair of binoculars from a captured British captain. In a 622-day, 102,000-mile cruise, he sank 22 ships (145,697 tons). His ship was sunk by the heavy cruiser *Devonshire* on November 22, 1941. Almost the entire crew was able to escape and were rescued by *U-126* and the supply ship *Python*. A few days later the *Python* was caught by another British cruiser and scuttled to avoid capture. The crews of the *Atlantis* and the *Python* boarded life boats and were at sea for a week before they were picked up by German submarines. When they finally got home, Hitler held a special reception for them in Berlin, promoted Rugge to rear admiral, and decorated him with the Oak Leaves to the Knight's Cross.

The handful of armed merchant raiders that Germany had were committed to operations in the spring of 1940. For a relative small investment (they represented only a tiny fraction of the German war effort), they caused relatively large disruptions in the British economy;

however, despite the headaches they caused the British Admiralty, they never posed a serious threat to British lifelines, and their effectiveness ended when the use of the convoy system became widespread. By November 1941, the glory days of the armed merchant raider were over, although the last one was not sunk until October 18, 1943.

Part of the German surface fleet also engaged in the dangerous business of surface raiding as well. One of the most successful such operations was directed by Theodor Krancke, the captain of the *Admiral Scheer*. On one four-month raid (ending April 1, 1941), the *Scheer* sank 17 enemy ships totaling 152,000 tons and damaged seven others. In addition, he disrupted British shipping from the North Sea to the Indian Ocean and evaded almost half of the British fleet, which attempted to run him down. He was awarded the Knight's Cross and, on the very day he docked at Kiel, was promoted to rear admiral. Shortly thereafter, he became naval liaison officer to Fuehrer Headquarters.

Meanwhile, at last, the Luftwaffe became interested in attacking shipping. OKM had long maintained that, if it tried, the Air Force alone could sink 300,000 tons of shipping a month and inflict heavy damage on the British harbors. This prediction proved correct, for, in April 1941, the Luftwaffe sank 296,000 tons of shipping, destroyed half of the docks in Liverpool, and put most of the Glasgow shipyards out of action for at least three months.[1] The Siege of Britain was tightening.

In the meantime, Admiral Guenther Luetjens, the commander of the German surface fleet, sailed from Kiel and began a major convoy raid with the battleships *Scharnhorst* and *Gneisenau*. This was his third attempt to reach the Atlantic, but this time he was successful, and he fell on British shipping lanes with his battleships. He sank five ships in one day and then turned southeast, to attack the route around the bulge of Africa; however, he was under strict orders from Raeder and SKL not to take any risks that might cause the loss of German capital ships. During this cruise, Luetjens intercepted two convoys with battleship escorts, but, in accordance with his take-no-risk orders, he did not attack them. Before the sortie was over, the two battleships had sunk 13 merchant vessels and sent three back to Germany as prizes. The British had lost 115,622 more tons of shipping and the convoy schedules had again been completely disrupted. Luetjens' run had also provided indirect cover for the returning *Scheer*. He then successfully evaded the Royal Navy and made his way to Brest, where he docked on March 23. He was summoned to Berlin in April.

THE SINKING OF THE BISMARCK

For his next mission, Grand Admiral Raeder ordered Gunther Luetjens to conduct a raid into the Atlantic with the heavy cruiser *Prinz*

Eugen and the battleship *Bismarck*. It would be the maiden voyage of the monstrous, 42,000-ton vessel.

Luetjens objected to Raeder's plan. He pointed out that the difference between the endurance of the two ships would prevent them from operating together as a homogeneous force. He wanted to wait until the *Scharnhorst* and *Gneisenau* were repaired and refitted and the *Tirpitz*, the sister ship of the *Bismarck*, completed her crew training period, which would mean a delay of about four months. As a combined force, these four ships would be difficult for even the Royal Navy to deal with; otherwise, Germany would be committing her forces piecemeal. Raeder, however, wanted to get them to sea while the Arctic nights were still long enough to provide cover. He felt that heavy ships were needed in the North Atlantic immediately, both to help the U-boats and to divert British naval strength from the Mediterranean, as well as to help the Afrika Korps and to provide indirect aid for the airborne invasion of Crete, which was scheduled for May 20.

Although he had by far the stronger case, and in spite of his own better judgment, Luetjens allowed himself to be persuaded. He remembered how his predecessors, Hermann Boehm and Wilhelm Marschall, had been sacked by the Grand Admiral, who was known to be overly sensitive to criticism, real or imagined. In fact, after leaving Berlin, Luetjens paid a visit to Marschall, a champion of the commander's right of freedom of action on the sea. The retired admiral urged Luetjens not to feel himself too closely bound by the instructions of SKL, the Naval Operations' Staff.

"No, thank you," Luetjens said as he rejected Marschall's advice. "There have already been two Fleet Commanders who have lost their jobs owing to friction with the Naval Staff, and I don't want to be the third. I know what they want, and shall carry out their orders."[2]

The stage was set for another disaster.

There was another reason for questioning the logic of this operation, which Admiral Luetjens did not use: Was it wise to employ battleships as commerce raiders—a mission for which they were not designed?

There were basically two reasons for doing so. First, Imperial Germany had lost World War I without utilizing her fleet to a faction of its capabilities—a fact that hung over the Naval Staff like a dark cloud during World War II. Admiral Raeder, among others, had strongly disapproved of the timid use of the Kaiser's fleet and was determined that the same mistake would not be committed in this war. Second, the German capital ships had enjoyed a surprising run of success as commerce raiders in the first two years of the war. The *Scharnhorst* and *Gneisenau* had sunk 22 British and Allied merchant vessels during the first two months of 1941, sending 115,622 tons of shipping to the bottom.[3] The heavy cruisers *Scheer* and *Hipper* had also experienced some success (especially the former). There was no reason not to expect a similar performance from the *Bismarck*, or so the German admirals thought.

Adolf Hitler visited Gotenhafen (now Gydnia, Poland) on May 5, to inspect both the *Tirpitz* and the *Bismarck*, and, like the Fleet Commander, expressed doubts about the advisability of this operation. Now, however, Luetjens strongly supported Raeder's point of view. Had he said what he really thought, it is quite likely that the tragedy of the *Bismarck* would have been avoided. Faced by the united front of his naval experts, however, Hitler decided not to interfere with Raeder's plans. Unlike the case with his army generals, the Fuehrer did not consider his ideas concerning naval warfare to be superior to those of his admirals. Not yet, anyway.

The *Bismarck*, accompanied by the *Prinz Eugen* (under Captain Helmuth Brinkmann) and three destroyer escorts, sailed for the Atlantic on May 18. They steamed out to sea through the Great Belt during the night of May 19–20 and were first spotted by a British agent in the Kattegat on the afternoon of the 20th. On May 21, the small German fleet entered Hellwerden, in the Korsfjord near Bergen, Norway, to refuel. Here they were positively identified by British aerial reconnaissance, and the hunt was on. The Admiralty's first step was to revoke the orders of the battle cruiser *Repulse* and aircraft carrier *Victorious*, which had been scheduled to sail to North Africa the following day, as escort for an important troop convoy to the Middle East.

The Denmark Strait was already blocked by the heavy cruiser *Norfolk*, the flagship of the 1st Cruiser Squadron. The squadron commander ordered the heavy cruiser *Suffolk*, then refueling at Hvalfjord, Iceland, to join him at once. Shortly before 11 P.M. that night, Admiral Sir Charles Tovey, the commander of the Home Fleet, sailed from Scapa Flow aboard the battleship *King George V*, escorted by the *Victorious* and the 2nd Cruiser Squadron, which included four cruisers and seven destroyers. Tovey also ordered the Battle Cruiser Squadron (led by Vice Admiral Lancelot Holland[4]) with the battleships *Hood* and the *Prince of Wales* to patrol the Denmark Strait north of the 62nd parallel. Tovey himself would take charge of covering the seas south of that parallel.

Luetjens, meanwhile, left the fjord during the night of May 21–22, with the *Bismarck* in the lead, sailing north, and dismissed his destroyer escorts at about the latitude of Trondheim. The weather was stormy, so he had decided to launch an immediate breakout attempt. Speed was of the essence. After crossing the Arctic Circle, Luetjens pushed through rains and heavy clouds, near the edge of the ice line. Suddenly, at 7:22 P.M. on May 23, near the northwest coast of Iceland, the British heavy cruiser *Suffolk* appeared out of a thick fog bank, seven miles from the battleship. Before the Germans could open fire, the *Suffolk* ducked back into the fog, circled back behind the battleship, and began sending radio signals. The *Bismarck*'s electronics specialists reported an ominous development: the British had a new type of tracking radar, and they were already trapped in its net. An hour or so later, the heavy cruiser *Norfolk* appeared out of the fog, and the battleship straddled her with 15-inch gun salvos, but she also escaped into the fog without serious damage.

That night, Luetjens reversed his order of battle and sent the *Prinz Eugen* ahead of the *Bismarck*, so that the battleship could threaten the British cruisers. In the low visibility, this move went unnoticed by the British. Both continued steaming southwest. Early the next morning, as the weather became increasingly clearer, the German lookouts spotted two new opponents: the battle cruisers *Hood* and *Prince of Wales*. The *Hood* was equal to the *Bismarck* in size, speed, and weaponry, but she was more than 20 years older and her deck armor was weak, so she was vulnerable to plunging fire. The *Prince of Wales* was a significantly better and more modern warship; however, its crew lacked experience; in fact, her guns had only been delivered three weeks before, and dockyard people were still on board, working on them.

The British battle cruisers and the *Bismarck-Prinz Eugen* team spotted each other almost simultaneously and both sides opened fire on each other at 5:52 A.M. The British commander, Admiral Holland, maintained radio silence until the firing began, in a vain attempt to achieve surprise against a task force that was already fully alert. By doing so, he forfeited the aid of the two heavy cruisers shadowing the *Bismarck*, as well as six nearby destroyers—a considerable loss of fire power.

The *Hood* opened up at a range of 12 miles. Admiral Holland ordered the fire be concentrated on the lead ship, which he supposed was the *Bismarck*. (The battleship and the *Prinz Eugen* had similar silhouettes, and the last reports from the cruisers indicated that the *Bismarck* was in the lead.) Captain John C. "Jack" Leach of the *Prince of Wales* realized that Holland had made a mistake, so he ordered his crew to fire on the *Bismarck*. The other British ships blazed away at the *Prinz Eugen*.

Despite the fire aimed at it, the well-trained crew of the *Prinz Eugen* trained accurate fire on the *Hood* and scored a direct hit on it within the first minute of the battle. It was soon blazing brightly from a large fire amidships. The *Bismarck* opened up about the same time, firing a salvo every 22 seconds, and she also found her range quickly. Meanwhile, the first salvo from the *Prince of Wales* missed the *Bismarck* by a half a mile.

The battle lasted about three minutes before Admiral Holland ordered his flagship, the *Hood*, to make a 20-degree turn to port. In the middle of this maneuver, the *Hood* was caught by a full salvo from the *Bismarck*. The 46,000-ton British battle cruiser erupted in a huge explosion that threw a fireball hundreds of feet into the air. The bow and stern were only momentarily visible before they buckled and plunged into the ocean, carrying 1,416 men with her. Only three men survived the disaster.

The *Prince of Wales* turned sharply to avoid the flaming wreck and, within 60 seconds, came under the same heavy, accurate fire. A 15-inch shell from the *Bismarck* hit her, killing or wounding everyone on the bridge except the captain and one crewman. Several of her new guns broke down, so she was firing salvos of three shells instead of 10. German shells were falling so thickly about her that she could hardly observe the effect of her own fire through the cascading water. One shell from the *Prinz Eugen* landed in a magazine but failed to explode. Two other shells (of 203 millimeters) penetrated the ship below the water line and let in 600 tons of water into the aft compartments. The *Prince of Wales* was only seven miles from the *Bismarck* when she turned about, pouring smoke, at 6:03 A.M. The German ships stopped firing at 6:09 A.M., when the Prince was about 21,000 yards away. The Battle of the Denmark Strait, which had only lasted 20 minutes, was over. Because of Captain Leach's insubordination, the *Bismarck* had suffered two hits from the 14-inch guns of the *Prince*. Her speed was reduced from 31 to 28 knots and (more important) she was losing fuel oil.[5] Ernst Lindemann, the captain of the *Bismarck*, wanted to follow the *Prince of Wales*, finish her off, and then return to Germany.[6] Admiral Luetjens, however, was determined to obey orders, no matter what. He allowed the British to break off the battle and headed for the Atlantic, despite the fact the *Bismarck* was trailing oil. Meanwhile, the remaining British ships in the vicinity continued to shadow the German battleship.

By early afternoon, Luetjens had decided to put into the port of St. Nazaire, probably the only French port with a drydock large enough to hold the *Bismarck*. He also released the *Prinz Eugen* and sent it off on an independent commerce raid. That afternoon the *Bismarck* turned on her pursuers, who quickly fell back out of range; meanwhile, the *Prinz Eugen* made good her escape.

In the meantime, the British Admiralty spared no effort to gather ships for use against the *Bismarck*. Chasing the German battleship was the bulk of the Home Fleet, Admiral Somerville's forces from Gibraltar (including the battle cruiser *Renown*, the aircraft carrier *Ark Royal*, and the cruiser *Sheffield*), and even the battleships *Rodney* and *Ramillies* and the cruiser *Edinburgh*, which were ordered to abandon the convoys they were escorting and to take an intercept course for the *Bismarck*. Shortly before nightfall on May 24, Admiral Tovey contacted the 2nd

Cruiser Squadron (four cruisers and an aircraft carrier) and ordered it to slow down the *Bismarck*. Shortly before midnight, it launched several Swordfish torpedo bombers from the new aircraft carrier *Victorious*. They conducted two torpedo attacks against the *Bismarck*, and one "eel" struck the battleship amidships but exploded on the heavy-side armor and did no damage. During the night, Luetjens turned southeast, heading straight for France. The British, meanwhile, lost contact with the *Bismarck*; Luetjens, however, did not realize it, because the radar beams were still hitting the ship. He did not know that the beams were no longer bouncing back to the *Suffolk*'s receiver. For this reason, he sent a long message back to Naval Group West, describing the Battle of the Denmark Straits. He thus gave his own position away; however, the eager British navigators misplotted the data and directed Admiral Tovey to head northeast, toward the Iceland-Faeroes Passage, instead of toward France. By the time the mistake was discovered seven hours later, most of the destroyers were low in fuel and had to give up the chase.

The *Bismarck* was not discovered again until 10:30 on the morning of May 26, when a flying boat from the Coastal Command reported that it was about 690 miles west of Brest. By this point, it seemed likely that the *Bismarck* would reach port. Only the ships of Vice Admiral Sir John Somerville's Force H from Gibraltar were now within range of the *Bismarck*, and he was ordered not to engage her, because nothing in his command could match her 380-millimeter guns. The only chance the Royal Navy had left was the Swordfish biplanes of the *Ark Royal*. In seas tossing so violently that the flight deck pitched through a 56-foot arc, 15 biplanes took off. Initially, however, 11 of them attacked a British ship, the *Sheffield*, at 2:50 P.M. Five of the torpedoes exploded prematurely, and the *Sheffield* avoided the other six. Valuable time was lost in this near tragedy, but it did cause the British to replace the defective magnetic detonators on their torpedoes with contact detonators. At 10:55 P.M., the 15 Swordfish found and attacked the correct target. This was definitely the last chance the British would have; if the biplanes failed, the *Bismarck* would be close enough to France to be under the protective umbrella of the Luftwaffe.

The *Bismarck*'s 56 anti-aircraft guns blazed away at the Swordfish, but the violent pitching of the sea spoiled their aim. Several of the biplanes were hit, but none were shot down. All 15 biplanes attacked. Two could not launch their torpedoes, and 11 missed their target. One torpedo struck the *Bismarck* amidships, causing little damage. The fifteenth torpedo smashed into the steering engine room at rear of the ship, apparently causing little damage. However, the rudders had been hard over when the torpedo struck, and now they were stuck, and nothing could move them. Had they been at their normal positions, the *Bismarck* could have steered with her three propellers by altering engine speeds, but not with the rudders hard over. This doomed the *Bismarck*, which began to circle, out of control. She swung within range of the surprised *Sheffield* and scored a hit on her, knocking out her radar and killing or wounding a dozen men. The *Sheffield* escaped under a smoke screen and reported the *Bismarck*'s condition to the capital ships of the Home Fleet, which quickly closed in.

During the night, German divers desperately tried to free the rudders, but without success. Luetjens signaled Hitler and promised to fight to the last. Hitler responded by thanking them for their sacrifice in the name of the German people. Luetjens also asked Grand Admiral Raeder to award the Knight's Cross to his gunnery officer, Commander Adalbert Schneider, for sinking the *Hood*. Hitler immediately granted the medal to the doomed officer. In an attempt to save at least part of his crew, Admiral Luetjens (who was now completely out of anti-aircraft ammunition) set his flak crews out to sea in rafts. None of them were rescued, however.[7]

The unequal battle began at 8:47 A.M. About 9 A.M., the bridge suddenly became an inferno of flames, and this is probably when Admiral Luetjens died, but because so few Germans lived to tell the tale of the last hours of the *Bismarck*, this is impossible to confirm. The German battleship was an easy target and was systematically pounded at long range by the British fleet. Once the German fire control system was destroyed, they came in closer, firing shells and torpedoes. Toward the end, the British battleships were firing salvo after salvo of one-tons shells into the *Bismarck* from a distance of only two miles. The battleship was also hit by seven torpedoes, but still did not sink. Fearing that the British might try to board the burning hulk, the crew detonated their scuttling charges. The *Bismarck* finally capsized to port and sank at 10:40 A.M. on May 27. Only 110 members of the *Bismarck*'s crew survived: 2,100 on were killed or drowned, including Captain Lindemann and the entire fleet staff, including Admiral Dr. Hans-Releff Riege, the fleet surgeon. The British made little effort to save them.

It had taken eight British battleships, two carriers, four heavy cruisers, seven light cruisers, 21 destroyers, and dozens of airplanes and supporting vessels to catch and destroy the *Bismarck*. In doing so, they had lost their biggest capital ship and a destroyer, and two battleships were so severely damaged that they were forced to spend months undergoing repairs in "neutral" American shipyards. They had, however, accomplished their mission: the pride of the German fleet was lost beneath the waves.

After the Bismarck debacle, Hitler never fully trusted Admiral Raeder's judgment again. Raeder wrote later,

Whereas before this he had given me a relatively free hand as long as government policies or the other armed services were not involved, he now became extremely critical and very apt to insist on agreement with his personal views ... now he issued directives to me that radically restricted the movements of these major units. He forbade their sorties into the Atlantic.[8]

Hitler's declining confidence in Admiral Raeder was not necessarily bad news for the German Navy. Raeder had exhibited questionable tactical and operational judgment since before the war began, and since 1939 had shown a tendency to dissipate the navy's strength on raids of dubious value—such as the *Bismarck* sortie. Raeder had also been slow to appreciate the value of the submarine and had assigned U-boat construction a relatively low priority, even after it had proven its effectiveness against the British. Indeed, Hitler's major naval failure—other than going to war far too early—was probably retaining Erich Raeder as commander-in-chief of the Navy as long as he did.

After the death of the *Bismarck*, the Naval Operations Staff also concluded that the days of the Atlantic sorties were over. They decided not to complete the aircraft carrier, because it could not possibly break out into the Atlantic. Henceforth, German capital surface ships only had two major missions: patrol the Baltic, and remain a fleet in being, to tie down the British Navy.

Meanwhile, the Luftwaffe redeployed to the East, in preparation for the invasion of the Soviet Union. It would no longer play a major role in the Battle of the Atlantic. Henceforth, the German war at sea (and thus the Siege of Britain) would be waged almost exclusively by the submarine.

NOTES

1. Edward P. von der Porten, *The German Navy in World War II* (1969), p. 131 (hereafter cited as Porten).

2. Ibid., pp. 133–34.

3. See Theodor Krancke and H. J. Brennecke, *Pocket Battleships* (1958) and Charles E. Pfannes and Victor A. Salamone, *The Great Admirals of World War II*, vol. 2, *The Germans* (1984).

4. Lancelot E. Holland was born in 1887 (the son of a doctor) and joined the Royal Navy in 1902. He served in the China sector and was a gunnery officer during World War I. Promoted to captain in 1926, he headed the British naval mission to Greece in the early 1930s and was captain of the battleship H.M.S. *Revenge* (1934–35). Later he was naval aide-de-camp to King George VI, commander of the 2nd Battle Squadron of the Atlantic Fleet, and Admiralty representative to the Air Ministry. He commanded the 7th Cruiser Squadron in the Mediterranean before assuming command of the Battlecruiser Squadron. Admiral Holland was intelligent and well read. He was married but his only child (a son) died of polio in 1935 at age 18.

5. After the Battle of the Denmark Strait, the *Prince of Wales* was sent to the Pacific. It was sunk by Japanese torpedo-bombers in the South China Sea on December 10, 1941. Captain Leach went down with the ship, along with 326 of his men. Almost 1,200 of the ship's complement were rescued.

6. Ernst Lindemann was born in Altenkirchen, Rhineland-Palatinate in 1894. He joined the Imperial Navy in 1913 and was commissioned in 1915. He became a gunnery officer on battleships (including the *Schleswig-Holstein*) and fought in World War I (where he earned both grades of the Iron Cross). Later he served in the Reichswehr and was chief of the Construction Department in the OKM in the late 1930s. He was promoted to *Kapitaen zur See* in 1938 and assumed command of the *Bismarck* in August 1940.

7. Gerhard Bidlingmaier, "Exploits and End of the Battleship *Bismarck*," U.S. Naval Institute *Proceedings* 84 (July 1958), pp. 77–78.

8. Raeder, *My Life*, p. 358.

CHAPTER **XXIX**

THE NORTH AFRICAN SIDESHOW

While Hitler's paratroopers were being slaughtered on Crete, two of his mobile divisions, the 5th Light and 15th Panzer, were busy in another secondary theater: North Africa. The corps commander here, Erwin Rommel, was quite junior in rank (he had only been promoted to lieutenant general at the beginning of the year) and, at age 49, was quite young for his post. These facts led many of the senior army generals to suspect that Rommel, the former commander of the Fuehrer's bodyguard, owed his appointment to his political connections, rather than to ability. It is true that Hitler admired Rommel, at least until the latter part of 1942; however, most of those who questioned his ability were soon silenced, because Rommel was a tactical genius and a natural combat leader. In fact, no other theater of war is as closely associated with a single individual as the desert theater is associated with Erwin Rommel—the "Desert Fox."

Rommel, who won the *Pour le Merite* for bravery against the Italian Army in World War I, was summoned to Fuehrer Headquarters on February 6, 1941, where he was named commander of German Troops in North Africa. Initially his command consisted only of the X Italian Infantry Corps and the German Afrika Korps, which was not yet in Africa. His own immediate superior would be Italian Marshal Rodolfo Graziani.[1]

Later that day, Rommel met with Field Marshal von Brauchitsch, who confirmed his appointment and told him that the 5th Light Division would disembark in Tripoli from mid-February until mid-April. The 15th Panzer would follow and should be totally disembarked by the end of May. Rommel was instructed not to assume the offensive until both divisions had been completely disembarked.

When Rommel left Fuehrer Headquarters shortly afterward, neither von Brauchitsch nor Halder knew that he was a man to whom orders were not sacred things; rather, throughout his career, he would depend on his own judgment of the situation and act accordingly. The idea of actually taking orders from an Italian general never entered his head, and it never would.

During the war, the rumor spread (and still has some believers) that the Afrika Korps was an elite, handpicked German force, specially trained for desert warfare. One Allied report stated that the men were forced to live in overheated barracks (to acclimate them to the heat) and had to run up and down the sandy beaches of Pomerania, dressed in heavy greatcoats, to get used to operating in desert terrain. This is simply not true. Due to the quickest of the Italian collapse, there was no time to institute a desert training program (although such a course was later set up at the Grafenwoehr Maneuver Area in northern Bavaria, to train replacements). Nor is it true that the men of the Afrika Korps were elite, handpicked volunteers. They were sent to Libya simply because they were available for immediate deployment.

The first unit to disembark in Tripoli was the 3rd Panzer Reconnaissance Battalion, which off-loaded on February 14–15. Rommel immediately sent them to the frontline, which he had set about 200 miles away. Rommel did not have a single tank on the ground in North Africa; nevertheless, he was already thinking of assuming the offensive, despite the fact that Hitler had intended for the Afrika Korps to serve as a blocking force (*Sperrverband*) only. When Rommel revealed his idea to OKH, however, he was called back to Germany, where Brauchitsch and Halder told him to forget all about attacking until the entire Afrika Korps had arrived (that is, at the end of May). Then—perhaps—he would be allowed to try to take Benghazi. Rommel argued against this timidity. Now was the time to strike, he declared, while the British were still weak from rushing so many of its veteran units to Greece. He spoke of winning a decisive victory in North Africa before they could return and of conquering Egypt and driving to the Suez Canal, possibly even recapturing German East Africa. Halder, who loathed Rommel from the beginning, smiled impolitely at this. What would Rommel need for such a purpose? he asked.

Two more panzer corps, Rommel replied.

"Even if you had them, how are you going to supply them and feed them?" Halder asked.

"That's quite immaterial to me," Rommel replied. "That's your pigeon."

After some mutual recriminations, Brauchitsch and Halder rejected Rommel's plans. He returned to Africa with orders not to assume the offensive until late May at the earliest. These orders were intercepted by British intelligence, which relayed them to North Africa, where the Allied generals took them seriously—quite unlike Erwin Rommel, who tended to ignore orders he did not like.

When Rommel attacked on March 31, the British were not ready, either physically or psychologically. Rommel's First Cyrenacian campaign was a devastating success. Despite serious logistical problems and the fact that he had only a fraction of his forces available, he quickly smashed the British 2nd Armoured Division. Pursuing relentlessly across the desert, he surrounded and destroyed the remnants of the division at Mechili (April 7–8). Benghazi was captured on April 4. Prisoners included Lieutenant General Sir Philip Neame, commander of the Cyrenacian Command (formerly Western Desert Force), and General Sir Richard O'Connor, who had been sent forward as an advisor by Wavell. Major General Michael D. Gambler-Parry, the commander of the 2nd Armoured, was also captured.

With the greater part of Cyrenacian Command now smashed by Rommel's sudden blitzkrieg, the Desert Fox thrust forward again. Very little now lay between him and the Suez Canal, except for two obstacles: the two Australian brigades of Major General Leslie J. Morshead's tough 9th Australian Infantry Division, now located north of Mechili and retreating along the Coastal Road as rapidly as they could, and the fortress of Tobruk. If Rommel could cut off Morshead's brigades before they reached the fortress, his changes of overcoming the garrison in one pounce would be great. On April 8, Rommel was reinforced with the 605th Anti-Tank Battalion, the vanguard of the 15th Panzer Division. At its head was Major General Heinrich von Prittwitz und Gaffron, an energetic and experienced tank commander who had led the 2nd Brigade in France. Rommel immediately placed him in charge of a combat group made up of the 3rd Recon, 8th Machine Gun, and 605th Anti-Tank Battalions, and ordered him to continue the pursuit. He realized if he took Tobruk, he might well deal the British Empire a crippling blow.

Winston Churchill had the same thought. On April 7, he instructed Wavell that Tobruk was to be defended "to the death, without thought of retirement."[2] Wavell immediately began to reinforce Morshead with everything available. The bulk of the 7th Australian Division was inside the Tobruk perimeter on April 9, and, by the time Rommel launched his first major attack on the fortress, it was defended by the equivalent of six full infantry brigades, four regiments of artillery, two anti-tank regiments, 75 anti-aircraft guns, 45 tanks, and a total of 36,000 men. This force would be too much for Rommel to bypass. He would have to reduce it before he could invade Egypt.

On April 8, von Prittwitz cut off and captured one of the Australian rearguards (800 men), but he was unable to prevent Morshead from retiring into the fortress. On April 9, Rommel sent the Brescia and later the 102nd Trento Motorized Division (just up from Italy) to attack Tobruk from the west, while the 5th Light swept across the desert to strike it from the southeast. Major General Johannes Streich, the commander of the 5th Light, was again slow, partially due to maintenance problems that Rommel felt should have been ignored. As a result, no attack could be launched against the fortress until April 12. Meanwhile, General von Prittwitz pushed too close to an Australian rearguard on April 10. An anti-tank gunner scored a direct hit on his armored car, killing him and his driver instantly.

Rommel's forces completed the encirclement of the Tobruk landfront on April 11. That same day, elements of Baron von Weckmar's 3rd Reconnaissance and Lieutenant Colonel Gustav Georg Knabe's 15th Motorcycle Battalion occupied Bardia, 65 miles east of Tobruk on the Libyan-Egypt frontier.

Rommel's first attack against Tobruk was launched by the Brescia Division and elements of the 5th Panzer Regiment. The Germans were surprised to find an anti-tank ditch that they could neither cross nor flank. After suffering several casualties to artillery fire, they retreated. The fierceness of the defense also surprised Rommel, who expected to meet only confused and disorganized opponents. Regretfully, he suspended his offensive until the rest of his combat forces could catch up.

The second attack came on the night of April 13–14. Lieutenant Colonel Gustav Ponath's 8th Machine Gun Battalion led the way, supported by a battalion of anti-aircraft guns. They crawled forward, demolished a section of the anti-tank ditch, and broke through the British perimeter. With Colonel Herbert Olbrich's 5th Panzer Regiment coming up behind him, Ponath formed a spearhead and drove toward the port of Tobruk.

Olbrich made good progress initially but advanced on too narrow a front. The Italians assigned the task of covering his flank failed to do so, and, within a few miles of the town, he met stiff resistance from Fort Pilastrino and the 1st Royal Artillery Regiment, firing over open sights. Worried about being cut off, Olbrich ordered a retreat when he was attacked by a detachment of British cruiser tanks—a move that was tantamount to abandoning Ponath and his men to their fate. When he learned what had happened, Rommel desperately tried to organize a rescue attempt, but it was afternoon before he could get the Ariete Armored Division into line. Then a few British shells landed nearby. "The confusion was indescribable," Rommel wrote later. "The division broke up in complete disorder, turned tail and streamed back in several directions."[3]

Rommel tried to break through again on April 16. His objective was Ras el Madauer (Hill 187), which dominated much of the Australian line. The attack was led by the Ariete Armored Division and part of the Trento Motorized Division. They were supported by several German companies (directly behind them) and German artillery. In this way, Rommel hoped to obtain better results from his allies.

Ariete, probably the best of the Italian divisions, was in pitiful mechanical shape. It had started the offensive with 100 tanks, but more than 80 percent of them had broken down before it even met the enemy. Those that were left were no match for the British tanks. In fact, there was a joke that went around the Afrika Korps. "Who," the question went, "are the bravest soldiers in the world?"

"The Italians," was the answer.

"Why the Italians?"

"Because they go into combat with the equipment that they have."

To Erwin Rommel, however, it was no laughing matter. "It made one's hair stand on end to see the sort of equipment with which the Duce had sent his troops into battle," he wrote.[4]

The Ariete made good progress at first. They pushed back the Australians and even succeeded in overrunning Ras el Madauer. Then one of their periodic panics seized the Italians, who broke for the rear or rushed to surrender to the Australians. Among the Germans killed in this battle was Colonel Max Eichstaedt, the commander of the 33rd Panzer Artillery Regiment.

Colonel Ponath, meanwhile, put up a fierce resistance. Surrounded by the Australians, he dug in and held out for days. Then, at 11 P.M. on April 20, with his unit reduced to a handful of men and his command post surrounded, Colonel Ponath, who had already been wounded twice, led a desperate breakout attempt. An Australian rifleman, firing at nearly point-blank range, blew his brains out. The 8th Machine Gun Battalion was nearly wiped out. Only 116 of the 500 men who had been surrounded on April 14 escaped.[5]

Rommel was embittered and blamed General Streich and Colonel Olbrich for the loss of the 8th Machine Gun. He believed in two qualities above all others: loyalty and efficiency. Now he set about clearing house with a vengeance, and he sacked everyone whom he believed lacking in either quality. Rommel had never been General Halder's choice for this post because he had never undergone General Staff training and because Halder felt that Rommel had been promoted beyond his capabilities and had used political influence to obtain advancement. In any case, several General Staff officers were allied with General Halder against Erwin Rommel and at least one of them tried to engineer his removal. There was also beyond doubt a secret correspondence taking place between Halder and an officer on Rommel's staff, and Rommel correctly felt that there was a conspiracy afoot; therefore, he conducted a bloodless Night of the Long Knives and sent those whom he considered disloyal or inefficient back to Germany. They included General Streich; Colonel Olbrich; Hans-Henning von Holtzendorff, commander of the 104th Panzer Grenadier Regiment; Lieutenant Colonel Count von Schwerin of the 200th Special Purposes Regiment; Major Wolfgang Hausser, Streich's operations officer; Major Ehlers, the operations officer of the Afrika Korps; and Colonel Claus von dem Borne, the chief of staff of the Afrika Korps. Major General Heinrich Kirchheim was named temporary commander of the 5th Light. Rommel lived to regret this appointment, because Kirchheim did not turn out to be a good divisional commander, so Rommel sacked him as well, and replaced him with Major General Johannes von Ravenstein. Meanwhile, Major General Baron Hans-Karl von Esebeck assumed command of the 15th Panzer Division.[7]

There were howls of protest from OKH concerning Rommel's actions; apparently Halder and his friends in Berlin, who were agitating for Rommel's dismissal behind the scenes, did not believe he would have the gall to strike down their spies and confederates in Africa. Halder had even gone so far as to send a special staff to Africa, under the direction of Colonel Alfred Gause, to coordinate supply matters and serve as a liaison officer between Rommel and the Italians. Major Frederick Wilhelm von Mellenthin, the future intelligence officer for the Afrika Korps, was a member of this special staff. Rommel's reception was frigid, and with good reason: Gause had orders not to place himself under Rommel's command. The Desert Fox gave him a quick and simple choice: subordinate himself to Rommel's direction or return home at once. The East Prussian quickly yielded; in fact, he turned out to be a loyal subordinate and good chief of staff, with little talent for, or interest in, intrigue.

Von Mellenthin wrote later,

Rommel was not an easy man to serve; he spared those around him as little as he spared himself. An iron constitution and nerves of steel were needed to work with Rommel, but I must emphasize that although Rommel was sometimes embarrassingly outspoken with senior commanders, yet once he was convinced of the efficiency and loyalty of those in his immediate entourage, he never had a harsh word for them.[8]

Rommel attacked Tobruk again on April 30, but was again repulsed. Both sides now settled down for a long siege, mercifully unaware that it would last another 221 days. Stalemate had set in on the North African Front. For the next eight months, breaking the Siege of Tobruk would be a matter of the highest priority in the British war effort. Rommel's forces, however, would remain a low priority in Berlin, and with considerable justification: on June 22, 1941, Adolf Hitler committed 3 million men to Operation Barbarossa—the invasion of the Soviet Union.

NOTES

1. Rodolfo Graziani (1882–1955) had commanded a regiment in World War I and emerged from that conflict as the youngest colonel in the Royal Army.

He later was named commander of Colonial Troops in Tripolitania and suppressed a rebellion in Libya with great severity; in fact, he gained the nickname "Breaker of the Natives." He served as vice governor of Cyrenaica (1926–30), governor of Cyrenaica (1930–34), governor of Italian Somaliland (1935–36), commander of the XI Corps (1936–37), viceroy of Ethiopia (1937–38), commander of the 10th Army (1939–40), and governor-general of Libya and commander-in-chief, North Africa (1940–41). Although a Fascist, he was anti-German. In 1941, after he wished aloud for the day when he could lead an Italian Army against the Germans, he was relieved of his command. Graziani, however, remained loyal to the Duce. After Mussolini was deposed and then restored to power by the Germans, he set up his Social Republic and named Graziani his minister of war and commander of the Ligurian Army (1943–45). After the fall of the Social Republic and Nazi Germany, Graziani was convicted as a minor war criminal and was imprisoned until 1950 for collaborating with the Germans.

2. Strawson, pp. 56–57.

3. Rommel Papers, pp. 125–26; Playfair, vol. 2, p. 37.

4. Rommel Papers, p. 127.

5. The survivors of the 8th Machine Gun Battalion were incorporated into the 200th Panzer Engineer Battalion.

6. Johannes Streich was sent to the Eastern Front, where he briefly commanded the 16th Motorized Division. He was not considered a success here, either, and also ran afoul of Heinz Guderian, then commanding the 2nd Panzer Army. Streich spent the rest of the war in staff assignments with the Replacement Army. He was promoted to lieutenant general in October 1943. He surrendered to the Western Allies at the end of the war. He died in Hamburg in 1977.

7. Kirchheim (1882–1973) spent the rest of the war in minor staff appointments.

8. F. W. von Mellenthin, *Panzer Battles* (1956), p. 54 (hereafter cited as Mellenthin).

CHAPTER XXX

PRELUDE TO BARBAROSSA

While Erwin Rommel struggled to take Tobruk with fewer than two German divisions, 75 percent of the German Army secretly deployed in assembly areas in northern Norway, Finland, East Prussia, occupied Poland, the Protectorate and Romania, for Hitler's invasion of the Soviet Union.

THE PLAN

German operational planning for the invasion of the Soviet Union had began in July 1940. After some initial studies by Colonel von Lossberg and Colonel Hans von Greiffenberg of the OKH operations staff, Halder gave Major General Erich Marcks, the chief of staff of the 18th Army, the task of drawing up a basic plan for the invasion of the Soviet Union on July 29.

Marcks looked like the stereotype of a studious college professor, down to his wire-rimmed glasses. He was, however, a highly capable General Staff officer. His final plan was ready on August 5, and it formed the basis for Operation Barbarossa in its final form. It envisioned a campaign of two phases: first, the Soviet armies close to the frontier would be destroyed in battles of encirclement; then, the most valuable industrial regions in the Soviet Union would be occupied, including Leningrad, Moscow, and the Donetz Basin of the Ukraine. To accomplish this task, Marcks proposed that two army groups, North and South, be created. They would be divided by the Pripyat Marshes (a vast swamp 150 miles from north to south, and more than 300 miles long), and their mission would be to attain the Archangel-Gorky-Rostov line. Moscow, he stated, "constitutes the economic, political, and spiritual center of the U.S.S.R. Its capture would destroy the coordination of the Russian state."[1]

Halder accepted Marcks's basic ideas and turned the detailed planning over to Lieutenant General Friedrich Paulus, the new deputy chief of the General Staff for operations, on September 17. Paulus retained Marcks's basic concepts, but added a third army group and specified that three major thrusts take place: Army Group North to Leningrad, Army Group Center to Moscow, and Army Group South to Kiev. Moscow was to remain the primary objective.

Brauchitsch and Halder presented the plan to Hitler on December 5. Hitler had only one major objection to it, but it was one of the greatest significance: he wanted to defeat the Russians on the northern and southern wings first and take the Ukraine and Leningrad. "Moscow," he said, "is of no great importance."[2] He was more concerned with capturing the Baltic States and the agricultural and industrial complexes to the south. The loss of the Ukraine and its Donetz Industrial Basin, he believed, would wreck the Soviet economy and cause the people to turn against the Communists. Then, he felt, the capture of Moscow would be an easy matter.

The OKH generals did not protest when Hitler changed the fundamental focus of their plan. They had learned that remonstrating with the Fuehrer did no good; nevertheless, they continued to regard Moscow as the main objective, for both political and military reasons. It was, after all, the transportation and communications hub of the Soviet Union. They believed that a thrust toward Moscow would compel the Red Army to oppose it with most of its divisions, which would give the German Army an opportunity to encircle and destroy them. Apparently Halder and von Brauchitsch felt that, once the campaign was under way, events would dictate the correct course of action. "A conspiracy of silence descended on the subject," Cooper wrote later.[3] Major General (later General of Artillery) Walter Warlimont, the deputy chief of operations at OKW, wrote, "It later became known that their reasoning was that, in time, the course of the campaign would compel even Hitler to go back to the original Army concept. This was to a certain extent taking the easy way out and it proved to be no more than self-deception."[4]

As a result, the campaign would begin with the Fuehrer and his senior generals divided over the issues of what was the major objective of the invasion. The seeds of disaster had been sown.

Hitler's decision to invade Russia at this time did not meet unanimous approval within the Wehrmacht. Field Marshal Fedor von Bock, for one, objected to the entire idea of invading Russia, as did Hermann Goering and Field Marshal Wilhelm Keitel. Rather than risk another scathing dressing down, Keitel sent him a written memoranda in

August 1940. Hitler, who now surrounded himself only with "yes-men," summoned him to his office and gave him a vicious reprimand. Deeply wounded, Keitel suggested that the Fuehrer find an OKW chief whose judgment he trusted more. Hitler flew into a rage and heaped a torrent of abuse on Keitel's head. He did not have the right to resign, the dictator shouted, but would serve until he had no further use for him. The humiliated field marshal left the room without saying a word. Now he saw clearly part of the price he would have to pay for accepting promotions he did not deserve and a position for which he was intellectually not qualified. His reaction to this impossible situation was to submit completely; he would carry out the will of the Fuehrer, no matter what that entailed. Keitel, of course, could not foresee that he was taking a road that would end at the gallows in Nuremberg in 1946.

In May 1941, Keitel signed the infamous Commissar Order, in which he commanded that German soldiers shoot Red political officers immediately after they were captured, without courts-martial or trials of any kind. Several generals protested against this criminal order (including von Bock and Guderian), which directed them to shoot unarmed prisoners of war, but Keitel insisted that it be obeyed to the letter. This order, which originated with Hitler, can be traced to a speech he made to his commanders on March 30, in which he ordered that all Soviet officials, civilian or military, were to be shot when captured, even if they surrendered. In Russia, he said, the German soldier was not to be bound by the ordinary rules of war.[5] This speech set the tone for one of the cruelest conflicts in modern history.

The Commissar Order was not the only controversial directive issued that spring. Reichsfuehrer-SS Heinrich Himmler, who calmly estimated that approximately 30 million Slavs alone would have to be allowed to starve in the East before German colonization began, secretly gave orders to the *Einsatzgruppen*: racially inferior types, such as Jews and gypsies, and in some cases Slavs, were to be exterminated, as were known Communists, former officials, homosexuals, residents of mental institutions, and so forth. The depopulated lands could then be recolonized by Germans and Germanic peoples, including Danes, Dutch, Swedes, Norwegians, and perhaps even Englishmen, after the war was won. Hitler himself urged his men to be ruthless. "This enemy consists not of soldiers but to a large extent only of beasts," he said. "This is a war of extermination." Neither the rules of the Hague Convention (on the law of warfare) nor the Geneva Convention (on prisoners of war) applied to this war, he said, since the Soviet Union was not a signatory to either agreement. In early May, he issued an order forbidding the army to prosecute German soldiers who killed or mistreated Soviet civilians.

THE NEW WAVES

While the political maneuvering continued behind the scenes, General Fromm and his men were working feverishly, raising new divisions for Operation Barbarossa. Hitler demanded that the army expand from 120 to 180 combat divisions for his invasion of the Soviet Union, and the Replacement Army and the Wehrkreise raised no fewer than five new waves of troops for the campaign.

The Wave 11 infantry divisions were created by transferring cadres from existing divisions to the new unit and then "rounding them out" with new recruits from the draft class of 1920. Simultaneously, other new draftees were transferred to the old divisions, so that no division was too badly depleted and each would have at least a sizable contingent of combat veterans. Each old division transferred three battalions back to its home Wehrkreis, where they were incorporated into a new division. All of the Wave 11 divisions were three-regiment divisions (that is, all had three infantry regiments). The Wave 11 divisions were numbered between 121 and 137.

The Wave 11 divisions were all more or less ready by October 1940; by then, the Replacement Army had already begun work on the Wave 12 divisions, which were formed in the same manner as the Wave 11 divisions. The divisions of the 12th Wave were the 97th, 99th, 100th, and 101st Jaeger and the 102nd through 113th Infantry Divisions. The Jaeger divisions (light infantry divisions) were formed from the same cadres, but controlled only two rifle regiments and were equipped as pursuit divisions. Ten Wave 12 divisions had been formed and activated by the end of December 1940.

The Wave 13 divisions were formed in a manner similar to the Wave 11 divisions. They were not, however, nearly as well equipped and were not designed for combat on the Eastern Front; rather, they were used as occupation or garrison units to free other divisions for employment in the East. All were posted to France or Belgium except the 319th Infantry Division, which was used to garrison the English Channel Islands of Guernsey, Jersey, Alderney, Sark, Herm, and Jethou. There were nine divisions in the 13th Wave, numbered between 302 and 327. All were infantry and all were formed and had completed their unit training by early 1941.

The Home Army began forming the Wave 14 divisions in November 1940. They were also designed to perform occupation duties in the West and the 333rd and 335th Divisions had a high percentage of Polish soldiers in German service. There were eight Wave 14 divisions (all infantry): the 332nd, 333rd, 335th, 336th, 337th, 339th, 340th, and 342nd.

During the first five months of 1941, the Replacement Army formed 15 Wave 15 divisions, all numbered in the 700 block. All were static (non-motorized) two-regiment divisions, composed mainly of older men (many of them from the *Landeschuetzen* battalions), Volksdeutsche, or foreign personnel. They reflected the shortage of young men of military age in the Third Reich and the growing shortage of equipment in the depots of the Home Army. They had an artillery battalion instead of the usual four-battalion artillery regiment, and most of them had engineer, signal, and reconnaissance companies, instead of battalions. They had no divisional anti-tank battalions, and their infantry regiments had no 13th and 14th Companies (that is, they had no infantry cannon, heavy weapons, or anti-tank units). They were all sent to France or the Balkans. The units sent to Yugoslavia and Greece were later renumbered and converted into Jaeger divisions.[7]

In addition to these units, the 90th Light Division was created from miscellaneous units in North Africa, the 199th Infantry Division was formed in Norway, and the 4th, 5th, and 6th Mountain Divisions were organized in southern Germany and Austria. In June 1941, four Wave 16 reserve infantry brigades were formed: the 201st, 202nd, 203rd, and 204th. All were designated security units, and the 201st and 203rd were upgraded to security divisions in the summer of 1942. None of them had organic artillery units initially, although some were added later on. Also, some later formed their on "unofficial" artillery units and even panzer platoons, using captured Soviet equipment.

As a result of the massive reorganization in the winter of 1940–41, 84 new divisions of all types were created, at a cost of 17 of the 1939 divisions (which were converted to other types of units or broken up). As a result, in June 1941, Hitler had 205 combat divisions—although they were not that much more powerful than 140 divisions that had invaded France and the Low Countries in 1940. The number of panzers had not increased, even though their quality was higher, because they had more PzKw IIIs and IVs and fewer PzKw Is, PzKwIIs, and tanks of Czech manufacture.

General Fromm, however, issued a clear warning: at the end of May, he had only 80,000 men in the reinforcement (march) battalions and they had only three months' training. In addition, only about 350,000 men (mainly from the classes of 1921 and 1922) would be available for the rest of 1941. In other words, if German casualties in Barbarossa exceeded 430,000, the Home Army would not be able to replace them. In addition, German tank production—although it had improved slightly—was still quite low. Less than 200 tanks had been produced per month in 1940. German industry would increase its quarterly tank production from less than 700 in the first quarter of 1941 to 1,100 in the last quarter of the year, but this would still be woefully inadequate for its task in Russia, as we shall see.

DEPLOYMENT

OKH had three army groups and several smaller formations at its disposal in the spring of 1941. In the north lay Field Marshal von Leeb's Army Group North, which included the 18th Army (Colonel General von Kuechler), the 16th Army (Colonel General Busch), and 4th Panzer Group (Colonel General Hoepner). Its missions were to annihilate the Soviet forces in the Baltic States and to capture Leningrad. The weakest of the army groups, it controlled 29 divisions, of which three were panzer and three were motorized. It was supported by Colonel General Keller's 1st Air Fleet (660 aircraft).

In the middle of the German line lay its strongest force: Field Marshal von Bock's Army Group Center. North to south, it controlled the 3rd Panzer Group (Colonel General Hoth); 9th Army (Colonel General Strauss); 4th Army (Field Marshal von Kluge); and 2nd Panzer Group (Colonel General Guderian). Its initial mission was to destroy the strong Soviet forces in the Brest-Vilna (Vilnius)-Smolensk triangle, near the German frontier, and then to wheel north or continue to drive toward Moscow, as ordered. Bock's forces totaled 50 divisions, of which nine were panzer and six were motorized. It was supported by Kesselring's 2nd Air Fleet, which had 1,180 airplanes.

Between southern Poland and the Black Sea lay Gerd von Rundstedt's Army Group South. It was divided into a northern wing, concentrated between the Pripyat Marshes and the Carpathians, and a southern wing in Romania. In the north lay the strike force: Reichenau's 6th Army, Kleist's 1st Panzer Group, and General of Infantry Carl-Heinrich von Stuelpnagel's 17th Army. To the south lay Colonel General von Schobert's 11th Army, as well as the 3rd and 4th Romanian Armies, under Generals Petre Dumitrescu and Nicolae Ciuperca, respectively. The northern wing was ordered to destroy Russian General Mikhail Kirponos's strong forces in Galicia and the Western Ukraine, secure the Dnieper crossings, and capture Kiev. The southern wing had the task of protecting the Ploesti oilfields and, for that reason, 11th Army's divisions were interlaced with the less dependable Romanian divisions as "corset stays." In all, Rundstedt had 41 German divisions, of which five were panzer and three were motorized. He also controlled 14 Romanian divisions (about 150,000 men) and was supported by Colonel General Loehr's 4th Air Fleet, which contained 930 aircraft.

To the north of the main battlefront, Finnish Marshal Carl Mannerheim deployed 14 divisions (500,000 men) in the Finnish sector. In July he also was to begin an offensive, on both sides of Lake Lagoda, in conjunction with Leeb's efforts to take Leningrad. Finland, however, was to enter the war as a co-belligerent and not as a German ally; its orders came from Mannerheim, not from Berlin.

North of Mannerheim's divisions lay the Far North sector, where Falkenhorst's Army of Norway deployed four German divisions in two corps (about 67,000 men) in northern Norway and northern Finland. It also controlled a Finnish corps. The objective of the Army of Norway was to capture the Soviet port of Murmansk. It was supported by Luftwaffe Command Kirkenes (of Stumpff's 5th Air Fleet), which had only 70 aircraft. (Hitler had ordered that Stumpff keep the bulk of his forces to the south, in case the British decided to invade Norway, which was a recurring fear with him.)

In addition, OKH initially held 28 divisions (including two panzer and three motorized divisions) in reserve. In all, OKH deployed 148 divisions, including 17 panzer and 13 motorized divisions. Its Barbarossa forces included 3,050,000 men, 3,350 tanks, 7,184 guns, 600,000 motor vehicles, and 625,000 horses, excluding the Far North sector, which was an OKW theater. OKH also earmarked a dozen additional divisions (including two panzer divisions and a motorized division) for Operation Barbarossa. Table 30.1 shows the Order of Battle of OKH's German forces on June 22, 1941.

Table 30.1
Order of Battle, OKH German Forces, Eastern Front, June 22, 1941

Army Group North: Field Marshal Ritter Wilhelm von Leeb
    18th Army: Colonel General Georg von Kuechler
    4th Panzer Group: Colonel General Erich Hoepner
    16th Army: Colonel General Ernst Busch

Army Group Center: Field Marshal Fedor von Bock
    3rd Panzer Group: Colonel General Hermann Hoth
    9th Army: Colonel General Adolf Strauss
    4th Army: Field Marshal Guenther von Kluge
    2nd Panzer Group: Colonel General Heinz Guderian

Army Group South: Field Marshal Gerd von Rundstedt
    6th Army: Field Marshal Walter von Reichenau
    1st Panzer Group: Colonel General Ewald von Kleist
    17th Army: Colonel General Heinrich von Stuelpnagel
    3rd Romanian Army: General Petre Dumintrescu
    4th Romanian Army: General Nicolae Ciuperca
    11th Army: Colonel General Ritter Eugen von Schobert

Note:
Army Excludes the Far North (Lapland) Sector, an OKW front, which included Mountain Corps Norway (General of Mountain Troops Eduard Dietl) and other elements of the Army of Norway (Colonel General Nikolaus von Falkenhorst). Mountain Corps Norway later became the Army of Lapland (January 14, 1942) and then the 20th Mountain Army (June 22, 1942).

OKH thus planned to conquer the Soviet Union with 160 divisions—18 more than it had employed in the conquest of France. The area of operations in Barbarossa, however, was more than 1 million square miles—about five times the size of France. In addition, although the number of panzer and motorized divisions had more than doubled (from 15 in May 1940 to 32 in June 1941), the number of tanks had increased only from 2,574 to 3,332.

The German armies were, in fact, a far cry from the highly mobile, incredibly well-equipped units that Goebbels' propaganda ministry made them out to be, and many people still believe they were. Only 46 of the German divisions available for the invasion were fully equipped with German arms. The rest were either deficient in equipment (mainly in assault and anti-tank guns) or were outfitted with captured arms and equipment, primarily from France and Czechoslovakia. Eighty-four infantry divisions and even three of the motorized divisions were equipped with foreign vehicles. In fact, counting foreign equipment, the German Army had 2,000 different types of vehicles, 70 different types of guns, and 52 models of anti-aircraft guns. As a result, maintenance would be a nightmare in the Russian campaign, and the breakdown rates in all units would be extremely high. In addition, most of the infantry divisions were still heavily dependent upon horsepower. Some 119 divisions were still horse-drawn, and 77 of these had horse-drawn supply units (including 15,000 Polish two-wheeled *Panjewagen* [peasant wagons]).[9] Most of the divisional artillery regiments depended solely on horses or mules. Hitler and his generals were clearly gambling on a war of short duration, although few of them appreciated the risk they were running. Most German commanders at all levels favored the invasion of the Soviet Union, because they felt that it was only a matter of time before Moscow tried to "stab Germany in the back" and because they were stimulated by their successes in Poland, France, and the Balkans, and felt that they could easily defeat Stalin's legions. They were probably right on the first point, but, in retrospect, it is clear that they overestimated their own abilities and greatly underestimated those of the Soviet Union. Overconfidence and German arrogance played a major role in the disaster that overtook the German Army in Russia at the end of 1941. Following the tremendous success of the blitzkrieg in France and the Balkans, the military technocrats abandoned their previous caution and were now convinced that no power in Europe could halt the Wehrmacht.[10] OKH, for example, had replacement equipment available for a campaign of only three months, but felt no need to press for the higher priority in armaments, because it felt its reserves would be adequate for the conquest of the Soviet Union. On December 3, 1940, General Jodl unequivocally stated that it was correct to reduce the armaments allocations for the army in favor of the navy and Luftwaffe, since Operation Barbarossa could be fought with existing equipment. General Fromm obviously agreed with Jodl.[11] Even more incredibly, OKH did not even bother to prepare for the possibility of a winter campaign and only purchased enough winter clothing to supply a greatly reduced army of occupation. This overconfidence and short-sightedness would cost a great many soldiers fingers and toes lost to frostbite in the months ahead.

While OKH directed operations in the East, German-held territories elsewhere came under the control of OKW, an arrangement that became more and more solidified as the war progressed. By 1942, it would become popular to refer to the Russian Front as an "OKH Theater" and to any other sector as an "OKW Theater," in effect creating another command division in the upper levels of the German armed forces. In June 1941, Germany had 38 divisions in western Europe, one in Denmark, seven in Norway, seven in the Balkans, and two in North Africa. All were under the control of OKW.

THE UNPREPARED LUFTWAFFE

Meanwhile, the Battle of Britain played itself out in the west. The last major raids occurred in April and May 1941, and they seemed to indicate that the German Air Force was resuming the battle with renewed vigor. During the raid of May 10, London suffered its worst night of the war. More than 1,400 people were killed and 1,800 wounded, and some fires continued to burn for 11 days. Despite their ferocity, these attacks were just part of a diversion, because the Luftwaffe was secretly redeploying to the East. On May 21, Kesselring moved his headquarters to Posen in occupied Poland, and Field Marshal Hugo Sperrle became the sole air commander in the West. Of the 44 bomber groups previously operating against Britain, only four remained in France and the Low Countries. Of the fighter wings, only JG 2 "Richthofen" and JG 26 "Schlageter" remained in the English Channel sector. By the end of June 1941, the West was strictly a backwater theater, looked upon more as a reservoir of reserves for the Eastern Front than anything else.[12]

OKL committed 2,840 aircraft to Operation Barbarossa, of which about 1,910 were combat aircraft. This amounted to 59 percent of all combat aircraft in the Luftwaffe. Its other 1,340 combat aircraft were divided among the 3rd Air Fleet in the West (660 aircraft), the 5th Air Fleet in Norway (120), the X Air Corps and Air Command Afrika in the Mediterranean sector (370 airplanes), and various air defense units in Germany (only 190 aircraft). Keller's 1st Air Fleet supported Army Group North, Loehr's 4th Air Fleet flew close air support for Army Group South, and Kesselring's 2nd (the largest) was assigned the task

Table 30.2
Strength of the Luftwaffe by Aircraft Type, May 10, 1940, and June 21, 1941

Aircraft Type	10 May 40	21 Jun 41
Short-Range Reconnaissance	335	440
Long-Range Reconnaissance	322	393
Single-Engine Fighter	1,356	1,440
Night-Fighters	—	263
Twin-Engine Fighters	354	188
Bombers	1,711	1,511
Dive-Bombers	414	424
Ground-Attack	50	—
Coastal	240	223
TOTAL:	4,782	4,882

Source:
Williamson Murray, *Strategy for Defeat: The Luftwaffe, 1933–1945* (1983), p. 80.

of supporting Army Group Center. In addition, the Luftwaffe committed two anti-aircraft corps (I and II) to the offensive.

One reason that Hermann Goering opposed the invasion of the Soviet Union was the fact that the Luftwaffe was in strategic disarray. Under the poor management of Ernst Udet and others, the German aviation industry and the office of air armaments had barely been able to maintain the strength the Luftwaffe had had the year before (see Table 30.2).

Other than allowing himself to be talked into accepting the post of *Generalluftzeugmeister*, Udet's major mistakes were in his selection of aircraft to succeed current models. He decided to base the Luftwaffe's offensive capability on four main combat types by early 1940—the Me-109, the Ju-88, the Me-210, and the He-177. Although handicapped by its short range, the Me-109 was a successful aircraft. The Ju-88, however, had a great many problems and never really achieved the results expected of it, while the Me-210 and He-177 were total failures and greatly inhibited the Luftwaffe's ability to wage war from 1940 on.

The Ju-88 was developed by Dr. Heinrich Koppenburg, the managing director of Junkers. It was originally designed as a superspeed, unarmed, six-ton bomber, and was successfully test-flown in March 1938. Nicknamed the "Wonder Bomber" by the Air General Staff, it never lived up to expectations, mainly because the Technical Office kept adding requirements for it and modifications to it—including the requirement that it be able to dive. Both Udet and General Jeschonnek were firm believers that an effective bomber had to be able to dive in order to make an accurate attack. Because of these constant modification, production was delayed time and again. Eventually some 25,000 changes were required and the weight of some models exceeded 13 tons—more than twice the weight of the original prototypes. Engineer General Marquardt later wrote, with considerable justification, that the dive-bombing concept ruined the Luftwaffe.[13] It certainly ruined the Ju-88. The maximum speed of the prototypes exceeded 400 mph (faster than the Spitfires or Hurricanes), but the Ju-88A-4 could not even reach 280 mph. Its climbing rate and handling characteristics were so badly reduced that the pilots referred to it as a "flying barn door" in 1939. The German aviation industry nevertheless manufactured 15,000 during the war, mainly because the Technical Office could develop nothing better. They were used in a variety of roles, including horizontal and dive-bombing, long-range reconnaissance, torpedo bombing, night-fighting, and others. The Ju-88 was effective in some of these missions, but this did not make up for the fact that Germany had no modern bomber in 1941.

If the Ju-88 was a disappointment, the He-177 was a disaster. In early 1938, Udet finally decided that Germany might need a long-range bomber after all. He issued specifications that it would have to carry two tons of bombs and have a range of more than 1,000 miles. That summer. Ernst Heinkel showed Udet and Jeschonnek the mock-up of the He-177, which featured four engines joined to two propellers by a coupling arrangement. A few months later Udet, with the approval of Jeschonnek and Lieutenant General Rulof Lucht (chief of staff of the Office of Air Armaments) added the requirement that the He-177 be capable of diving at a 60-degree angle. "The He-177 must be capable of diving at all costs," Udet told Heinkel.

Heinkel was horrified. "You can't make a dive-bomber out an aircraft that size!" he exclaimed. The He-177 weighed 15 tons at the time.

"For all practical purposes it's a twin-engine aircraft," Udet responded. "If the twin-engined Ju-88 can dive, why shouldn't the He-177?"[14]

As a result of the new requirement, Heinkel was forced to increase the weight of the He-177 to 32 tons, at a considerable sacrifice of speed, maneuverability, and safety. On November 19, 1938, it was test-flown at Rechlin and was declared unsatisfactory because of high engine oil temperatures. Udet nevertheless authorized production, but at a low priority. Only three He-177s per month were being produced in June 1940.

When the Luftwaffe was defeated in the Battle of Britain, Udet's failures were also made public for the entire world to see. It was clear that Germany had lost its technological lead in military aviation. In an effort to regain it quickly, Udet gambled. In October 1940, he ordered the He-177 into mass production, despite its negative test results. This demanded a time-consuming reorganization of the German aircraft industry. The He-111 was taken out of production, the bomber factories were retooled, and mass production of the He-177 began. All of this took months. Only when it came off the production line were the defects of the aircraft fully discovered. Most serious was its tendency to explode in mid-air while in straight and level flight for no apparent reason. Apparently the fuel lines dripped on the hot manifolds. It also broke apart during dives, and its connecting rods were prone to breaking, penetrating the crankcase, and letting hot oil fly everywhere. Even if fire and explosions were avoided, the valves fouled after a maximum of six hours' flying time. Wood and Gunston described it as "possibly the most troublesome and unsatisfactory aircraft in military history ... no engines in bomber history have caught fire so often in normal cruising flight."[15] The He-177 became known as the *Luftwaffenfeuerzueg* (the Luftwaffe's lighter). More than 50 prototypes broke up during dives or exploded in level flight, killing their entire crew. Despite the fact that 1,446 were manufactured during the war, only 33 had been accepted for service by late 1942. Of these, only two were still operational a few weeks later.[16]

Because of the loss of so many prototypes, the He-177 had to be withdrawn from the production lines. The aircraft industry had to be reorganized and retooled again, at the cost of tens of thousands of man hours, so it could resume the production of the He-111, a bomber that was already known to be obsolete. The waste of raw materials was tremendous.

The Me-210 was another Udet disaster. It was designed by Professor Willi Messerschmitt as a multipurpose replacement for the Me-110, the Ju-87, and the Hs-123. The plans for the Me-210 were approved by the Udet's Technical Office in the summer of 1938, and Jeschonnek had required 1,000 airplanes, even before the first prototype was flown, so great was their confidence in the designer. They had both been taken in. Udet was "no match for the tricks of the industrialists," his adjutant, Colonel Max Pendele, noted later,[17] and, in this case, neither was General Jeschonnek. The Me-210 prototypes were unstable and unpredictable in flight and whipped into spins at high angles of attack. Even so, Udet ordered the progressive phasing out of the unsatisfactory Me-110; reliance on the Me-210 was total.

When it was brought into production in 1941, the Me-210 proved to be a total failure. Airplane after airplane crashed, and pilots looked on it as a deathtrap. State Secretary Milch finally cancelled the program altogether. He estimated that the Me-210 project cost the Luftwaffe 600 aircraft.

As a result of the failure of the Technical Office and the German aviation industry, the Luftwaffe was rapidly becoming an outmoded branch by the spring of 1941. The situation was bad enough when it was just fighting the British. Now, however, three-fifths of the

Luftwaffe was committed to a second front. It was now clear to many in the air force that Germany had better successfully eliminate Stalin and his party in 1941, as Hitler envisioned, or face a war of attrition with the Soviet Union. If that occurred, the situation for Nazi Germany in general and the Luftwaffe in particular would be grim indeed.

SOVIET PREPARATIONS

On the other side of the frontier, Joseph Stalin, the general secretary of the Soviet Communist Party, had become the official chief of the Soviet government on May 1941, when he made himself chairman of the Council of People's Commissars. Several agencies were subordinate to this body, including the Defense Committee of the Council of People's Commissars, the People's Commissariat of Defense, under Marshal Semen Timoshenko, and the People's Commissariat of the Navy. The Soviet Union had no separate air force.

Subordinate to the Defense Commissariat was the General Staff (Marshal Georgi Zhukov), which was responsible for war plans. In the event of a general war, it intended to establish a general headquarters, the *Stavka* (staff), which would direct the war effort of the Soviet military forces. The highest army field commands before the outbreak of hostilities were the 16 military districts. The day Hitler invaded the Soviet Union, five became fronts (army groups), and others were converted shortly thereafter.

Soviet military command functions at all levels were complicated by political surveillance. Political commissars were posted to every staff down to the regimental level, and *politruks* (political leadership officers) extended down to platoon level. The commissars, looking over the commanders' shoulders, had the authority to review every decision and could revoke them if they felt so inclined. They were also trained to see sabotage in every reversal and treason in every retreat, no matter how necessary it might be. In addition, the commanders had to deal with the secret police of the People's Commissariat of Internal Affairs (NKVD), which had authority over state security and maintained surveillance over officers and men in the armed forces. It also had troops of its own, which often formed blocking detachments and were used to halt or prevent retreats. They could pass summary judgments on anyone and were authorized to carry out executions. The Commissars, the NKVD, and other agencies provided Stalin with a constant stream of information outside military channels concerning the actions, behavior, and attitudes of his officers.

At the beginning of 1941, the leadership of the Red Army was in considerable disarray. During the Stalinist purges of 1937 and 1938, it had lost all 11 of its deputy commissars for defense, all of its military district commanders, 13 of its 15 army commanders, 57 of its 85 corps commanders, 111 of 195 division commanders, 220 of its 406 brigade commanders, and half of its regimental commanders—almost all executed. The Officers' Corps had only just begun to recover from Stalin's rash and drastic actions, and the Soviet armed forces would continue to be handicapped by a lack of competent officers throughout the war.

It suffered from no such shortages in the realm of equipment. "[I]n strictly numerical terms, the Soviet forces may actually have been the best equipped in the world at that time," the U.S. Official History records.[19] According to Stalin, the Soviet Union had 24,000 tanks when the war broke out. Military aircraft production totaled 17,745 airplanes between January 1, 1939, and June 1941, a figure that far exceeded the German total. In addition, the army had 67,335 artillery pieces and mortars (larger than 50 millimeters) when Barbarossa began.

The newest Soviet tanks, the T-34, KV-l, and KV-2, were far superior to anything the Germans had or had even designed. The T-34 was a medium tank of 28 tons (three tons heavier than the heaviest PzKw IV) and had a top speed of 32 mph (eight mph faster than the PzKw IV). The German short-barreled 75-millimeter gun was inferior to the T-34s long-barreled 76-milimeter gun in both range and power. The heavy KV-2 (Kliment Voroshilov-2) weighed 52 tons, and, at 20 mph, was slower than the PzKw IV, but much more heavily armored. Its 76-millimeter gun outgunned the PzKw IV and III. In addition, despite their greater weights, the T-34 and KV-2 had such wide treads that they had as much as 25 percent lower ground pressure per square inch than the German tanks and thus had much better traction and maneuverability in mud and snow. They also featured welded, sloping hulls and turret armor, which made them invulnerable to all but the heaviest German anti-tank weapons.

The new Soviet light tank, the T-60, weighed 6.5 tons, mounted a 20-millimeter main battle gun, and was roughly equal to the PzKw II. It was inferior to either the PzKw III and IV, but it could be built rapidly in ordinary automobile plants, using standard automotive components. In 1940, the Soviets built 2,421 T-60s, 117 T-34s, and 256 KVs. By June 1941, they had constructed 1,225 T-34s and 639 KVs.

The Wehrmacht might have found the Soviet armored forces almost unbeatable had not Russian armored doctrine been so badly flawed. The Soviets dissolved their tank branch as an independent arm in 1939 and its forces were distributed as brigades throughout the infantry armies, much like those of the French Army. Following the victories of the panzer divisions in Poland, France, and the Balkans, the Soviets fanatically tried to reestablish the tank corps, but this process was still in its early stages in the summer of 1941. Also, most of the Soviet tanks did not have radios, but virtually all of the panzers did. As a result, the Red Army would not be able to duplicate or match the combined arms tactics of the Wehrmacht on the battlefields of 1941.

Like the rest of the Red Army, the Soviet air forces were in a transition process in June 1941. The vast majority of the Soviet aircraft were technologically inferior to their German counterparts at that time. The most modern Soviet airplanes with the squadrons were the Mikoyan-Gurevich (MIG-3), Yakovlev (YAK-1), and Lavochkin-Gorbunov-Goudkov (LAGG) fighters and the Ilyushin (IL-2) dive-bomber, a ground attack aircraft that was slow but heavily armored and difficult to shoot down. The Soviet air units had 2,739 aircraft of these modern designs with their squadrons in 1941. Most of its more than 15,000 airplanes were much older, and many were biplanes. Some of their fighters actually featured gunsights *painted* on their cockpit windshields.

Soviet military preparations were also flawed by an overconcentration of weapons, at the expense of auxiliary and supplementary equipment needed to make the weapons effective. Much of the artillery, for example, depended on ordinary farm tractors as prime movers. The Red Army also lacked radios, trained technical personnel (including signals personnel), and even some of the most basic infantry equipment. During the first German offensive, many Soviet troops tried to dig foxholes with their helmets, because they had no entrenching tools. In short, the Red Army would prove to be a vast, primitive, and cumbersome opponent in the summer of 1941.

PRELUDE TO WAR

Although he had been preparing for a major war at a rapid pace since the mid-1930s, Stalin stubbornly refused to believe that Hitler was planning to invade his country, even after the German buildup on his borders became too large to be concealed. As early as March 20, 1941, Filipp Ivanovich Golikov, the head of the GRU, the military intelligence directorate of the General Staff (and a future marshal of the Soviet Union), presented an intelligence appreciation that spelled out the evidence of the apparent German plan in some detail. By May, he was reporting that more than 100 German divisions were concentrated near the Soviet frontier.

Stalin received warnings from many sources, especially from secret Communist agents and spies in Berlin, Berne, Paris, and other capitals, but also from foreign diplomats. In March, U.S. Secretary of State Cordell Hull gave Konstantin A. Oumansky, the Soviet Ambassador to Washington, a copy of Hitler's invasion plans. The Americans had obtained it from Sam Edison Woods, the American commercial attaché in Berlin. Woods, who had been in Berlin since 1934, had developed reliable relationships with the secret anti-Nazi underground, and one of these contacts had given him the plan. Ambassador Oumansky turned pale when he read the document.

The most convincing warning of what was to come, however, came from the most important man in the Soviet secret service, Dr. Richard Sorge. A Berliner by birth, Sorge was a dedicated Communist and, posing as a journalist, carried out successful spy missions in Scandinavia, Great Britain, and China, before being sent to Japan in 1933. In 1941, he was the press assistant at the German Embassy in Tokyo and learned about the impending invasion from the German military attaché. Later, in late 1941, his reports that Japan was not planning to attack the Soviet Union enabled Stalin to shift his Siberian divisions from the Far Eastern Front to the Moscow sector, where they helped turn the tide of the war. On May 12, he informed Moscow that about 150 German divisions would invade the Soviet Union on June 20. Three days later, he revised this report, setting the date as June 22. Sorge's warnings, however, were also ignored.

Washington and London continued to try to warn Stalin throughout the spring of 1941, but he continued to ignore them. The Soviet dictator believed that the Allies were trying to deceive him to provoke him into a confrontation with Hitler, because a war between Soviet Russia and Nazi Germany could only benefit the West. The few measures that the Soviet Union took were precautionary, but by no means extensive. A number of former officers who had survived the purges were released from concentration camps and prisons and returned to active duty. There was a special call-up of 800,000 reservists in the spring of 1941, bringing the strength of the Soviet armed forces to about 5 million men, and 28 divisions (four armies) were moved from the interior to the western frontier. Finally, Stalin concluded a treaty of neutrality with Japan on April 13.[18]

Why Stalin did so little to prepare for the German invasion and allowed the Wehrmacht to achieve tactical surprise over his forces on the frontier is one of the mysteries of World War II. Certainly the indications of an impending invasion were present. There was almost no German shipping in Soviet ports in the late spring of 1941, for example, but Soviet shipping in German ports was being delayed on all kinds of pretexts. The Soviet boundary commission had been expelled from the German side of the Polish frontier and had not been allowed to return. German aerial reconnaissance was violating Soviet airspace on a daily basis, although Stalin had given orders that they should not be fired on, in case Hitler was looking for a provocation. Stalin, however, still would not believe that an invasion was imminent. He put himself in Hitler's place and concluded that, if he were Hitler, he would engage in a war of nerves with the Soviet Union, to frighten it away from the Balkans and Finland, possibly as a prerequisite to making some new territorial demands of his own. "Stalin could not bring himself to believe that the Germans would defy all reason and enter into a war on two fronts," Colonel Seaton concluded. His mistake was analyzing the situation and drawing conclusions based on his own cold and logical mentality. He did not study Hitler's mentality, which was certainly not cool and logical, and then try to draw conclusions based on the world view of the more passionate Fuehrer. And that is where he went wrong.[20]

While the Soviet intelligence and espionage network formed a clear picture of German intentions and a fair idea of its dispositions, German military intelligence failed disastrously. Two German military organizations were responsible for obtaining data on the Soviet armed forces: Admiral Canaris's Abwehr and O Qu IV, the military intelligence staff of the Army High Command.

O Qu IV was headed by Major General Gerhard Matzky, who, after a tour of duty as military attaché in Tokyo, had become director of army intelligence on January 5, 1941. O Qu IV was divided into two main sections: Foreign Armies West under Lieutenant Colonel Ulrich Liss and Foreign Armies East under Lieutenant Colonel Eberhard Kinzel. These titles are somewhat misleading, since Liss was responsible for gathering information concerning the armies of western Europe exclusively, while Kinzel was responsible for the rest of the world, including Scandinavia, China, Japan, the United States, and South America. Gathering intelligence concerning the Red Army was only a minor part of Kinzel's duties before 1941. Since OKH had not designated the Soviet Union as a major potential target, Kinzel's section devoted little time or money to it. Even less was done in 1939 and 1940, because Hitler had forbidden either the Abwehr or OKH from collecting and evaluating data on the Red Army. Finally, Kinzel was not particularly well qualified for his duties. He was an infantry officer by trade and not an intelligence expert; he had no specialized knowledge of the Soviet Union; and he could not speak Russian.

OKH was not impressed with what little it knew about the Red Army. It had made a poor impression in Poland, an even worse one in Finland, and the military attaché and his deputy, Colonel Hans Krebs, expressed low opinions of it. The Soviets, however, through their police state and totalitarian government, had been successful in blocking the flow of information out of their country. Encouraged by their government, most Soviet citizens were unfriendly to and suspicious of both strangers and foreigns. As a result, the Germans were able to obtain a good idea of the dispositions of Soviet troops in the border zones (thanks to aerial reconnaissance), but had almost no idea of what to expect in the interior. It had almost no knowledge of the Soviet strategic reserves, had no grasp of the extent of Soviet industrial complex, and no idea of the ability of the Soviet Union's economy to sustain a major war effort.

As a result of all of this, a number of totally erroneous intelligence estimates were made. On July 22, 1940, Halder estimated that the Soviets had 50 to 75 divisions.[21] In August, General Marcks estimated that the Red Army had 151 infantry divisions, 32 cavalry divisions, and 38 motorized brigades, of which 96 infantry divisions, 23 cavalry divisions, and 28 motorized brigades were arrayed against Germany.[22] At the beginning of the campaign, however, OKH estimated that the Red Army had 200 divisions. Within six weeks, it was discovered that it had at least 360.[23] In addition, the German General Staff did not even know the T-34 existed, had never heard of the superheavy KV tanks, and had no knowledge of the terrifying multiple-barrel rocket launchers the soldiers would nickname "Stalin's pipe organs." Their estimate on the number of Soviet tanks was very low. In the mid-1930s, Guderian had been ridiculed by the senior generals for estimating that the Soviets had 10,000 tanks, and General Beck even accused him of exaggerating and spreading alarm. Guderian's estimates were, in fact, conservative. The Soviets had 24,000 tanks available when Operation Barbarossa began and enough industrial capacity to produce 1,000 more each month. German industry only produced 2,800 tanks throughout 1941.[24]

Luftwaffe intelligence estimates were also, as usual, wrong. General Schmid's branch placed the strength of the Red Air Force at 8,000 airplanes, three-quarters of which were in European Russia. Actually, the Soviets had 10,000 aircraft in the western areas alone, and at least 3,000 in the East; furthermore, they were supported by an average production of 1,131 per month.[25] The Luftwaffe commanders had no idea that they were about to take on an enemy that outnumbered them at least seven to one.

NOTES

1. United States Department of the Army, "The German Campaign in Russia—Planning and Operations (1940–1942)," United States Department of the Army, Pamphlet 20-261a (1955) (hereafter cited as DA PAM 20-261a).

2. Cooper, *German Army*, p. 263; Halder Diaries, December 5, 1940.

3. Cooper, *German Army*, p. 265.

4. Walter Warlimont, *Inside Hitler's Headquarters*, R. H. Barry, trans. (1964; reprint ed., n.d.), p. 139 (hereafter cited as Warlimont, *Inside Hitler's Headquarters*). Warlimont was born in Osnabrueck in 1894 and joined the army as a Fahnenjunker in 1913. He served in the artillery in World War I and became a brigade adjutant. After serving in the Freikorps, he was accepted into the Reichsheer and began his secret General Staff training in 1922. He visited the

United States and England in the interwar years and served in the Spanish Civil War. After commanding the 26th Artillery Regiment in Duesseldorf (1937–38), he was assigned to the staff of OKW and eventually became deputy chief of operations. For future historians, he proved to be a valuable witness to events at Fuehrer Headquarters. Brilliant and arrogant, he was severely wounded during the July 20, 1944, attempt to assassinate Adolf Hitler, and was not reemployed. He was sentenced to life imprisonment as a minor war criminal but was released in 1957. He retired to Kreuth, Upper Bavaria, where he died in 1976.

5. Ibid., pp. 168–69.

6. Bethell, p. 26.

7. These were the 104th, 114th, 117th, and 118th Jaeger Divisions.

8. Seaton, *German Army*, p. 160.

9. Koch, *Aspects*, pp. 328–29; Foerster, "Volkegemeinschaft," p. 202

10. Kroener, "Manpower Shortage," p. 294.

11. Foerster, "Volkegemeinschaft," pp. 195–96.

12. Cooper, *GAF*, pp. 173–75; Musciano, p. 42.

13. General a.D. Marquardt, "Die Stuka-Idee hat der deutsch Luftwaffe den Untergang gebracht," in Karlsruhe Document Collection; Hermann Plocher, "The German Air Force versus Russia, 1941," United States Air Force Historical Studies, no. 153, United States Air Force Historical Division, Aerospace Studies Institute, Maxwell Air Force Base, Alabama (1965) (hereafter cited as Plocher MS, 1941); Hermann Plocher, "The German Air Force versus Russia, 1942," United States Air Force Historical Studies, no. 154, United States Air Force Historical Division, Aerospace Studies Institute, Maxwell Air Force Base, Alabama (1965) (hereafter cited as Plocher MS, 1942); Hermann Plocher, "The German Air Force versus Russia, 1943," United States Air Force Historical Studies, no. 155, United States Air Force Historical Division, Aerospace Studies Institute, Maxwell Air Force Base, Alabama (1965) (hereafter cited as Plocher MS, 1943); Irving, *Milch*.

14. Irving, *Milch*.

15. Wood and Gunston.

16. Plocher MS 1942.

17. Irving, *Milch*.

18. Earl F. Ziemke and Magna E. Bauer, *Moscow to Stalingrad: Decision in the East* (1985), p. 11 (hereafter cited as Ziemke and Bauer).

19. Ibid., p. 99.

20. Seaton, *Russo-German War*, pp. 18–21.

21. Cooper, *German Army*, p. 259; Halder Diaries, July 22, 1940.

22. DA PAM 20-261a.

23. Paul Carell, *Hitler Moves East, 1941–1943* (1965; reprint ed., 1966), p. 53 (hereafter cited as Carell, *Hitler Moves East*).

24. Albert Seaton, *The Battle of Moscow* (1980; reprint ed., 1981).

25. DA PAM 20-261a; R. J. Overy, *The Air War, 1939–1945* (1980), p. 62; Werner Baumbach, *The Life and Death of the Luftwaffe* (1960), p. 62.

CHAPTER XXXI

OPERATION BARBAROSSA: THE INVASION OF THE SOVIET UNION

Operation Barbarossa took the Soviet defenders in the frontier zones completely by surprise. Only in Colonel General Mikhail P. Kirponos's Kiev Military District was there a degree of readiness. Many of the trucks and tractors used to tow the Soviet guns were away at construction sites or in the fields. The Red Air Force had just completed a series of night training exercises, and its pilots were in bed and their machines short of fuel. Many men were on leave, and several important border fortress units were away from their positions, on field training exercises to the east.

Those who were on the border were taken completely by surprise. At one post on the Bug River, German frontier guards called out the Soviet guards, as if an emergency was taking place. When the unsuspecting Reds came out, the Germans shot them down. Then, all along the border, Soviet positions and installations were rocked by the roar of 6,000 guns—all German. Barracks, supply depots, communications centers, forward headquarters, and military and civilian targets of every description went up in flames. On the western bank of the Bug, engineers began putting down pontoon bridges, while infantrymen and motorcycle troops moved quickly across the river in rubber dinghies and assault boats. At one point, an entire battalion of underwater tanks—originally designed for Operation Sea Lion—crossed the Bug. South of the important fortress of Brest, Geyr's XXIV Panzer Corps bolted across the river, capturing every important bridge in its sector, overrunning Soviet border guards and the rearguards of retreating troops, and smashing Soviet anti-tank positions. North of Brest, in the zone of the IX Corps, everything also went according to plan. Dinghies and assault boats crossed the river under the cover of artillery fire, and a bridgehead was quickly established. By 9 A.M., a heavy equipment bridge had been completed, and trucks, artillery, and assault guns poured across the river. In fact, along the entire 500-mile length of the Bug, not a single German attack miscarried.

Simultaneous with the ground attack, the Luftwaffe pounced on targets further to the rear and on the Red Air Force. By noon, they had knocked out dozens of Soviet airfields, blasted their fuel dumps, cut their supply lines, pulverized troop units as they attempted to assemble, and destroyed 1,200 Soviet airplanes—800 of them on the ground. They ranged as far east as Sevastopol, where they bombed one of the most important Soviet naval bases. The Germans lost only 10 planes.

At the Officers' Club in Minsk, General Dmitry Pavlov, the commander of the Western Military District, was watching a comedy when his intelligence chief arrived and whispered in his ear that the Germans were attacking. Pavlov turned to his deputy and said that the message was some "nonsense" about Germans firing along the border. He continued watching the play.[1]

When the Soviet generals were finally jolted into reality, they found themselves hamstrung by orders from Moscow. Timoshenko told General Bolden, "No actions must be taken against the Germans without our consent. Comrade Stalin has forbidden our artillery to open fire."

"It's not possible," Boldin shouted into the receiver. "Our troops are retreating. Whole towns are in flames. Everywhere people are being killed." But the order stood.[2]

That morning, Moscow ordered Major General Ivan Ivanovich Kopets to bomb the enemy. He knew that his slow Ilyushin and Tupolev bombers, unescorted by fighters, would have little chance against the Messerschmitts, but he did as he was told. Almost every Soviet general tried to carry out his orders, many of which were ridiculous, because the memory of Stalin's Great Purge was still fresh on everyone's mind, and there was a suspicious Commissar looking over every general's shoulder. Kopets was right: his aircraft were shot down so easily that Field Marshal Kesselring called it "infanticide." By June 23, Kopets had lost all of his bombers—more than 500 aircraft. Then he killed himself.[3]

Lieutenant General Pavel Rychagov, the commander-in-chief of aviation units, also did as he was told, with equally disastrous results. Within a week he was sentenced to death for treason (that is, for having failed) and was executed without trial.

Meanwhile, back in Moscow, Defense Commissar Semen Timoshenko had no idea what was happening at the front. Generals, who knew that Stalin equated failure with treason, were afraid to report the truth to the Kremlin, and even General Zhukov thought that the situation was developing favorably. Timoshenko therefore ordered a general counterattack. Colonel General Kirponos's armies were ordered to surround and destroy the German forces that had attacked them and to push on to Lublin, a Polish city well behind German lines, within two days. Kirponos knew that this order was crazy; some of his divisions had disappeared entirely, communications were down, the Red Army was in complete disarray, and the Germans had broken through in several places. His political commissar, however, was Nikolai N. Vashugin, who had played a major role in the Great Purge. Vashugin told him to carry out his order. Noting the commissar's threatening tone, Kirponos nodded and attempted to do so. The counterattack was unsuccessful, robbed Kirponos of much of his reserve, and was very costly in terms of Russian lives.

During the first two months of Operation Barbarossa, the Luftwaffe was successful everywhere it struck. German bomber units flew up to six missions a day in the first few days of the campaign, while dive-bombers and fighters flew up to eight missions, depending on the distance from their forward airfields to their targets. The German pilots were amazingly successful in their attempts at establishing aerial supremacy from the outset. "It was like shooting ducks," Colonel Johannes Steinhoff recalled.[4] This sense of individual superiority over the Russian pilot remained with the German aviator throughout the war. "The German pilot gained and retained the ascendancy over his Russian counterpart mainly because of his superior ego factor," Constable and Toliver wrote.

All the qualities of individual intelligence, independence initiative, and enterprise which fitted him temperamentally for the highly individualized art of aerial combat were encouraged and developed in his training. The Soviet system with its leveling tendencies and opposition to individualism was less than an ideal environment in which to breed fighter pilots. Even as the Russians got steadily better with the passage of time, the individual German fighter pilot never lost the inner conviction that he was a better man than his foes.... The capacity of the German fighter pilots to sustain themselves in the air under such adverse conditions show that what a fighter pilot thinks of himself will manifest itself in what he achieves.[5]

In the zone of General of Fliers Helmuth Foerster's I Air Corps alone, German pilots attacked 77 Soviet airfields in 1,600 sorties during the first three days of the campaign. The I Air Corps shot down 400 enemy airplanes and destroyed another 1,100 on the ground. By August 23, it had shot down 920 enemy airplanes and destroyed 1,594 more on the ground, a total of 2,514 Soviet airplanes destroyed—more than three times the number of aircraft in the entire 1st Air Fleet.

This success was matched all along the front. Kesselring's 2nd Air Fleet virtually wiped out the Red Air Force in the central combat zone within 48 hours of the beginning of the invasion. Kesselring claimed to have destroyed 2,500 Soviet airplanes during the first week of the campaign. Hermann Goering did not believe this claim, so he ordered an investigation to determine whether Kesselring had inflated the size of his victory. The investigators reported that Kesselring had underestimated the number of airplanes his pilots had destroyed by 200 to 300.[6] Goralski wrote that, as of June 24, "About 2,000 Soviet planes had now been destroyed. In just seventy-two hours the largest air force in the world had been reduced to an ineffectual remnant."[7] On June 29, at the end of the first week of the campaign, OKW reported the destruction of 4,017 enemy aircraft, at a cost of 150 German airplanes destroyed or heavily damaged—a ratio of 27 to 1.[8]

By June 24, with most of the Red Air Forces smashed, the Luftwaffe turned almost all of its attention to direct and indirect support missions for the army. In these types of operations, Wolfram von Richthofen excelled. On June 24, the Army's VIII and XX Corps of Strauss's 9th Army came under heavy tank and cavalry attack near Bialystok and Lunna. Richthofen committed his entire corps to their aid and destroyed 105 tanks by nightfall. Throughout the campaign of 1941, the Luftwaffe—and especially the Stukas of VIII Air Corps—continued to support the army in an outstanding manner. The "flying artillery" destroyed command posts, tanks, bunkers, smashed troop concentrations, and caused all manner of destruction to the Red armies and the Soviet war machine.

Unfortunately for the Germans, the Luftwaffe bombers did not have the range to disrupt rail traffic east of the Dnieper. Because the Third Reich had no strategic air forces, Soviet engineers were able to hastily dismantle every possible piece of industrial machinery and send it east, where it would be reassembled in the Urals or beyond. In all, nearly 300 industrial complexes were evacuated from the Ukraine alone, along with nearly 150 smaller factories. Almost 500 factories were transferred from the Moscow area to the east. In all, some 1,300 large plants were shipped east, a move requiring 6.5 million railroad cars. Although dislocated and badly hurt, the industrial potential of the Soviet Union had not been destroyed; if the blitzkrieg did not conquer the U.S.S.R. before the onset of winter, Russia, with a population almost three times that of Germany, would be able to recover.

For the Germans, the first unpleasant surprise of the campaign came on the night of June 23, on the left wing of the 4th Panzer Group, in the zone of Army Group North. Here, east of the Lithuanian village of Rossizny (Raseiniai), the 1st and 6th Panzer Divisions of Georg-Hans Reinhardt's XXXXI Panzer Corps came under heavy attack from the

Soviet 3rd Armored Corps, which was equipped mainly with KV-1 and KV-2 tanks, which weighed 43 and 52 tons, respectively. The KV-2, in fact, weighed twice as much as the heaviest German tank. "[A]ll armored-piercing shells simply bounced off them," the 1st Panzer reported. One KV-2 was hit more than 70 times by German anti-tank fire, but not a single round pierced the armor. The anti-tank gunners soon took to aiming at their tracks, hoping to immobilize them, and then finish them off with artillery or anti-aircraft guns, or blow them up at close range with HE devices. Fortunately, the Soviets showed no tactical skill or understanding of combined-arms methods and merely launched repeated frontal attacks. The battle was not decided until June 26, when the more experienced Germans (now reinforced with the 36th Motorized and 269th Infantry Divisions) launched a flank attack, drove them into a swamp, and smashed the 3rd Armored. The Reds lost 200 tanks in this battle.[9]

On Reinhardt's right flank, General Erich von Manstein's LVI Panzer Corps did not face such determined opposition. Even resistance from Soviet tank units was ineffective because, as was the case along most of the front, they had been supplied with HE ammunition (good for close support missions against infantry) and not armor-piercing, anti-tank shells. His spearhead, Major General Erich Brandenberger's 8th Panzer Division, broke through quickly and drove toward Daugavpils, scattering the Russians as it went. In four days, it covered more than 200 miles, and on the morning of June 26, captured its first important objectives of the campaign: the road and railroad bridges over the Dvina River at Daugavpils.

Manstein wanted to continue the pursuit while the Soviets were still off balance. "The safety of an armored formation in the enemy's rear depends on its continued movement," was an adage coined by Manstein.[10] Hitler, however, was getting jittery again and was afraid of his own success. He ordered LVI Corps to halt and await the arrival of the left wing of the 16th Army, which was more than 60 miles back.

Manstein, whose corps already posed a threat to Leningrad, was quite displeased with this order. He realized that speed was of the essence, and the entire concept of Barbarossa demanded that a breakthrough and a rapid advance be maintained. But orders were orders, and he obeyed them.

The LVI Panzer Corps, which had gained 200 miles in four days and was only 300 miles from Leningrad, sat still for six days. During that time, General Kuznetsov drew all of his forces back to the old Stalin Line, on the former Russian-Estonian frontier, between Lake Peipus and Sebezh, and threw the 21st Mechanized Corps into a counterattack against Daugavpils. Manstein quickly defeated the Soviet attack but, when he at last received permission to advance again on July 2, he found that his opponent was no longer a beaten mass of men on the run; he was organized, prepared, and much more difficult to deal with. Leningrad was much farther away than it had been on June 26th.

This battle and the subsequent delay highlights once of the principle features of the Soviet soldiers and High Command during the entire war. Whenever they were surprised by a swift and powerful blow, even if it was delivered by a numerically inferior foe, the cumbersome and inflexible Soviet command would be seized with paralysis. However, when they were given time to organize and prepare a resistance, they would resist fiercely, even if they knew that they were deliberately being sacrificed.

AUFTRAGSTAKTIK AND THE FIRST BATTLE OF ENCIRCLEMENT

On the ground, the German Army in Russia was outnumbered from the beginning. On June 22, it struck the Soviet Union with 146 divisions: 3 million men, 600,000 vehicles, 750,000 horses, and 3,580 armored vehicles. They were met in the frontier zones by 139 Soviet divisions, 29 independent brigades, and several independent tank and mechanized corps—a total of 4.7 million men.[11] Yet the Germans seized and maintained the initiative in every sector. Unlike the Russian officers, the German commanders and NCOs had been trained to exercise personal initiative and to think for themselves when orders from above were lacking. "[T]he German higher commander rarely or never reproached their subordinate unless they made a terrible blunder," General Balck recalled.

They left him room for initiative and did not reprimand him unless he did something very wrong. This went down to the individual soldier, who was praised for developing initiative. Of course there were exceptions, but generally independent action along the line of the general concept was praised and was accepted as something good.[12]

The Germans called this mission-oriented tactical doctrine *Auftragstaktik*, and it was superior to the tactical doctrine of the Soviets—and to the order-oriented tactical doctrine that the Fuehrer later forced on the Wehrmacht—in every respect. The first major ground battle of the campaign was the Battle of Bialystok-Minsk, which was fought in the zone of Fedor von Bock's Army Group Center, and it is a good example of Auftragstaktik. It consisted of two double envelopments. The deeper envelopment was directed against Minsk, the capital of Belorussia, which was 170 miles in the Soviet rear. Bock planned for Hoth's 3rd Panzer Group to attack it from the north, while Guderian's 2nd Panzer Group enveloped it from the south. Simultaneously, the shorter double envelopment would take place to the west. It focused on the Bialystok salient, with the infantry of Strauss's 9th Army attacking from the north and von Kluge's 4th Army advancing from the south. When the encircled Soviet forces were destroyed, Bock planned yet another double envelopment, this time against Smolensk, using the 3rd and 2nd Panzer Groups. This encirclement would advance the German front yet another 150 miles to the east, across the Dnieper River, and well over halfway to Moscow.

It should be noted here that there was a tremendous amount of rivalry and ill-feeling between the senior members of the German armed forces, and Army Group Center provides a prime example of this phenomena. The most prominent characteristic that distinguished the cold, humorless, and arrogant Bock, for example, was his overwhelming ambition. He did not like Brauchitsch, apparently because he felt he should have been named commander-in-chief of the army in 1938, instead of Brauchitsch, who had been junior to him in seniority at the time. Bock, who was stubborn and intolerant, had also developed bad relations with Kluge, Strauss, and especially Guderian, who was equally intolerant and had a running feud with most of the senior generals in the army. Bock, Halder, and Brauchitsch all disliked Jodl, whom they considered an interloper, and the commander-in-chief of OKH and his chief of staff deliberately excluded him from army planning; and, of course, everyone considered Keitel a blockhead, including Hitler himself. In addition, Halder considered Brauchitsch a gutless wonder, and their relationship was quite cool. Of the senior generals of Army Group Center, only the calm, level-headed, and highly professional General Hoth seemed to maintain a correct relationship with everybody—which is a tremendous compliment to his diplomatic balm. In view of all of these personality disputes, the successes that Field Marshal von Bock achieved during the opening stages of the Russian campaign are nothing short of remarkable and were achieved only because he did not interfere in the tactical affairs of his subordinates— and did not let anyone else interfere with them, either.

As the infantry of the 9th and 4th Armies converged on Bialystok from the north and south, General Dmitri Pavlov, the commander of the Soviet West Front, moved his remaining reserves from the Minsk area west, to attack the German infantry. Apparently, he was unaware that an even greater danger existed in the rapidly moving panzer columns, north and south of Minsk. The Soviet reserves were quickly engaged in heavy fighting against the infantry of Kluge and Strauss, while Hoth and Guderian pushed well east of Bialystok with their tanks and motorized formations.

At this point, Hitler panicked. On June 25, only three days into the war, he began to interfere in the tactical business of his generals;

bypassing Brauchitsch, he ordered von Bock to abandon the Minsk encirclement, in favor of a much shorter one. Bock fiercely objected to this change with every argument he could muster, and this time Hitler gave way. The result was a tremendous victory for the Germans. The 3rd and 2nd Panzer Groups continued to push east, against scattered resistance. Then, suddenly, Hoth's columns turned abruptly south, while Guderian's broke to the north; both converged on Minsk, a city of a million people, which was now virtually undefended. The Belorussian capital fell on June 28, the same day that Strauss and Kluge closed the jaws on Bialystok. The next day, Hoth's vanguard linked up with Guderian's spearhead, forming a giant double pocket, trapping three Russian armies and parts of two others—40 divisions in all. The Russians made several uncoordinated attempts to break out of the pockets, and a few units did manage to escape through the deep forests of Belorussia. The 29th Motorized, 18th Motorized, and 19th Panzer Divisions kept the Minsk Pocket sealed until Bock could replace them with infantry units from the 4th and 9th Armies. The pockets were finally cleared on July 3. Bock's forces took 290,000 prisoners and destroyed or captured 3,332 Soviet tanks and 1,809 pieces of artillery. Two Soviet armies had been totally destroyed, along with most of three others. Stalin had lost 22 infantry divisions and the equivalent of seven tank divisions and six mechanized brigades, as well as a province containing almost 10 million citizens. On June 29, even before this battle was over, Guderian ordered Major General Walter Nehring, the commander of the 18th Panzer Division, to drive south of Minsk and head east, toward Borisov on the Berezina River, to form a bridgehead there. The division would be alone, 60 miles behind enemy lines. It jumped off on June 30. The bridge, which the defenders had not been authorized to blow up, was captured the next day. Fifty miles farther south, Lieutenant General Walter Model's 3rd Panzer Division had already crossed the Berezina at Bobruysk, and, still farther south, 4th Panzer Division also crossed the river and headed for Mogilev.

General Pavlov himself escaped the Minsk encirclement and was summoned to Moscow, where he was promptly arrested, court-martialed and shot, along with his chief of staff and several of his top advisors. His political commissar was not punished. Marshal Timoshenko, the commissar of defense, personally assumed command of the West Front and Marshal Semen Budenny's Reserve Front (four armies) on July 2, but could do nothing to halt the panzers on the Berezina, which had already been penetrated in a number of places. He dug in on the line of the upper Dvina and upper Dnieper and awaited the panzer onslaught.

Guderian's spearheads reached the Dnieper the next day. They were already 320 miles inside the Soviet Union, and had already covered about half of the distance to Moscow.

STIFFENING RESISTANCE AND SLOWER PROGRESS

Meanwhile, Soviet resistance stiffened. There were a number of reasons for this, and Hitler himself is to blame for much of the opposition. Thousands of men, including commissars, Jewish soldiers, officers, and others, knew that they had nothing to gain by surrendering. Stories of German atrocities spread rapidly throughout the Red Army from the first day of the invasion. Many of them were not true, but all too many of them were completely accurate. By the end of the first week of the war, SS Lieutenant General Otto Ohlendorf's *Einsatzgruppe* was already at work in Belorussia, which had a large Jewish population. Even by Nazi standards, the murders here were indiscriminate. One day in Minsk, for example, the SS men hauled 280 prisoners out of the Minsk jail, lined them up in a ditch, and shot them all. Then, since the ditch was not yet full, they went back to the jail, brought out 30 more, and shot them, too. It was discovered later that this second group included 23 skilled workers who had come from Poland as German employees. They had been billeted in the jail only because there was a housing shortage in war-torn Minsk.

Naturally stories about atrocities of this nature, often embellished in the telling, spread like wildfire through the Soviet ranks. Commissars and others had little trouble convincing their often illiterate and unsophisticated enlisted men that a horrible fate awaited them if they allowed themselves to be captured by the Germans. Tales of unspeakable torture and unprovoked German cruelty and sadism also made the rounds throughout the Red Army in 1941.

On the heels of the Einsatzgruppen came Hitler's *Reichskommissionaren* and civil administrators selected to rule the occupied lands. These administrators were major contributing factors to Soviet resistance at the front and to the proliferation of partisan bands behind it.

When the soldiers of the German Army entered the Ukraine, they were greeted as liberators. "In every village we're showered with bouquets of flowers, even more beautiful ones than we got when he entered Vienna," one soldier wrote in June 1941. The Ukrainians (and the Poles living in the western Ukraine) disliked the Russians and hated the Communists, who had closed down their churches and murdered their upper class. The villagers and peasants greeted the troops in their native costumes, carrying bread and salt (the traditional Ukrainian welcome for honored guests), serenaded them with balalaika music, offered them food and drink, and erected arches bearing such slogans as, "The Ukrainian peoples thank their liberators, the brave German Army. Heil Adolf Hitler!"[13]

That was before they met Erich Koch, the new Reichskommissionar for the Ukraine. Koch, a former railroad clerk from the Rhineland and a close friend of the insidious Martin Bormann (now Hitler's principle advisor), had been appointed Gauleiter of East Prussia in 1928, on the recommendation of Julius Streicher, the notorious Jew-baiter. He was already known for his ruthlessness, sadism, and corruption. Koch's first official act upon taking charge of the Ukraine was to close the local schools, declaring that "Ukraine children need no schools. What they'll have to learn later will be taught to them by their German masters."[14] He quickly destroyed or plundered several Ukrainian museums and libraries, including every university library as well as the library of the Ukrainian Academy of Sciences at Kiev. The Gauleiter made it clear to everyone that he had nothing but contempt for Slavic *Untermenschen* (subhumans) and, in his inaugural speech, told his subordinates:

Gentlemen: I am known as a brutal dog. Because of this reason I was appointed Reichskommissar of the Ukraine. Our task is to suck from the Ukraine all the goods we can get hold of, without consideration of the feeling or property of the Ukrainians. Gentlemen: I am expecting from you the utmost severity toward the native population.[15]

Later he declared, "We are a master race, which must remember that the lowliest German worker is racially and biologically a thousand times more valuable than the population here."[16] As if to emphasize the point that the Ukrainians would have no say in the governing of the Ukraine, Koch drove thousands of villagers out of the Zuman district, which he converted into a 175,000-acre private hunting estate for himself.

Koch agreed with Goering that "[t]he best thing would be to kill all men in the Ukraine over fifteen years of age, and then to send in the SS stallions."[17] He soon made an informal deal with the Reichsmarschall and Himmler, whereby the SS would be given a free hand in its extermination program, in return for the allocation of economic resources and "general loot" to Goering.[18] Both, in turn, would support Koch against his archenemy, Alfred Rosenberg, the head of the Eastern Ministry. They made an effective unholy triumvirate. Koch's particular forte was to have prisoners whipped to death in public squares or parks, to encourage the Ukrainians to be obedient. Naturally, such acts had the reverse affect. Due to his policies of repression, "Germanization," murder, and exploitation, his region was soon infested with partisans. Koch's contempt extended to the German Army, which, in turn, refused to protect his hunting lodge from guerillas, who eventually burned it down; in fact, in September 1942, a gunman fired at Koch, but missed, and then made good his escape—in an army Mercedes. Koch was later charged with responsibility for murdering 400,000 Poles, as well as tens of thousands of Jews and Ukrainians.

Wilhelm Kube, the Landeskommissar of Belorussia, was another of the infamous Nazi administrators who wielded vast power in the newly conquered territories. He had been a Nazi member of the Reichstag and a civil servant in West Prussia but had been "retired" because of his scandalous behavior. In Belorussia, he was delighted to find high-quality vodka, beer, and attractive, blonde-haired, blue-eyed female peasants, whom he called "blondies" and incorporated into his domestic service, which soon became a harem. His administrative staff, one author wrote, consisted of "woefully unprepared personnel.... Nazi waiters and diary men, yesterday's clerks and superintendents, graduates of quick training courses ... dizzy with power, yet quite unfit for their jobs.... In practice Kube's instructions were often disregarded by his subordinates."[19]

Kube's administration of Belorussia (White Russia) was, needless to say, a disaster, but he continued to amuse himself with his harem and alcohol until September 1942. Then, he went to bed, only to find that one of his "blondies" had put an antipersonnel mine under his hot water bottle. It blew off both of his legs and he died within a half an hour. Kube was succeeded by SS Major General (later SS Lieutenant General) Kurt von Gottberg, whose rule was considerably harsher than Kube's. Naturally, neither were able to "win the hearts and minds" of the Belorussian people, and the region was soon heavily infested with partisans.

In addition to the blunders of the Nazis, patriotism also played a part in the increasingly stiff Russian resistance. Many of the Soviet peasants fought out of a simple love for Mother Russia. Communist propaganda played on this theme skillfully, which helped rally the troops at the front, increase industrial production in the rear, and begin partisan movements in the German communications zones. Ihor Kamenetsky recalled,

The tradition of military glory was symbolized not by the heroes of the Russian Revolution or of International Communism but by such old Russian "bourgeois" and "reactionary" national heroes as Czar Ivan the Terrible, Peter the Great, General Kutusov, etc. By reviving Russian nationalism and pretending to be a savior of "Holy Russia," the Soviet government grasped one of the main assets of its survival, and it used this asset with a great skill in the time to come.[20]

Finally, fear of their Communist masters was a major motivating factor in the increasingly fanatical Soviet resistance. Soviet soldiers who were captured were declared traitors for allowing themselves to be taken alive. Even a Russian prisoner who escaped and made it back to his own lines could expect nothing but a prison sentence—or worse.

The fact that families of prisoners of war had their food rations taken away—which often meant they starved to death—further inspired the Russian soldier to fight to the end. "There are no prisoners of war, there are traitors," Stalin declared. When Stalin's eldest son, Yakov Djugashvili, was captured in July 1941, the dictator had Yakov's wife, Yulia, thrown into prison for two years. Even when Hitler offered to trade Yakov for one of his nephews who had been captured at the front, Stalin refused to make the swap. Yakov was killed by the SS on April 14, 1943, when he deliberately crossed a "death line" at Sacksenhausen. According to the sentry who shot him, Yakov grabbed the perimeter wire and yelled at him, "Hey, you are a soldier, so don't be a coward. Shoot me!" He died instantly.[21]

Such brutality from the top permeated the Soviet armed forces and citizenry with fear from top to bottom, thanks largely to the Commissars, the politruks, the Narodnyy Kommissariat Vnutrennikh Del (The People's Commissariat for Internal Affairs or The Secret Police) (NKVD), and the Komitet Gosudarstvennoy Bezopasnosti (The Committee for State Security, the premier security agency and intelligence bureau of the U.S.S.R.) (KGB), and many other agencies that flourished in the ruthless totalitarian system that was the Soviet Union.

Russian patriotism, Nazi atrocities, and Stalin's brutal police state methods were not the major factors in slowing the German advance. In early July 1941, the Soviet transportation system was a major drawback to the Wehrmacht. In 1941, the Soviet Union had 850,000 miles of "roads," but 700,000 of them were little more than cart tracks. Only 150,000 were classified as all weather, and only 40,000 miles were paved.[22] Even the major roads were dirt, and the dust was tremendous. The infantry marched behind the panzers, often covering 30 miles a day, becoming harder and more physically fit each week. As their stamina improved as the brutal summer sun beat down upon them, hotter and hotter every day, as their uniforms became more and more infested with dirt, vermin, and lice, the morale of German infantry actually improved, the deeper they advanced into Soviet Russia. By July 1941, morale was higher than it had ever been.

Panzer units were another matter. Unlike the infantry, with its horse-drawn supply wagons, they needed more than just rations and a few rounds of light ammunition. They required fuel, maintenance, oil, grease, and spare parts of every kind. The dirt roads of the Soviet Union soon turned to dust under the heavy treads of the tanks, and it clogged the engines and caused the moving parts of the panzers to wear quickly. The supply units had a difficult time keeping up, even in good weather. As a result, spare parts could not reach the maintenance units quickly enough or in sufficient quantities, and the German tanks and trucks were soon breaking down faster than their motor pools could repair them. The combat strengths of the German motorized and panzer divisions began to fall dramatically. By early August, 30 percent of the German motor vehicles had broken down and were awaiting repair, and casualties and mechanical breakdowns had reduced the army's tank strength to less than 50 percent of its establishment. By the end of August, 4th Panzer Group had only 70 percent of its authorized number of operational tanks—and it was in better condition than any other group in the east. Kleist's 1st Panzer Group was at 53 percent of its authorized strength, and 3rd Panzer Group was at 41 percent. Only one-quarter of Guderian's tanks were still operational.[23]

THE BATTLE OF THE SMOLENSK POCKET

Despite their problems, Hitler's panzer spearhead continued to advance on the central sector of the Russian Front. By July 10, they had already covered half of the distance to Moscow, but resistance was stiffening and progress was becoming more difficult. At Hitler's personal orders, and over the objections of Field Marshal von Bock, Army Group Center was reorganized. The 2nd and 3rd Panzer Groups were placed under the command of Kluge's 4th Army, which was temporarily and unofficially dubbed 4th Panzer Army, for the advance on Smolensk. Weichs's 2nd Army Headquarters, now up from Yugoslavia, took over the infantry divisions that had previously belonged to 4th Army.

The new command arrangement was not a good one, because Kluge did not have much talent for leading panzer armies. For example, he wanted to advance on a broad front, which merely pushed the Soviet armies east, instead of destroying them by encirclement. The plan to encircle Smolensk was devised by Guderian and Hoth, behind Kluge's back. Guderian, of course, was harsh in his criticism of Kluge, whom he hated, but the more level-headed and objective Hoth also described Kluge's advance as a showpiece on how not to conduct armored warfare.[24] Hoth's advance toward Smolensk was relatively slow, partially due to Kluge, partially due to Hitler, partially due to stiffening Soviet resistance, and partially due to heavy summer rains turning the dirt roads into bogs. He advanced on the city from the north, but was held up by heavy Russian flanking attacks. On the southern flank of the envelopment, however, Guderian advanced much more rapidly. He crossed the Dnieper on July 10 and 11, secured two bridgeheads, and then quickly drove on Smolensk, shoving the Soviet 13th Army before him, and encircling four rifle divisions and part of the 20th Mechanized Corps near Mogilev on the 12th. Hoth, meanwhile, captured

Figure 31.1
The Battles of Encirclement on the Eastern Front, 1941

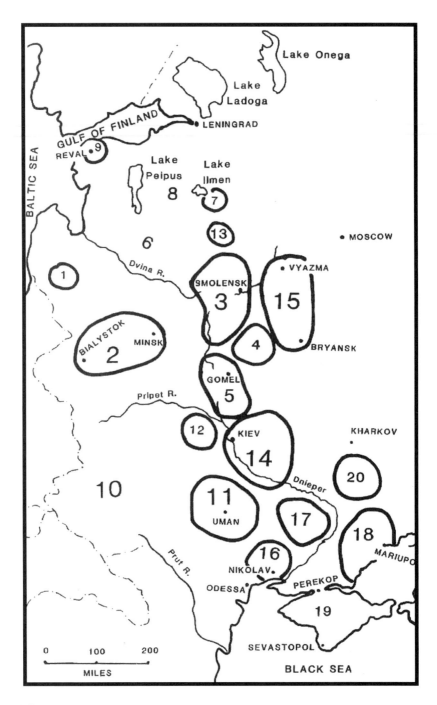

THE BATTLES OF ENCIRCLEMENT OF THE EASTERN FRONT, 1941

1. **Rossizny:** 200 tanks
2. **Bialystok-Minsk:** 290,000 captured, 3,332 tanks, 1809 guns
3. **Smolensk:** 310,000 men, 3,205 tanks, 3,120 guns
4. **Roslavl:** 38,000 men, 250 tanks, 359 guns
5. **Gomel:** 84,000 men, 144 tanks, 848 guns
6. **Divina:** 35,000 men, 355 tanks, 655 guns
7. **Staraya Russa:** 53,000 men, 320 tanks, 695 guns
8. **Luga:** 250,000 men, 1,170 tanks 3,075 guns
9. **Reval:** 12,000 men, 91, tanks, 293 guns
10. **Galacia:** 150,000 men, 1,970 tanks, 2,190 guns
11. **Uman:** 103,000 men, 317 tanks, 1,100 guns
12. **Zhitomir:** 18,000 men, 142 tanks, 123 guns
13. **Valdai Hills:** 30,000 men, 400 guns
14. **Kiev:** 667,000 men, 884 tanks, 3,718 guns
15. **Vyazma-Bryansk:** 663,000 men, 1,242 tanks, 5,412 guns
16. **Nikolav:** 60,000 men, 84 tanks, 1,100 guns
17. **Dnieper Bend:** 84,000 men, 199 tanks, 465 guns
18. **Mariupol (Sea of Azov):** 106,000 men, 212 tanks, 672 guns
19. **Crimea:** 100,000 men, 160 tanks, 700 guns
20. **The Donetz:** 14,000 men, 45 tanks, 69 guns

Note: Soviet losses in men refers to those captured only; losses in tanks and guns refer to those captured or destroyed.

Yartsevo, a cotton milling city, on July 15, at the same time Guderian's 29th Motorized Division took Smolensk. To the astonishment of General Halder, the two joined hands the following day, trapping the Soviet 20th and 16th Armies, and forming another large pocket. This did not end the battle, because the Soviets launched repeated breakout attempts, which were fierce but uncoordinated, and Timoshenko made several attacks designed to relieve the pocket from the east. Against Hoth's forces alone he threw three armies, but without success. To the south, the Soviet 28th Army struck from the important communications center of Roslavl against 2nd Panzer Group and made some progress until it fell into a Guderian trap and was surrounded by XXIV Panzer and VII Corps. Figure 31.1 shows the pockets at Smolensk and Roslavl, as well as the other battles of encirclement on the Eastern Front, where the Red Army of 1941 was devastated.

The Battle of the Smolensk Pocket ended on August 5, when the last resistance was crushed. About 310,000 Soviet soldiers were captured, and 3,205 tanks and 3,120 guns captured or destroyed. Three days later, the Battle of the Roslavl Pocket ended. Guderian took another

38,000 prisoners, along with 250 tanks and 359 guns, captured or destroyed.[25]

As soon as the Battle of the Smolensk Pocket was over, Guderian hurled the XXIV Panzer Corps into the Russian rear, west and north of Gomel, in coordination with von Weichs's 2nd Army, which attacked from the east. By the time the battle of the Gomel Pocket was over on August 24, two more Russian armies were gone and another 84,000 prisoners had been captured, along with 144 tanks and 848 guns.[26]

By the first of September, Field Marshal von Bock's Army Group Center had carried out its initial mission brilliantly. From June 22 to the end of August, it had inflicted more than three-quarters of a million casualties on the Russians and had destroyed several Soviet armies, captured more than 600,000 men, and destroyed or captured some 7,000 Soviet tanks and more than 6,000 guns. In the meantime, it had suffered fewer than 100,000 casualties. More important, it had advanced more than 500 miles, was well beyond the Dnieper, and was only about 185 miles from Moscow at its closest point.

The Communists feverishly dug in and prepared to defend their capital, but Fedor von Bock was absolutely confident that he could brush these remnants aside and be in Moscow within a month. His optimism was shared by Hoth, Guderian, Halder, and most of the other German commanders. There is, in fact, little question that he could have done just that, had he been given permission to do so. Hitler, however, was not much interested. On August 4, he gave his orders for the next phase of the campaign. Hoth's 3rd Panzer Group was to turn north, to join Army Group North in the capture of Leningrad; simultaneously, Guderian's 2nd Panzer Group was to turn south, to assist Rundstedt's Army Group South in the conquest of the Ukraine and the capture of Kiev. This order had the effect of stripping Bock's army group of four of its five panzer corps. Richthofen's VIII Air Corps, which had provided Bock with excellent air cover, was also transferred to the north.

THE DRIVE TO LENINGRAD

While Bock was crushing his opponents in the massive double envelopments of Bialystok, Minsk, and Smolensk, Field Marshal Ritter von Leeb's Army Group North was having a more difficult time in the Baltic States. His problems in this campaign were mammoth. The terrain was flat, thickly forested, and sandy, with much marshland and many swamps. Like Bock, his objectives were unclear. He had been ordered to capture the Baltic States and seize Leningrad, but no priority had been assigned to these assignments. Was he suppose to clear the

Baltic States first or take Leningrad and then mop up the Baltic States? He still had not received an answer when the campaign began. Finally, Leeb himself was a defensive expert; he was neither trained nor suited for directing large mobile formations, which he handled here for the first time in his long career. His senior tank commander, Hoepner, was a capable panzer leader but independent minded and difficult to direct. Friction soon developed between them, because Hoepner considered Leeb too slow, and Leeb became nervous when the advances of the panzer generals, in keeping with their standard tactics, put them dozens of miles ahead of the infantry, with nothing in reserve to cover their rear.

Leeb attacked into the Soviet Union at 3:15 A.M. on June 22, with Kuechler's 18th Army on the left, Hoepner's 4th Panzer Group in the center, and Busch's 16th Army on the right. He was initially faced by General Fedor I. Kuznetsov's Northwest Front, which consisted of some 30 divisions, including two mechanized corps (four armored and two mechanized divisions), as well as a few independent tank brigades. To the Soviet rear lay Markian M. Popov's Leningrad Military District (later North Front), which had another 20 divisions.

Leeb's forces initially advanced rapidly, breached the Dvinsk River line, and won important victories at Daugavpils and Rossizny. Leeb, however, did not object to Hitler's order paralyzing Manstein's LVI Panzer Corps at Daugavpils for almost a week. On July 1, he met with General Hoepner and proposed that 16th Army (on the southern flank of the army group) wheel north and seal off the Baltic States, while 4th Panzer Group protect its eastern flank. Hoepner vigorously objected; he wanted to advance between Lake Peipus and Ilmen, on the direct route to Leningrad, with his entire command. Leeb, therefore, proposed a compromise: Manstein would drive on Novorzhev (in the direction of Lake Ilmen), along with the 16th Army, while Reinhardt's XXXXI Panzer—Hoepner's other corps—advanced on Ostrov, in the direction of Leningrad. Hoepner did not like this plan either, because it was a broad-front approach. The bold General Hoepner favored a narrow, quick-thrust advance on Leningrad, but was overruled by Marshal Leeb.

Leeb continued to push forward on a broad front until July 7, when Brauchitsch appeared at his headquarters and approved Hoepner's plan for an advance on Leningrad: XXXXI Panzer Corps would advance along the Pskov-Luga-Leningrad road, while Manstein's LVI Panzer drove on Novgorod, and then on to Leningrad. These were the only two routes to the capital of the Czars, which meant that the element of surprise would be totally lacking, and the two panzer corps would be separated from each other by more than 100 miles of forests and swampland, and well out in front of the infantry.

Reinhardt began his advance on July 10, but faced stiff resistance and difficult terrain. He was stopped on July 12, after a gain of only a few miles. Two days later, Manstein was attacked by the reinforced Russian 11th Army, and at one point was completely cut off from the rest of the German Wehrmacht. Hoepner, meanwhile, executed a bold move: he sent Manstein's entire command to the north, to turn the flank of the Russian units barring Reinhardt's way. The maneuver worked; by July 17 the Luga position had been overcome and 4th Panzer Group was only 80 miles from Leningrad. Unfortunately, Hitler and OKH became nervous and ordered Hoepner to halt Manstein's corps until the infantry of the 16th Army could come up and secure his right flank. Leeb, who for once favored the bold solution, appealed to OKW, but could not get the order rescinded. He considered letting Reinhardt proceed alone, but did not. The ensuing delay gave the Russians three weeks to rally their forces and prepare their defenses.

Leeb's army group had now advanced 430 miles into Soviet Russia and had cleared most of the Baltic States of Russian forces, but was at the end of a long supply line that was subject to attack by Russian partisans, bypassed units, and stragglers. Also, as one moves east, European Russia opens up like a funnel. Army Group North's frontage increased with every step his men advanced. To add to his problems, Hitler had finally decided that 18th Army must complete the conquest of the Baltic States before attempting to take Leningrad. Finally, the Fuehrer required Busch to cover the left flank of Army Group Center, to the extent that 60 percent of the 16th Army's infantry was engaged in this task by the middle of July. As a result, there were no foot soldiers to spare for 4th Panzer Group, which was exposed to probing attacks by new Russian armies. Leeb's rate of advance, which had averaged 17 miles a day for the first three weeks of the campaign, slowed to barely one mile a day in August.

Hoepner resumed his drive on Leningrad on August 8, with Reinhardt on the left and Manstein on the right. The swampy, forested terrain was utterly unsuited for armor, and Soviet resistance was well-prepared and fierce. Reinhardt's three divisions suffered so many casualties that Hoepner considered abandoning the offensive. Finally, on August 14, Hoepner at last broke out, but Leeb had to take away half of his panzer group almost immediately, because a major crisis had developed to the south.

On August 1, on the left flank of 16th Army, General of Artillery Christian Hansen's X Corps had begun an advance on Staraya Russa, an important transportation center on the southern side of Lake Ilmen, to provide cover for the deep right flank of Army Group North for its final advance on Leningrad. The Soviets were fully ready for this onslaught and committed the entire 11th Army to the defense, behind deep minefields, dug-in tanks, bunkers, and extensive field fortifications. It took three German infantry divisions a week of heavy fighting to penetrate the last nine miles to Staraya Russa, where they were soon engaged in house-to-house fighting.

On August 12, Soviet Marshal Voroshilov, the latest commander of the Northwest Front, threw his newly activated 34th Army (eight infantry divisions, a tank corps, and a cavalry corps) into an attack on Staraya Russa, with the objective of pinning X Corps against the southern shore of Lake Ilmen and destroying it. On August 15, Leeb had to hurriedly transfer LVI Panzer to the 16th Army to save Hansen and his men. On August 19, after a forced march of more than 100 miles, Manstein hurled his two divisions (the 3rd Motorized and the SS Motorized Division Totenkopf) into the rear of the 34th Army, trapping it between himself and Hansen. By August 23, the Soviet army had been destroyed and 246 guns had been captured. Manstein could not return to the north, however, because Voroshilov threw three more armies into an offensive against the land neck between Lakes Peipus and Ilmen, pinning down both 16th Army and the LVI Panzer Corps in the process.

Meanwhile, in accordance with Hitler's orders, 18th Army was reinforced with Schmidt's XXXIX Panzer Corps (from Army Group Center) and VIII Air Corps. With this help, Kuechler was able to push back the Soviet 48th Army to the north of Lake Ilmen. He took Novgorod and, on August 25, seized Chudovo, on the main Moscow to Leningrad railroad line. The Soviets reinforced this sector to a strength of four armies but were unable to prevent Leeb from taking Mga on August 30. By September 4, the 18th Army had cleared Estonia of Soviet troops, as well as the entire southern shore of the Gulf of Finland, except for a small bridgehead at Oranienbaum, opposite Kronstadt, where the Soviet 8th Army was besieged by Albert Wodrig's XXVI Corps. In the center, Leeb's troops were nearing the suburbs of Leningrad.

This city, the second largest in the Soviet Union, was formerly St. Petersburg, the capital of the Czars. It had a population of 3 million in 1941, contained major munitions plants, tank factories, textile mills, and shipyards, and was the home port of the Soviet Baltic Fleet. It was of major importance to the Soviet war effort, and its fall very well could have endangered the continued existence of the Soviet Union. It was defended by troops in two major rings of fortifications, which had been constructed around the city, mainly by the women and children of Leningrad. The inner ring focused on Duderhof Hills, the key point in the defensive line.

The first German artillery shells landed in the city on September 4. Two days later, it was subjected to its first bombing attack. With the Germans clearly closing in, Stalin reinforced Leningrad with three newly formed armies. In the city itself, the Soviets formed 300,000 factory workers into 20 Red militia divisions. The troops was so raw and untrained, however, that they did little to impede the progress of the Germans, and most of them never came home again.

During the first week of September, Field Marshal von Leeb received the loan of General Hoth's 3rd Panzer Group (LVII and XXXIX Panzer Corps) from Army Group Center. He used it to smash the three Soviet armies between Staraya Russa and Kholm. This enabled him to anchor his right flank and bring up the XXVIII Corps and XXXIX Panzer Corps (under Busch), for the decisive attack on the city.

For the final offensive, Reinhardt's XXXXI Panzer Corps (36th Motorized, 1st Panzer, and 6th Panzer Divisions) was chosen to launch the main attack, while, on the extreme eastern flank, Rudolf Schmidt's XXXIX Panzer Corps had the task of capturing Schluesselburg on the southern shore of Lake Ladoga, which would seal off the city from the rest of the Soviet Union, except by water.

On September 8, Leeb began his final assault on the city. Simultaneously, the 1st Air Fleet subjected Leningrad to a massive aerial bombardment, during which it dropped tons of incendiaries. The bombs set fire to the Badayev warehouses, which were wooden buildings, each separated from the next by only a few feet. Inside the warehouses lay Leningrad's entire reserve food supply. This is exactly the wrong way to store such critical provisions. The city's entire food reserve was burned, except for the sugar. It melted, all 2,500 tons of it, and flowed into the cellars, where it solidified into a substance that resembled hard candy. Later it was sold to the population "as is," when almost all the other types of food were gone.

Despite fierce resistance, Reinhardt's troops pushed slowly forward, until, at last, at 11:30 A.M. on September 11, Hill 167—the famous "General's Hill" of the Czars—fell to the 6th Panzer Division, and one of the spearhead commanders signaled that he could see St. Petersburg and the sea. In the meantime, the men of the 291st Infantry Division knocked out 150 concrete pillboxes in a single day, while the 58th Infantry Division captured a Leningrad tram car in the suburb of Uritsk, only six miles from the center of the city. Schleusselburg also fell, closing the system of rivers, lakes and canals that linked Leningrad with the White Sea and the Arctic Ocean, and sealing off the city to the east. By now, the forward tanks crews could see the golden spires of the Admiralty building. Leningrad was doomed—or so it seemed. Then on September 12, Adolf Hitler ordered Ritter von Leeb not to take the city. He was to merely blockade it and starve it into submission. Simultaneously, Army Group North was ordered to give up XXXXI Panzer Corps, LVII Panzer Corps, and the VIII Air Corps, as well as Headquarters, 3rd and 4th Panzer Groups—a total of five panzer and two motorized divisions, and the bulk of its air support. In return, Hitler promised to sent Leeb a German infantry division then in France, as well as the 250th (Spanish) "Blue" Infantry Division and two parachute regiments.

Leeb immediately protested this strategically ridiculous order but was overridden by Hitler, who had committed one of the greatest tactical blunders of the war. Thirty Soviet divisions were trapped in the city but not destroyed. As winter descended on northern Russia, the Soviets were able to build a "Road of Life" across the ice of Lake Ladoga and even constructed a railroad across it. Although thousands starved to death, just as Hitler had planned, Leningrad was nevertheless able to hold out for 28 months, tying down the desperately needed 18th and 16th Armies in the process. In the end, the Soviets managed to break the siege. Leningrad was never taken.

Meanwhile, far to the north, Colonel General Nikolaus von Falkenhorst's Army of Norway could not capture the Arctic Ocean port of Murmansk. Displeased with Falkenhorst, Hitler created the Army of Lapland under Colonel General Eduard Dietl on November 7. He would also prove unable to capture the port. The Far North front would remain stalemated until September 1944.

THE FINAL DECISION

And what was happening in the critical zone of Army Group Center during the first two weeks of August, while Stalin and Timoshenko were moving heaven and earth to scrape together every available formation for the defense of Moscow?

OKH and Army Group Center were virtually paralyzed with indecision. Bock and his subordinates were still almost unanimously in favor of resuming the offensive toward the Soviet capital, in spite of Hitler's decision; however, no one wanted to confront the wrath of the Fuehrer. Meanwhile, Guderian, once again on the edge of insubordination, was still planning for a drive against Moscow, despite Hitler's orders to the contrary. On August 11, however, Bock notified Guderian that his plan had been rejected by OKH as "completely unsatisfactory."[27]

On August 15, the Soviet offensive against Leeb's right flank at Staraya Russa began. As a result, Hoth was ordered to send another panzer corps (Schmidt's XXXIX, with the 12th Panzer and two motorized divisions) to Army Group North, to help rescue Busch's 16th Army. "We reckoned with 200 Russian divisions" when Barbarossa began, Halder noted in his diary that evening. "Now we have already counted 360. Our front on this broad expanse is too thin, it has no depth. In consequence the enemy attacks often meet with success."[28] Bock's ability to continue the drive on Moscow was severely curtailed by the loss of the XXXIX Panzer, but still no final plans were made for the resumption of the offensive and vital time was wasted. On August 18, Brauchitsch finally mustered up enough courage to submit a memorandum to Hitler, calling for a drive against Moscow, but Hitler emphatically rejected it. In a handwritten answer, he informed the commander-in-chief of the army that the maximum effort was to be placed on the southern attack; furthermore, he criticized OKH for allowing the panzer units to operate too independently and to push too far ahead of the infantry, which, he said, had allowed too many enemy units to break through the loose encirclements and escape. Thus reprimanded and cowed, Brauchitsch meekly relayed Hitler's orders to Halder and Army Group Center.

The final chapter in the crisis began on August 22, when Guderian was ordered to move his XXIV Panzer Corps to the Klintsy-Pochep area, on the left flank of Weichs's 2nd Army. Once again Guderian protested, stating that the idea of sending his panzer group to the south was "criminal folly."[29] The next day, Halder arrived at von Bock's headquarters at Novy Borisov. Here he met with Bock and Guderian, and, on Bock's suggestion, it was decided that the panzer leader should personally appeal to Hitler and talk him out of the drive to the south. Halder and Guderian boarded a Ju-52 and took off for Loetzen that very afternoon.

When they landed at the airfield near Fuehrer Headquarters just before nightfall, they were met by Field Marshal von Brauchitsch, who was in a state of nervous agitation. "I forbid you to mention the question of Moscow to the Fuehrer," he told Guderian. "The operation to the south has been ordered. The problem now is simply how it is to be carried out. Discussion is pointless."

Guderian replied that, in that case, he would fly back to his headquarters immediately, since any conversation he had with Hitler would be a waste of time. No, Brauchitsch answered, he must see the Fuehrer and report on the condition of the panzer group, "but without mentioning Moscow!"[30]

When the meeting took place, Guderian had a large audience, including Keitel, Jodl, and several OKW officers; neither Brauchitsch nor Halder was present. Hitler listened in silence to Guderian's report, and then asked, "In view of their past performance, do you consider that your troops are capable of making another great effort?"

"If the troops are given a major objective, the importance of which is apparent to every soldier, yes."

"You mean, of course, Moscow?" the Fuehrer asked.

"Yes," Guderian responded, and then gave him the reasons for his opinions. Hitler listened impassively until Guderian had finished. Then Hitler spoke in great detail about the economic reasons behind his decision, concluding, "My generals know nothing about the economic aspects of war."

As the Leader spoke, Guderian noticed the attitude of the OKW officers in attendance. "I saw here for the first time a spectacle with which I was later to become very familiar: all those present nodded in agreement with every sentence that Hitler uttered, while I was left alone with my point of view."[31]

Since he saw that the decision to attack into the Ukraine was not going to be reversed, Guderian recalled later, he begged Hitler not to split the panzer group as was intended, but to commit the entire 2nd Panzer to the operation. Hitler agreed to back Guderian on this point, and as a result, Army Group Center was also deprived of XXXXVII Panzer Corps, leaving it with only von Vietinghoff's XXXXVI Panzer (7th Panzer, 11th Panzer, and 14th Motorized Divisions). Had the XXXXVII been allowed to remain with Army Group Center and rebuild its tank strength, instead of being committed to a long and strength-consuming drive to the south, the ensuing drive on Moscow might have been successful. This is doubtful, but, in any case, Halder felt betrayed. Guderian reported that, when he heard the news, the chief of the General Staff "suffered a complete nervous collapse, which led him to make accusations and imputations which were utterly unjustified."[32] Unjustified or not, it is obvious that Halder believed that Guderian had allowed Hitler to bribe him. He telephoned Bock and told him that Guderian had let them down, and the relationship between the panzer group commander and the chief of the General Staff was never the same. Halder then urged Brauchitsch to join him in resigning in protest of the decision to forego Moscow. This Brauchitsch would not do, and Halder (who was no Beck) would not resign alone. So Hitler had his way; Army Group Center lost four of its five panzer corps, as well as three infantry corps and most of its air support, and Moscow was saved.

ARMY GROUP SOUTH

On June 22, it will be recalled, Rundstedt's Army Group South consisted of two wings. In the north, between the southern edge of the Pripet Marshes and the foothills of the Carpathians, lay Reichenau's 6th Army, Kleist's 1st Panzer Group, and Stuelpnagel's 17th Army. The other German army (Schobert's 11th) was intermixed the Romanian and Hungarian units and was not scheduled to go over to the offensive until July.

Facing Rundstedt was the bulk of the Red Army. Led initially by Colonel General Kirponos, the commander of the Kiev Military District, the forces defending west of the Ukraine included four armies, with three mechanized corps in close support of the infantry and three others further back. The legions Rundstedt struck on June 22 were thus much stronger than his own formations, but they were too scattered; nevertheless, Kirponos's divisions gave a much better account of themselves than did the Red units facing either Leeb or Bock.

The day the invasion began, Kirponos ordered up all three of his mechanized corps, with the intention of concentrating them northeast of Rovno (where the 22nd Mechanized Corps was already in position) and launching a massive counterattack from there against 1st Panzer Group's left flank. General von Kleist, however, was too fast for him. He broke through the Soviet frontier defenses and headed directly for Rovno, where he smashed the 22nd Mechanized Corps on the very first day of the invasion. The 15th Mechanized Corps tried to reach Rovno from the south, but was blocked by von Kleist and received a bloody check. A series of uncoordinated counterattacks developed, in which Kleist defeated each Soviet unit piecemeal. The 8th Mechanized Corps (which was equipped with modern T-34 tanks) attacked alone and was severely battered, while the 9th and 19th Mechanized Corps struggled for four days to reach the battlefield, under relentless bombardment from the Luftwaffe. They were already at about half strength when they went into action on June 26 and were promptly swamped by the veterans of the 1st Panzer Group. In all, Kleist's 600 panzers defeated 2,400 Soviet tanks, many of which were technologically superior to his PzKw IIIs and IVs, which were the best tanks the Third Reich had in 1941. Kirponos's counterattacks, however, had at least slowed down the German advance. "The enemy leadership in front of A. G. South is remarkably energetic," Halder recorded in his diary, "his endless flank and frontal attacks are causing us heavy losses." The next day he added, "One has to admit that the Russian leadership on this front is doing a pretty good job."[33]

Kirponos's tank losses in the frontier battles were extremely heavy; by June 28 he was in full retreat, covered by the survivors of his mechanized corps. Kleist took Lvov (Lwow) on June 30, reached the old Stalin Line on July 3 and broke through it on July 6, despite several strong Soviet counterattacks. On July 10, Kleist took Zhitomir (about 90 miles west of Kiev) after defeating heavy attacks from three mechanized corps. That same day the Soviet 5th Army, reinforced with the surviving elements of the 9th, 19th, and 22nd Mechanized Corps, emerged from the southern edge of the Pripet Marshes and cut Kleist's main supply line. Field Marshal von Reichenau, following behind with his 6th Army, had to commit much of his infantry to restore contact with von Kleist.

The terrain of Galacia and the western Ukraine was far from ideal for armored operations. It was heavily forested, much of it was swampy, and the roads were predominately made out of sand or dirt. Bypassed Red Army or partisan units operating in the German rear constantly disrupted German supply lines, to the point that, between

June 22 and July 10, 1st Panzer Group could only average an advance of 10 miles a day and even less after that—far from the blitzkrieg that Hitler was hoping for.

Meanwhile, on July 10, Stalin reorganized his forces in the south. The South and Southwest Fronts, under F. V. Tyulenev and Kirponos, respectively, were merged to form the Southwest Theater, under Marshal Semen M. Budenny.

Semen Budenny bore a superficial resemblance to the American General Patton, with his love of horses, the cavalry charge, his mahogany-handled revolvers, his womanizing, and his unorthodox manner. He had none of Patton's ability to lead men in battle, however; Stalin's appreciation of his reliability was the sole reason that he had advanced to this high rank. The dictator ordered Budenny to hold Kiev at all costs and gave the southern sector priority in the allocation of men and equipment. Aided by the rail system of the Ukraine (the most highly deployed in the Soviet Union), Budenny was soon able to assemble formidable forces in two areas (as dictated by the railroads): one in Kiev itself, the second at Uman. By the second week in July, he had about 1.5 million men—roughly half of the strength of the Red Army in the field at that time.

Kleist, meanwhile, concentrated his three panzer corps (III, XIV, and XXXXVIII) at Zhitomir and, on July 12, started an offensive aimed at separating Uman and Kiev. He made rapid progress against Budenny's predominately infantry ("infantry heavy") forces and, during the night of July 15–16, cut the vital Berdichev-Kazat railroad, effectively splitting the Red forces in two. Meanwhile, Reichenau's 6th Army followed Kleist and applied pressure to the flanks of the Kiev concentration, while Carl-Heinrich von Stueplnagel's 17th Army pinned down the Uman forces from the west and north. At the same time, the infantry of Schobert's 11th Army pushed across the Bug River at Gaivoron, 30 miles south of Uman, and headed toward Novo Ukrainka, deep in the Soviet rear. Marshal Budenny reacted very slowly and did not seem to appreciate the danger his Uman concentration was in. In any event, Wietersheim's XIV Panzer Corps of Kleist's group rapidly turned due south and linked up with Stueplnagel's vanguard at Pervomaysk, forming the first large encirclement on the southern sector of the Eastern Front. By the time the Uman Pocket was cleared by the 11th and 17th Armies on August 8, the Reds had lost 103,000 men captured, including two army commanders, along with 317 tanks and 1,100 guns captured or destroyed.[34] By this time, Kleist's spearheads had advanced as far as Kirovgrad, more than 100 miles southeast of Kiev. By August 17, the III Panzer and XIV Panzer Corps had captured Krivoy Rog (the principle iron-ore center of the Soviet Union) and had pushed into the great bend of the Dnieper. In the meantime, Schobert, supported by Germany's Hungarian and Romanian allies, was threatening Odessa and was advancing on the Dnieper estuary against light opposition. He crossed the mighty river above Kherson on August 21. General von Mackensen's III Panzer Corps crossed the river above the huge industrial city of Dnepropetrovsk the following day and entered the place on the 25th. Now nothing stood between Kleist's panzers and the occupation of the Donetz Basin (the Ukraine's huge industrial complex) except a few scattered militia units and local defense troops.

In the meantime, as we have seen, Guderian prepared to advance behind Kiev from the north. Elements of Reichenau's hard-marching army had already worked their way behind Kiev and were nearing Cherkassy, while the seven infantry divisions of Stuelpnagel's 17th Army (freed by the fall of Uman) marched 30 to 40 miles a day and seized a bridgehead over the Dnieper at Kremenchug on August 22 and 23. The encirclement of Kiev was already taking shape.

While all of this was going on, Budenny sat in the capital of the Ukraine, doing nothing. His few surviving tanks were largely immobilized by lack of fuel, but, even so, he did very little to prevent the encirclement of Kiev. He assigned the task of defending the north bank of the Dnieper (southeast of Kiev) to the 48th Army, which was much too weak to hold a 120-plus mile frontage against the 17th Army and the 1st Panzer Group. But Stalin had ordered Budenny to hold Kiev at all costs, and that is what he intended to do, oblivious to the encirclement that was developing behind him.

THE BATTLE OF THE KIEV POCKET

General Guderian wheeled south and began his drive behind Kiev on September 9, taking the Russians completely by surprise. The gap between Timoshenko's armies (facing Army Group Center) and Budenny's northern flank was more than 120 miles, defended only by remnants of the Soviet 5th Army, which could do little to even slow the panzertruppen down. The 2nd Panzer Group was delayed as much by the poor roads through the deep forests as by the Soviets.

Guderian's group was divided into two columns (one for each corps), which advanced about 30 miles apart. Geyr's XXIV Panzer Corps was spearheaded by Model's 3rd Panzer Division, while the 17th Panzer Division (under the temporary command of Ritter von Thoma) led the advance of Joachim Lemelsen's XXXXVII Panzer. By the third day of the offensive, Model had already covered 60 miles and captured the bridge over the Desna at Novgorod-Severski, thus overcoming the last natural barrier between the 2nd and 1st Panzer Groups. Kleist, meanwhile, took over the 17th Army's footholds north of the

Figure 31.2
The Battle of Kiev

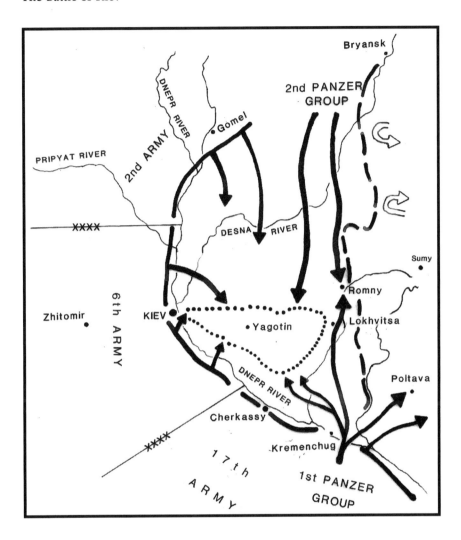

Dnieper and attacked to the north on September 10. He was held up for two days, but on September 12 broke out from his bridgeheads at Cherkassy and Kremenchug and barreled into the Russian-rear, spearhead by Major General Hans Valentin Hube's 16th Panzer Division. The one-armed Hube advanced with incredible speed, covering 43 miles in the first 12 hours. He made contact with Model near Romny, 130 miles east of Kiev, on September 14, closing the ring on the largest encirclement achieved during World War II (see Figure 31.2).

Inside the pocket, the confusion was total. Stalin relieved Budenny on September 13 and had him flown out of the pocket, to command reserve forces in the interior. With his departure, the last semblance of central command also disappeared. On September 16, Stalin finally authorized the forces in the pocket to withdraw, but the breakouts were made by individual armies and corps, without central direction. As a result, they amounted to little more than human wave attacks. Kiev, the third-largest city in the Soviet Union, fell on September 19, and by September 26, the battle was over. The final bag was 667,000 prisoners, and 3,718 guns and 884 tanks captured or destroyed. Among the dead was Colonel General Kirponos, one of Russia's most capable generals, who was killed by a German shell, presumably while trying to find an escape route out of the pocket. Four Soviet armies were destroyed, along with part of two others, and the Ukraine—the bread-basket of the Soviet Union—was now lost to Stalin, as was the critical Donetz industrial region, including Kharkov, the fourth-largest city in the Soviet Union. As a reward for their part in this victory, the 1st and 2nd Panzer Groups were upgraded to panzer armies on October 6.

To date, since the beginning of Operation Barbarossa, the Soviets had lost 2.5 million men, 22,000 guns, 18,000 tanks, and 14,000 air-planes. Hitler's strategic objectives had been largely achieved and OKH was already discussing plans to withdraw and demobilize about 80 divisions from the Soviet Union after it surrendered. A wave of opti-mism swept through the General Staff at Zossen, where the general feeling was that one more major victory would finish off the Soviets. At the front, however, the feelings of the troops were not nearly so op-timistic. One German soldier wrote—

The billet is full of lice.... Socks which we put there to dry were white with lice eggs. We've caught fleas—absolute prize specimens.... What a country, what a war, where there's no pleasure in success, no pride, no satisfaction; only a feeling of suppressed fury now and then.[35]

The soldiers felt a deep sense of foreboding, as if they were advanc-ing deeper into another world, a strange and dangerous world, from which many of them would not return.

They were right.

THE DOUBLE BATTLE OF VYAZMA-BRYANSK

When Hitler deprived Bock of 80 percent of his tank units in the sec-ond half of August, the road to Moscow was clear. By the end of the month, Stalin had rushed several new armies to the threatened sector, and Bock had no choice but to go over to the defensive with the 9th and 4th Armies. By the end of September, Stalin had concentrated 15 armies (1.5 million to 2 million men) against Army Group Center. These were, however, the weakest armies Moscow would ever put in the field. They were made up almost entirely of reservists, who had little or no basic training. They also had few tanks or trucks, and even horses were in short supply. Their sole mission was to buy time, until "General Winter" could arrive and save the Soviet Union.

After the fall of Kiev, OKH thinned out Army Groups North and South and reinforced Army Group Center to a strength of 70 divisions, including 14 panzer and eight motorized infantry divisions. In addition, it was supported by Kesselring's 2nd Air Fleet, which now controlled about 1,000 of the 2,400 aircraft operating on the Eastern Front. Field Marshal von Brauchitsch met with Bock and his principle subordinates on September 15, to discuss the next phase of operations: the destruction of Timoshenko's forces and the final drive to Moscow. Now that Soviet resistance in the Ukraine had been broken, Hitler no longer objected to seizing Stalin's capital before the onset of winter. Only Gerd von Rundstedt spoke emphatically against this course of action. He wanted to go into winter quarters at once, arguing that the Red Army could not be defeated before winter arrived, but his ideas were firmly opposed by Brauchitsch, Halder, Bock, Kluge, Hoth, Guderian, Kesselring, and others.

Specifically, Brauchitsch planned to commit three of Germany's five panzer groups/armies to the attack. Due to the lateness of the season and the poor mechanical condition of the tanks, OKH decided not to return the 2nd Panzer, 3rd Panzer, or 2nd Army to Smolensk; they would attack from where they were. This gave Army Group Center a total frontage of about 400 miles.

From north to south, as shown in Figure 31.3, Bock deployed the 3rd Panzer Group (Hoth); the 9th Army (Strauss); the 4th Army (Kluge); the 4th Panzer Group (Hoepner); the 2nd Army (Weichs); and the 2nd Panzer Army (Guderian). His plan was for Hoepner to break through the Soviet center and split the Red Army into two parts, which would then be destroyed in separate battles of encirclement. After he achieved his breakthrough, Hoepner was to wheel north and link up with Hoth (advancing to the south), to form a huge pocket around Vyazma. Meanwhile, Strauss and Kluge were to attack the Soviets frontally, to pin them down north of the Smolensk-Yelnya line, while Hoth and Hoepner cut them off. Simultaneously, to the south, Weichs and Guderian were to converge on Bryansk and Zhizdra, in a separate envelopment.

Bock began his offensive on the morning of September 30. Hans-Karl Schmidt (writing under the pseudonym of Paul Carell) later called the double battle of Vyazma-Bryansk "the most perfect battle of

Figure 31.3
The Vyazma-Bryansk Encirclement

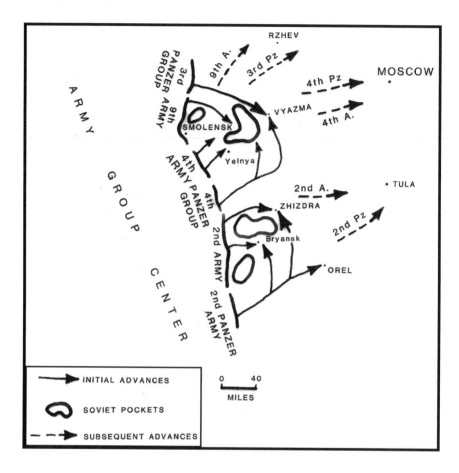

encirclement in military history."[36] To everyone's surprise, Guderian easily broke through the Soviet 13th Army, and his spearheads covered 80 miles on the first day of the battle. On October 6, 17th Panzer Division took Bryansk in a surprise coup, and later that day Guderian linked up with Weichs's 2nd Army, encircling 26 divisions (three Soviet armies). The next day, 10th Panzer Division of Hoepner's 4th Panzer Group took Vyazma and linked up with 3rd Panzer Group's vanguards, encircling six more Soviet armies and sealing the fate of 55 enemy divisions. The fighting continued until October 17, and several Russian units did succeed in breaking out to the east, but the Battle of Vyazma-Bryansk cost Stalin another 663,000 men, 1,242 tanks, and 5,412 guns.[37]

The Vyazma encirclement was an auspicious beginning for the 3rd Panzer Group's new commander, Georg-Hans Reinhardt. Brauchitsch had fallen out with Carl-Heinrich von Stuelpnagel, the commander of the 17th Army (who had proven to be an unsatisfactory field commander) and relieved him of his post on October 5. Hoth was chosen to replace him, and Reinhardt succeeded Hoth. (At OKH, this was looked upon as a promotion for Hoth.) Walter Model took Reinhardt's place as commander of XXXXI Panzer Corps.

THE BATTLE OF MOSCOW

Long before the Vyazma-Bryansk Pockets were cleared by the infantry, von Bock's panzer spearheads turned toward Moscow, the "grand prize" of Operation Barbarossa. The going by now was difficult, even though resistance was light, due to the fact that the Red Army had been crushed. The first snow fell on October 7. It melted quickly, but it began to rain incessantly on October 9, turning the Russian roads into rivers of mud. It was virtually impossible to bring up fuel, ammunition, food, replacements, or winter clothing to the front. There was very little winter clothing available in any case, because OKH had accepted Hitler's conclusion that there would be no winter campaign and had only ordered enough for about one-third of its divisions. There were also no replacements. When the campaign began, General Fromm, the commander-in-chief of the Home Army and an opponent of Operation Barbarossa, had warned that he could only furnish about 430,000 replacements in 1941, and these had been used up by September. In spite of their successes, German casualties had not been light. As of the beginning of September, 14 divisions reported personnel deficiencies of greater than 4,000 men; 40 divisions were short between 3,000 and 4,000 men, while 30 divisions were 2,000 to 3,000 men below their authorized strength levels.[38] Naturally, most of the shortages were found in the combat units, especially the infantry. By September 26, the German Army had suffered 534,000 casualties on the Eastern Front—15 percent of its total establishment in the East.[39] Bock nevertheless continued his offensive with a tenacity that bordered on stubbornness. On October 14, Reinhardt's panzers, followed closely by the infantry of the 9th Army, took Kalinin, the northern hinge of Moscow's defenses, and rolled down the Volga as far as the Moscow Canal, only 70 miles north of the Kremlin. For the next three days, there was panic in the capital of the Soviet Union, heightened by the news that the government offices were being evacuated to Kuybyshev in the Ural Mountains. There was widespread looting, the food distribution system broke down, and Communist Party members were assaulted on the streets. No one knew where Stalin was, and all sorts of rumors proliferated. Order was not restored until the 19th, when the city was declared under a state of siege and special units of NKVD security troops took charge of the capital.

Since October 9, all of the forces defending Moscow had been under the command of Marshal Zhukov, whose primary objectives were to hold the city and keep his command "in being" until the winter arrived in earnest. The harsh and often brutal Zhukov organized "workers' battalions" from the Moscow factories and hurled them into battle with little or no training and often armed only with Molotov cocktails. Meanwhile, more than 500,000 of the city's other inhabitants (mostly women) were drafted into construction battalions and spent day and night digging anti-tank ditches and trenches, and building bunkers.

Due to the broken, forested nature of the terrain north of the Soviet capital, Reinhardt never had the best chance of capturing Moscow. The real danger was to the south, where Heinz Guderian's 2nd Panzer Group had debouched in reasonably good tank country and was driving on Tula, a major industrial city south of Moscow. Consequently, Zhukov committed the bulk of his best forces here. Meanwhile, Stalin brought up his last strategic reserves: the Siberian divisions of General Iosif Apanasenko's Far Eastern Front. These were some of the best-trained and well-equipped units in the entire Red Army. The Soviet dictator could afford to take this step, because he knew that the Japanese were not going to attack in the East. He had learned this from Richard Sorge, his master spy in Tokyo.

Another valuable source of information was "Lucy," the code name for Rudolf Roessler, a German writer living in Switzerland. A severely wounded World War I veteran, he hated Nazism with a passion and, prior to the outbreak of the war, set up a spy ring within the Wehrmacht. His agents included eight officers in OKW and two in OKL. They worked in the army's operations, logistical, transportation, military economics, and communications offices, and five of them were generals. They apparently included Hans Oster, the deputy chief of the Abwehr; Major General Fritz Thiele, the deputy of General Fellgiebel, the chief signals officer of the High Command of the Armed Forces; Abwehr agent Hans Bernard Gisevius; and Carl Goerdeler, the former Lord Mayor of Leipzig and the civilian leader of the German resistance.[40]

Lucy's information was extremely accurate and included day-to-day changes in the German order of battle. His intelligence dispatches to Moscow eventually totaled 12,000 closely typed pages: the equivalent of about 40 average length books. By 1942, scarcely 10 hours elapsed between the making of a decision at OKW and Lucy's learning about it.[41] "[I]n the end," one Soviet intelligence expert said later, "Moscow very largely fought the war on Lucy's messages."[42] This state of affairs continued until November 1943, when Walter Schellenberg (the chief of the SS intelligence branch) almost tracked Roessler down and forced the Swiss (who pretended they knew nothing about it) to shut down the spy ring. In any case, Stalin knew that he could safely move his Siberian divisions to the Moscow sector in November 1941.

By this point, the forward German units were in particularly bad shape. The infantry had received no new boots, socks, or shirts for weeks, and their footwear was literally falling apart. The supply difficulties were simply insurmountable. The German Army was now at the end of a 1,000-mile-long supply line, and the snow and the primitive road system severely limited the amount of food, fuel, and ammunition that the forward units could receive. The 3rd Panzer, 9th, and 4th Armies, for example, all used just two roads: the same number two divisions would have used in France. Hoepner's 4th Panzer Group had to share the only hard-surfaced road in his zone of operations with Weichs's 2nd Army, and Guderian had no hard-surfaced roads at all. Due to the cold, it was necessary to run the engines of the trucks and tanks every four hours, which further exacerbated the fuel crisis. In addition, the railroads were virtually useless. Most of the Soviet rolling stock had been evacuated or destroyed as the Red Army retreated (only 500 Soviet locomotives and 21,000 cars had been captured—about 10 percent of what was needed), and German trains were built for standard-gauge rails, not for the wide gauge of the Soviet Union. The process of converting the broad-gauge Russian rail system to standard European gauge had just begun.

Getting spare parts to the motor pools was also a major problem. At the end of October, for example, Walter Nehring's 18th Panzer Division had lost 59 tanks due to accidents and enemy action, but 103 tanks were inoperative due to a lack of spare parts.[43] The story was the same in every panzer division, which were down to the strength of reinforced regiments as the Battle of Moscow began.

Off of the roads, progress was virtually impossible, except on foot. The mud was so bad that the 292nd Infantry Division reported that a team of 16 horses was not able to move a single howitzer of the 292nd Artillery Regiment. Motorized supply columns were averaging less than five miles a day, and more than 2,000 vehicles were stuck on the Moscow Highway alone.[44] "[T]he internal combustion engine is a dead loss in winter warfare," one German soldier wrote. "Everything has to go by sledge. Where all the sledges come from is a mystery. But how all the horses survive is a greater one still. . . . The native ponies live by water and straw and beating."[45] The Luftwaffe was grounded, but not the Red Air Force, which was operating on paved airfields in the Moscow area.

Due to all of these difficulties, von Bock halted his offensive on October 30 to await freezing weather. Then the ground would again be hard enough to bring up food and ammunition, and resume the advance. Meanwhile, most the infantry remained rationless and, after they consumed their Iron Rations (a concoction of chocolate laced with caffeine, to be eaten only in emergencies), they subsisted mainly on tea and potatoes they looted from local farms. Some units lived on almost nothing but horsemeat for up to six weeks at a time. Soon sickness, the cold, dysentery, and malnutrition were causing more casualties than the enemy bullets.

The final effort to take Stalin's capital began on November 15. North to south, Bock attacked with the 9th Army, the 3rd Panzer Group, the 4th Panzer Group, 4th Army, and the 2nd Panzer Army. Weichs's 2nd Army, while still part of Army Group Center, had to be moved far to the south, to try to maintain contact with Army Group South, and played no further role in the Battle of Moscow. Figure 31.4 shows Bock's dispositions and his final thrusts toward the Soviet capital.

During the first two weeks of November alone, Stalin had brought up 100,000 men, 2,000 guns, and 300 tanks from the Far East. By mid-November, Zhukov was able to deploy three fronts: West Front (six armies); Kalinin Front (three armies); and South-West Front (two armies). In all, he had 60 rifle divisions, 17 tank brigades, and 14 cavalry divisions—a total of 91 major combat formations. Stalin, however, was not through bringing up units from the East. By the end of the winter of 1941–42, he brought up 15 rifle divisions, three cavalry divisions, and eight tank brigades (1,700 tanks), as well as 1,500 airplanes, in addition to the units already at the front.[46] Bock, on the other hand, had only 38 infantry, 13 panzer, and seven motorized divisions—a total of 58 major formations.[47] Needless to say, many of the Soviet formations and all of the German units were well below their authorized strength.

By now, large sections of the German Army were virtually immobilized. On November 19, Halder informed Hitler that 30 percent of the half a million trucks that entered Russia had been destroyed or damaged beyond repair. Another 40 percent were nonoperational and awaiting overhaul or major repairs. Only 30 percent were still on the roads.[48] Most the army was now being supplied by two-wheeled *panje* (peasant) wagons, pulled by local Russian ponies, which lived where the heavier European horses died—even though they usually had nothing to eat except straw from the local thatched roofs.

Bock's progress toward Moscow was slow. Hoth's 3rd Panzer Group captured Klin on November 23, and Baron von Funck's 7th Panzer Division reached the Moscow-Volga Canal on November 28. A battle group under the command of Colonel Baron Hasso von Manteuffel crossed the canal but was soon under attack by the Siberians and could

Figure 31.4
Army Group Center, November 15 to December 5, 1941

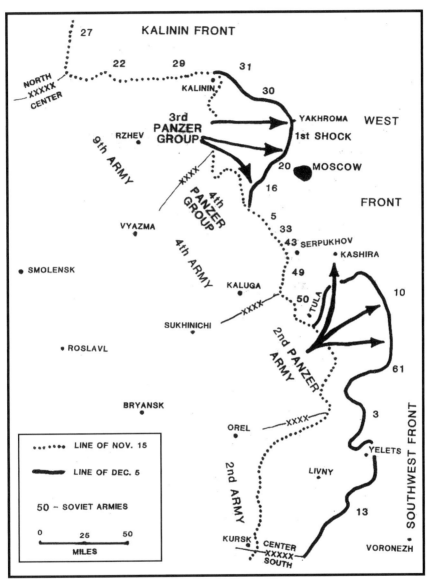

advance no further. Lieutenant General Rudolf Veiel's 2nd Panzer Division, however, made a superhuman effort and pushed into the outskirts of Moscow, and its reconnaissance battalion even managed to get Nazi Germany's only glimpse of the Kremlin, less than 15 miles away.

It was the high water mark of the Third Reich.

To the south, Guderian forced his way up toward Oka, but was unable to take Tula, which was defended by the entire Soviet 50th Army, reinforced by several workers' battalions. Guderian then bypassed it to the east and continued his advance to the north, screening his long flanks with infantry formations. One of these was Lieutenant General Friedrich Mieth's 112th Infantry Division, which was posted on Guderian's right (eastern) flank. All three of its infantry regiments had suffered more than 50 percent casualties due to frostbite, its machine guns were so badly frozen that they could only fire single shots, and the packing grease on its anti-tank ammunition had frozen so solid that it had to be scraped with a knife before it would fit into the breech of the AT guns. On November 18, the 112th was attacked by a fresh Siberian infantry division, outfitted in white quilted uniforms and armed with tommy guns, and supported by an entire brigade of T-34 tanks. It was too much for the weary, lice-infested survivors of the 112th, who broke and ran away. This was the first time such an incident had occurred on the Russian Front.

Zhukov wanted to hold his Siberians in reserve until the Germans had exhausted themselves, then commit them all in one devastating offensive. Guderian's advance, however, forced him to throw three Siberian divisions and two tank brigades into counterattacks against the 2nd Panzer Army. These attacks halted the German advance and convinced Guderian that it would be impossible to take Moscow. On November 24, he turned up at Bock's headquarters and convinced the field marshal (who was ill and in bed) to telephone OKH and ask permission to call off the offensive. Brauchitsch, however, replied that he was not allowed to make such a far-reaching decision. He ordered Guderian to continue to try to reach the Zaraisk-Mikhailov line and to cut the Ryazan railroad.

Meanwhile, Veiel's drive and Manteuffel's advance across the Moscow-Volga Canal had brought the wrath of the Siberian divisions down on Reinhardt, whose 3rd Panzer Group was brought under heavy counterattack for five days. While this was going on, Guenther von Kluge was conserving his strength (that is, doing nothing), so Hitler personally commanded that his 4th Army resume the offensive on December 2. The next day, Kluge broke the line of the 33rd Soviet Army north of Naro Fominsk and forced Zhukov to commit the reserves of his 33rd and 43rd Armies near the railroad town of Golizno. Kluge suffered heavy losses during this operation and, on his own responsibility, withdrew the 258th Infantry Division from the front, on the grounds that it was no longer battleworthy. The next day the temperature dropped to $-4°$ Fahrenheit (F). and 4th Army was forced back in a heavy snowstorm. The following day, December 5, Field Marshal von Bock called off the offensive, with the acquiescence of OKH. The nighttime temperatures by now had dropped to −25° F, and quite a few men had frozen to death. Dozens of tanks would not start because the oil in their engines had frozen, and artillery and machine guns would not fire because their lubricants had frozen. Hitler would not accept Bock's decision until December 8, but by then the Battle of Moscow was clearly over. The Soviet winter offensive had already been in progress in the central sector for two days, and Army Group Center was fighting for its very survival.

NOTES

1. Bethell, p. 30.
2. Ibid.
3. Kesselring, p. 98.
4. Constable and Toliver, *Horrido*, p. 64.
5. Ibid.
6. Brett-Smith, p. 137.
7. Goralski, p. 164.
8. Cooper, *GAF*, p. 222.
9. Carell, *Hitler Moves East*, pp. 23–24.
10. Ibid., p. 28.
11. Samuel J. Newland, *Cossacks in the German Army* (1991), p. 7.
12. Hermann Balck and F. W. von Mellenthin, "Generals Balck and von Mellenthin on Tactics: Implications for NATO Military Doctrine, Dec. 19, 1980," United States Army Command and General Staff College, Publication M-313-5 (1981), p. 21.
13. Bethell, p. 78.
14. Robert Wistrich, *Who's Who in Nazi Germany* (1982), p. 175 (hereafter cited as Wistrich).
15. Ihor Kamenestsky, *Hitler's Occupation of the Ukraine* (1956), p. 35.
16. Wistrich, p. 175.
17. Alexander Dallin, *German Rule in Russia* (1957), p. 123 (hereafter cited as Dallin).
18. Alan Clark, *Barbarossa* (1965), p. 65.
19. Dallin, pp. 204–5.
20. Kamenestsky, p. 21.
21. Wayne M. Dwonchya, "Armored Onslaught Frozen," *World War II*, vol. 4 (May 1989), pp. 22–23.
22. Ziemke and Bauer, p. 14.
23. Mueller-Hillebrand, *Das Heer*, vol. 3; Foerster, "Volkegemeinschaft," p. 202.
24. Hoth, *Panzeroperationen*, p. 78.
25. James Lucas, *War on the Eastern Front, 1941–1945* (1979), p. 176 (hereafter cited as Lucas, *Eastern Front*); Seaton, *Russo-German War*, p. 130.
26. Ibid.

27. Clark, p. 106.

28. Halder Diaries, August 15, 1941.

29. Clark, *Barbarossa*, p. 110.

30. Guderian, p. 159.

31. Ibid., pp. 159–60.

32. Ibid., p. 162.

33. Clark, p. 54; Halder Diaries.

34. Plocher MS 1941; Seaton, *Russo-German War*, pp. 139–40. Also see James Lucas, *Alpine Elite* (1980), pp. 86–126, for a detailed account of the Battle of Uman.

35. Helmut Pabst, *The Outermost Frontier* (1957), p. 35 (hereafter cited as Pabst).

36. Carell, *Hitler Moves East*.

37. Guderian, p. 82.

38. Mueller-Hillebrand, *Das Heer*, vol. 2, chap. 10.

39. Seaton, *Russo-German War*, p. 175; also see Halder Diaries.

40. Pierre Accoce and Pierre Quet, *A Man Called Lucy* (1966), p. 45; Geoffrey Jukes, *Kursk* (1968), pp. 46–47; Martin Caidin, *The Tigers Are Burning* (1974; reprint ed., 1975), pp. 79–80; Jack Finnegan, "A Man Called Lucy," *World War II*, vol. 3, no. 5 (January 1989), pp. 12–16.

41. Ibid.

42. Clark, p. 151.

43. Foerster, "Volkegemeinschaft," p. 202.

44. Deighton, pp. 231–32.

45. Pabst, p. 54.

46. Clark, p. 170.

47. Seaton, *Russo-German War*.

48. Ibid., pp. 200–201; also see Halder Diaries.

CHAPTER **XXXII**

STALIN'S WINTER OFFENSIVE, 1941–42

THE ZONE OF ARMY GROUP CENTER

With the falling temperatures, Marshal Zhukov launched his counteroffensive at dawn on December 6. The temperature was −38° F. Fortunately for the Germans, the Russian attacks were poorly coordinated and slow in forming in many sectors. The only significant progress the attackers made took place in the zone of the 30th Army, which broke through the 3rd Panzer Army's flank northeast of Klin and penetrated eight miles. By the next day, the Soviet attack had spread north, to the zone of the 9th Army, and 3rd Panzer had begun to pull back from the Moscow-Volga Canal, abandoning 15 tanks and dozens of trucks and other vehicles because they would not start, along with nine guns and assorted other equipment. In all, due to the cold, the panzer army had to leave behind more equipment in one day than they would ordinarily lose in a week of heavy fighting. And the retreat was just beginning.

Meanwhile, back in Berlin, Field Marshal von Brauchitsch worked up the courage to submit his resignation on December 6. He had been contending with Hitler's ruthlessness and deliberate rudeness for four years and had lived on a steady diet of anger, humiliation, frustration, and fear. On November 10, he had suffered his first heart attack. In the hospital, he was told that he had a malignant cardiac disease that was probably incurable.[1] He had nevertheless returned to duty within a few days, determined to take Moscow before he retired. When this proved to be impossible, he resigned. Hitler paced up and down the room for 10 minutes before telling Brauchitsch that he could not allow a change of command at that moment. The marshal got up and walked out without a word.[2]

On December 8, Guderian began to evacuate the salient east of Tula. Here, one corps alone had more than 1,500 frostbite cases that day, and

350 of them required at least one amputation. South of Guderian, Rudolf Schmidt's 2nd Army was in an even more difficult position. (Schmidt had temporarily replaced Baron von Weichs, who was ill.) It held a front 180 miles long with only seven divisions, an average of more than 25 miles per division, or two miles per understrength company. Behind it lay Kursk, its only railhead and major supply depot, and Orel, the railhead and major supply depot for the 2nd Army. That same day, Soviet tanks tore a hole between the 45th and 95th Infantry Divisions and the Red generals pushed a cavalry division through the gap. The next day, they sent two more cavalry divisions and a rifle division into the breakthrough area and expanded the gap to 16 miles. By the end of the day, the Soviet spearheads were 50 miles in the German rear, the 95th Infantry had lost half of its strength, and the 45th had lost more than that. The Luftwaffe promised to help, but was grounded by snow and freezing rain, and Schmidt had no reserves. He signaled Bock that 2nd Army was about to be cut in two; he made contingency plans to fall back on Orel and Kursk, leaving a 85-mile gap in between.

Bock had no reserves either. On the morning of December 9, he telephoned Halder and told him that Army Group Center had to have reinforcements because it could not repulse a major attack anywhere on its front. All of his specialists except tank drivers had already been pressed into the infantry. Halder speculated that the Soviets had committed untrained troops and cadres, which meant, he said, that the situation could be quieter by the end of the month. "By then the army group will be *kaputt*," the field marshal told him.[3] After this conversation, it was clear to Bock that Halder did not appreciate the gravity of the situation. He instructed his subordinate commands to prepare to retreat 60 to 90 miles, to the Rzhev-Gzhatsk-Orel-Kursk line, even though he did not believe he could hold even this.

Zhukov's relentless attacks continued on December 10. The Soviets cut the road west of Klin, 3rd Panzer Army's only route to the west. Reinhardt signaled Army Group Center:

[D]iscipline is breaking down. More and more soldiers are heading west on foot without weapons, leading a calf on a rope or pulling a sled loaded with potatoes.... All the hangers-on (corps troops, Luftwaffe, supply trains) are pouring to the rear in full flight. Without rations, freezing, irrationally.[4]

Bock's problems continued to multiply, as ice and snow tore down telephone lines and he had difficulty communicating with his subordinate units. Traffic jams in the rear were horrendous, especially on bridges, and, had it not been for the panje wagons, ammunition and rations would not have reached the frontline troops at all. By

December 15, 9th Army was evacuating Kalinin, and 3rd and 4th Panzer Armies were retreating, either on the roads or cross country. Hoepner's army had already lost most of its artillery. "The roadside scenes were shocking," Lieutenant Gerhardt Linke of the 185th Infantry Regiment wrote in his diary. "I thought such things were possible only on the retreat of the French.... Everywhere smashed up vehicles were lying upside down, the goods they were carrying scattered all over the place."[5]

"Discipline began to crack," General of Panzer Troops Ferdinand Schaal, the commander of the LVI Panzer Corps, recalled "the entire [corps] supply train—except where units were firmly led—was streaming back in wild flight. Supply units were in the grip of psychosis, almost of panic.... Without food, shivering with cold, in utter confusion, the men moved west."[6]

The case of the LVI Panzer Corps was not unique: it was typical of the entire army group. No doubt about it—the German Army was on the verge of disintegration. Meanwhile, as if the soldiers of the Wehrmacht did not have enough problems, Hitler brought another enemy into the war against them.

On December 7, 1941, the Japanese Navy launched a surprise attack against the major U.S. Pacific Ocean base at Pearl Harbor, Hawaii. Since Japan was clearly the aggressor, there was nothing in the Tripartite Pact that required Germany to declare war on the United States. Nevertheless, on the afternoon of December 11, amid the cheers of his puppets in the Reichstag, Adolf Hitler hurled insults at Roosevelt and the New Deal and concluded his address by declaring war on the United States.

He had made a fatal blunder.

"NOT ONE STEP BACK"

In the meantime, the situation on the Russian Front continued to deteriorate. On December 11, Guderian withdrew from the Tula salient and fell back in the direction of the upper Don, closely pursued by the Soviets. All of the German spearheads aimed at Moscow were thrown back. Stalin's forces pushed the German northern flank back 30 miles and gained up to 50 against the 2nd Panzer Army, smashing three German infantry divisions. The commander of the 134th Infantry, Lieutenant General Conrad Cochenhausen, committed suicide on the 13th. By the end of the day, half of the 9th Army—100,000 men—were in danger of being cut off. Its only remaining escape route was the road from Kalinin to Staritsa, and it was threatened by four Siberian divisions. General Strauss had only one battalion left—the Bavarians of the III/18th Infantry Regiment of the 6th Infantry Division. It was hastily committed to the battle, with orders to keep the Kalinin road open.

The men of the III Battalion knew that they had been given a suicide mission, but they held their thin line on December 14, despite repeated Soviet attacks. By the end of the day, they were near exhaustion and had lost 182 of their 800 men. They had suffered more casualties in one day than they had suffered in the entire campaign up to that point, but the battle was still not over.

That night, a 15-man Russian patrol captured a four man observation post. They killed three, took the fourth prisoner, and gouged out his eyes with a knife. "There," one of them said in broken German. "Go straight forward, to your brothers, the other German dogs, and tell them we'll destroy them all. We'll cut out their eyes and send what's left to Siberia—that will be Stalin's revenge. Now get going." Like Hitler, the Red Army never learned that such barbaric tactics are usually counterproductive. The soldier, blind and sobbing, reached German lines, and his story threw the III Battalion into a white fury. Sergeant Schnittger, a veteran of considerable bravery, grabbed his machine gun and, followed by nine men, set out after the Soviet patrol. They ambushed the Siberians and riddled them with bullets. Not one escaped, and they took no prisoners.

The next day, the close-quarter fighting was extremely bitter. A pile of Russian corpses stacked up in front of the III Battalion, but it held its positions, in spite of the efforts of four Siberian divisions. Meanwhile, the trapped divisions of the 9th Army made good their escape. When the Bavarians finally retreated, they carried another 150 wounded and frostbitten men with them and left another 120 dead on the battlefield. But their heroic stand saved half of the 9th Army. They were awarded 64 Iron Crosses (an incredible number for a single battalion in a single action) and the German radio dedicated a special program "to the little battalion that had withstood the onslaught of four Siberian divisions so that half an army could escape."

"We did not hear the broadcast," one of the survivors wrote later. "Retreating armies jettison their radio sets."[7]

Meanwhile, the Soviets captured Klin on December 15, and reoccupied Kalinin the next day. Dozens of stuck or disabled German vehicles and guns were captured. As usual on the Eastern Front, the Germans had no reserves, other than four security divisions, which had only two infantry regiments each and little or no artillery. On December 16, von Bock (who was reluctant to talk to Hitler personally) spoke to General Schmundt and asked him to relay his concerns to the Fuehrer. He then poured his heart out. He said that he his ulcers were acting up again, he had the "Russian disease" (diarrhea), that his health was shaky at best, and that the Fuehrer might need someone in better physical condition to command the army group. Militarily, he said, it was difficult to tell whether the army group should stay put or retreat; either way it was likely to be destroyed. At midnight that night, Hitler telephoned Bock and told him that there was only one correct decision: not to go a step back, to close the gaps and hold.[8] By this one command, Hitler took all the initiative out of the hands of his generals and concentrated all of the decision-making power into his own.

Reaction to this order at the higher levels of the German Army varied from resigned acceptance to near rebellion. Bock accepted without protest, but Guderian refused to obey. Brauchitsch, who was now sick in body and spirit, began secretly discussing limited withdrawals to a winter line with Bock, Kluge, and Guderian. Colonel Schmundt, however, got word of these discussions and informed Hitler, who immediately cancelled the plans for a winter line and demanded that the troops hold where they were, regardless of the situation on their flanks or rear. He called in Brauchitsch on December 19 and dismissed him. Their final meeting was acrimonious and ended with Hitler shouting that he was assuming command of the army himself, because he knew of no general who was capable of instilling the spirit of National Socialism into it. But, he added softly, "We will remain friends."[9]

News of Brauchitsch's retirement was announced to the world without preface that same day. Hitler named himself commander-in-chief of the Army, and the disgraced field marshal—the scapegoat of the Russian campaign—left Zossen the following day. He never saw Hitler again and died, a broken man, in American captivity in 1947. Privately, Hitler called Brauchitsch "a vain, cowardly wretch."[10]

Hitler's assumption of direct command of the army effectively left the army with no commander-in-chief and removed the last vestiges of opposition to Hitler's directives at Fuehrer Headquarters. On December 20, he called Halder in and told him how he wanted the war in the East conducted. "Fuehrer holds forth at great length on need of holding the line. Every man must fight back where he stands. No falling back when there are no prepared positions in rear," Halder noted in his diary.[11]

Meanwhile, on December 18, Field Marshal Keitel telephoned Fedor von Bock and told him that the Fuehrer suggested that he (Bock) apply for an extended leave to restore his health. Bock promptly did so. The following day, he was replaced by von Kluge. Hitler sent Bock word that he did not hold him responsible for the failure to take Moscow.

In the ranks, Hitler's assumption of command of the army led to a collective sigh of relief. The morale of the average German soldier was boosted, because most of the troops still had unbounded faith in the Fuehrer and were ignorant of his true personality. The changes, however, did nothing to improve the deteriorating situation at the front. On December 20, General of Infantry Richard Ruoff (the commander of the V Corps) and General of Panzer Troops Heinrich von Vietinghoff, the commander of the XXXXVI Panzer Corps, reported to General Hoepner that they could no longer hold their positions. They had had to destroy most of their vehicles due to lack of fuel, and they had lost more than half of their weapons. Hoepner relayed these reports to Kluge. Strauss also reported that his 9th Army was in danger of being crushed.

Kluge obeyed Hitler's orders blindly, because he was a man who placed his own career above all other considerations. If scapegoats were needed, Colonel Seaton wrote, "von Kluge could find them; if heads must fall, von Kluge took good care to see that his would not be among them." He later recorded that "Kluge had in fact replaced von Brauchitsch as the Fuehrer's postman."[12] In justice to Kluge, however, it must be noted that he did propose several retreats to Hitler and even succeeded in obtaining the Fuehrer's permission to conduct some of them.

Meanwhile, Stalin became overly ambitious and aimed at nothing less than the total destruction of the entire German Wehrmacht on the Eastern Front. Kluge's armies would be destroyed, Stalin ordered, by a double envelopment; the two pinchers were to join hands at Smolensk. To accomplish this task, Stalin employed 16 armies, including 78 rifle, 22 cavalry, and three tank divisions, and 19 independent rifle and 17 tank brigades.[13] Kluge had a total of 67 divisions (including 2nd Army, which was too far to the south to be of any help).

Much has been made of Hitler's fanatical, stand-fast order, and how it saved the German Army. No doubt it did improve the morale of many soldiers and helped speed the rally that was already taking place. However, it must be pointed out that Army Group Center did not stand fast; it was gradually pushed back 100 to 200 miles and a good case can be made for a rapid strategic withdrawal to a shorter defensive line, in the vicinity of Vyazma or Smolensk, which would have enabled Army Group Center to create a reserve, without suffering the excessive casualties it sustained in the winter of 1941–42. The supply situation would then have been reversed: Kluge would have then been near his supply depots, and Stalin's divisions would have had to contend with long and uncertain supply lines. It must be recalled that the Red Army had lost thousands of trucks and motorized vehicles during the summer and fall, and it had yet to obtain the tens of thousands of trucks it would eventually receive from the United States. It is highly doubtful that it would have been able to defeat the Germans in a major defensive battle if a proper and militarily sound retreat had been conducted. Of course, some might question whether or not the main body of Army Group Center could have broken contact with the Soviets to a sufficient degree to allow them to successfully execute such a far-ranging retreat, but the evidence (although inconclusive) seems to suggest that they could have. After the fall of Klin, 3rd and 4th Panzer Groups broke contact with the Soviets and, during the week of December 15, dug in unmolested behind the Lama and Ruza Rivers, turned the nearby villages into strongpoints, and even had time for several hot meals and to get up to two full nights of sleep, before the Russians caught up with them and resumed the battle.

Whether or not Hitler's "stand-fast" and "hold-at-all-costs" ideas were correct, the propaganda ministry made sure that the soldiers of the Wehrmacht and the civilian population heard only that Hitler was right. "[T]he German Army and public firmly believed that the Fuehrer was the savior of the German Army," Colonel Seaton wrote.

This in itself did great and permanent damage to the German war direction. Hitler was even more convinced of his own military genius and became certain that any crisis could be weathered by will-power and rigidity; he was throughout the course of the war to quote what he believed to be his success before Moscow as a justification for his obdurate and often senseless attitude towards German withdrawals.[14]

Hitler had, in reality, gone a long way toward eliminating Auftragstaktik and replacing it with an order-oriented command system. He defined the essence of defense as holding the main line of resistance at all costs. In the fall of 1942, he restricted the independence and operational control of the field general even further by ordering, "No army group commander, let alone army commander, is entitled to order a so-called tactical withdrawal without my explicit approval."[15] He thus formally institutionalized the command system that he had already introduced in December 1941 and largely eliminated one of Germany's most potent military weapons: the tactical initiative of the average German commander.

As the campaign evolved, the German Army suffered an average of 2,800 to 3,500 casualties a day from November 30, 1941, to April 1, 1942. Soviet losses were also high, but German equipment losses were extremely serious. By December 19, 2nd Panzer Army had only 70 operational tanks left and another 168 in repair, out of the 970 it had had when the campaign began or had received since June. As it retreated during the first two weeks in December, 3rd Panzer Group had to abandon or destroy 289 tanks. The 35th Infantry Division lost all but two anti-tank guns and six howitzers. The elite 23rd Infantry Division from Potsdam lost all but about 1,000 of its infantry, and its commander, Lieutenant General Heinz Hellmich, collapsed under the strain, like a great many other commanders. Casualties among officers and senior NCOs were very heavy in the winter battles of 1941–42, because they went to the forefront of the battle every day to rally their men and—although generally successful—they paid a high price for their success. A partial list of the senior casualties includes:

- General of Infantry Kurt von Briesen, the one-armed hero of the Polish campaign and commander of the LII Corps, killed in action on November 20, 1941
- Colonel Otto von Kries, chief of staff of the I Corps, killed on November 26
- Lieutenant General Herbert Geitner, commander of the 295th Infantry Division, mortally wounded on December 8 and died on January 22, 1942[16]
- Major General Hugo Ribstein, commander of the 81st Infantry Division, mortally wounded on December 8 and died on December 26
- Lieutenant General Friedrich Bergmann, commander of the 137th Infantry Division, killed on December 21
- General of Infantry Hermann Metz, commander of the XXXXIV Corps, severely disabled on December 23 and forced to retire
- Colonel Max-Hermann von Loefen, commander of the 190th Infantry Regiment, killed on January 4, 1942
- Major General Gerhard Berthold, acting commander of the XXXXIII Corps, killed in action on January 24
- Lieutenant General Georg Hewelke, commander of the 339th Infantry Division, killed in January 18, 1942
- Colonel Hans Berger, commander of the 18th Artillery Regiment, killed, February 9
- Colonel August-Heinrich Wassmuth, C.O. of the 413th Infantry Regiment, killed on February 23
- Major General Cord von Buelow, commander of the 10th Rifle Brigade, killed near Vitebsk, March 1
- Colonel Botho von Frantzius, commander of the 504th Infantry Regiment, killed at Nevel, March 14
- Lieutenant General Otto Gabcke, C.O. of the 294th Infantry Division, killed, March 22
- Major General Bruno Hippler, commander of the 329th Infantry Division, killed, March 23
- Lieutenant General Kurt Himer, the conqueror of Copenhagen and commander of the 46th Infantry Division, mortally wounded on March 26 and died in the hospital at Simferopol on April 4
- Major General Karl Fischer, C.O., 267th Infantry Division, killed on March 31
- and Major General Franz Scheidies, commander of the 61st Infantry Division, killed on April 7[17]

And there were dozens of others, killed or crippled by mortar fire, shot down by enemy snipers or machine guns or crushed beneath the heavy Russian tanks. Others simply collapsed under the strain or were relieved of their commands for refusing to obey some senseless "hold-at-all-costs" order. Divisions were now often commanded by colonels, battalions were led by captains and lieutenants, and companies (or what was left of them) were frequently commanded by second lieutenants or sergeants. By late December, for example, the remnants of the 329th Infantry Regiment (162nd Infantry Division) were led by Lieutenant Scheel, until he, too, was wounded at the end of the year. The III Battalion of the 18th Infantry Regiment was now commanded by its senior surviving lieutenant, Count Franz Joseph von Kageneck, a young military genius. He was shot through the head during the street fighting at Schitinkovo on December 29, the day after he learned that his wife, the Princess of Bavaria, had given birth to twin sons. By the time the III/18th Infantry was taken out of the line, it was commanded by Lieutenant Rudi Becker—its only surviving officer, other than the battalion physician. Its total strength was two officers, five NCOs, and 22 men.[18]

By the end of 1941, the German soldiers looked on the wounded as lucky, provided their wounds were not too serious but were severe enough to earn them an evacuation to the rear or—best of all—a trip to the Fatherland. Willi Nolden, a *Landser* (the German equivalent and companion in misfortune to the British "Tommy" or American "G.I."), was hit in the hand by a piece of shrapnel. "I'll give you a thousand marks for your hand!" one of his buddies joked to him, because he knew that Nolden was going home. (Until almost the end of the war, any German soldier who spent eight consecutive weeks in the hospital was given four weeks' medical leave in Germany.)

By December 22, the Soviet 49th Army had broken through the center of 4th Army's front and XXXXIII Corps was in danger of being encircled. Kluge appealed to Hitler several times to allow it to retreat and finally obtained permission on the afternoon of the 23rd. Meanwhile, in Guderian's sector, the Soviets broke through Lieutenant General Wilhelm Stemmermann's 296th Infantry Division in several places, and the commander of the 2nd Panzer Army had two choices: disobey Hitler's orders and pull back the 296th Infantry, or sacrifice it to a senseless command. Guderian pulled it back, opening up a 25-mile gap in the German line. The following morning, Kluge signaled Halder that Guderian had withdrawn without authorization. Halder, who at this time was also parroting Hitler's orders, declared that Guderian should be court-martialed. Guderian was relieved of his command the next day (Christmas Day) and was replaced by Rudolf Schmidt, who was promoted to colonel general on January 1. Also on Christmas Day, General of Mountain Troops Ludwig Kuebler took command of the 4th Army. It had taken him almost a week to reach his headquarters.

(When Kluge moved up to army group command, General Reinhardt had been named acting commander of the 4th Army, but the weather was so bad that he could not reach army headquarters, even by sled. Kluge retained command of both the army and army group until Kuebler could reach his new headquarters.)

The next day, the temperatures fell to −25° F. The German Army was practically immobilized. Infantry marching on the roads could only cover a maximum of eight miles a day, and motorized infantry could cover a maximum of 20—on the roads. At the front, it took four days for an infantry battalion to shift 12 miles, but the Russians, equipped with skis, sleds, and horses, moved much more quickly and were soon in the rear of Army Group Center in several points. The Germans were amazed at the Russians' ability to live in the open under such conditions. West of Volokolamsk, in the zone of the 4th Panzer Group, Ruoff's V Corps was on the point of collapse, and Hoepner had to send in his last replacement battalion. It had just arrived from the Reich, was clad in shoes, and was armed only with pistols. Strauss's 9th Army was also near the point of collapse and was in danger of being surrounded at Rzhev, and General Kuebler was planning the defense of his own headquarters. On December 30, Kluge telephoned Hitler and asked for freedom of action. It was refused. Army Group Center was to hold its present positions without thought of withdrawal, the Fuehrer declared.

Despite the odds against them and the chaotic situation in the rear, the frontline units and their rear guards generally fought on with great courage and saved much of the German Army from destruction. The 3rd SS Engineer Battalion, for example, held the Lowat River bridge at Korowitschina for more than a week against three Soviet Guard regiments, two battalions of ski troops, and approximately 30 tanks. They faced constant mortaring, artillery fire, dive-bomber strikes, and human wave attacks almost every day, and the fighting was often hand-to-hand. After a week, the battalion was surrounded and had to be resupplied by air drop. The unit commander, SS Lieutenant Colonel Karl Ullrich, was everywhere, standing with his men throughout the thickest fighting. "Always calm and composed despite the desperate situation, his steadfastness and confidence, his concern for his men's welfare and his own gallantry gave them the strength to hold out," Gordon Williamson wrote later. On February 19, Ullrich received word that he had been awarded the Knight's Cross. He signaled back that he would rather have fresh reinforcements. When he finally broke out on the night of February 22–23, he left nearly 2,000 Russian soldiers lying dead on the battlefield.[20] The 3rd SS Engineer Battalion probably had fewer than 300 men when the battle began.

Near Wyborgskaja, Corporal Bruno Sassen of the 3rd Parachute Regiment exhibited similar tenacity and held his position despite tremendous odds. Then, realizing that the Russians were massing for an overwhelming attack, Sassen infiltrated through their frontline with his five remaining men. Then they jumped up and attacked the Soviet assembly area with machine pistols blazing. Taken by surprise, the Russians bolted and ran. The next day, many of the demoralized and leaderless Red survivors surrendered to the paratroopers.[21]

Part of the stubborn German resistance was due to the courage of desperation and can be directly attributed to Soviet brutality. No one wanted to surrender to the Russians. It was well known that they frequently tortured and murdered prisoners and mutilated the bodies of the wounded. During the retreat from Rostov, for example, they captured a German hospital. They threw the wounded out into the snow, poured buckets of cold water on them and left them to die; then they killed the doctors and raped and murdered the nurses. Their behavior toward their own people was often equally barbaric. Nina Markovna was a pretty Russian girl in her late teens whose 48-year-old father had been drafted into the Red Army before her village was captured by the Wehrmacht. When Stalin's counteroffensive reached the edge of her village, however, Nina's mother knew what to expect. "Those drunken soldiers are more scared of tuberculosis than bullets," she cried to her daughter. "What followed was an elaborate masquerade," Nina recalled.

I became a tuberculosis-wasted girl lying in bed, a hanging sheet meant to protect others in the home from the infectious germs. I held a bloodstained handkerchief with countless bright spots of blood spattered on the top sheet near my face—blood that Slava [her younger brother] had donated by cautiously cutting his leg.... Uneven red spots on my cheeks were there with the help of juice from a grated beet, diluted with water.

The Red Army entered the village about noon. "Piercing, animal-like screams from the women rose in an anguished chorus. The children began to cry ... dishes were heard breaking, windows shattered with rifle butts, sacks of food were dragged out of the apartments," Nina recalled

"Leave us some food! We'll starve!" one civilian begged.

"So starve, bastards!' a soldier shouted back. "Greeting the fascists German dogs with bread and salt!"

Three soldiers broke into Nina's apartment but halted when they saw the "dying" girl. "Poor child, dying of tuberculosis. Not long now," her mother said. "Mama ... thirsty," Nina whined. The leading soldier spat on her and left, followed by his comrades.

Mother threw herself on her knees by my bed and wept in prayerful gratitude ... I, too, prayed—a bit ashamed that even as I prayed for my own deliverance, someone else was being raped. That someone was my neighbor, Nadia, and the girl's screams filled the air."[22]

Small wonder that the Germans fought so desperately to avoid capture.

The comradeship of the unit also played a decisive (if unquantifiable) role in the salvation of Army Group Center. Martin Roller recalls:

The greater the pressure on a unit, the more it held together, Soldiers at the front had an especially close relationship. Your outfit was almost like a family.... I believe that even if there were no more goals, even if you saw that it was pointless and that everything was over, you would have kept on fighting so as not to shame yourself in front of your comrades. You had to stick together to survive.[23]

Back in the Reich, everyone was alarmed over the German Army's first major defeat. On December 20, Goebbels addressed the nation on public radio and announced that because winter had come earlier than expected, the Wehrmacht was not prepared for the winter campaign in Russia; therefore, between December 27 and January 4, a gigantic collection of equipment and clothing for the armed forces would be conducted by the party.

Swedish journalist Arvid Fredborg recalled hearing sarcastic remarks as to whether or not it was reasonable to expect winter in December, but nevertheless "catastrophe was in the air. The prospect of the Russian masses welling over into Europe made even the most fanatical anti-Nazi prepared for sacrifice. The collection campaign actually produced a moral shake-up."[24] During the collection campaign, the German people voluntarily donated 1.5 million furs and skins and 67 million woolen garments. Much of it was collected by the Hitler Youth. It was a major propaganda victory for the party, although it did the soldiers no good for some time. The vehicle losses and the chaotic state of the Russian railroads meant that only supplies of the highest priority reached the frontline troops. These included ammunition, food, and very little else. Sergeant Pabst of the hard-pressed 129th Infantry Division and his lice-infested men did receive some blankets from Germany in February 1942. He recalled that they smelled clean. "You could see the parlor with the sofa," he wrote, "or the child's bed, or perhaps the young girl's room from which they came. We held them in our hands for a moment, smiling. How far away it all seemed, it could have been on another planet."[25]

At dawn on New Year's Day, 1942, the temperature stood at −25° F. In Rastenburg, Adolf Hitler raised 3rd and 4th Panzer Group to army status, no doubt to improve their morale. General Reinhardt tartly noted that his command was more nearly a corps than an army in terms of strength. Since June 22, the Wehrmacht had been decimated. It had lost 173,722 men killed, 621,308 wounded, and 35,873 missing. According to Halder, losses on the Eastern Front in 1941 totaled 25.96 percent of the 3.2 million men engaged.[26]

The New Year brought another crisis of confidence between the Army and the Fuehrer. On January 2, Adolf Hitler was furious because General Strauss had ordered a withdrawal without his authorization. General Halder recalled his "mad outbursts" and how "OKH is charged with having introduced parliamentary procedures in the army, and with lacking incisiveness of direction. These ravings interspersed with utterly baseless accusations waste our time and undermine any effective cooperation." Halder also noted that Kluge was "at the end of his wits." The next day he recorded, "Another dramatic scene with the Fuehrer, who calls in question the generals' courage to make hard decisions. The plain truth however is that with the temperature down to thirty below freezing our troops simply cannot hold any longer."[27]

The troops certainly were nearing exhaustion. One man, who did an hour's outpost duty every three hours, wrote, "Sleep comes in snatches; in 48 hours I have slept for eight. Not all nights are as quiet as this one."[28] The junior officers also performed miracles. One of his men wrote of Lieutenant von Hindenburg, the descendent of the famous military family and an company commander:

Strain has drawn rings under his eyes. In moments when he thinks he's not being watched, a great tiredness overcomes him and he grows quite numb. But as soon as he takes the receiver in his hand, his quiet low voice is clear and firm. He talks to his platoon commanders with such convincing warmth and confidence that they go away reassured. His own courage is self-sufficient, he wears it as naturally as his uniform.[29]

Meanwhile, three new divisions arrived by rail to reinforce Army Group Center. At the front, the Soviet 10th Army bypassed Sukinichi, surrounding 4,000 German troops in the process. On January 2, the Soviets broke through 4th Army and, by January, 8, XX Corps was threatened with encirclement. In vain, Hoepner begged Kluge for permission to allow it to retreat, but the field marshal refused to sanction it, because Hitler would not approve. Hoepner then ordered the retreat on his own responsibility. At 11:30 P.M. that same evening, Hoepner was relieved of his command on Hitler's personal orders—one of more than 30 generals he would dismiss before the spring of 1942. Hitler also instructed that he be expelled from the army with loss of retirement pay and benefits and the rights to wear the uniform and his decorations. (Hoepner took his case to the army courts, which upheld his contention that he could not be deprived of his pay or rights without a court-martial. This Hitler did not wish to risk, so Hoepner continued to draw full pay and lived in a garrison house until he was arrested for his part in the July 20, 1944, attempt on Hitler's life.) Richard Ruoff succeeded Hoepner as commander of the 4th Panzer Army.

As New Years approached, it was still highly doubtful that Army Group Center could survive until the spring thaw, and there were several major crisis points in its zone. One of the main objectives of the Soviet offensive was now Vyazma, a small railroad city 125 miles west of Moscow and 90 miles east of Smolensk. Its railroads ran due north to Rzhev, south to Bryansk, northeast to Moscow, and southeast to Kaluga and Tula, carrying the bulk of the supplies bound for the 3rd Panzer, 9th, 4th Panzer, and 4th Armies. During the critical battles of early 1942, it was the key to survival for Army Group Center. Figure 32.1 shows the Battle of Moscow and Army Group Center's deteriorating situation from January 1 to 14, 1942.

On the German left flank, the major crisis developed around Rzhev, where the 9th Army was in danger of being encircled and where VI Corps alone was under attack by three Soviet armies. The Reds opened a gap northwest of Rzhev before nightfall on January 2, but the temperature dropped to −40° F that night. The Soviet troops, fighting in the open, were not invulnerable to the cold, particularly when the temperatures fell this low. Consequently, they were unable to exploit the Rzhev gap the following day. By now, 9th Army had partially clothed itself in furs and felt boots (taken from Russian civilians) and had figured out ways of keeping warm in the cold temperatures. One battalion collected the bodies of 73 frozen Russian soldiers. It sawed their legs off at the knees, put them in ovens until they thawed, removed their felt-lined boots, and gave them to German soldiers. This battalion had been so depleted by casualties that this desperate measure provided footwear for almost every man in the unit.[30] Even so, the situation remained desperate. On January 5, the Soviet 39th Army burst into the rear of and behind the 9th Army. Strauss countered by committing his last reserves: the SS Cavalry Brigade, which was led by SS Major General Hermann Fegelein, a noted horseman and womanizer who had no military qualifications for his post. His troops fought well but ran out of ammunition and were forced to withdraw on the afternoon of January 8. Four Soviet divisions pushed into the rear of 9th Army, with nothing between them and the Vyazma-Rzhev railroad— the lifeline of the 9th Army. On the afternoon of January 12, they attacked Sychevka (Strauss's headquarters) and 9th Army's staff had to defend its own command post. On the right flank of 3rd Panzer Army, V Corps was under Soviet armored attack and was slowly bleeding to death, losing village after village. It was almost out of fuel, rations, and ammunition. Before nightfall, Reinhardt signaled Kluge and threatened

Figure 32.1
The Battle of Moscow, January 1–14, 1942

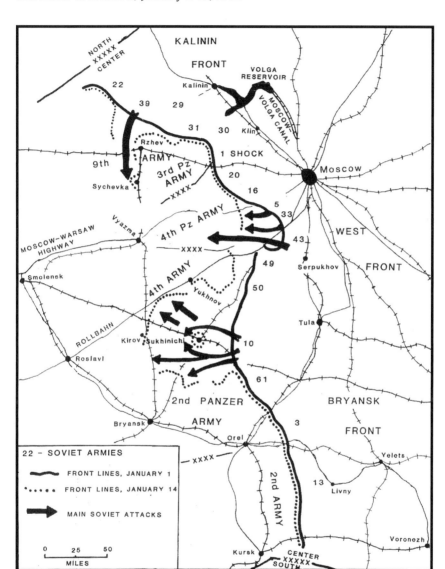

to give the order to retreat himself, if Army Group Center did not do so.

Sychevka fell on the afternoon of January 13, and 9th Army's main supply line was cut. That afternoon, 4th Army's main *Rollbahn* (main supply road) was also cut and four of Kuebler's five corps were effectively surrounded.

By January 15, the situation had become so bad that even Hitler was forced to admit that his "stand-fast" order no longer had any basis in reality, so he authorized a general withdrawal. Most of the supplies 4th Army received for the next few days were flown in by Ju-52s. On the 19th, General Kuebler had enough and reported himself sick, and was replaced by General of Infantry Gotthard Heinrici, the commander of the XXXXIII Corps. Heinrici had spent 36 years in the service. He was not a dynamically inspirational leader in the same sense that Guderian, Rommel, or Patton were, but he inspired a quiet confidence in his soldiers, who considered him as solid as a rock and felt that there was no situation too difficult for him to master. Heinrici did, in fact, exhibit a sure hand in all of the many crisis he was called on to overcome. With this tough, stoic, and extremely competent veteran in charge, the sagging morale of the 4th Army instantly recovered.

The faith that the soldiers had in General Heinrici was fully justified by subsequent events. The temperature on January 21st was −40° F, and there was no fighting until the next day, when it rose to −10° F. On the 22nd, Heinrici committed Major General Hans Zorn's XXXX Panzer Corps to clearing the Rollbahn and simultaneously launched a surprise attack against Zhukov with General Friedrich Kirchner's LVII Panzer Corps. Both maneuvers were successful. Zorn reestablished a narrow corridor to the rear and, despite the Soviet forces behind his frontlines, Heinrici was able to keep his divisions supplied and conduct a staged retreat. He successfully evacuated the Yukhnov salient in phases and reestablished his army's line behind the Ugra on March 6.

RZHEV

Meanwhile, to the north, 3rd Panzer and 4th Panzer Armies put up a fierce defense on the Lama-Ruza River Line, bringing the right flank of Zhukov's West Front to an abrupt halt. Except for a few local retreats, Reinhardt and Ruoff were able to hold their positions throughout the rest of the winter—although just barely.

Following Heinrici's assumption of command of 4th Army, the most dangerous sector in Army Group Center was around Rzhev, where the badly outnumbered 9th Army was again on the verge of disaster. So far, it had survived this long almost solely because of the courage of its individual soldiers, NCOs, and officers. One sergeant recalled what happened when his division was attacked by five Soviet divisions:

[W]e reached the limit of human endurance. And yet I saw moving instances of valor and courage. There was a staff-sergeant who in all those days stood like a rock in no-man's land: he never once left his post, never once let his machine-gun jam, but roared at his men to stand their ground. There was a red-bearded sergeant who didn't make a sound when they dressed his wounds, who laughed and called out cheerfully, as two comrades held him up: "I'll soon be back, sir!" And then there was a tall company commander who would edge himself slowly above the parapet, take aim carefully and fire, saying "Round away," just as if he were on a rifle range. Such men still exist, and they can be worth more than a whole company.[31]

On January 14, Kluge earmarked Headquarters, XXXXVI Panzer Corps and the "Das Reich" SS Motorized Division for transfer from the 4th Panzer to the 9th Army, transferred Major General Walter Krueger's veteran 1st Panzer Division from the 3rd Panzer Army to the 9th, and replaced 9th Army commander General Strauss with General of Panzer Troops Walter Model, the commander of the XXXXI Panzer Corps.

Model was the very best of the "Nazi generals" on the Eastern Front in the winter of 1941–42. In appearance, he looked like an arrogant East Prussian general from an earlier era, complete with his ever-present monocle. He was, however, an indefatigable leader and a brilliant tactician who was well liked by his men, with whom he was quite friendly. On the other hand, he was often harsh and frequently unreasonable when dealing with his officers. Later he was to receive the nickname "the Fuehrer's fireman," because he was only used in the most critical and dangerous situations.

The situation at Rzhev was certainly critical when Model arrived at 9th Army's Headquarters on January 18. The Soviets had already pushed through the 100-mile gap between the 9th Army and the 16th Army of Army Group North and were now west of Rzhev. Ninth Army was defending in three directions, and the Russian 9th Cavalry Corps was heading in the direction of Vyazma, the vital rail junction for three German armies. Fortunately for the 9th Army, the Soviets were also in trouble. They had been on the offensive for a month and a half in the dead of winter; they were also having serious supply troubles (having outrun their supply lines) and were experiencing heavy casualties due to the cold and due to poor and inexperienced leadership at all levels. Model took advantage of the Russian weaknesses and of the reinforcements he had received from Kluge to launch a counterattack at Sychevka, and by January 20 the 1st Panzer Division had reopened the railroad all the way to Rzhev. On January 22 and 23, the VI Corps, spearheaded by the "Das Reich" SS Division, pushed forward west of Rzhev and made contact with the spearheads of the XXIII Corps. This breakthrough also severed the two "snow roads" over which the Russians were resupplying the 39th and 29th Armies, as well as the XI Cavalry Corps. If contact could not be reestablished, these forces were doomed. For the 29th Army, the end came quickly. On January 30, von Vietinghoff's XXXXVI Panzer Corps launched a surprise attack from Sychevka, covered 30 miles in six days, and by February 5 had the 29th Army surrounded in a tight pocket southeast of Rzhev. The Kalinin Front launched a desperate offensive to rescue it, but in vain. After several breakout attempts, the 29th collapsed on February 20.

Realizing that the success of his winter offensive was in danger, Stalin reactivated West Theater under Zhukov on February 1. It controlled the Kalinin, West, and Bryansk Fronts, but this move came too late to have much of an impact on the campaign. By February 6, Army Group Center had halted its retreat and sealed most of the major gaps in its front. The Soviet 33rd, 39th, and 29th Armies were either cut off, isolated, or surrounded, along with the 11th Cavalry, 1st Guards Cavalry, and 4th Airborne Corps. Stavka, however, was not convinced that the Germans could not be destroyed. On February 16, it reinforced Zhukov with two guards rifle corps, 10 rifle divisions, two airborne brigades, 60,000 additional replacements, and 200 tanks. The quality of these reinforcements was low, however, and many lacked adequate military training. On the other hand, all of Army Group Center's units were seriously depleted. By February 16, for example, 2nd Panzer Army was down to a strength of 45 operational tanks—less than the peacetime components of a panzer battalion.[32]

In repeated attacks, Zhukov hurled his Kalinin Front against the 9th Army; the 43rd, 49th, and 50th Armies against Heinrici's 4th Army; and the 16th and 61st Armies against Schmidt's 2nd Panzer. The German line held firm. The crisis had passed.

After the Red armies had exhausted themselves all along the German front, Army Group Center now went about the business of liquidating the Soviet forces cut off in their impetuous and unsystematic raids and breakthroughs. With the no immediate crisis to deal with, Kluge was able to withdraw some of his combat units from the front to handle this task. (Zhukov did launch several more attacks, but none seriously threatened Army Group Center.) During the first week in March, the 5th Panzer Division (Major General Gustav Fehn) smashed and destroyed a large part of the 1st Guards Cavalry Corps south of Vyazma. Then the rest of the V Corps went over to the offensive, pushing through watery snow and mud, slowly encircling and crushing the Soviet 33rd Army, which ceased to exist on April 15. Its commander committed suicide.

By now, the *rasputitsa*—the spring thaw—was setting in. During the winter, the ground (saturated by the fall rains) had frozen to a depth of eight feet or more, and several feet of ice and snow had accumulated on top of that. Now it began to melt from the top downward, creating a progressively deepening layer of water and mud on top of frozen ground. The water could not go anywhere until the lowest layer of frozen soil had completely thawed, a process that usually took five or six weeks. During the worst three weeks of the rasputitsa, the mud was too deep for movement by motorized vehicles, or even by horse-drawn vehicles, other than panje wagons (which had high wheels and low weight). By mid-April, operations were virtually at a standstill throughout the zone of Army Group Center. Stalin's first winter offensive was over.

ARMY GROUP SOUTH

And what was happening in the zones of the other army groups while the divisions of Kluge and Zhukov were exhausting themselves west of Moscow?

To the south, Kleist's 1st Panzer Army captured Rostov on November 21, but it was immediately counterattacked by 10 Soviet divisions (see Figure 32.2). Then the Red armies shifted their attacks to the north, against Kleist's overextended left flank, where the XIV Panzer Corps was attacked by three Soviet armies. Kleist had no choice but to shift his 13th and 14th Panzer Divisions to the north and northwest, to avert disaster. Then, on November 25, Marshal Timoshenko launched his main attack with 21 divisions against General of Cavalry Eberhard von Mackensen's III Panzer Corps (the SS Motorized Division "Leibstandarte Adolf Hitler" (SS-LAH) and the 60th Motorized Infantry Division), which was defending Rostov itself. The Don River, which would have been a tremendous defensive asset in summer, was frozen solid, many of the line companies were down to one-third of their authorized strength, and those that were left were still dressed in summer uniforms. Even so, the two German divisions held on for three days, in temperatures of −14° F. On November 28, just as he had predicted, Kleist was forced to evacuate Rostov.

Adolf Hitler was not at the *Wolfsschanze*, his Rastenburg headquarters, at the time. When he did return on November 30, he learned that von Kleist (with Rundstedt's permission) had ordered III Panzer Corps to withdraw behind the Mius River, 45 miles west of Rostov.

Hitler, of course, was opposed to such a move, and browbeat Brauchitsch into ordering Rundstedt to hold his positions. On November 30, the commander-in-chief of Army Group South signaled back to Hitler that his order was "madness." If the Fuehrer did not rescind it, Rundstedt's dispatch continued, he should find someone else to carry it out. At 2 A.M. that very night Gerd von Rundstedt was relieved of his command and replaced by Field Marshal Walter von Reichenau.[33]

Figure 32.2
Army Group South, November 28 to December 3, 1941

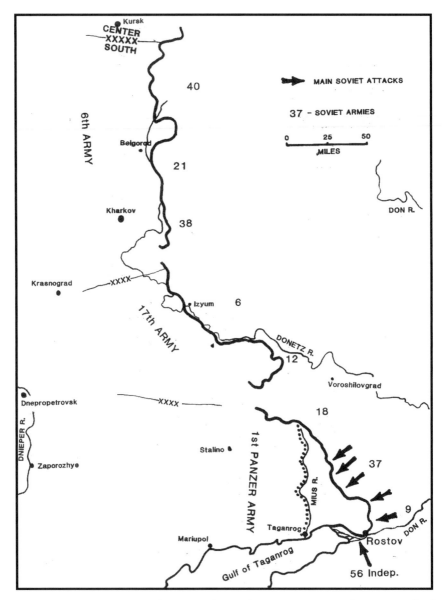

Lieutenant General Friedrich Paulus (who was promoted to general of panzer troops on January 1, 1942), the deputy chief of the General Staff of the Army and Reichenau's former chief of staff, was chosen to command 6th Army.

Reichenau initially insisted that Kleist hold his present positions but, at 3:30 P.M. on December 1, reversed himself and allowed Kleist to complete his withdrawal to the Mius during the night of December 1–2. That morning, Hitler flew to Kleist's headquarters at Mariupol on the Black Sea. As soon as he landed he conferred with *SS-Obergruppenfuehrer* (General of SS) Sepp Dietrich, the commander of the Leibstandarte. This conversation saved the careers of Rundstedt, Kleist, and Colonel Kurt Zeitzler, the chief of staff of the 1st Panzer Army. Hitler had already decided to sack the last two until Dietrich frankly told him that he had been wrong on the Rostov issue and wrong to fire Rundstedt. If an army general had told him this, Hitler would probably have flown into a tirade or (at best) ignored him. But he believed his old party comrade, Dietrich. Halder described the entire incident as "a senseless waste of strength and time, and to top it, we lost von Rundstedt also."[34]

The next crisis occurred on the Crimea. The 11th Army (under Manstein since Ritter Eugen von Schobert was killed on August 30) had overrun most of the peninsula in November, but the Soviets continued to hold the naval fortress of Sevastopol, one of the most heavily fortified places in the world. Manstein besieged it with his XXX and LIV Corps. He planned to launch an all-out offensive against the place that winter, using six of his seven German divisions. The task of defending the 170 miles of coastline from Yalta to Kerch (that is, east of Sevastopol) he assigned to Count von Sponeck's XXXXII Corps, which controlled only the German 46th Infantry Division and three Romanian brigades, plus a few corps troops.

Eleventh Army began its attack on Sevastopol on the morning of December 17, and by the end of the day, the 22nd Air Landing Division had penetrated the Outer Perimeter, the first of the three defensive rings around the city. By the 22nd, it had cracked the Main Line (the middle defensive belt), but the Soviets brought up reinforcements by sea and launched heavy counterattacks, pinning down the 22nd Division. Then, in the early morning darkness of December 26, the Soviet Azov Naval Flotilla began landing troops of the 51st Army along a 40-mile strip on the eastern end of the Kerch Peninsula (see Figure 32.3). Count von Sponeck did not have enough troops to counterattack every landing, so he struck systematically. By the morning of December 29, he had wiped out two major beachheads and was planning to attack another, when the Soviet Navy landed some 5,000 troops at Feodosiya within two hours. By the next morning, it had 20,000 troops ashore and was depositing more every hour. Sponeck had little choice but to order a general withdrawal.

The retreat of the 46th Infantry was extremely difficult. Only 250 of its 1,400 motorized vehicles were operational, and the men had to

Figure 32.3
The Soviet Kerch Offensive, December 26, 1941 to January 18, 1942

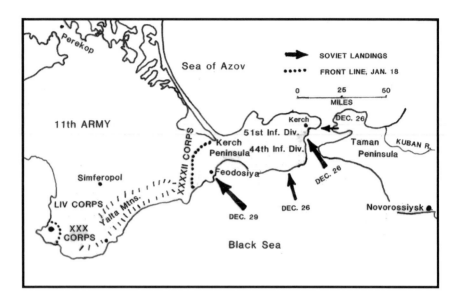

march through a driving sleet and snow storm, in below-zero temperatures. Vehicles that skidded into ditches could not be pulled out, and
many others broke down. Major General Kurt Himer, the divisional
commander, ordered that the equipment that could not be carried to
the rear be abandoned; in his view, his mission was to save as many of
his men as possible, before the Soviets could drive across the Kerch
Peninsula and cut off his retreat. The 46th left behind a trail of abandoned equipment as it headed west, and the retreat deteriorated into a
shambles. The mobile elements of the division were already northwest
of Feodosiya when orders arrived from Manstein to attack the Soviet
bridgehead. Himer dutifully turned about and attacked Feodosiya on
December 31, without artillery support. The infantry put forth little
effort, and that night the retreat continued.

On the last day of 1941, Manstein found that the 46th Infantry Division was now virtually valueless as a combat unit. It had lost 80 percent of its trucks, almost all of its engineer equipment, and half of its
communications gear, as well as about 25 pieces of artillery and dozens
of other weapons and items of equipment. He hurriedly cancelled his
assault on Sevastopol and began sending regiments to the east. He was
slowed down by weather, but on January 15, he launched a major
attack with three German infantry divisions, as well a Romanian infantry division and two Romanian brigades. The two Soviet armies were

unable to check his assault, and, during the night of January 18–19, fell back into the isthmus and occupied a trench line left from the 1941 fighting. Manstein then switched over to the defensive on both of his fronts until the spring.

Meanwhile, Count von Sponeck was arrested for flagrantly disobeying Hitler's orders to hold at all costs. He was tried by court-martial (with Hermann Goering presiding) and was sentenced to death. Lieutenant General Walter von Seydlitz-Kurzbach, a member of the court, strongly protested the verdict, which may explain why the sentence was not carried out at the time. Sponeck was shot by the SS on Himmler's orders on July 23, 1944, three days after the Stauffenberg attempt on the Fuehrer's life. By that time, Seydlitz was in a Soviet prison.

Manstein ordered an investigation of the conduct of the 46th Infantry Division during its retreat. It was a source of embarrassment to him that a German division could be reduced to a wreck without having actually made contact with the enemy. Field Marshal von Reichenau, the new commander-in-chief of Army Group South, did not wait for the results of the inquiry. He stripped the division of its honor and decreed that its men would receive no promotions or decorations until it had redeemed itself in combat. Strangely enough, Lieutenant General Himer was not court-martialed and was only relieved of his command for 10 days. He was still command of the 46th when he was mortally wounded on March 26, 1942.

Reichenau's tenure as army group commander was destined to be short. On January 12, 1942, he went on his usual cross-country run of six or more miles in temperatures well below −20° F. Later that morning, in the mess hall, he collapsed with a severe heart attack. He was at the point of death on January 17 when it was decided to fly him back to Germany, on the thin chance that doctors there might be able to save his life. En route, the airplane crashed. We do not know if he died of heart failure or as a result of the injuries he suffered in the crash. Possibly it was a combination of the two; in any case, he was replaced by Field Marshal Fedor von Bock, who immediately officially restored the 46th Infantry Division to a state of honor.

ARMY GROUP NORTH

When Operation Barbarossa ended, the 18th Army of Field Marshal Ritter Wilhelm von Leeb's Army Group North was besieging Leningrad, and the 16th Army was covering its right flank and rear. In addition, Lieutenant General Juergen von Arnim's XXXIX Panzer Corps held Tikhvin, at the end of a 230-mile salient, and was dangerously overextended. Hitler, however, assured Leeb in October that the Moscow offensive would prevent the Soviets from counterattacking in his zone.

He was wrong. When Arnim attempted to advance north to the Svir River (to link up with the Finns), he was promptly counterattacked by Stalin's Siberian divisions. By November 25, XXXIX Panzer and its supporting I Corps were under attack from four Soviet armies. By December 7, when a blizzard descended on the battlefield, Arnim's badly outnumbered vanguard was almost surrounded at Tikhvin and had only five tanks left. That afternoon, Leeb ordered him to evacuate the town. He continued to hold the salient until December 15, when the temperature dropped to $-33°$ F. That morning, Leeb telephoned Hitler and told him that he would have to give up the idea of holding positions near Tikhvin. Hitler objected, but Leeb insisted that he be allowed to withdraw 45 miles west, to the Volkhov River line. Hitler, as was often the case, could not make up his mind, so Leeb assumed that the decision was his, and at noon ordered von Arnim to begin his withdrawal. Several hours later, Keitel called Leeb and ordered him to stop the retreat, because Hitler had not made his decision. The frustrated marshal took matters into his own hands and flew to Fuehrer Headquarters that very afternoon.

The following morning, Hitler met with Leeb and agreed to the withdrawal from the Tikhvin salient without an argument. With Field Marshal Brauchitsch present, he blamed Army Group North's present predicament on OKH, which had given him bad advice, he said. He had suspected all along that Tikhvin could not be held, he declared. Hitler also blamed his decision to transfer 3rd Panzer Army to Army Group Center on bad advice from OKH. Leeb must have thought that he had landed in a lunatic asylum, but, since he had gotten what he wanted, he signaled Arnim to continue his withdrawal and flew back to his headquarters. On December 22, XXXIX Panzer Corps finally limped back through the ice and snow behind the Volkhov. It had been decimated. The 18th Motorized Division alone had lost 9,000 men in the Tikhvin operation and was reduced to a strength of 741—the size of a peacetime battalion.

The Soviet victory at Tikhvin saved Leningrad. With Tikhvin in their hands, the Reds were able to repair the railroad through that town and open connections from Lake Lagoda to points east, and ferry supplies across the lake to the city. It would not be operational until January, however, and, in the meantime, the people of the city starved. By early November, the average manual worker was receiving 400 grams (14.1 ounces) of bread per day—about 500 calories. Children and nonmanual workers received about half this amount. Most days there was no meat, milk, grains, or cereals available. On November 20, the rations were reduced to 250 grams (seven ounces) of bread a day for manual workers—about one-sixth of the minimum amount actually needed by the normal adult. Office workers, children, and other dependents got about half this amount. Cattle and horse feed was now being issued to humans, who were glad to get it. Sheep guts were processed into jelly, flavored with herbs (to disguise the smell), and sold as part of the meat ration. Dogs and cats disappeared from the city, as did sparrows, rats, and mice. Even leather and glue was cooked and eaten; nevertheless, 11,000 people starved to death in November and 53,000 died in December, according to official figures. The actual number is not known, but it was much higher. Western historians have estimated that 1 million people starved to death during the Siege of Leningrad, and that figure excludes tens of thousands killed by artillery and bombs. Notices were posted on public bulletin boards, offering to sell furniture, clothing, jewelry, and even grand pianos for a few slices of bread. By the beginning of 1942, there were no takers. Finally, cannibalism broke out in the city. Soldiers—the best-fed people—were murdered on their way home from the front and eaten. It was rumored that children had begun to disappear, so families kept their youngsters off of the streets. Anyone who looked well fed and healthy was suspect. By the end of December, a third of the labor force was too weak to work.[35]

By January 1942, ice had formed on Lake Lagoda. Soon it was thick enough to support three-ton trucks, and a 60-mile-long ice road was constructed across the lake. Up to 400 three-ton trucks a day crossed the ice road, bringing in supplies and carrying out residents of the city. Some 221,000 civilians were evacuated in February alone. More than 1,000 vehicles were lost on the ice road, either to German airplanes or because the drivers got lost in snow storms and froze. Not a few trucks actually fell through the ice, which constantly shifted, and the route had to be adjusted accordingly.

In the meantime, Stalin's legions tried to break the siege.

The winter offensive in the sector of Army Group North began on January 7, 1942 (see Figure 32.4). It was ill-coordinated, but the weight of 11 Soviet armies was too much not to experience some success against 31 exhausted German divisions, some of which were still in summer uniforms. By January 13, General Vlasov's elite 2nd Shock Army had broken through the 16th Army on a 20-mile front between Novgorod and Chudovo and forced its way across the Volkhov. Temperatures in the northern sector now dropped as low as −49° F. Leeb was losing thousands of men to frostbite and wounded soldiers were freezing to death by the score because of the lack of blankets. The marshal committed his last reserves, but still the Reds continued to gain ground. Headquarters, 281st Security Division (under Lieutenant General Theodor Scherer) was on the verge of being surrounded at Kholm with 5,500 men, and II Corps (General Count von Brockdorff-Ahlefeldt) and elements of the II Corps were threatened with encirclement at Demyansk. On January 12, Leeb asked permission to pull II Corps back

Figure 32.4
Army Group North, January to March 1942

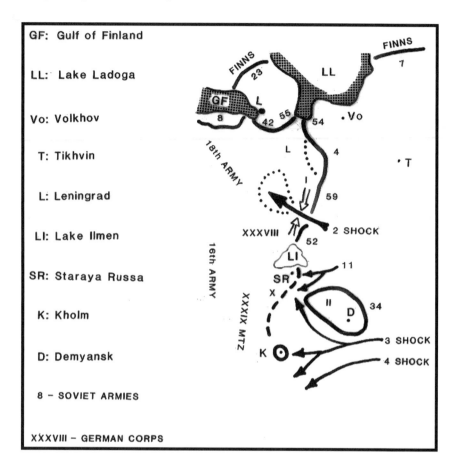

and conduct a general retreat to the Lovat River. Hitler refused to abandon Demyansk, because he believed that such salients tied down more Russians than Germans. Leeb, who by now was wondering aloud whether Hitler and Stalin were not secretly allied against the German Army, refused to accept this reasoning.[36] On January 16, he asked to be relieved of his command. He was replaced the next day by Colonel General von Kuechler. General of Cavalry Georg Lindemann assumed command of the 18th Army.

The winter offensive in the northern sector was a battle for the control of the crossroads, of which there were only a few. Kuechler simply did not have enough men to hold a continuous line against the massive Russian assaults, so he tried to hold the major road junctions, reasoning that, without control of the primitive road net, the Reds would not be able to resupply their spearheads once the spring thaw set in. He was exactly right in this prediction.

Kholm was surrounded on January 22 and Demyansk (20 miles southeast of Staraya Russa) was encircled on February 9, forming a pocket 20 miles deep and 40 miles wide, with a garrison of six divisions and 103,000 men. Both garrisons were supplied solely by the Luftwaffe, despite terrible casualties to the weather, Soviet anti-aircraft fire, and the fighters of the Red Air Force. Another Soviet drive was stopped just north of Novgorod, and the Soviet attacks on Starva Russa (the main supply depot of 16th Army) were turned back only after hand-to-hand fighting in the streets.

For all of their efforts and the seemingly impressive amount of ground they had gained, the Soviets had not forced the Germans to relax their grip on Leningrad one notch since the fall of Tikhvin. Halder, for one, was appalled by the poor Soviet tactical execution, which he dubbed "senseless." "Unable to conceive that the Stavka would deliberately fritter away strength in secondary attacks," Ziemke and Bauer wrote, "Hitler, Halder, and Kuechler concluded that the main blow was yet to come.... They were wrong. The 'brawl' was going to continue."[37]

Had the Red armies in the northern sector exhibited any tactical skill at all, Army Group North probably would have been smashed. As events worked out, they gained thousands of square miles of useless forests and swamps, but all of the key positions remained in German hands.

Throughout the winter of 1941–42, Army Group North had resorted to patchwork measures to prevent or contain Soviet breakthroughs and to hold strongpoints. By early March, however, the Soviets had generally shot their bolt and Kuechler was able to begin a series of counterattacks, designed to destroy the Russian penetrations and reestablish his line. On March 15, he launched his most ambitious offensive, designed to cut off General Andrey Vlasov's elite 2nd Shock Army in the Volkhov salient. The mouth of the bulge was only six miles long, and it was attacked on the northern face by elements of the I Corps, and on the southern edge by XXXVIII Corps. The 58th Infantry Division spearheaded the southern attack, while the SS Motorized Division "Police" led the trust from the north. Russian resistance was extremely heavy and the temperature fell to −30° F, but the German forces joined hands late in the afternoon on March 19. The 2nd Shock Army was surrounded.

The attacks aimed at relieving Demyansk began two days later. Because they did not trust the pro-Nazi General Busch, Kuechler and Halder arranged to have the relief forces placed directly under the control of Army Group North. Halder also considered the corps commanders involved (Christian Hansen of the X and Brockdorff of the II) as insufficiently strong for the task. As a result, Lieutenant General Walter von Seydlitz-Kurzbach, an arrogant but straight-laced and strong-willed minion of an old and legendary Prussian military family, was charged with the mission of forming a five-division battle group for the relief of the fortress. Within the pocket, Lieutenant General Hans Zorn was placed in charge of the forces that would break the encirclement and join hands with Seydlitz, when the relief force reached Ramushevo.

Against the Russians, Seydlitz used the loose order infiltration tactics pioneered by the Finnish Army to surround, bypass, and eliminate Soviet strongpoints. The Reds reacted with surprise, confusion, and disorganization. In some places, they fought like fanatics; in others, they collapsed altogether. The temperature rose above the freezing mark on March 23, and, after that, the snow melted rapidly. Seydlitz's leading regiments reached the Redya River, the halfway mark, on the fourth day of the offensive. Meanwhile, the Soviets fiercely struck at the Demyansk perimeter and dropped two parachute brigades inside the pocket. Progress was extremely limited the next four days, as the troops had to push through three feet of snow, covered by a foot and a half of water. On March 30, Seydlitz halted, regrouped, and shifted his main line of attack north to the Starya Russa-Demyansk Road. He resumed his advance on April 4, and it took eight days of heavy fighting to push six miles. By now he had suffered more than 10,000 casualties. On April 14, Zorn launched his counterattack, even though Seydlitz had not yet reached Ramushevo. His action was a bit of a gamble, but he felt it was necessary, because the rasputitsa would soon bring all operations to a halt.

The gamble paid off. Zorn and Seydlitz linked up on the Lovat River on April 20, restoring land contact between II Corps and the rest of the German Army. They consolidated their gains over the next few days and the first supply trucks rolled into the Demyansk salient on May 2.

Meanwhile, the 2nd Shock Army, ignoring the fact that it had been cut off, continued its relentless drive toward Lyuban. It pushed to within eight miles of the city before it was halted by I Corps and could go no further. To the northeast of Lyuban, the Soviet 54th Army pushed to within five miles of the town, but it was also stopped. The Russians had come very close to rescuing the 2nd Shock from the north, surrounding I Corps, and threatening the German hold on Leningrad, but they had failed by approximately 13 miles.

The Russians were unable to resupply 2nd Shock Army. By April 23, the pocket was beginning to shrink. Fighting continued until July, but the 17 divisions and eight independent brigades trapped in the Volkhov Pocket were slowly crushed out of existence by the 18th Army. Most of the trapped Russians fought to the end, and only 32,000 allowed themselves to be taken alive. Among the prisoners was General Andrey Andreyevich Vlasov, who was captured (along with a female companion) by the pro-German headman of a Russian village and handed over to the Germans on July 11. The total Soviet losses totaled almost 100,000 men.

While the 18th Army mopped up the Russian forces trapped in the Volkhov swamps, General Theodor Scherer's Kholm garrison was near the end of its strength. It was now besieged by the entire 3rd Shock Army. The melting snow had filled its trenches to a depth of two feet with ice water, which froze the infantrymen to their bones. By the end of March, more than half of the garrison had been killed or wounded, and the Russians—determined to annihilate the stubborn defenders—launched up to eight attacks a day against the pocket. By May 1, the garrison had lost 1,550 dead and 2,200 wounded. That day, the Reds launched another full-scale assault and overran the eastern sector of the pocket. Kholm was saved only by the guns of the stalled relief force, the Stukas from the Luftwaffe, and the desperate courage of Scherer and his men.

It was the last thrust of the 3rd Shock Army. On May 5, a relief force from the 8th Panzer Division finally pushed its way into the pocket, breaking the siege after 96 days.

Like Army Groups Center and South, Army Group North had survived all of Stalin's attacks—barely.

NOTES

1. Halder Diaries, November 10, 1941.
2. Irving, *Hitler's War*, p. 360.
3. Ziemke and Bauer, p. 76.
4. Ibid., p. 82.
5. *True to Type: A Selection from Letters and Diaries of German Soldiers and Civilians Collected on the Soviet-German Front*. 1945, p. 39.
6. Carell, *Hitler Moves East*, p. 339.
7. Heinrich Haape, *Moscow Tram Stop* (1957), pp. 226–29 (hereafter cited as Haape).
8. Ziemke and Bauer, pp. 81–82.
9. Irving, *Hitler's War*, p. 351.
10. Paul Joseph Goebbels, *The Goebbels Diaries*, Louis P. Lochner, ed. and trans (1948; reprint ed., 1971), p. 157 (hereafter cited as Goebbels Diaries).
11. Halder Diaries, December 20, 1941.
12. Seaton, *Moscow*, pp. 211, 245.

13. Seaton, *Russo-German War*, pp. 225–26.

14. Ibid.

15. Foerster, "Volkegemeinschaft," p. 210.

16. Geitner died in early 1942.

17. Keilig, p. 1 ff.

18. Haape, p. 343.

19. Johannes Steinhoff, Peter Pechel, and Dennis Showalter, *Voices From the Third Reich* (1989), p. 144 (hereafter cited as Steinhoff et al.).

20. Gordon Williamson, *Infantry Aces of the Third Reich* (1991), p. 57 (hereafter cited as Willlamson, *Infantry Aces*).

21. Ibid.

22. Nina Markovna, *Nina's Journey* (1989).

23. Steinhoff et al., pp. 147–49.

24. Terry C. Charman, *The German Home Front, 1939–1945* (1989), p. 93 (hereafter cited as Charman).

25. Pabst, p. 54.

26. Halder Diaries, January 5, 1942.

27. Ibid., January 2 and 3, 1942.

28. Pabst, p. 46.

29. Ibid., p. 48.

30. Haape, p. 254.

31. Pabst, p.

32. Ziemke and Bauer, pp. 176–78.

33. Brett-Smith, p. 31; Seaton, Moscow, p. 172.

34. Halder Diaries, December 1, 1941.

35. Bethell, pp. 110–13.

36. Brett-Smith, p. 55.

37. Ziemke and Bauer, p. 149.

CHAPTER **XXXIII**

THE HOLOCAUST BEGINS

While the panzers surged across Russia to within sight of the Kremlin, an event of unprecedented horror occurred: the Holocaust—the systematic extermination of the European Jews—began.

No other aspect of the history of Nazi Germany is remembered so frequently or has defined the Third Reich so thoroughly as its program of genocide against the Jews. Called "the Final Solution" by those who engineered it, it destroyed most of European Jewry in a state-supported program of mass murder. Soon after the war, the Nuremberg Tribunal estimated that 4.5 to 5.5 million Jews had been murdered in the Holocaust. Subsequent research and the discoveries of more mass graves, however, have established that the first figure was far too conservative. Estimates of those killed now run between 5.5 million and 6 million, with the latter being a commonly accepted figure. At least 60 percent of the European Jews were put to death, but this estimate is probably conservative. Seventy percent is more likely, and the total may run as high as 75 percent.

The idea of exterminating an entire race, class of people, or ethnic group did not begin or—alas—end with Hitler. In the Middle Ages, for example, it was considered quite natural to try to annihilate unbelievers or heretics, an idea which led to the Spanish Inquisition and the Saint Batholomew massacre, when the French Catholics attempted (with some success) to exterminate the Huguenots. During the French Revolution, the Jacobins had as their objective the extermination of an entire class. The Russian revolutionaries of 1917–18 had a similar objective toward the ruling class; according to many reports, the sailors in Sevastopol and Odessa shot everybody who had clean fingernails.[1] The Turks murdered more than a million Armenians during their genocidal campaign in the 1920s, and Stalin murdered or was responsible for the deaths of somewhere in the neighborhood of 4.5 million Kulacks in the 1930s. Since the death of Hitler, the Soviets committed tens of thousands of mass murders in Eastern Europe, the Chinese Communists murdered more than 1 million people, and the Khmer Rouge in Cambodia murdered some 3 million of their own people, out of a population of 8 million. In an attempt to exterminate all opposition, they murdered anyone who wore glasses. Many readers could no doubt cite other examples of attempted extermination, the most recent of which may still be taking place in the former Yugoslavia or in the Dafur region of the Sudan. The Nazi efforts were different, however, because here, for the first time, the techniques of the Industrial Revolution were applied to mass murder, which made it even more terrifying. It involved mass murder on an assembly-line basis and, for some reason, the brain recoils at the thought. Even half a century later, the enormity of the horror is still hard to grasp.

Adolf Hitler hated the Jews since his boyhood in Linz and probably acquired the anti-Semitic virus from his father Alois, a harsh and violent man who subscribed to several anti-Jewish papers and journals. In 1920, very early in his rise to power, Hitler shocked Joseph Hell, a journalist with the weekly magazine *Der Gerade Weg* (The Straight Path) by saying,

When I really am in power, then the annihilation of the Jews will be my first and most important task. As soon as I have the power to do it I shall, for example, have erected in the Marienplatz in Munich gallows and more gallows, as many as can be fitted in without stopping the traffic. Then the Jews will be hanged, one after another, and they will stay hanging, until they stink. They will hang as long as the principles of hygiene permit. As soon as they have been taken down, the next ones will be strung up, and this will continue until the last Jew in Munich is destroyed. The same thing will happen in the other cities until Germany is cleansed of the last Jews.[2]

Adolf Hitler was bitterly unhappy to have 503,000 Jews in Germany when he took power in 1933. He soon adopted a policy of emigration, and some 149,000 Jews did emigrate from Germany by the end of 1938, but then Hitler annexed Austria and, with it, 200,000 Jews. The bloodless conquest of the Sudetenland and Czechoslovakia added 100,000 more—and then came Poland and 3 million more. The conquests of Denmark, Norway, the Netherlands, Belgium, France, Greece, and Yugoslavia added tens of thousands more. Finally, the conquest of most of European Russia added approximately 3 million more Jews to Hitler's domain. In all, it has been estimated that perhaps 10 million Jews lived within the Nazi-occupied realm at the peak of its expansion period.

In the meantime, Hitler had reached the peak of his power and self-assurance. All of the forces that had restrained him before 1939 were dead, gone, or impotent. The political opposition had been suppressed;

Hindenburg was in his grave, and the forces he represented were neutralized, eliminated, or actively collaborating with the regime. Minister of Economics Hjalmar Schacht had been sacked; the press had been muzzled and the German people now heard only what the Fuehrer and Goebbels wanted them to hear; international opinion no longer meant anything to Hitler; the dissident generals (Hammerstein, Beck, von Witzleben, von Fritsch, and others) were dead, in retirement, or in relatively powerless positions; and (at least on the surface) the General Staff was now firmly under Hitler's thumb. Hitler was, in short, in a position to act against the Jews in any way he saw fit.

"Nature is cruel," the dictator declared,

[S]o we must also be cruel. If I send the flower of the German people into the inferno of war without the slightest compassion ... for the precious blood that is shed, we certainly have the right to eliminate millions of human being belonging to inferior races that multiply like vermin.[3]

Himmler would have agreed with this assessment; as far as he was concerned, Hitler had the right to do anything he pleased, no matter how outrageous it was, although, as late as May 25, 1940, he personally preferred forced expulsion to the East to extermination. "Each individual case may seem cruel and tragic," he said, "but this method [expulsion] is the mildest and best if we are to reject as ungermanic, impossible and incompatible with our convictions the Bolshevik method of physically exterminating a race." Himmler went on to state that the Eastern peoples would be taught how to sign their names and count to 500, but not how to read. They would then be used as a labor pool for the Reich. He added that Hitler "warmly approves" of these ideas.[4] After the fall of France, however, Hitler decided that Madagascar would make a suitable location for the exiled European Jews.

Certainly, Reinhard Heydrich did not have any reservations about committing mass murder or any compassion toward his victims. "I care nothing about what happens to Russians or Czechs," he said. "Whether other peoples live in prosperity or die of starvation interests me only insofar as we need them as slaves. . . . If 10,000 Russian women die of exhaustion while digging an anti-tank ditch, it interests me only insofar as the anti-tank ditch is completed for Germany."[5]

Himmler was taken aback by the order to initiate the Holocaust. "When the Fuehrer gave the order to carry out the total solution of the Jewish question, I at first hesitated, uncertain whether I could demand of my worthy SS-men the execution of such a horrid assignment," he told an assembly of high-ranking military officers on January 26, 1944. "But this was ultimately a matter of a Fuehrer order, and, therefore I could have no misgivings."[6] Whatever he thought about the idea personally, an order was an order to Heinrich Himmler, and should be carried out without question. He never voiced the slightest opposition to the Holocaust.

After Hitler gave the order, he did his best to carry it out. In fact, the only person known to have confronted Hitler in opposition to the extermination process was Henrietta von Schirach, the daughter of Heinrich Hoffmann, who had known Hitler for years. She had witnessed Jews being rounded up in Amsterdam and told him what she had seen and that she was horrified by it.

"You're sentimental," he snapped. Henrietta, did not back down, however, and "there was a terrible row." She recalled that Hitler said, "Every day 10,000 of my best soldiers die on the battlefield, while the others carry on living in the camps. That means the biological balance in Europe isn't right anymore."[7]

We do not know the exact date on which Hitler ordered the Holocaust to begin, because he avoided signing his own name on any orders directly concerning the extermination progress. This has led one historian to suggest that Hitler may not have known about the systematic mass murders of the Jews until as late as 1943.[8] If this were true, it would fundamentally change the way we look at Nazi Germany. But it is not true. The evidence is abundant enough to prove beyond a doubt that Hitler not only knew about the Holocaust, but also ordered it.[9] "Responsibility in this kind of hierarchy is always with the Fuehrer," Axel von der Bussche said later. "There is absolutely no doubt that Number One had to know and had given verbal orders … Anybody who thinks differently just doesn't know how this type of organization works."[10]

In trying to avoid having his name directly linked to the Holocaust, Hitler was not doing anything he had not done before. At the beginning of the euthanasia program, he had told Philip Bouhler, "The Fuehrer's Chancellery must under no circumstances be seen to be active in this matter."[11] Hitler's order to exterminate the Jews was initially given to his deputy, Hermann Goering, in the spring of 1941. He, in turn, passed the order on to Heydrich and ordered him to prepare the "total solution of the Jewish problem in all the territories under German control."[12] The Reichsmarschall, in fact, was a middle man whose role in this disgusting process was mainly a formal one. Heydrich's real superior was Himmler.

The first veiled reference to the mobile killing operations is found in the Operation Barbarossa directive of March 13, 1941 (signed by Keitel), which stated that, by the order of the Fuehrer, Reichsfuehrer-SS would carry out special duties in Russia. Because they were to operate in the same zones as the army, the SS entered into negotiations with Brauchitsch's representative, Major General Eduard Wagner, the

Quartermaster General of the Army. Heydrich, the chief of the Reich Main Security Office (RSHA), designated Heinrich Mueller, the head of the Gestapo, to negotiate on behalf of the SS. Mueller and Wagner could come to no agreement, however, so, at Wagner's request, Heydrich replaced Mueller with SS Major General Walter Schellenberg, then the chief of the counterintelligence branch of the Gestapo. Under the final arrangement, which was signed in late May, Heydrich's Einsatzgruppen (mobile killing squads) were allowed to operate right up to the frontline, instead of merely in the rear areas, as had been the case in Poland. For his operations in Russia, Heydrich set up four battalion-size Einsatzgruppen, which were divided into company-size Einsatzkommandos and Sonderkornmandos. The Einsatzgruppen were assigned north to south (that is, Einsatzgruppe A was assigned to the zone of Army Group North, B to the zone of Army Group Center, C to the area of Army Group South, and Einsatzgruppe D to the 11th Army's zone).

The officers of the Einsatzgruppen were mainly professional men and varied from a physician to a professional opera singer. Few sought employment in the murder squads. Otto Ohlendorf, the commander of Einsatzgruppe D, was an intellectual who had attended the Universities of Leipzig, Goettingen, and Pavia, and held a doctorate. A lawyer and an economist by training, he joined the party in 1925, the SS the following year, and the SD in 1936. He worked in the Institute for World Economy and Maritime Transport in Kiel before the war and did not look upon his SS activities as his primary career, even after he became chief of SD-Inland (Amt III), one of the main offices of the RSHA (Amt IV was the Gestapo). Perhaps that is why Himmler forced him to accept command of the Einsatzgruppe: he did not like his SS officers to have divided loyalties.[13]

Einsatzgruppe C was led by Otto Rasch, the former security police inspector for Koenigsberg. This older man later claimed to have protested his assignment as soon as he learned its true nature, but he was nevertheless involved in the great massacre of Jews at Kiev in September 1941. He became involved in a dispute with Erich Koch shortly thereafter and went on leave to Germany. He prolonged his furlough (and, in effect, was absent without leave) until he could arrange a transfer. Later he became mayor of Wuerttemburg and director of Continental Oil AG. Near the end of the war, he was offered the post as Higher SS and Police Leader for France and North Italy, but declined it.

Franz Stahlecker led Einsatzgruppe A in the Baltic states. The former head of Amt VIa, the foreign intelligence department of the RSHA, he apparently lost his job through the intrigues of Martin Luther, Ribbentrop's state secretary. He viewed his posting to the Einsatzgruppe as a demotion and was determined to excel, so that he could resume his advancement in the SS. He never made it. Although Einsatzgruppe A was considered the most efficient of the murder groups, Stahlecker was killed by partisans on March 23, 1942.

Einsatzgruppe B was led by Artur Nebe, a former police detective who had been with the Gestapo since 1933. In September 1939, he became chief of the criminal police or Kripo, Amt V of the RSHA. Nebe was a contradiction. He was one of the few SS members of the anti-Hitler conspiracy, but, as far as I know, Nebe was also the only person who ever volunteered to command an Einsatzgruppe. Earmarked to handle the Moscow area, Nebe's Einsatzgruppe committed thousands of murders in White Russia. Nebe himself returned to the criminal police in November and was succeeded by Erich Naumann.

The total strength of the Einsatzgruppen was about 3,000 men, most of whom were drawn from the Security Police and SD. Others included Waffen-SS men, Order Police, and auxiliaries (that is, Lithuanians, Estonians, Latvians, Ukrainians, and others).

When the Wehrmacht crossed the Soviet frontier on June 22, 1941, there were roughly 5 million Jews living in the Soviet Union; however, they were concentrated in the cities of European Russia. According to Hilberg, 4 million Jews lived in the areas eventually overrun by the German Army. Of these, 1.5 million managed to flee before the Germans arrived.[14] The strategy of the Einsatzgruppen was to follow as closely on the heels of the army as possible, in order to trap as many Jews as possible before they had a chance to learn what was in store for them and flee.

Those who were captured were driven to burial pits, where the actual shooting was done by German police troops, who were armed with Schmeisser or Sten machine guns. At his trial, Otto Ohlendorf described a typical "operation" of his Einsatzgruppe:

The unit would enter an occupied village or city and order the leaders of the Jewish community to call all Jews together at a specified place. They were told that they were about to be "resettled." This kept down panic and made our task easier.

The Jews were then requested to hand over their valuables to our squad leaders. Just before the executions, the victims were ordered to remove their clothes.

The men, women and children were then led to the place of execution which was usually a tank ditch dug extra deep for the occasion, or a large natural ditch of some kind.

Then they were shot, kneeling or standing, and the corpses thrown in the ditch.[15]

In the initial phases of the extermination process, the murderers seldom achieved security, and some commandos do not seem to have even tried. Hermann Graebe, a German civilian construction engineer, was in Rovno, in the Ukraine, on the night of July 13–14, 1941, when the Einsatzgruppe struck. He later testified:

Shortly after 2200 hours [10 P.M.], the ghetto, the Jewish section, was surrounded by a large detachment of SS troops and about three times as many Ukranian militiamen [collaborators]. Huge electric arc lights that had been erected in and around the ghetto were switched on, and detachments of 4 to 6 SS men and militia troops began forcing their way into the houses, smashing doors and breaking windows and shouting for the people inside to get out of bed and come outside.

The people were driven into the streets just as they were, some half dressed, some undressed. When they resisted, they were beaten with whips and rifle butts. At last the houses were empty. Some of the parents were driven from the homes before they could gather up their children, and in the streets the mothers were wailing and crying for their young ones. That didn't stop the troops from driving the people through the streets like cattle toward waiting freight cars.

Amid the screams of the women and the crack of the whips and the sound of rifle fire, the people were jammed into the freight cars.

Some of the younger and stronger broke away and ran for freedom into the dark beyond the arc lights. To catch them or shoot them down, the Germans sent up rocket flares.

All night long, these beaten, hounded and wounded people streamed through the brightly lighted streets toward the waiting train. Women carried dead babies in their arms. Children pulled the dead bodies of their parents along, sometimes dragging them by an arm or leg.

I saw dozens of corpses of all ages and both sexes in the streets as I walked along. The doors of the houses were open, the windows smashed. Scattered about in the streets were shoes, stockings, jackets, caps, hats, coats, and so on. At the corner of one house lay a little child of less than one year old with a smashed skull. Blood and brains were smeared on the wall of the house and on the street. The child was wearing only a little shirt.[16]

Graeber later witnessed another "action," which occurred near the Dubno Airport, in the former Volhynian province of Poland, in full view of German soldiers and anyone else who happened to be in the area. He later testified:

An old woman with snow-white hair was holding this one-year-old child in her arms and singing and tickling it. The child was cooing with delight. The parents were looking on with tears in their eyes. The father was holding the hand of a boy about 10 years old and speaking to him softly; the boy was fighting his tears. The father pointed towards the sky, stroked the boy's head, and seemed to explain something to him. At that moment the SS man at the pit shouted something to his comrade. The latter counted off about 20 persons and instructed them to go behind the earth mound. The family I have described was among them. I well remember the girl, slim and with black hair, who, as she passed me, pointed to herself and said: "Twenty-three years old."

I then walked round the mound and found myself confronted by a tremendous grave. People were closely wedged together and lying on top of each other so that only their heads were visible. Nearly all had blood running over their shoulders and their heads. Some of the people shot were still moving. Some lifted their arms and turned their heads to show that they were still alive. The pit was already two-thirds full. I estimate that it held a thousand people. I looked for the man who did the shooting. He was an SS man who sat at the edge of the narrow end of the pit, his feet dangling into it. He had a tommy gun on his knees and was smoking a cigarette. The people—they were completely naked—went down some steps which were cut in the clay wall of the pit and clambered over the heads of those who were lying there to the place to which the SS man directed them. They lay down in front of the dead and wounded. Some caressed the living and spoke to them in a low voice. Then I heard a series of shots. I looked into the pit and saw that their bodies still twitched or that their heads lay motionless on top of the other bodies before them. Blood ran from their necks. I was surprised that I was not ordered off, but I saw that there were two or three postmen in uniform near by. Already the next batch was approaching. They went down into the pit, lined themselves up against the previous victims and were shot. When I walked back round the mound, I noticed that another truckload of people had arrived. This time it included sick and feeble people. An old, terribly thin woman was undressed by the others, who were already naked, while two people held her up. The woman appeared to be paralysed. The naked people carried her round the mound. I left . . .

On the morning of the next day, when I visited the site, I saw about 30 naked people lying near the pit—about 30 to 50 meters away from it. Some of them were still alive; they looked straight in front of them with a fixed stare and seemed to notice neither the chilliness of the morning nor the workers of my firm who stood around. A girl of about 20 spoke to me and asked me to give her clothes and help her escape. At that moment we heard a fast car approaching and I noticed that it was an SS detail. I moved away to my site. Ten minutes later we heard shots from the vicinity of the pit. Those Jews who were still alive had been ordered to throw the corpses into the pit, then they themselves had to lie down in the pit to be shot in the neck.[17]

One is compelled to ask: "How could anyone except a complete pervert commit such abominable and unspeakable crimes? How could one function as a member of an Einsatzgruppe and retain one's sanity?" In answer to the first question, I have no idea. In answer to the second question, many did not. Hardened SS men cracked under the strain of slaughtering thousands of innocent men, women, and children. They heard their screams for mercy in their dreams and woke up screaming themselves. Quite a few could stand it no longer and deserted. Others committed suicide. Hundreds of them became hopeless alcoholics and were unable to perform their duties unless they were blind drunk.

Discipline and morale deteriorated, and it even effected the senior officers. SS Colonel Karl Jaeger, the commander of Einsatzkommando 3, had a nervous breakdown and had to be sent home. General Erich von dem Bach-Zelewski, the Higher SS and Police Leader Center (who was abnormal anyway), was plagued with hallucinations in which he relived the murders in which he had participated and had to be hospitalized. Major General of Police Heinz Jost, who replaced the dead Stahlecker in March 1942, held his post only three months before he, in effect, deserted to the Eastern Ministry and became Rosenberg's liaison officer to Field Marshal von Kleist. Himmler arranged for him to be demoted to second lieutenant and sent to the front. Worse still from the standpoint of Himmler and his cronies, many of the executioners talked freely when they were drunk, which was most of the time, and were careless about their "actions." Word began to spread from ordinary soldiers to their friends and families about what was going on in the East—about what the Third Reich was really like. Soon there were not enough volunteers to replace the lost executioners, even though the members of the Einsatzgruppen did not have to fight at the front, received home leave every three months, were paid triple the ordinary pay for their rank, and were given a generous alcohol ration. Himmler and Heydrich soon had to resort to SS men who were discipline problems and soldiers in trouble. SS Major General Georg Keppler, the commander of the "Das Reich" Division, explained this process to Dr. Felix Kersten, Himmler's masseur:

They are late or they fall asleep on sentry duty. They are court-martial led but are told that they can escape punishment by volunteering for special commandos. For fear of punishment and in the belief that their career is ruined anyway, these young men ask to be transferred to the special commandos. Well, these commandos, where they are first put through a special training, are murder commandos. When the young men realize what they were being asked to do and refuse to take part in mass murder, they are told that the orders that have been given them are a form of punishment. Either they can obey and take that punishment or they can disobey and be shot. In any case their career is over and done with. By such methods, decent young men are frequently turned into criminals.[18]

General Keppler knew of what he spoke. His own "Das Reich" Division had been ordered to supply a commando to conduct an "action" and was responsible for the September 9, 1941, massacre at Lachoisk (near Minsk), in which 920 Jews were liquidated.[19]

Meanwhile, a second set of officials responsible for mass murders of Jews and other undesirables arrived in the occupied territories: the Higher SS and Police Leaders. The Higher SS and Police Leader North (HSSPf) was Obergruppenfuehrer (full general of police) Hans Adolf

Pruetzmanni, General of Police Erich von dem Bach-Zelewski was HSSPf Center, and Franz Jeckeln was HSSPf South. Each HSSPf arrived with a regiment of police, which assisted the Einsatzgruppen and, in several cases, conducted the massacres themselves. Jaeckeln was particularly aggressive in this regard and was soon ordered to exchange commands with Preutzmann, who was less active, although he did put about 10,000 Jews to death in the Riga area. Jaeckeln's Order Police Regiment South, however, liquidated about 20,000 Jews in the Kiev area in a two-day period. At the request of Field Marshal von Reichenau, he helped clear out a nest of partisans in 6th Army's rear, killing 240 guerrillas and Communists and 1,658 Jews in the process. Then he shot 23,600 Jews at Kamenets Podolski, 1,303 Jews at Berdichev (mostly women), 10,000 at Dnepropetrovsk, and 15,000 at Rostov. Bach, meanwhile, assisted Einsatzgruppen B in murdering 2,278 Jews in Minsk and 3,726 in Mogilev.[20]

The Einsatzgruppen and HSSPfs did not act alone: they were supported, and often assisted, by local populations, extreme nationalists, and frequently by the Wehrmacht. In the Lithuanian capital of Kovno, 1,500 Jews were killed on the night of June 25 and 2,300 the following day. In his after-action report, Franz Stahlecker, the commander of Einsatzgruppe A, praised the anti-Communist Lithuanian partisans and "the understanding attitude of the Wehrmacht." Unfortunately for him, Field Marshal Ritter Wilhelm von Leeb, the straight-laced commander-in-chief of Army Group North and a man of considerable character, did not understand at all. He ordered the more cooperative General von Kuechler, the commander of 18th Army, to prevent such incidents from recurring. Henceforth, Stahlecker received no further help from the army, but plenty from the Lithuanians. In mid-July, they assisted a Sonderkommando in removing 700 Jewish hostages from the city of Vilna to a railroad stop variously known as Ponary, Punar, or Panarai, where the Russians had dug huge pits for petroleum storage tanks. Here they were shot by the Germans and Lithuanians. According to Reitlinger, these pits were to become the first of the permanent extermination camps. In early 1942, Stahlecker reported that, in his firing squads, Lithuanians outnumbered Germans by a ratio of 8 to 1.[21] By mid-1942, entire battalions of Lithuanian police were assisting the SS in every way possible, including committing mass murders and guarding concentration camps and ghettoes. Meanwhile, Stahlecker was compiling what Berlin considered a record of success. By mid-September, he had cleared the main town of Vilna of Jews, killing 25,000 to 30,000 in the process. The Jews of this city were now isolated in a ghetto. On October 28, the Einsatzgruppe raided Kovno, carrying off 10,000 people in a single day. They were taken to the death pits of Fort Number 9 and shot. On November 7, a similar number of Jews were taken from Dunaburg (Dwinsk) to Zolotaya Gorka and shot. The Jewish ghettoes in Riga were raided on November 30 and more than 10,000 more Jews were liquidated. Two more "actions" followed, and, by the beginning of 1942, 27,800 Riga Jews had been murdered and fewer than 5,000 remained alive. The Riga ghetto, meanwhile, had received its first shipment of "Reich Jews" (that is, Jews from Germany), and other Jewish ghettoes had been established in Libau and Dwinsk.

In many places, the Einsatzgruppen was also assisted by the Wehrmacht; in fact, several of the Einsatzkommandos reported that the armed forces were surprisingly eager to assist them. Ritter von Leeb refused to honor the RSHA-OKH agreement and forbade his troops to cooperate with the murder squads in any way, but men of his high morale and religious character are, unfortunately, rare. Some of the names of men who cooperated are surprising. Dr. Stahlecker, the commander of Einsatzgruppe A, for example, praised Colonel General Hoepner and reported that his relations with 4th Panzer Army were "very close, yes, almost cordial." General of Infantry Carl-Heinrich von Stueplnagel, the commander of 17th Army, actually requested that Einsatzkommando 4a wipe out the Jews in Kremenchug, because of partisan attacks on his communications.[22] Hoepner called Operation Barbarossa the continuation of an age-old struggle between the Germanic and Slavic peoples and represented the "defense of European culture against Moscovite-Asiatic inundation, and the repulse of Jewish Bolshevism." He added that the destruction of Russia "must be conducted with unprecedented severity."[23] Both Hoepner and von Stueplnagel later played prominent roles in the July 20, 1944, anti-Hitler coup, and both were hanged after it failed. As commander of the 17th Army, Colonel General Hermann Hoth called on his men to understand the "necessity of harsh punishment of Jewry."[24] General of Infantry Karl von Roques, the rear area commander, Army Group South, assisted in reprisals against Jews, and 11th Army (Erich von Manstein) provided the Einsatzkommandos in its area of operation with gasoline, trucks, and sometimes even soldiers.[25] Meanwhile, Field Marshal von Reichenau issued an order, "Conduct of Troops in the Eastern Territories," which so impressed Hitler that he held it up as a model for others to follow. It read in part, "We have to exact a harsh but just retribution on the Jewish subhumans. This serves the added purpose of stifling at birth uprisings in the rear of the Wehrmacht, since experience shows that these are always conceived by Jews."[26]

Field Marshal von Rundstedt had the Reichenau order duplicates and copies were sent to 11th, 17th, and 1st Panzer Armies. Kuechler, the commander of the 18th Army, issued an order that was largely a copy of Reichenau's. Manstein wrote an elaboration of the order, informing his men that the Jews were the liaison man between the Red Army and the partisans. General of Infantry Hans von Salmuth, the commander of the XXX Corps, asked Ohlendorf to exterminate the Jews of Kodyma (in Transdniestria) and sent 300 men to help him. He also issued directives to his subordinates, ordering them to cooperate with the SD (that is, the Einsatzgruppen).

With such orders and examples from many of the senior generals, there can be little wonder that some of the junior commanders also cooperated with the Einsatzgruppen, and sometimes even went into the mass murder business themselves. In the summer of 1941, for example, after mopping up in the Mirgorod vicinity (in the zone of Army Group South), Lieutenant General Rudolf Friedrich's 62nd Infantry Division shot the entire Jewish population (168 people), in addition to 45 partisans. In October and November 1941, Major General Baron Gustav von Mauchenheim gennant von Bechtoldsheim's 707th Infantry Division, operating in the rear area of White Russia, shot 10,431 out of a total of 10,940 "captives." During the same period, the division suffered only seven casualties (two killed and five wounded).[27] Under Reichenau, 6th Army was especially active in slaughtering civilians, especially Jews.

Despite the fact that their zone of operation was small, the Romanians also played a prominent role in the mass murders, although their killings resembled atrocities that got out of hand. On October 16, 1941, the 4th Romanian Army finally took Odessa after a long struggle. Before the war began, this city had a Jewish population of about 175,000—ranking it with Berlin, Lodz, Vienna, and Kiev; but more than 100,000 of them were able to flee to the east before the city fell. Six days later, a delayed action bomb exploded and destroyed the former NKVD building, which now served as the headquarters of the 10th Romanian Infantry Division. Two hundred twenty people were killed, including the port captain and several other Germans. Marshal Antonescu, the Romanian dictator, ordered 100 Jews to be killed for every soldier who died in the explosion, as well as 200 Jews for every officer. During the night of October 22–23, 19,000 Jews were driven into the harbor area and shot. Their bodies were doused with gasoline and burned. Meanwhile, another 40,000 Jews were transported to a collective farm at Dalnic and shot in anti-tank ditches. Nearly 60,000 Jews are killed in these two operations—more than twice the number called for by Antonescu's decree.

Elsewhere, the mass murders were less successful. In Belorussia (White Russia), for example, Nebe and his successor, Erich Naumann, had to cover an area half the size of Western Europe. It featured forests, swamps, and marshes, and was characterized by a lack of all-weather roads. Geography enabled many of the Jews to escape. By the end of February 1942, Einsatzgruppe B had only killed 33,000 Jews in eight months; there had been approximately 850,000 Jews in the region when Operation Barbarossa began. More than half of the murdered Jews had come from Minsk.

In White Russia, the Jews acquired a totally unexpected protector: Wilhelm Kube, the *Generalkommissar*. Upon inspecting the ghetto in Minsk, the lecherous Kube was moved to find that many of the Jewish girls and women looked like Aryans. In February 1942, however, Minsk was transferred from the zone of Einsatzgruppe B to Einsatzgruppe A, which was commanded by Stahlecker, who was more successful than Nebe or Naumann (from Heydrich's point of view). Stahlecker made Einsatzkommando 2 responsible for Minsk, and Kube was forced to take on one of the most brutal of Heydrich's murderers, SS Major Dr. Eduard Strauch. Strauch soon reported Kube for his efforts, leading to a visit by Heydrich, who gave the Generalkommissar a severe dressing down. He demanded that Strauch and Kube completely liquidate the Jewish populations in the Minsk area at once. Heydrich's visit definitely had its effect: there were very few Jews left in White Russia by the end of 1942.

In 1941, some 2 million Soviet Jews lived in the Ukraine, which included the former Polish territory of Eastern Galicia, which had been annexed by Stalin in 1939. These areas were the responsibility of Einsatzgruppen C and D (commanded by Otto Rasch and Otto Ohlendorf, respectively). Although most of the Jews escaped to the east as the Red Army retreated, the SS carried out mass murders in Lvov, Zhitomar, Uman, Kherson, Kharkov, Dniepropetrovsk, and others. The most famous of the executions, however, was carried out by Commando 4a, which was led by Paul Blobel, a former Duesseldorf architect turned drunkard and mass murderer.

Blobel's commando was attached to 6th Army, which was led by Field Marshal von Reichenau, a notorious Nazi. Reichenau took Kiev on September 19. Five days later, a tremendous explosion wrecked the Continental Hotel, the headquarters of 6th Army's Rear Area Command. Before the fires could be contained, dozens of German soldiers had been killed, Blobel had been forced to abandon his headquarters and 25,000 people had been made homeless. Before the fires could be extinguished, Blobel, Otto Rasch, and army Major General Kurt Eberhard, the commandant of Kiev, had decided to retaliate against the Jews. On September 26, notices were posted ordering the Jews to report for "resettlement." The Germans expected 5,000 to 6,000 to actually show up; but more than 30,000 reported. In two days, September 29 and 30, Blobel's commando exterminated 33,771 Jews in the Babi Yar ravine—a two-day record that was never equaled—not even by the death factories of Auschwitz and Treblinka.[28]

With the failure of Army Group Center to capture Moscow, the "first sweep" was over. Of the 4 million Jews in the area of operations, about 1.5 million had escaped with the Soviets, 500,000 had been killed, and at least 2 million remained alive. Himmler was not particularly pleased with the result of the Einsatzgruppen operations. They were too public, they were unsystematic, and they were too hard on his SS men. Himmler had a little experience in this area himself. In July 1941, he asked Nebe to shoot 100 prisoners, so he could see what the executions were like. Nebe did so, but Himmler could not watch: he looked at the ground before every volley. The murders made him physically ill.

After the shooting stopped, von dem Bach-Zelewski, the HSSPf Center, approached him. "Reichsfuehrer, those were only a hundred," he said.

"What do you mean by that?" Himmler asked.

"Look at the eyes of the men in this Kommando, how deeply shaken they are! These men are finished for the rest of their lives. What kind of followers are we training here? Either neurotics or savages!"

Himmler was clearly moved by Bach's words. He assembled the commando and gave a speech, in which he pointed out that it was their lot to carry out a repulsive duty, but that their consciences should in no way be impaired, since they were soldiers who had to carry out every order unconditionally.

After the speech, Himmler and Bach inspected an insane asylum. Himmler ordered SS General Karl Wolff, the chief of his personal staff, to end the suffering of these people as quickly as possible, but to use some method other than shooting. Nebe asked permission to try dynamite. Himmler consented, but the results were woeful.[29] Efforts continued, however, to find more efficient means and methods for committing mass murder, while a second sweep of the Jews in the occupied territories began.

NOTES

1. Ernst Nolte, "Between Myth and Revisionism? The Third Reich in the Perspective of the 1980's," in Koch, *Aspects*, p. 35.

2. Flood, *Hitler*, p. 244.

3. Calic, *Heydrich*, p. 11.

4. Irving 1977, p. 123.

5. Calic, *Heydrich*, p. 11.

6. Gerald Fleming, *Hitler and the Final Solution* (1986), p. xxxii (hereafter cited as Fleming). Even after the extermination of the Jews began, there were two schools of thought within the SS regarding the Jews. Oswald Pohl's SS Main Economic Office (Wirtschaftshauptamt), which wanted to gradually take over the entire German economy, felt (correctly) that the wholesale destruction

of the Jews was counterproductive to the German war effort. These men believed the Jews should be treated in such a manner as to retain their productive capacity. The second school of thought were the views of Hitler and the SS racial fanatics, represented by Reich Security Office (*Reichssicherheltshauptamt*), who advocated extermination. Even after Himmler issued orders to halt the mass murders of the Jews in September 1944, they continued to gas Hungarian Jews.

7. "The Fatal Attraction of Adolf Hitler," *Biography*. Peter Graves, narrator. A BBC Production in Association with the A & E Network, 1989 (hereafter cited as "Fatal Attraction").

8. Irving *Hitler's War*.

9. See Fleming.

10. "Fatal Attraction."

11. Fleming, p. 20.

12. Saul Friedlaender, "Introduction," in Fleming, *Final Solution*, p. xiii.

13. Ohlendorf commanded Einsatzgruppe D until June 1942. He became a ministerial director and deputy to the state secretary of the ministry of economics in 1943.

14. Raul Hilberg, *The Destruction of the European Jews* (1961), p. 190.

15. Richard Hanser, *True Tales of Hitler's Reich* (1962), p. 176; Ohlendorf was tried at Nuremberg and hanged on June 7, 1951. His Einsatzgruppe D killed more than 90,000 Jews. It killed 14,300 people (mostly Jews) at Simferopol (Crimea) in a single day.

16. Trial of the Major War Criminals Before the International Military Tribunal at Nuremberg, November 14, 1945, to October 1, 1946, vol. 19(1948), p. 457 (hereafter cited as IMT).

17. Ibid.

18. Felix Kersten, *The Memoirs of Doctor Felix Kersten* (1947), p. 153.

19. Gerald Reitlinger, *The Final Solution* (1961), p. 211. Georg Keppler was born in Mainz in 1894. He served in the infantry in World War I, where he was wounded three times, won both grades of the Iron Cross, and earned a commission. An early Nazi, he was a police officer until 1934, when he briefly rejoined the army. He transferred to the SS-VT in 1935. He rose rapidly and, during World War II, commanded the SS Regiment "Der Fuehrer," served as acting commander of the Totenkopf Division in 1941 (when Eicke was in the hospital with wounds), and commanded the SS Division "Nord," the 2nd SS Panzer Grenadier Division "Das Reich," the I SS Panzer Corps, the III (germ.) SS Panzer Corps, and the XVIII SS Corps. He was a prisoner of war until 1948, but was never prosecuted for war crimes. He settled in Hamburg, where he died in 1966.

20. Hilberg, pp. 193–96.

21. Reitlinger, pp. 213–14.

22. Hilberg, pp. 199–200.

23. Foerster, "Weltanschauungen," p. 309.

24. Ibid., p. 315.

25. Hilberg, pp. 199–200.
26. Irving 1977, p. 385.
27. Foerster, "Weltanschauungen," p. 315.
28. Reitlinger, pp. 233–34.

Field Marshal Wilhelm Keitel (*left*), the commander-in-chief of the High Command of the Armed Forces (1938–45), shaking hands with his chief, Adolf Hitler. In Keitel, Hitler found the yes-man he was looking for to conduit his orders and policies to the armed forces without questioning them. Even though Hitler said Keitel had the "brains of a cinema usher," he held his post throughout the war. Promoted to field marshal on July 19, 1940, Keitel was executed at Nuremberg on October 16, 1946 (U.S. National Archives).

Hitler's personal bodyguard, the Leibstandarte Adolf Hitler, November 9, 1935. From 133 men, this unit grew to a strength of more than 20,000 men by 1943, when it became the 1st SS Panzer Division Leibstandarte Adolf Hitler. Throughout this period, it was commanded by Joseph "Sepp" Dietrich (Courtesy of Dr. Waldo Dalstead).

A German reconnaissance unit advances in Norway, 1940. Contrary to popular myth, most German Army units in World War II were not motorized (U.S. National Archives).

Field Marshal Erich von Manstein (1887–1973), considered by the German Officer Corps to be its most brilliant general. A strategic genius, it was Manstein who devised the plan that led to the fall of France. During World War II, Manstein served as chief of staff of Army Groups South and A and commanded the XXXVIII Corps, LVI Panzer Corps, 11th Army, and Army Group Don and South. He conquered Sevastopol in 1942 and saved the southern sector of the Eastern Front during the winter of 1942–43. Hitler sacked him on March 31, 1944. He was never reemployed. He was sentenced to 18 years imprisonment in 1950 but was released for medical reasons in 1953 (U.S. National Archives).

Hermann Hoth was born in Neuruppen, northern Brandenburg, in 1885 and was educated in cadet schools. He entered the army as a Faehnrich in 1904 and was commissioned in 1905. Although an infantryman by trade, he proved to be an excellent commander of motorized and armored forces. During World War II, he commanded the XV Motorized Corps (1938–40), 3rd Panzer Group (later Army, 1940–41), 17th Army (1941–42), and 4th Panzer Army (1942–43). He was promoted to general of infantry in 1938 and to colonel general on July 19, 1940. Hitler did not appreciate his opinions on the deteriorating situation on the Eastern Front and forced him into retirement on November 30, 1943. He was never reemployed. He was captured by the Americans, tried as a war criminal, and was sentenced to 15 years in Landsberg prison in late 1948. He was released in April 1954 and retired to Goslar am Harz, where he died on January 25, 1971 (U.S. National Archives).

A German infantryman stops for a snack in the Crimea, 1941 (U.S. National Archives).

Junkers Ju-52 transport airplanes landing on an emergency field near Demyansk, Russia, 1942. The transports were able to resupply and save the encircled II Corps. They were unable to save 6th Army a year later (U.S. National Archives).

General of SS Theodor Eiche, commander of the Dachua Concentration Camp, Inspector General of Concentration Camps, and commander of the Totenkopf (Death's Head) SS Division (later the 3rd SS Panzer Division) in Belgium, France, and Russia. A ruthless murderer, Eiche personally shot Ernst Roehm, commander of the Brownshirts, in his jail cell in 1934, and mocked him as he lay dying. A poor commander in France, Eiche's performance improved in Russia and he distinguished himself at Demyansk. He was killed in action on the Eastern Front in February 1943 (U.S. National Archives).

The desert in flames, December 1941. Under the Desert Fox, Panzer Army Afrika and the Afrika Korps distinguished themselves against numerically superior forces from throughout the British Empire (U.S. National Archives).

British and South African soldiers march off to the prisoner-of-war camps, 1942. These soldiers were captured near Ain el Gazala, when the Gazala Line was abandoned (U.S. Military History Institute).

An infantry company on the Russian Front, 1943. When Germany invaded the Soviet Union on June 22, 1941, the average authorized strength of a German infantry company was 180 men. After the Battle of Moscow, the size of the average company was reduced to about 80 men. Due to experience and the introduction of more automatic weapons, the combat effectiveness of the typical German infantry company did not diminish drastically as a result of these changes (U.S. National Archives).

A German 20mm anti-aircraft gun, mounted on a panzer chassis, prepares for action on the southern sector of the Eastern Front, 1942 (U.S. Military History Institute).

Friedrich Paulus (1890–1957), the commander of the 6th Army at Stalingrad. A capable General Staff officer, Paulus proved too conservative and indecisive to lead an army effectively. He was captured by the Russians on January 31, 1942, only hours after Hitler promoted him to field marshal. (Since no German field marshal had been captured before, this promotion was an invitation to commit suicide.) This he would not do. He was a Soviet POW until 1954 (Courtesy of John Angolia).

Colonel General Kurt Zeitzler (1895–1963), the chief of the General Staff of the Army, 1942 to 1944. A highly energetic officer (he was nicknamed Fireball), he was chief of staff of OB West and a relatively junior major general when Hitler named him chief of the General Staff and promoted him to general of infantry. He bypassed the rank of lieutenant general altogether. Hitler hoped Zeitzler would be a yes-man like Keitel, but he was not. He firmly advocated allowing 6th Army to break out of the Stalingrad encirclement. He also apparently knew of the Stauffenberg assassination plot in 1944 and made sure that he was not in the room when Stauffenberg's bomb detonated. Zeitzler's deputy, General Heusinger—who was in the room and was severely injured—never forgave Zeitzler for this act. Zeitzler ended the war in a concentration camp (U.S. National Archives).

Soviet infantry in the attack, Stalingrad, 1942 (U.S. Military History Institute).

CHAPTER XXXIV

THE DESERT WAR

When Hitler's legions crossed into the Soviet Union on June 22, 1941, Erwin Rommel's Afrika Korps and its accompanying Italian units were besieging Tobruk. Although the battles in North Africa were to occupy much of the attention of the people of the Western Powers, they were considered to be strictly of secondary importance by the German people, whose attention was riveted on the Eastern Front. Indeed, to Rommel's constant frustration, the North African theater never amounted to more than 3 percent of the Nazi war effort until after the desert war was irrevocably lost. By the end of June, for example, OKH had committed 160 divisions to the Eastern Front. Rommel had only two German divisions in North Africa.

SLATEMATE

When Rommel's last assault on Tobruk failed on May 1, his forces were experiencing severe supply difficulties and could not continue their drive toward Egypt and the Suez Canal. In the meantime, however, his reconnaissance forces had penetrated as far as the Egyptian frontier, giving him an early warning system, in case the British tried to break the siege.

In the meantime, Sir Archibald Wavell, the British commander-in-chief, Middle East, reestablished the Western Desert Force, under the command of Lieutenant General Sir Noel Beresford-Peirse. The units at his disposal included the 4th Indian Division, what was left of the 7th Australian Division, the British 6th Infantry Division, and Brigadier William H. E. Gott's Mobile Force (22nd Guards Brigade, 11th Hussars Regiment, and the 2nd Support Group). Beresford-Peirse was reinforced with 238 tanks, of which 35 were Matilda IIs, the latest-model heavy infantry support (or "I") tanks, which weighed 26.5 tons. Most of the rest were Mark II cruiser tanks (14 tons). Both were a match for most of Rommel's panzers.

From Ultra and other intercepts, the British learned that Rommel's supply situation had deteriorated drastically. In May, for example, the Afrika Korps needed 50,000 tons of supplies, but received only 29,000.[1] Soon the German soldiers were short of almost everything. Food, for instance, was universally bad. The troops besieging Tobruk, for example, received only one meal a day. It arrived in the front trenches about midnight and consisted of a poor-quality soup, processed cheese, sardines, and black bread. They had to eat olive oil instead of butter, which spoiled too quickly in the desert. Sometimes they were given Italian rations marked with the brand name "A.M." The Germans called it *armer Mussolini* (poor Mussolini), but the less charitable Italians referred to it as *asino morte*: dead donkey.

Conditions were also bad in the tank units. Temperatures in the desert reached 107° F, and temperatures inside the panzers reached 160° F. Many undersupplied and underfed young men of the Afrika Korps ended up in the hospital with dysentery or heat exhaustion. Their morale nevertheless remained incredibly high. Under Rommel's inspiring leadership, they had already begun to think of themselves as an elite unit, capable of astonishing feats against tremendous odds. They were about to prove the correctness of their attitude to the entire world.

The first British attacks (Operation Brevity) began on May 15. Gott's Mobile Force overran the vital Halfaya Pass (the northern anchor of Rommel's frontier defenses) and the inland frontier fortress/town of Capuzzo. The German screening force continued to retreat the following day, but on May 17 Rommel came up with 160 tanks (the bulk of the Afrika Korps) and counterattacked. He destroyed 18 British tanks and pushed Gott back to the Sidi Omar-Sidi Suleiman line. Rommel attacked again on May 18, using a perfect coordination of artillery, armor, and infantry that characterized the operations of the Afrika Korps. The British, as was often the case in the first years of the war, sent their armor into battle unsupported by the infantry, and vice versa. In "Brevity," the superior tactics of the Afrika Korps resulted in the isolation of the 3rd Coldstream Guards Battalion at Halfaya Pass. It broke out during the night of May 26–27, but lost 173 men, four guns, eight AT guns and five infantry support tanks ("I" tanks) in the process. Operation Brevity had accomplished nothing. Rommel only lost three tanks during the entire operation.

OPERATION BATTLEAXE

For their summer offensive, the British badly outnumbered Lieutenant General Rommel. They had more than 300 tanks, against 80 for the 15th Panzer Division and perhaps a few less in the 5th Light. In terms of modern tanks, Rommel had only 95 PzKw IIIs and IVs, the only tanks of real value in his arsenal. The British also had superior artillery forces and the Royal Air Force outnumbered the Luftwaffe 116 to 60 in fighters and 128 to 79 in bombers and dive-bombers. Overall, the odds against Rommel were about 2.5 or 3 to 1. Meanwhile, in June, 40 percent of his supplies were sunk before they could reach Africa. His forces needed 1,500 tons of supplies per day but were receiving less than 1,000.

Operation Battleaxe began on June 15, when Major General F. W. Messervy's 4th Indian Division (with 22nd Armored Brigade in support) made its first effort to storm Halfaya Pass. It was defended by a garrison led by the Reverend Captain William "Papa" Bach, a battalion commander from the 104th Panzer Grenadier Regiment. The British attack was spearheaded by a large detachment of Mark IIs, perhaps their most deadly tank, but it was met by an even more dangerous foe: the 88-millimeter anti-aircraft gun. This weapon could effectively engage an opponent at a range of 11,000 yards—more than six miles— and a good crew could fire 20 rounds a minute with accuracy. The Indian infantry advanced courageously, but was decimated; British tanks were ripped apart long before they could get within range of their enemies. Eleven of the 12 British tanks advancing south of the pass were destroyed, and four others (attacking north of the pass) ran into a minefield and were blown up.

Just inland from the coastal plan, a steep ridge (called the "Coastal Escarpment") parallels the Coastal Road. It could only be crossed by armored vehicles at a very few points. Without Halfaya Pass, the 4th Indian and its supporting armor would be unable to join the 7th Armored Division and Gott's Mobile Force to the south. Messervy, therefore, railed against the pass all day on June 15 and 16, but Bach turned him back every time. Five major attacks were repulsed on June 16 alone. Meanwhile, Beresford-Peirse tried to outflank Rommel to the south.

Rommel's desert flank was anchored at Point 208 (Hafid Ridge), which was defended by the 1st Oasis Company, a machine gun section, a battery of 37-millimeter anti-tank guns, and a battery of legendary 88s, all under the command of Lieutenant Paulewicz. Late on the morning of June 16, he was attacked by 70 tanks from the 7th Armored Brigade. Paulewicz held his fire until the Mark IIs were well within range; then he blasted them with a concentrated volley. Within a few minutes, 11 Mark IIs were burning wrecks, and the rest had retreated out of range. The British attacked again that afternoon and lost another 17 tanks. A third attack late that afternoon (this one involving only infantry) was also halted.

By nightfall on June 16, the British had been checked in the north and the south. In the center, however, the 8th Panzer Regiment had been involved in a free-for-all around Capuzzo with elements of the 4th Armored and 22nd Guards Brigades and the 31st Royal Field Artillery Regiment. It had lost 50 of its 80 tanks. Despite this local Allied victory, however, Rommel still had the advantage, because he still had almost a division in reserve, and the British had practically no reserves left.

That afternoon, Rommel ordered von Ravenstein's 5th Light to move far to the south. As nightfall approached, this division launched Rommel's decisive attack. It caught the 7th Armored Brigade in an exposed position six miles west of Sidi Omar and still shaken from its defeat at Point 208. By nightfall, the 7th Armored had only 21 operational tanks.

With the Allied southern flank wavering, Rommel boldly stripped his center of mobile forces and sent the bulk of the 15th Panzer Division (including what was left of the 8th Panzer Regiment) to reinforce the 5th Light. This was a dangerous maneuver, for a major Allied attack from Capuzzo toward Tobruk would have resulted in a decisive defeat for the Afrika Korps. The British, however, did not attack, but Rommel did. Beginning at dawn on June 17, he drove deep into the rear of the Western Desert Force, which only escaped with difficulty, leaving behind dozens of vehicles, some of which had to be abandoned due to lack of gasoline. The Allies lost 100 tanks that day, as opposed to 25 for the Afrika Korps. Nazi Germany had won its first major defensive battle. As a result, Rommel was promoted to general of panzer troops effective July 1 and was named commander of Panzer Group Afrika. Lieutenant General Ferdinand Schaal was named commander of the Afrika Korps, but he was in poor health and was only able to remain in North Africa a few days. His announced successor was Major General Philip Mueller-Gebhard, a man with no panzer experience. Rommel succeeded in having his appointment cancelled. The fourth commander of the Afrika Korps was Lieutenant General Ludwig Cruewell, who had led the 11th Panzer Division in the Balkans. His appointment turned out to be a fortunate one indeed. General Gause moved up to the post of chief of staff of Panzer Group Afrika, and Colonel Fritz Bayerlein was named chief of staff of the Afrika Korps. The 5th Light was simultaneously upgraded and redesignated 21st Panzer Division (but with no new units). Ravenstein remained its commander, and the popular Major General Walter Neumann-Silkow continued as commander of the 15th Panzer.

At the same time, Rommel received authorization to form a new division from the miscellaneous German units in Libya. Initially dubbed the Afrika Division, it was soon redesignated the 90th Light Division. At first it had only four non-motorized infantry battalions, but was eventually fleshed out to a full three regiments of motorized troops, as well as the 190th Panzer Battalion. Its first commander was Major General Max Suemmermann. Improvised units of this type seldom become elite formations, but for some unexplainable reason this one did. Because it was immobile, the 90th was initially used in the trench lines, to steady the four Italian divisions involved in the Siege of Tobruk.

THE SUPPLY WAR

Following Rommel's victory in Operation Battleaxe, a long lull descended on the North African Front. Prime Minister Churchill relieved General Wavell of his duties and replaced him with Sir Claude Auchinleck. Shortly thereafter, the Western Desert Force was redesignated XIII Corps and placed under the command of Lieutenant General Sir Alfred R. Godwin-Austen; it was subordinated to the 8th Army, which was activated in Egypt under the leadership of General Sir Alan Cunningham. The 8th Army also included the XXX Corps (under Major General C. Willoughby M. Norrie) and X Corps (Lieutenant General Sir William G. Holmes).

From July to November 1941, both sides engaged in a race to build up enough supplies and forces to assume the offensive. Churchill sent 8th Army lavish amounts of supplies and equipment, including a good quantity of war equipment obtained from the theoretically neutral United States. From July to the end of October, for example, 8th Army received 300 British cruiser (main battle) tanks, 300 American Stuart tanks, 170 "I" (infantry) tanks, 34,000 trucks, 600 guns, 80 anti-aircraft guns, and 900 mortars, plus tons of other equipment. Cunningham was reinforced with the 1st and 2nd South African Infantry Divisions, the British 70th Infantry Division (which took over garrison duties in Tobruk), the newly organized 1st and 32nd Army Tank Brigades, and New Zealand 2nd Infantry Division (rebuilt after Crete), and the 22nd Armoured Brigade of the 1st Armoured Division (the rest of the division was still on the way when the "Crusader" offensive began). Meanwhile, on the German side of the "wire" (as the Egyptian-Libyan border was called), the Desert Fox could barely even supply his men. In October, British air and naval forces operating out of Malta sank a whopping 63 percent of the tonnage bound for Rommel, and only 18,500 tons reached North Africa. The troops' rations, which were already bad, grew even worse.

The disastrous supply situation forced Hitler to take action to restore the balance of power in the central Mediterranean or else run the risk of losing the Afrika Korps to starvation. He withdrew the 2nd Air Fleet from the Russian Front and sent it to Italy. Its commander, Field Marshal Kesselring, was simultaneously named commander-in-chief, South (OB South) on November 28. Although for the moment he was only allowed control over the II and X Air Corps and the relatively small

Air Command Afrika, this energetic officer was determined to restore German control over the sea lanes to Libya. By the time his air wings arrived in strength, however, Rommel had already lost the supply race and the British Winter Offensive of 1941 was well under way. Panzer Group Afrika faced it with only 15 percent of the supplies that it needed. Table 34.1 shows the Order of Battle of both sides in November 1941.

OPERATION CRUSADER

General Cunningham's plan to relieve Tobruk (dubbed Operation Crusader) called for XXX Corps (with all three British armored brigades) to cross the frontier on the desert flank between Sidi Omar and Fort Maddalena and attack northwest, towards Tobruk. This, the British thought, would force Rommel to engage them in a tank battle early in the campaign. Meanwhile, the British XIII Corps on the coastal flank would put down the German coastal garrisons. When General Norrie thought the time was right, Major General Ronald M. Scobie (the new commander of Tobruk) would break out of the perimeter and link up with XXX Corps in the vicinity of Sidi Rezegh, breaking the siege and possibly cutting off a substantial part of the Afrika Korps. Events, however, did not unfold according to plan.

The British had 748 tanks when the battle began: 213 Matildas and Valenines, 220 Crusaders, 150 other heavy cruiser-model tanks, and 165 light American Stuarts, which the British used as main battle tanks in this battle. The Matilda (26.5 tons) was heavily armored and boasted a two-pounder main battle gun, but, like almost all British-manufactured tanks, it was slow and could average only six mph over the desert. Its replacement, the Valentine, weighed 16 tons and averaged eight mph in the desert. The Crusader, the main British cruiser in this offensive, weighed 19 tons, fired a two-pounder gun, and equaled the PzKw III and IV in speed, but was mechanically unreliable. The American M-3 Stuart tank was probably the best Allied tank in Operation Crusader. Originally designed as a light or reconnaissance tank, it weighed only 12.5 tons, had a 37-millimeter main battle gun (which was slightly better than the two-pounder), and was the fastest tank in 8th Army. Like the Americans, the British called it the "Honey," because it was easy to handle and was so mechanically reliable.

On the other side of the line, Panzer Group Afrika could commit only 249 German and 146 Italian tanks.[2] The latter varied in quality from marginal to almost useless. The Germans were also heavily outnumbered in the air—650 airplanes to 120 for the Luftwaffe. Two hundred Italian airplanes were also available, but they were of no great value. Figure 34.1 shows the initial phase of the battle.

Table 34.1
Order of Battle of Opposing Forces, Operation Crusader, November 1941

Panzer Group Afrika: General Erwin Rommel
  Afrika Korps: Lieutenant General Ludwig Cruewell
    21st Panzer Division
    15th Panzer Division
  90th Light Division[a]
  Italian XX Motorized Corps[b]
    Ariete Armored Division
    Trieste Motorized Division
    Trento Motorized Division[a]
  Italian XXI Infantry Corps[c]
    Pavia Division[c]
    Bologna Division[c]
    Brescia Division[c]
    Savona Division
British 8th Army: General Sir Alan Cunningham
  XXX Corps: Lieutenant General C. W. M. Norrie
    7th Armoured Division: Major General W. H. E. Gott
      7th Armoured Brigade
      22nd Armoured Brigade
      4th Armoured Brigade
      7th Support Group
    1st South African Infantry Division: Major General George Brink
      1st South African Infantry Brigade
      5th South African Infantry Brigade
    22nd Guards Brigade: Brigadier J. C. O. Marriot
  XIII Corps: Lieutenant General A. R. Godwin-Austen
    2nd New Zealand Infantry Division: Major General J. C. Freyberg
      4th New Zealand Infantry Brigade
      5th New Zealand Infantry Brigade
      6th New Zealand Infantry Brigade
    4th Indian Infantry Division: Major General F.W. Messervy
      5th Indian Infantry Brigade
      7th Indian Infantry Brigade
      11th Indian Infantry Brigade
    1st Army Tank Brigade: Brigadier H. R. B. Watkins
  Tobruk Garrison: Major General R. M. Scobie
    70th Infantry Division: Scobie
      14th Infantry Brigade
      16th Infantry Brigade
      23rd Infantry Brigade
    32nd Army Tank Brigade: Brigadier A. C. Wilson
    1st Polish Carpathian Infantry Brigade: Major General S. Kopanski

Table 34.1 (*continued*)

8th Army Reserve:
2nd South African Infantry Division: Major General I. P. de Villiers
3rd South African Infantry Brigade
4th South African Infantry Brigade
6th South African Infantry Brigade
29th Indian Infantry Brigade: Brigadier D. W. Reid

Notes:
[a]Not completely formed.
[b]Ordered to coordinate with Rommel but not officially subordinated to Panzer Group Afrika until late November 1941.
[c]Besieging Tobruk.

The British XXX Corps first met the enemy (elements of the Savona Division) on the morning of November 18 and began a desert battle of unprecedented fury which lasted, almost without pause, for three weeks. Even today it is difficult to describe.

On November 18, the British pushed back Savona, the 21st Panzer Division and the two German panzer reconnaissance battalions. On the morning of the 19th, however, Rommel committed 15th Panzer Division to the battle on the frontier. His improvised plan was a bit of a gamble and was based on the assumption that the British would scatter their armor all over the desert, as usual, and not concentrate them in a single thrust aimed for Tobruk. He was right, and this enabled Rommel and Cruewell to defeat the Allied tank units piecemeal, even though the 21st Panzer Division was totally immobilized all morning on November 20, due to a lack of fuel. The British 22nd Armoured Brigade and the 5th South African Infantry Brigade did succeed in reaching Sidi Rezegh, a village less than 10 miles from the Tobruk perimeter, on November 20, but Rommel contained it with the 90th Light and the Afrika Korps' artillery reserve (the 104th Artillery Command under Major General Karl Boettcher); meanwhile, Cruewell looped behind the British and slowly crushed them with the Afrika Korps, despite fierce and courageous resistance. The battle lasted until November 23. More than 300 British tanks had been destroyed since the offensive began and another 150 were heavily damaged. The Afrika Korps, however, also suffered heavy losses and had only 90 operational panzers remaining.

At this point, Rommel convinced himself that the 8th Army was on the run, and that a thrust into the British rear would stampede it into a headlong retreat, if not a rout. General Cruewell opposed the raid, but Rommel could not be swayed. At 10:30 A.M. on November 24, he began his famous "dash to the wire" with the Afrika Korps. He quickly broke through and scattered several British corps staffs and rear area units,

Figure 34.1
Operation Crusader, Phase 1

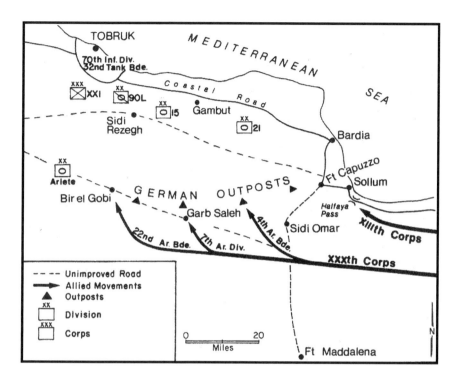

but did no real damage to the 8th Army's capacity to wage war. His raid also strung out the Afrika Korps over 40 miles of desert. While Rommel raced about in the rear of the 8th Army for three days, the British recovered. Auchinleck sacked Cunningham and replaced him with Major General Sir Neil Ritchie, a man of little command experience but one who knew how to take orders. In this case, his orders were uncompromising: 8th Army was to win this battle or never return. As a result, General Ritchie rallied his forces southeast of Tobruk and did not retreat, as Rommel expected.

The "dash to the wire" was a disastrous failure. When Rommel returned to his headquarters after his fruitless raid, the situation had changed markedly. The British XIII Corps had encircled the German and Italian garrisons at Halfaya Pass, Sollum and Bardia on the coast, and the reinforced 2nd New Zealand Division had retaken Sidi Rezegh, while the 32nd Army Tank Brigade of the Tobruk garrison had broken out and taken El Duda, only three miles north of Sidi Rezegh. The Afrika Korps arrived at almost the last possible moment and prevented the two Allied forces from linking up. The Italians wanted to abandon the Siege of Tobruk and retreat, but—despite his exhaustion and that of his men—Rommel decided to attack instead. On November 28, the DAK struck but was unable to destroy the New Zealanders, and General von Ravenstein, the dashing commander of the 21st Panzer, was captured. He was replaced by Major General Boettcher.

By now, both sides were at the end of their tether. Rommel's decision to attack again on November 30 is striking proof of his will power and determination. Taking the chance that the Tobruk garrison would not launch a major offensive, Rommel hit the New Zealanders with all available forces, including the entire Afrika Korps and elements of the 90th Light Division. By December 1, he had overrun one brigade, surrounded the division, and cut it in two. That night, the New Zealanders broke out of the pocket, losing another 1,000 men and 26 guns in the process. The 1st Army Tank Brigade also escaped, but it was down to a strength of only 10 tanks. Rommel had restored the Siege of Tobruk and, for the moment at least, seemed to have won the battle. During of night of December 1–2, Rommel signaled Hitler that his forces had destroyed 814 enemy tanks and scout cars, 127 enemy airplanes, and had taken 9,000 prisoners. His own losses were 142 tanks and 25 armored cars and more than 4,000 German soldiers, including 17 commanding officers. The Afrika Korps had only 80 operational tanks left and was virtually out of supplies.[3] Many of the tanks were running on captured British fuel.

Contrary to Rommel's hopes, the Crusader battle was not yet over. General Ritchie had a strong streak of the famous bulldog tenacity that characterizes the British, and resolutely he rallied his forces, summoned his reserves (two infantry divisions and two independent brigades), and struck again on December 4. By nightfall, Ritchie's spearheads were near Sidi Rezegh, only two miles from the garrison. That night, Rommel withdrew the Italian Bologna Infantry Division and his few mobile forces east of Tobruk through this narrow corridor. This move effectively lifted the Siege of Tobruk after 242 days.

Rommel, always the last to give up, regrouped rapidly and launched another attack (this one on Bir el Gubi) on December 6 and 7, in one last attempt to disperse Ritchie's forces and chase the garrison back into the fortress. The attempt failed, and Major General Neumann-Silkow, the commander of the 15th Panzer Division, was mortally wounded by a shell burst in one of the last attacks (he died on December 9). That night, Panzer Army Afrika began retreating to the west. Erwin Rommel had suffered his first defeat.

On December 9, Major General Max Suemmermann, the commander of the 90th Light Division, was killed in an air attack. He was soon replaced by Major General Richard Veith. Rommel had lost all three of his German divisional commanders in a single campaign and the

Afrika Korps was now down to 33 operational tanks. It evacuated Benghazi on December 24 and finally halted at the Mersa el Brega line on January 12, 1942. Meanwhile, 450 miles to the east, back on the Libyan-Egyptian frontier, time was running out for the trapped garrisons at Bardia, Sollum, and Halfaya Pass.

Major General Artur Schmitt, the former commander of the panzer group's rear area and now leader of the ad hoc Division Bardia, put up a skillful defense, even though he knew his position was hopeless in the long run. He surrendered the town on January 2, 1942, about 48 hours after he lost his last water hole. Some 2,200 German troops (mostly from the administrative services) and 4,400 Italians were captured, and more than 1,100 Allies prisoners were liberated when Bardia fell.

Sollum was defended with equal skill by the two companies of the 300th Oasis Reserve Battalion. It fell on January 12, when the Germans ran out of ammunition. The agony of Sollum ended after a siege of 56 days.

Halfaya Pass was defended by Italian Major General Fedele de Giorgis of the Savona Division and by Major Reverend Wilhelm "Papa" Bach, the former Mannheim chaplain and commander of the I Battalion of the 104th Motorized Infantry Regiment. The defenders included 4,200 Italians and 2,100 Germans. They did not surrender until January 17, 1942.

The loss of the frontier garrisons cost Rommel 14,000 men, of whom 4,000 were German. These losses ran Rommel's casualties for Crusader to 38,200 men or 32 percent of his original force. Most of them were Italian infantry; the Savona Division, for example, had ceased to exist. A total of 14,600 Germans were killed, wounded, or captured. The Allies lost 17,700 men killed, wounded, or captured.

THE SECOND CYRENAICAN CAMPAIGN

The senior British generals thought that their victory in Operation Crusader signaled the beginning of the end for Erwin Rommel and the Afrika Korps and began building up for a final drive on Tripoli. In the process, they scattered their units all over the map (see Figure 34.2). All they left in the forward zone was one brigade of the inexperienced 1st Armoured Division and the 201st Guards Brigade. In all, the British had only about 150 tanks at the front.

Meanwhile, however, Field Marshal Kesselring's 2nd Air Fleet began to pound Malta, which rapidly lost its offensive capacity. In January 1942, a major convoy docked in Tripoli. It delivered 55 new panzers, 20 armored cars, and a large quantity of fuel, food, and ammunition. Rommel at once began to think about taking the offensive again. By January 19, the Afrika Korps had 111 tanks, with 28 in reserve. Realizing that the higher councils in Rome were thoroughly infiltrated by the

Figure 34.2
British Dispositions, January 1942

British Secret Service, Rommel informed the Italians that he was planning to abandon the Mersa el Brega line. Auchinleck received word of this "plan" within hours. British aerial reconnaissance also revealed that Rommel was preparing to retreat. They did not know that he was secretly bringing his tanks up at night or under the cover of sandstorms and hiding them under camouflaged nets. The Desert Fox also withheld information from OKW, OKH, and Fuehrer Headquarters as well, because he was afraid his enemies there (Keitel, Jodl, and Halder) might try to interfere with his plans or inform the Italians as to what he was up to.

To everyone's surprise, Rommel unleashed his attack on the night of January 21–22, and the 1st Armoured Division was slaughtered. By the time the campaign was over, it had lost 100 of its 150 tanks, 33 artillery pieces, most of its divisional staff, and thousands of men. "Now the tables are turned with a vengeance," Rommel wrote to his son. "We've got the British by the short hairs, and I'm going to tear their hair out by the roots."[4]

By January 25, the forward elements of the 8th Army had totally panicked. Colonel von Mellenthin recalled that "the pursuit attained a speed of 15 mph, and the British fled madly over the desert in one of the most extraordinary routs of the war."[5] The 15th Panzer Division advanced an incredible 50 miles in only four hours. After the first five days of the counteroffensive, the British had lost 299 tanks and armored vehicles, 147 guns, and 935 prisoners. Rommel reported his own losses at three officers, 11 enlisted men, and three tanks.[6]

The Desert Fox retook Benghazi at noon on January 30. The Arab population cheered the Germans and greeted them as liberators, just as they had done for the British less than two months before. A thousand men from the 4th Indian Division were trapped inside the city and surrendered when it fell. Shortly after he reentered the Cyrenaican capital, Rommel received a message from Mussolini, suggesting that he retake Benghazi. Rommel sent back a curt reply, "Benghazi already taken."[7]

During the Second Cyrenacian campaign, the 8th Army lost more tanks than Erwin Rommel had. For the Desert Fox, this victory was filled with honors. On January 22, Panzer Group Afrika was upgraded to Panzer Army Afrika, and Hitler awarded him the Knight's Cross with Oak Leaves and Swords and promoted him to colonel general to date from January 30, the day Benghazi fell.

NOTES

1. Strawson, p. 61.
2. Mellenthin, p. 63. These figures exclude British Mark VIB light tanks and Italian L-3s, which Mellenthin described as "quite useless."
3. Carell, *Foxes*, p. 90, W. G. F. Jackson, *The Battle for North Africa* (1975), p. 178 (hereafter cited as Jackson, *North Africa*).
4. David Irving, *The Trail of the Fox* (1977), p. 156 (hereafter cited as Irving, *Trail*).
5. Mellenthin, p. 104.
6. Irving, *Trail*, p. 155; Playfair, vol. 3, pp. 148–49; Carell, *Foxes*, pp. 134–35.
7. Mellenthin, p. 105.

CHAPTER XXXV

CRISIS IN THE DESERT

Following Rommel's second conquest of Cyrenaica, a lull descended on the North African Front. This time, however, Rommel's sea lanes were clear and supplies poured into Tripoli and Benghazi. In March, 93 percent of the supplies dispatched from Italy actually arrived, and in April the total reached an unprecedented 99 percent. Kesselring's air raids against Malta continued with unabated fury; the Luftwaffe dropped 2,000 tons of bombs on the island in March and 7,000 in April. The Royal Air Force was driven off of the island, and now it was Malta's turn to starve. In March, for example, only 5,000 of the 26,000 tons of supplies bound for the island-fortress actually reached port.

At the same time, Grand Admiral Raeder persuaded a lukewarm Hitler to cooperate with the Italians for a joint invasion of Malta. The airborne and seaborne landings were timed for the full-moon phase of June. Six Italian divisions were assigned to take part in the invasion, along with 30,000 German and Italian paratroopers, who were training under the elite Nazi airborne specialist, Major General Hermann Ramcke. The total force involved 100,000 men and 500 transport aircraft, excluding Kesselring's fighters, bombers, and dive-bombers. The British had only 30,000 men on the island to oppose the invasion, with little prospect for reinforcement.

Meanwhile, in the desert, Ludwig Cruewell (now a general of panzer troops) was named deputy commander of Panzer Army Afrika, and Lieutenant General Walter Nehring replaced him as commander of the Afrika Korps. Major General Georg von Bismarck was named commander of the 21st Panzer Division and Major General Gustav von Vaerst, a veteran of Poland, Belgium, France, Yugoslavia, Greece, and Russia, took charge of the 15th Panzer Division.[1] All were experienced and talented leaders.

On the other side, the British were busy constructing an extremely strong defensive position, extending from the Mediterranean Sea to

Bir Hacheim, 40 miles inland. (A Bir, in theory at least, is a water hole.) Colonel von Mellenthin described it as a mining operation "on a scale never yet seen in war."[2] More than a million mines were laid. The position, called the Gazala Line, included several isolated strong-points, called "boxes," which were designed to cover the minefields and prevent the Axis forces from breaching them. The boxes were usually two miles in diameter and garrisoned by a reinforced brigade.

Even without the Galaza Line, the Allies had tremendous advantages, including a two to one superiority over the Germans in armor. Rommel's chief intelligence officer put the Panzer Army's strength at 333 German and 228 Italian tanks, against 900 British tanks.[3] Major General Playfair's figures are similar (see Table 35.1). In addition, the Nazi war machine had lost whatever technical superiority it had over the Western Allies when the Grant tank arrived in the desert. This American-made vehicle weighed 30 tons (more than any existing panzer) and had two main battle guns: a 75 millimeter and a 37 millimeter. The only tank Rommel had which could equal the 75-millimeter cannon was the high-velocity 50-millimeter gun on the PzKw III (Special), and there were only 19 of these in the entire panzer army. Ritchie had 167 Grants with his armored divisions when the battle began. In addition, the Allies had a 10 to 1 superiority in armored cars, 8 to 5 in artillery, and 6 to 5.5 in aircraft, even if the inferior Italian airplanes are taken into account.[4] "Perhaps fortunately, we underestimated British strength," Rommel's chief of intelligence admitted later, "for had we known the full facts even Rommel might have balked at an attack on such a greatly superior enemy."[5] Table 35.2 shows the opposing forces in May 1942.

Table 35.1
Opposing Tank Strength, North Africa, May 1942

	Allies		Axis	
Medium tanks	Grants	167	PzKw IIIs	242
	Crusaders	257	PzKw IVs	40
Total with armored divisions		424		282
	"I" tanks	276	PzKw IIs	50
Light tanks	Stuarts	149	Italian Mediums	228
GRAND TOTALS		849		560

Source:
I.S.O. Playfair, *The Mediterranean and Middle East*, Volume III (1960), p. 220.

Table 35.2
Opposing Forces, Battle of the Gazala Line, May 1942

ALLIED FORCES: British 8th Army: General Sir Neill Ritchie
  Front Line:
  XIII Corps: Lieutenant General William H. E. Gott
    1st South African Division
      3rd, 2nd, and 7th South African Brigades
    50th Infantry Division
      151st, 69th, and 150th Infantry Brigades
    1st Free French Brigade
  Reserves:
  XXX Corps: Major General Willoughby Norrie
    2nd South African Division
      6th and 4th South African Brigades, 29th Indian Brigade
    32nd Army Tank Brigade
    1st Army Tank Brigade
    1st Armoured Division
      2nd and 22nd Armoured Brigades, 201st Guards Brigade
    7th Armoured Division
      4th Armoured Brigade; 7th and 3rd Indian Motor Brigades
    29th Indian Motor Brigade
AXIS FORCES: Panzer Army Afrika: Colonel General Erwin Rommel
  Pinning Forces: General of Panzer Troops Ludwig Cruewell
    15th German Rifle Brigade[a]
    XXI Italian Infantry Corps
      Sabratha Infantry Division
      Trento Infantry Division
    X Italian Corps
      Brescia Infantry Division
      Pavia Infantry Division
  Strike Forces: Colonel General Rommel
    XX Italian Motorized Corps
      Trieste Motorized Division
      Ariete Armored Division
    Afrika Korps: General of Panzer Troops Walter Nehring
      21st Panzer Division
        5th Panzer Regiment, 104th Motorized Infantry Regiment, 155th
        Panzer Artillery Regiment, 3rd Reconnaissance Battalion,[b] 200th Panzer
        Engineer Bn.
      15th Panzer Division
        8th Panzer Regiment, 115th Motorized Infantry Regiment, 33rd
        Panzer Artillery Regiment, 33rd Reconnaissance Battalion,[b] 33rd Panzer
        Engineer Bn.
      90th Light Division
        155th, 200th, and 361st Motorized Infantry Regiments, 190th
        Motorized Artillery Regiment, 580th Reconnaissance Battalion, 900th
        Motorized Engineer Battalion.

Notes:
[a]Consisted mainly of the 361st Motorized Infantry Regiment and other detached elements of the 90th Light Division.
[b]Temporarily attached to the 90th Light Division.

THE BATTLE OF THE GAZALA LINE

As impressive as the Gazala Line defensive network was, it had one major deficiency: it could be outflanked. Once again, the British leaders refused to recognize that their left (desert) flank was vulnerable. Rommel planned to divide his forces into two parts: Group Cruewell in the north and center, and the strike force in the south. Group Cruewell was to feint against the Gazala Line, while Rommel rounded it to the south. Then the XX Italian Motorized Corps was to capture the southern anchor of the Gazala Line at Bir Hacheim (a box held by the 1st Free French Brigade), while Rommel smashed the British armor in 8th Army's rear. Figure 35.1 shows the details of this plan and the first

Figure 35.1
The Gazala Line, Phase 1

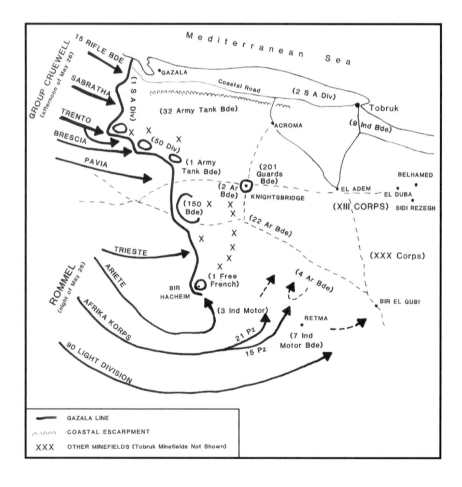

phase of the battle. Events proved that Rommel's plan was overly ambitious.

As usual, Rommel struck before the Allies were ready. He launched his offensive at 10:30 P.M. on the night of May 26 and was well behind the Gazala Line by daybreak. He wheeled north with the bulk of the Afrika Korps and smashed the 3rd Indian Motor Brigade, while the 90th Light captured the Retma Box, overran the 7th Motor Brigade, and disrupted the rear of the British XXX Corps. Meanwhile, with the main body, the Afrika Korps caught the 4th Armoured Brigade before it could completely deploy. Here, Rommel had his first nasty surprise of the campaign: the Grant tank. Colonel Gerhard Mueller, the commander of the 5th Panzer Regiment, led his men directly into the middle of the fray, and he was followed by Rommel, Nehring, and von Vaerst. The fighting was fierce and the panzer units suffered severe casualties, but the superior numbers and the greater tactical skill of the German commanders made the difference in the end. One of the two regiments of the 4th Armoured was almost wiped out, and the other suffered heavy losses, including 16 Grants.

As the remnants of the 4th Armoured fell back, the Afrika Korps surged forward into the rear of the 7th Armoured Division, capturing its divisional headquarters and temporarily eliminating it as a cohesive combat unit.

Seeing the confusion and disorganization his surprise offensive had caused, Rommel decided to pursue in the direction of the Trigh Capuzzo. He wanted to be at Acroma by nightfall—a move which would isolate the bulk of Gott's XIII Corps in the Gazala Line. He expected this maneuver to force Ritchie to commit the rest of his armor into a frontal battle against the Afrika Korps—one he felt sure he would win. For once, however, he was outwitted by his opponent. Ritchie avoided a frontal confrontation with the DAK; instead, he let the panzer spearheads pass west of Knightsbridge and then struck Rommel's supporting columns in both flanks with the 2nd Armoured and 1st Army Tank Brigades. The unexpected counterattacks completely cut off the Afrika Korps from the rest of the panzer army. Now, Rommel was in the trap.

During the night of May 27, the Germans located the 150th Brigade Box, which was just a few miles west-southwest of Rommel's camp. The British 150th Infantry blocked Rommel's path to the west and prevented the Trieste and Pavia divisions from breaching the Gazala minefields and sending supplies to the trapped strike force. The Afrika Korps was reduced to a water ration of a half a cup per day and was in real danger of annihilation.

General Cruewell promptly devised a plan to break through to his encircled comrades and flew toward the front in a Storch light observation plane to make the final preparations for the attack. A junior officer was supposed to have fired flares when Cruewell's airplane neared friendly lines but, as fate would have it, he was called to the telephone just as the general's airplane appeared. Cruewell suddenly found himself over enemy lines at an altitude of only 500 feet. Enemy machine-gun bullets ripped through the light airplane, killing the pilot instantly and knocking out the engine. The general, who was in the back seat (there was only one in the front), was helpless. Miraculously, the stricken airplane landed itself. An unwounded Ludwig Cruewell was pulled out of the Storch by British soldiers. For him, the war was over. Germany had lost one of its best and most promising panzer commanders; and, without him, the attack by the Italian Sabratha Division produced nothing.

Meanwhile, in the pocket, the British failed to concentrate their greatly superior strength against the Afrika Korps, and the fighting was indecisive. During the night of May 29–30, Rommel established defensive positions in an area that soon became famous as "the Cauldron." He decided to turn back to the east, destroy the 150th Brigade in its box at Got el Ualeb, and reestablish contact with the rest of the panzer army. Meanwhile, Ritchie made a number of unconcentrated and uncoordinated attempts to destroy the Afrika Korps. He and Norrie, however, were preoccupied with the planning of "Limerick," an offensive against the Italian contingent facing the Gazala Line. They never seemed to be fully prepared to launch it and kept postponing it from day to day, leaving Rommel free to deal with the 150th Brigade with the majority of his original strike force.

On May 30, the 150th (with the 44th Royal Tank Regiment attached) had more than 3,000 men, 124 guns, 80 heavy Matilda tanks, and plenty of food, water, and ammunition. It was attacked by the entire Italian XX Motorized Corps, as well as the 90th Light Division and the bulk of the Afrika Korps. The stubborn defenders put up a valiant fight and held off the equivalent of two corps for three days, but were finally forced to surrender on the afternoon of June 1. The Gazala Line had been breached and the Afrika Korps had been saved. The cost to the Afrika Korps had not been light, however. Among others, Rommel had lost Colonel Siegfried Westphal, his operations officer, who had been seriously wounded by British mortar fire. General Gause, the chief of staff of the Afrika Korps, had also been wounded, as had General von Vaerst, the commander of the 15th Panzer Division, who would be convalescing for months. Many generals would have called off the battle at this point, after narrowly escaping annihilation and losing so many of his top subordinates; Rommel, however, turned south, to deal with the southern anchor of the Gazala Line.

The Bir Hacheim Box was defended by the 1st Free French Brigade, which was supplemented by a battalion of Jews: more than 4,000 determined and desperate men, holding a well-prepared position behind deep minefields. As was the case with the 150th Infantry, the British generals remained inexcusably inactive while Rommel concentrated against Bir Hacheim. They did not attack until June 5; then, using about half of their available armor, they launched another unconcentrated and poorly coordinated series of frontal assaults against the Cauldron. The worst of these was against Sidra Ridge, the northern face of the Cauldron, where the 32nd Army Tank Brigade conducted what Colonel von Mellenthin later denounced as "one of the most ridiculous attacks of the campaign."[6] Supported by only 12 guns, it attacked frontally, with very little infantry (one battalion), in broad daylight across open terrain: a perfect target for the defenders. It was slaughtered by the 21st Panzer Division. Then it retreated—into a minefield. The 32nd lost 50 of its 70 tanks and was temporarily finished as a factor in the battle. On the eastern side of the pocket, the 22nd Armoured Brigade lost 60 tanks. The 10th Indian, 2nd Armoured, and 4th Armoured Brigades also suffered losses in the piecemeal frontal assaults. After the Allies had shot their bolt, Rommel launched a double envelopment, with the 21st Panzer Division forcing the British right flank back on its center, while the 15th Panzer Division (now led by Colonel Eduard Crasemann) emerged from the minefields and hit the British left. The Afrika Korps overran the headquarters of the 5th Indian and 7th Armoured Divisions and encircled the 9th and 10th Indian Brigades, four artillery regiments, and much of the 22nd Armoured Brigade. Some of the trapped soldiers managed to escape during the night, but, when the pocket was cleared the next day, the Desert Fox took 3,100 prisoners and captured 96 guns and 37 anti-tank weapons. Many Allied tanks and guns were destroyed, to keep them from falling into German hands.

With the Allied armor temporarily neutralized, Rommel created a new combat group from his engineer units (the 33rd, 200th, and 900th Panzer Engineer Battalions), placed it under Colonel Hans Hecker, the Panzer Army engineer officer, and ordered him to penetrate the minefields, so the 90th Light could crush the Bir Hacheim pocket. On June 8, Hecker succeeded in killing or capturing most of the Jewish battalion. When Hitler heard the news, he sent Rommel an order to shoot his Jewish prisoners. As was often the case with orders he did not like, this one simply disappeared. The Jewish soldiers were treated humanely and then turned over to the Italians, who treated them as regular prisoners of war.

Rommel regrouped on June 9 and reinforced Group Hecker with Lieutenant Colonel Ernst Baade's 115th Panzer Grenadier Regiment. The next day, the defenses began to crack. That night, French General Pierre Koenig broke out with most of his command. The following morning, when Bir Hacheim finally fell, the 90th Light took only 500 prisoners, and most of these were wounded; however, the 1st Free French was temporarily eliminated, and the road to Tobruk was clear of all obstacles but one: the British armored forces in the vicinity of the Knightsbridge Box.

As late as June 11, more than two weeks after the Battle of the Gazala Line began, Ritchie still had about 330 tanks (250 cruisers and 80 infantry tanks), as opposed to Rommel's 230 tanks, of which only 160 were of German manufacture. (Many of the tanks on both sides had been hastily repaired.) German casualties had been heavy, and the 90th Light was down to a strength of 1,000 men. That night, General Norrie, the commander of the XXX Corps, gave his orders for the next day. The 7th Armoured Division would deal with the 15th Panzer, while the 1st Armoured Division took on the 21st Panzer. Unfortunately for the Allies, they violated radio security, the German Wireless Intercept Service picked up the signal, and informed Rommel of the British plans. The Desert Fox was thus able to set up an ambush and caught the 7th Armoured Division between the two panzer divisions of the Afrika Korps. The 2nd and 4th Armoured Brigades were smashed; between them they lost 100 to 120 tanks.

THE FALL OF TOBRUK

Erwin Rommel wasted no time in ordering a pursuit of his battered opponents. On June 13, he defeated the 1st Armoured Division in the Battle of Acroma and temporarily finished it as a battleworthy unit. By now, Ritchie had only 70 operational tanks, and the 1st and 7th Armoured Divisions were retreating toward the frontier. The 1st South African Infantry Division now pulled out of the Gazala Line, which Rommel had outflanked, but it was too late for the 50th (Northumbrian) Infantry Division. It had to break out to the west, through the surprised Italians, and execute a wide sweep to the south, and then trek across the desert to the east. This bold move saved the division, but it had to abandon all of its heavy equipment in the process, temporarily eliminating yet another British division as a viable combat force. The Italians finished mopping up the Gazala Line on June 16, capturing 6,000 prisoners, thousands of tons of supplies, and entire convoys of undamaged vehicles in the process.

At this point, General Auchinleck wanted to abandon Tobruk and ordered Ritchie not to allow any part of 8th Army to be encircled in the fortress but, despite a categorical statement from the Royal Navy that it was not prepared to supply a second siege, Churchill ordered Tobruk held at all costs. Ritchie did have the promise of early help. With the U.S. Army arriving in the United Kingdom in strength,

Figure 35.2
Rommel's Plan of Attack on Tobruk, June 17, 1942

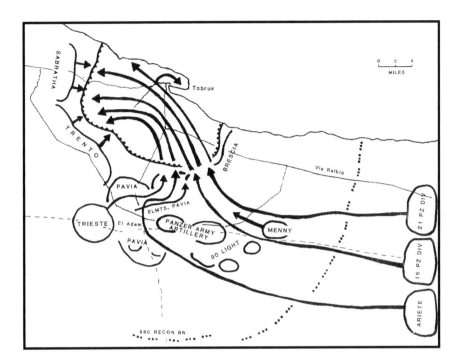

Churchill was able to release large forces for North Africa, including the 8th Armoured and 44th Infantry Divisions and 11 regiments of artillery. In addition, the 2nd New Zealand Division (now rebuilt) was on the way from Syria, and the 10th Armoured Division was already in Egypt. Churchill made a terrible mistake, however, for the situation in 1942 was fundamentally different than it was in 1941, and most of the brigades manning the defenses were no longer battleworthy. From June 16 to 18, Erwin Rommel invested the fortress and cut off the 2nd South African Infantry Division, along with the 11th Indian, 29th Indian, 201st Guards and 32nd Army Tank Brigades, inside of the Tobruk perimeter. Next, Rommel feinted to the east with his panzer forces, as if he intended to invade Egypt; then he doubled back on Tobruk to launch a surprise frontal attack on the fortress (see Figure 35.2).

At 5:20 A.M. on June 20, the Allied perimeter was blasted by hundreds of dive-bombers. By 8:30 A.M., the 15th Panzer Division (personally led by General Nehring) was rushing north, and Rommel had his breakthrough. The remnants of the 32nd Army Tank launched a belated counterattack at 10 A.M., but it was too late, and the brigade was wiped out. By 2 P.M., Rommel was deep in the British rear. He sent the 15th Panzer Division in the direction of Fort Pilastrino, to deal with the 201st Guards Brigade and finish off the British armor; the honor of capturing Tobruk went to Georg von Bismarck and the 21st Panzer Division.

Bismarck broke into Tobruk with such speed that several British ships were sunk by the divisional artillery and the panzers. By nightfall, two-thirds of the fortress was in German hands. It capitulated at 9:40 A.M. on June 21. Rommel had captured 32,000 men (19,000 British soldiers, 10,500 South Africans, and 2,500 Indians) and huge quantities of supplies.[7]

Erwin Rommel reached one of the pinnacles of his military career on June 22, 1942, when a grateful Hitler promoted him to field marshal. At 50, he was the youngest man yet to attain this, Nazi Germany's highest military rank. He celebrated in a typically restrained fashion. He ate a can of pineapples and had a small glass of well-watered whiskey from captured British supplies. After dinner, he wrote his wife, "Hitler has made me a field marshal. I would much rather he had given me one more division."[8]

THE INVASION OF EGYPT

When Tobruk fell, Rommel captured more than 2,000 vehicles and 14,000 tons of fuel. With this, he believed that he could lead his victorious but nearly exhausted army all the way to the Suez Canal. He was so carried away by his undeniably brilliant series of successes that he forgot his own earlier warning: "Without Malta the Axis will end by losing control of North Africa." He cabled Lieutenant General Enno von Rintelen, the German military attaché in Rome, and requested that he ask Mussolini to lift the restriction on his freedom of maneuver and give him permission to invade Egypt. Kesselring, however, argued that Malta must be captured before an invasion of Egypt, or the Luftwaffe would not be able to properly support ground operations, because the pressure on the island would have to be maintained; even then the island might be able to recover its offensive potential and cut off Rommel's supplies. The Italian General Staff, the German Naval Staff, Mussolini, and von Rintelen all sided with Kesselring, but the final decision was, of course, left to the Fuehrer, and, since Crete, Hitler had not been an advocate of parachute operations. On June 22, he endorsed Rommel's plan to invade Egypt. Now definitely the junior member of the Axis partnership, Mussolini accepted Hitler's decision without a single argument. He was also lured east by the possibility of a triumphal march into Egypt and the further expansion of the Fascist Empire, after so many defeats.

Rommel's arguments did have considerable merit. With American industrial potential beginning to make itself felt on the side of the 8th Army, and with the bulk of the Wehrmacht decisively engaged on the Eastern Front, any chance of scoring a decisive victory had to be taken, because such an opportunity would not likely present itself again. Although he was proven to be wrong in fact (that is, in hindsight), he was certainly correct in theory, and, although Rommel failed, he failed striving for victory, not prolonged indecision. Had Kesselring's conservative approach been adopted, defeat in North Africa undoubtedly would have been delayed, but it would have happened nonetheless. At least Rommel's alternative offered the hope of victory.

Everything now depended on how fast Rommel could advance and how rapidly the British could recover. The Desert Fox began his invasion on June 23, barely allowing his own men time to pause.

The Afrika Korps had only 44 operational panzers when it crossed into Egypt, and the XX Italian Corps had only 14 tanks, 30 guns, and 2,000 men.[9] Despite the fact that it was bombed and strafed by more than 500 British combat airplanes, the DAK advanced more than 100 miles during the first 24 hours of the campaign. Rommel neared Matruh as night fell on June 25, and, because of the need for speed, threw his mobile forces into battle without conducting a thorough reconnaissance. He assumed that the British had four infantry divisions holding a line from Matruh and the sea to the southern edge of the coastal escarpments, and that their left (desert) flank was covered by the 1st Armoured Division. In fact, the 8th Army was divided into two wings. The X Corps on the north held Mersa Matruh and the sector from the sea to the Northern Escarpment with two infantry divisions. The sector south of the Southern Escarpment was held by Gott's XIII Corps, which included the 2nd New Zealand, 1st Armoured, and 5th Indian Divisions. In between the two forks of the escarpment, Ritchie had only two thin minefields and two battalion-sized motorized battle groups from the 29th Indian Brigade.

Rommel struck early on the afternoon of June 26. Thanks to the fast work of his mechanics, he now had 60 operational panzers; Auchinleck (who had relieved Ritchie and had taken personal command of the 8th Army) had 160 tanks, including 60 of the superb Grants. As luck would have it, however, the 90th Light and 21st Panzer Divisions struck the weakest part of the British line. The following morning, the 90th Light (reduced to 1,600 effectives) smashed the famous Durham Light Infantry Regiment 17 miles south of Matruh, and, shortly after nightfall on June 27, cut the Coastal Road east of Matruh, effectively isolating the X Corps. Meanwhile, to the south, the 15th Panzer and Italian XX Corps raged unsuccessfully against the British XIII Corps, while the 21st Panzer drove into the rear of the 2nd New Zealand

Division and scattered its main transport park. General Gott, who witnessed the flight of the New Zealand trucks, incorrectly concluded that Freyberg's division had been routed. Acting on this misconception, he ordered a general retreat for that night. Due to poor communications, however, this news did not reach Holmes's X Corps until early in the morning of June 28—too late from it to break out until the following evening.[10]

On June 28, Rommel sent the Afrika Korps in the direction of Fula and El Alamein, in pursuit of the XIII Corps, while the 90th Light Division and elements of the X and XXI Italian Infantry Corps stormed the fortress of Mersa Matruh. The attack began at 5 P.M. that evening and lasted all night. Another confused breakout attempt took place in the darkness, and approximately 60 percent of the X Corps escaped. Matruh fell the following morning. A rear guard of 6,000 men was captured, 40 Allied tanks were destroyed, and the 50th British and 10th Indian Infantry Divisions were temporarily *hors de combat*.

On June 29, numerous columns of the Axis and British X Corps vehicles streamed across the desert and along the Coastal Road, trying to avoid each other, all heading eastward. Rommel's leading elements were only 60 miles from Alexandria and the western distributary of the Nile. All that stood between him and a decisive victory was the British XXX Corps at El Alamein, the position that all of the British commanders now realized was the Allies' last ditch in North Africa.

NOTES

1. Bismarck had been in motorized or panzer units since 1923. He had served in Rommel's 7th Panzer Division during the French campaign.

2. Mellenthin, p. 93.

3. Ibid.

4. Ibid., p. 94; Rommel Papers, p. 197; Warlimont, *Inside Hitler's Headquarters*, p. 190.

5. Rommel Papers, p. 195.

6. Mellenthin, p. 109; also see Playfair, vol. 3, p. 232.

7. James P. Werbaneth, "Helpful Conduct by the Enemy," *World War II*, vol. 7, no. 1 (May 1992), p. 28.

8. Young, *Rommel*, p.100.

9. Michael Carver, *El Alamein* (1962), p. 25 (hereafter cited as Carver); Rommel Papers, p. 236; B. H. Liddell Hart, *History of the Second World War* (1972), vol. 1, p. 277.

10. General Freyberg was seriously wounded during this battle and was replaced by Brigadier Lindsay M. Inglis (1894–1966), who normally commanded the 4th New Zealand Brigade. He later commanded the 4th New Zealand Armored Brigade in Italy.

CHAPTER XXXVI

THE BATTLES
OF EL ALAMEIN

THE FIRST BATTLE OF EL ALAMEIN

The Alamein position was almost the only unflankable position in the Western Desert. Forty miles south of El Alamein lay the Qattara Depression: a huge mixture of salt marshes and quicksand that was impassable to wheeled or tracked vehicles. This time, Rommel would not be able to go around the enemy's left flank. He would have to launch a frontal assault. Figure 36.1 shows the situation as of July 1.

Meanwhile, in Alexandria, panic set in. Diplomats, soldiers, and civilians alike had lost faith in the 8th Army's ability to deny Rommel his goals. The British fleet left the port of Alexandria as Rommel approached, and demolition squads prepared to blow up the harbor installations. Many civilians fled to Cairo, which suffered terrible traffic jams due to the emigration. Telltale smoke appeared from the British embassy: the diplomats were burning their secret papers. Meanwhile, various military headquarters evacuated the city; long columns of army trucks sped off in the direction of Palestine, while the few remaining combat worthy units of the X Corps dug in on the Nile; and General Auchinleck actually considered giving up Egypt and sending the 8th Army to the Sudan, Palestine, and Iraq.[1] The Rommel legend had grown to such an extent that his very name was enough to spread terror in the enemy's capitals. Unfortunately for him, Rommel had little left but his name. His entire German contingent consisted of 55 worn-out panzers, 15 armored scout cars, 77 field guns, 65 anti-tank guns (including a few 88s), and about 2,000 tired infantrymen. To make matters worse, his supply lines now collapsed completely. Of the 60,000 tons he needed each month, the Axis authorities could deliver only 3,000, mainly because the British were forewarned of the departure

Figure 36.1
El Alamein, July 1, 1942

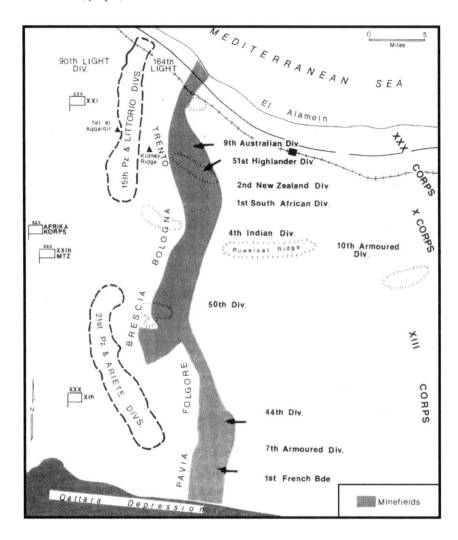

times and routes of merchant convoys via ULTRA intercepts and by spies and traitors in Rome.

Rommel began the First Battle of El Alamein with only the vaguest idea of the British dispositions; however, at El Alamein, he was not as lucky as he had been at Mersa Matruh. The 90th Light lost its way and ran into the Alamein box instead of bypassing it. The 3rd South African Brigade kept it pinned down until a sandstorm provided it with cover to withdraw. Under the cover of the blowing sand, the 90th moved south, but when the dust finally settled, the division found itself in open terrain among the South African brigades and within range of the 1st Armoured Division's artillery, which tore it to pieces; some elements panicked and the tough, veteran division was almost routed. Meanwhile, to the south, General Nehring led the Afrika Korps forward and ran into the 18th Indian. The courageous Indian brigade was annihilated, but the DAK lost 18 of its 55 remaining tanks. "[T]he fighting edge of the Afrika Korps was finally blunted," Mellenthin wrote.[2]

Rommel attacked again on July 2, but was turned back by the South Africans and the 1st Armoured Division. He planned to launch a concentrated assault on the Alamein Box on July 3, but Auchinleck beat him to the punch, and sent the 2nd New Zealand Division forward in a bayonet charge against the Ariete. The best Italian unit in Panzer Army Afrika broke and ran, leaving behind 28 of its 30 field guns and several tanks. To meet this threat to his desert flank, the field marshal was forced to pull the 15th Panzer Division out of his main attack and send it south. As a result, the attack on the Alamein Box failed.

Rommel now had no choice but to admit defeat and go over to the defensive, awaiting the arrival of the X and XXI Italian Infantry Corps, which were marching toward the front—perfect targets for the Royal Air Force. Then he would be able to withdraw his mobile elements from the front, create a reserve, and attack again. Grimly, the weary and filthy survivors of the Afrika Korps and 90th Light dug in. Mercifully they did not know what was in store for them, but one thing was clear: the glorious advance to the Nile was at an end.

Now that it was too late to achieve decisive results, Rommel was finally reinforced. Kesselring flew in more elements of the 164th Infantry Division from Crete to Tobruk, where they joined units already in Africa to form the 164th Light Afrika Division. In addition, the Luftwaffe began ferrying the 2nd Parachute Brigade across the Mediterranean, and the Italians contributed the Folgore Parachute Division and two infantry divisions—units released by the cancellation of the Malta invasion. To bolster his badly undermanned defenses, Rommel employed what for him was a new weapon: the land mine. He requested thousands from Berlin and dug up thousands more from the Galaza Line, Mersa Matruh, and Tobruk. Rommel's natural grasp of mine warfare was fantastic, and the mine soon became a major part of the Axis defensive line at El Alamein.

On the other side of the line, Auchinleck hastily rebuilt his units and brought up the 9th Australian and 8th Armoured Divisions. By August, 8th Army had 400 tanks, 500 guns, 7,000 vehicles, and 75,000 tons of supplies. Rommel's men, on the other hand, continued to live almost exclusively on supplies captured at the Gazala Line and at Tobruk.

During this brief lull, Auchinleck came up with a plan designed to destroy Panzer Army Afrika once and for all. He realized that the Italian divisions were used up, so he deliberately concentrated against them, forcing Rommel to use the Afrika Korps as a fire brigade, so it he would be too busy restoring his front and saving Italians to have no opportunity to launch a major offensive itself.

Auchinleck began his offensive on July 5, when the XIII Corps attacked Rommel's southern flank. This advance was checked in three days of fighting, after Rommel committed much of his depleted reserve. Then, on the 8th, Auchinleck struck Rommel's northern flank with a huge artillery bombardment (10,000 shells were fired), followed by an infantry attack, which was turned back by the 15th Panzer Division.

On July 10, Auckinleck struck again. Along the Coastal Road, the fresh 9th Australian Infantry Division attacked the Italian Sabratha Division, which melted away in minutes. The panzer army's tactical headquarters was only a few miles behind the Italian infantry. The senior officer present, Colonel von Mellenthin, recalled driving to the front and seeing

[H]undreds of Italians streamed towards me in panic-stricken rout ... I immediately got in touch with [Panzer Army Afrika] Headquarters and scraped together everything I could in the way of staff personnel, flak, infantry, supply units, field kitchen companies ... and with these heterogeneous troops faced the Australian attack. In bitter hand-to-hand fighting, in which staff officers manned machine guns, we managed to halt the first enemy rush. [3]

At this most opportune moment, a new German unit, the 382nd Grenadier Regiment of the 164th Light Afrika Division, arrived on the battlefield. It had no vehicles, but marched straight into the combat and halted the Australian attack within 3,000 yards of panzer army headquarters. Unfortunately, most of the Wireless Intercept Service, including its commander, had been killed. "The Tommies have netted two battalions of the Sabratha shits," Rommel reported, "It ... makes you puke."[4]

Auchinleck launched several more major attacks in July 1942. All were repulsed. The First Battle of El Alamein ended on July 27. The British 8th Army, which was shaken by the failure of 10 successive attacks, had lost 13,000 men, as opposed to 7,000 for Panzer Army Afrika (fewer than 1,500 of them German). It is ironic that Auchinleck stopped attacking when Rommel was on the verge of defeat. His artillery was out of ammunition and the few remaining panzers had only a few shells left. He had already decided to retreat to the frontier if the attacks were resumed.

BATTLE OF ALAM HALFA RIDGE

With the failure of Auchinleck's last attack, a lull descended on the North African Front. Churchill visited Egypt near the end of the month, relieved Sir Claude Auchinleck of his commands, and replaced him as commander-in-chief, Middle East, with General (later Field Marshal) Sir Harold Alexander. General Gott was named commander of 8th Army, but he was killed by a Luftwaffe fighter on July 26 and was replaced by General Sir Bernard Law Montgomery. General Sir Brian Horrocks succeeded Gott as the commander of the XIII Corps.

Meanwhile, the Allies won the supply war. In the central Mediterranean, they now had 250 British airplanes on Malta, and they (along with Malta-based submarines and surface vessels) were able to choke off Rommel's supply lines and defeat the II Air Corps' efforts to neutralize the island. In North Africa, Anglo-American naval forces unloaded 500,000 tons of supplies for 8th Army in the second half of August, as opposed to 13,000 tons for Rommel: a supply imbalance of 38 to 1. Rommel, therefore, decided to launch one, last, desperate effort to break through to the Nile. The Panzer Army General Staff informed Rommel that he would be outnumbered three to one in tank strength and five to one in aircraft when the battle started. Even the Desert Fox considered abandoning the offensive, but, on August 27, met with Cavallero and Kesselring and demanded a minimum fuel reserve of 6,000 tons. "The outcome of the battle depends on the punctual delivery of this fuel," the Desert Fox declared, emphatically. "You can start your battle, Field Marshal," Cavallero replied. "The fuel is already on the way."[5] The chief of the Italian High Command did, in fact, try his best to deliver the fuel by sending four tankers to Africa. The British sank all four. Rommel was nearly out of fuel and virtually defeated before the battle began.

Montgomery correctly assumed that Rommel would attack his southern flank, so he assembled an overwhelming force of 700 tanks in this sector. Rommel had only 259 panzers (most of them worn out) in his entire army. The Desert Fox waited until the last possible moment to attack, but the full moon that the engineers needed to breach the minefields was already on the wane, so he struck on August 30, despite the fact that he had not received his promised fuel. Figure 36.2 shows the Battle of Alma Halfa Ridge.

The attack was a nightmare. The DAK broke through the frontline of the XIII Corps quickly enough, but then ran into a dense minefield, which was covered by the 7th Armoured Division. As the Axis attack stalled in the open terrain, the Royal Air Force shot up the motorized columns and lit up the area with a new magnesium flare called the Christmas tree. The entire battlefield was soon as light as day. Among

Figure 36.2
The Battle of Alam Halfa Ridge

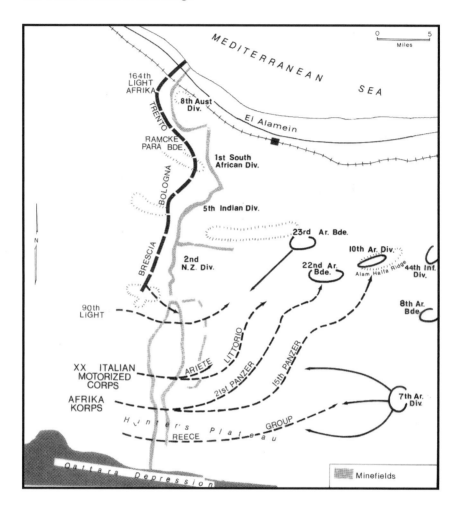

those killed were Major General Georg von Bismarck, who was personally leading the 21st Panzer Division forward when his tank was incinerated. General of Panzer Troops Walter Nehring, the commander of the Afrika Korps, was seriously wounded by a fighter-bomber. Colonel Fritz Bayerlein, Nehring's chief of staff, temporarily assumed command of the DAK. Major General Ulrich Kleeman, the commander of the 90th Light, was also seriously wounded. Rommel had lost three of his top four German commanders within three hours of the start of the offensive.

The Afrika Korps did not succeed in breaching the minefield until after dawn. Rommel struck his first blow at Alam Halfa that evening but was met by the entire British 44th Infantry Division (a fresh unit) and the 22nd Armoured Brigade, with dug-in tanks and heavy artillery support. One British tank squadron was wiped out, but Horrocks' line held.

The decisive attack came on September 1. The 21st Panzer Division was so low in fuel that it could not be used, so Rommel (who was now so sick that he could not get out of his cot most of the time) struck with only the 15th Panzer, which had only 70 operational tanks left. Horrocks met it with two infantry and two armored divisions, as well as much of the 8th Armoured Brigade—more than 400 tanks in all. Colonel Crasemann led his division up the face of the ridge, only to be taken in the flank by the 7th Armoured Division. A fierce but unequal tank battle ensued; meanwhile, British artillery fired round after round into German ranks, and the Royal Air Force fighters and fighter-bombers roamed all over the battlefield, striking again and again. In all, they dropped an estimated 1,300 tons of bombs on Axis positions from August 30 to September 4. By late afternoon the whole battlefield was littered with burning tanks and motorized vehicles—most of them German. The attack had failed; Erwin Rommel had suffered his "Stalingrad of the Desert."

Panzer Army Afrika began its retreat on September 1, but it was all too slow, because it was virtually out of fuel. The relay bombing continued for the next four nights, inflicting even heavier casualties on the Afrika Korps. Had Montgomery launched a major counteroffensive at this point, he might well have won a decisive victory, but he did not. The retreat finally ended on September 6. Rommel wrote, "With the failure of this offensive, our last chance of gaining the Suez Canal had gone. We could now expect that the full production of British industry and, more important, the enormous potential of America ... would finally turn the tide against us."[6]

It already had. Panzer Army Afrika was doomed.

DISASTER: THE SECOND BATTLE OF EL ALAMEIN

After his defeat at Alam Halfa Ridge, Rommel fell back and incorporated the captured Allied minefields into his own defensive network. He manned his frontline with six Italian infantry divisions, along with the 164th Light Afrika Division, which held his northern flank. Behind the front lay his mobile reserve and his best divisions: the 90th Light in the north, the 15th Panzer in the center, and the 21st Panzer to the south. The 90th Light was now commanded by Major General

Count Theodor von Sponeck; Major General Hans von Randow took charge of the 21st Panzer; and Lieutenant General Ritter Wilhelm von Thoma (a general of panzer troops as of November 1) succeeded Nehring as commander of the Afrika Korps. Vaerst, meanwhile, resumed command of the 15th Panzer Division, and General of Panzer Troops Georg Stumme arrived in Africa as Rommel's deputy commander. (Goering had persuaded Hitler to release Stumme and his former chief of staff, Colonel Gerhard Franz, who were in prison because of a security violation.) The Desert Fox then returned to Europe, to undergo liver and blood-pressure treatment at Semmering, a mountain resort in Austria, and Stumme assumed command of the panzer army.

General Stumme did what he could to prepare for Montgomery's offensive, but he was badly outnumbered in every category (see Table 36.1). Strawson called the Second Battle of El Alamein "the antithesis of the blitzkrieg."[7] Rommel called it "a battle without hope." Montgomery began it at 9:40 P.M. on the night of October 23, when a massive artillery bombardment blasted a five-mile sector of the German lines. Fifteen artillery regiments—more than 1,200 guns—took part in the shelling. More than 500 of these guns had a caliber heavier than 105 millimeters. The density of guns was 240 guns per mile, or one cannon for every 7.3 yards of frontage. The main concentration was against Major General Carl-Hans Lungershausen's 164th Light Afrika Division, which endured five hours of uninterrupted fury. Entire units were buried alive; command posts were wiped out, communications were totally disrupted, and a large part of Rommel's minefields (called Devil's Gardens) were detonated prematurely by the concussion of the blasts. The attack had a particularly bad effect on the Italians, entire battalions of which fled to the rear in complete disarray.

Table 36.1
Strengths of Opposing Forces, Second Battle of El Alamein, October 1942

Category	Allies	Axis	German Only
Men	195,000	104,000	50,000
Tanks	1,029[a]	489	211[a]
Artillery	1,400[b]	475	200
Antitank Guns	1,403	744	444
Aircraft	750	675	275
Serviceable Aircraft	530	350	150

Note:
[a]Excluding light tanks
[b]Approximate total
Sources:
Kershaw, p. 42; Playfair and Molony, pp. 2–30.

At 1 A.M. on October 24, the Allied ground attack began. Montgomery's plan was to launch his major attack in the north. Lieutenant General Sir Oliver Leese's XXX Corps struck with five infantry divisions, supported by two armored brigades. Once they achieved the decisive breakthrough, Monty's plan called for the X Corps (Lieutenant General Herbert Lumsden) to exploit the situation with the 1st and 10th Armoured Divisions.[8] Meanwhile, to the south, Horrocks' XIII Corps would attack with three divisions and three brigades and pin down the forces on Stumme's right and center. This phase of Montgomery's battle plan, however, did not survive contact with the enemy.

Many of the South Africans and New Zealanders who led the advance on the northern flank did not expect to find a single German left alive. Instead, they ran into the remnants of the 125th Motorized Infantry Regiment of the 164th Light, which fought with unbelievable tenacity and turned back two full Allied divisions. South of the 125th, the 382nd Motorized Infantry Regiment checked the 9th Australian and 51st Highlander Divisions, but could not prevent a breakthrough when the Aussies found the gap created by the rout of the 62nd (Trento) Italian Infantry. Lungershausen and Major General Fritz Krause, the commander of Arko 104 (the 104th Artillery Command—the Panzer Army Artillery), however, had wisely ordered their artillery not to fire during Montgomery's initial bombardment; as a result, it had survived the barrage and now opened up on the Allied infantry with devastating effect. Finally, Lungershausen threw in his reserve (the 433rd Motorized Infantry Regiment) into the battle, halting the 9th Australian and 51st Highlander. Casualties had been heavy on both sides, but Montgomery had been denied his breakthrough—for the moment, at least.

Meanwhile, General Stumme followed the tradition of the German panzer commander and was leading from the front. En route to the headquarters of the 90th Light Division, he took a detour to observe the enemy's advance. Suddenly he came under machine gun fire. Colonel Andreas Buechting, the chief signal officer of the panzer army, was hit in the head and fell back into the staff car, mortally wounded. Stumme jumped on the running board of the car and ordered the driver to get out of there—an order which he obeyed with audacity. In the excitement, the driver did not notice that the general suffered a heart attack and fell off of the running board. For several hours no one knew what had happened to him. Lieutenant General von Thoma, the commander of the Afrika Korps, reported to Berlin that Stumme was missing in action and assumed command of the panzer army himself.

Montgomery's attacks, like blows from a sledgehammer, continued all night and into the daylight hours of October 24. The Italians south of the 164th Light were attacked by more than 100 American Grant and Sherman tanks. They panicked and fled to the rear, yelling ''Front kaput, front kaput!" Thoma restored the situation by launching a counterattack with the 8th Panzer Regiment, which forced the Allied armor back into a minefield, where 35 Shermans were destroyed. This setback did not deter Montgomery, however; he simply called for massive Royal Air Force airstrikes against the 8th Panzer and launched another attack on the southern flank. This one was turned back by the 21st Panzer and Ariete Divisions, Thoma's last reserves in that sector.

Monty's crumbling operations continued all afternoon on the 24th. Hitler personally telephoned the Desert Fox in Austria and asked him to start for Egypt immediately. Rommel took off from Wiener Neustadt a short time later. Aboard a Storch reconnaissance airplane, Rommel landed near his tactical headquarters at nightfall on October 25. Thoma met with him a few hours later and briefed him on the desperate situation. By now, Stumme's body had been found, Trento had been smashed, the 164th Light badly damaged, the Afrika Korps fuel was almost gone, and the 15th Panzer Division had only 3,294 men and 31 battleworthy tanks left. "Rommel could do nothing," Colonel Bayerlein recalled. "No major decisions which could alter the course of events were possible."[9]

Despite the odds against him, Rommel checked every Allied attack for a week. At the end of October, Monty regrouped for another major offensive, which he appropriately codenamed "Supercharge." He planned to have the Australians attack north for the Coastal Road during the night of October 30–31, in an effort to force Rommel to commit his reserves; then he would launch the main attack against Rommel's center, just west of Kidney Ridge. According to the plan, the 2nd New Zealand Division (supported by the 23rd Armoured Brigade and two British infantry brigades) would break through and would be followed by 400 British tanks at dawn on November 2. They would destroy whatever was left of the Afrika Korps.

The Australian attack began on the night of October 30–31. With generous artillery support, they broke through the remnants of the 125th Motorized Infantry Regiment and cut the Coastal Road. General von Thoma led an immediate counterattack with all available forces but could not reach the encircled regiment. The next day, Rommel personally scraped together a battle group, consisting of elements of the 21st Panzer and 90th Light Divisions, and broke through the Aussies, rescuing the gallant 125th. However, this move drew most of the German reserves into the northern sector, well away from Montgomery's intended point of attack—just as the British general had planned.

By this point, Rommel's men were almost out of ammunition and had only 90 operational panzers and 140 nearly useless Italian tanks left, as opposed to 800 operational tanks for the 8th Army.

The main attack began on both sides of Kidney Ridge on the night of November 1–2, and the fighting was savage. The northern prong broke through the 15th Panzer Division, but was checked by elements of the 90th Light. To the south, Lumsden's X Corps overran a regiment of the Trieste Division and a battalion of German infantry. Colonel Wilhelm Teege's 8th Panzer Regiment lost 35 of its tanks—half of its total strength. British losses were also heavy. The 9th Armoured Brigade alone lost 70 of its 94 tanks, but Lumsden had torn a 4,000 yard hole in the German front. Rommel knew that he would have to close this gap, or the battle was lost.

On November 2, Ritter von Thoma launched two major attacks against the "Supercharge" forces, and again the fighting was desperate. "The enemy fought with all the certain knowledge that all was at stake, and with all the skill of his long experience in armored fighting," Montgomery wrote later.[10] Both of Thoma's attacks were thrown back. Then 400 of Lumsden's tanks surged forward again. The 15th Panzer Division quickly rallied and made a last-ditch stand that has since been known as the Battle of Tel el Aqqaqir—one of the most desperate battles in the history of armored warfare. It was the death ride of the 8th Panzer Regiment. Willi Teege led his men forward into the counterattack with reckless abandon. Soon the battlefield was littered with burning British vehicles, but weight of numbers decided the battle in the end. All 35 of Teege's panzers were destroyed; the colonel died with his men. The elite 8th Panzer Regiment was effectively wiped out, and the 33rd Panzer Artillery Regiment lost all but seven of its guns. The once mighty 15th Panzer Division—half of the Afrika Korps—was thus reduced to a strength of zero tanks and seven guns.

Disaster overtook the panzer army all along the line. Shortly before noon, the Trieste and Littorio Divisions finally broke under the strain and headed for the rear. Rommel, who now had only 35 German tanks left, took the desperate step of throwing the Ariete Armored Division into battle against the Lees, Grants, and Shermans. "The dead are lucky," Rommel wrote to wife.[11]

Montgomery did not attack on November 3, the day Rommel began his retreat from the Alamein line. For a time it looked as if he would be able to at least get his motorized formations back to Tripolitania, but, at 1 P.M., a message arrived from Fuehrer Headquarters. It commanded Rommel to—

[S]tand fast, yield not a yard of ground, and throw every gun and every man into the battle.... It would not be the first time in history that a strong will has triumphed over bigger battalions. As to your troops, you can show them no other road than that to victory or death.[12]

Rommel was stunned. When he finished reading the dispatch, he simply sat down and stared blankly out the window. The sound of artillery fire was distinctly audible.

Rommel, for perhaps the first time in his life, did not know what to do. Finally he told Colonel Westphal: "So far I have always insisted upon unqualified obedience from my men ... even if they do not understand my orders or consider them wrong. Personally I cannot depart from this principle and I must submit to it."

"That means the end of the army," the chief of staff said.

"I am a soldier," Rommel answered.[13] Shortly thereafter he ordered his regiments to reoccupy their former positions and to hold them at all costs. He would live to regret this decision.

Hitler's order greatly affected the German soldiers, most of whom still believed in the Nazi dictator. "At the Fuehrer's command they were ready to sacrifice themselves to the last man," Rommel wrote later.[14] The 164th Light beat back several Allied attacks on the northern flank, but a South African armored car regiment pushed through Rommel's broken center and into his rear, destroying transport and supply columns and generally spreading confusion and disorganization. They also cut the supply lines of the troops to the south, adding food and water shortages on top of everything else.

That night, Rommel agonized over his situation. Did he have the right to disobey his Supreme Commander or not? He sought out Major Elmar Warning of Westphal's staff and argued with himself. Warning, a tall, bald, bullet-headed man, was a good listener. Finally, Rommel declared, "My men's lives come first! The Fuehrer is crazy."[15] Even so, he signaled Rastenburg and requested that the order be rescinded. He was still awaiting a reply when daylight broke.

The first major Allied attack, which was spearheaded by 200 tanks, began at 8 A.M. Ritter von Thoma met it with 20 panzers; nevertheless, despite odds of 10 to 1, he turned it back. By now, the 8th Army had lost more than 500 tanks, or roughly three times the number lost by Rommel.[16] Montgomery, however, could afford the losses; Rommel could not. The British attacked again, and von Thoma made his last stand with Rommel's old *Kampfstaffel* (personal battle group–approximately 350 men) around a dune called Tel el Mampsra. He lost his last tank about noon. With his command virtually wiped out, he stood, tall and erect, beside a burning panzer, facing the enemy. Almost miraculously, he survived a hail of machine gun fire without being touched. Then the firing suddenly stopped, and several Shermans and a British jeep slowly approached his position. The general walked toward the jeep and got in without saying a word. That night, General von Thoma dined with Bernard Montgomery, who liked him and treated him with great courtesy. Thoma, in turn, invited Monty to visit him at his home in Bavaria after the war. This mutual admiration by two opposing soldiers was the subject of considerable criticism by the news media in England, the United States, and Germany. It was not criticized in North Africa by either side. Churchill, however, commiserated with the German. "Poor von Thoma!" he declared. "I, too, have dined with Montgomery."

Of course, he was only joking. I think.

South of Tel el Mampsra, the Italian XX Motorized Corps resisted courageously, but its "mobile coffins" were no match for modern Allied tanks. By the evening of November 4, the Ariete and Littorio Armored and Trieste Motorized Divisions had been destroyed, except for a few rear-area units—all because of a senseless order issued by a Supreme Commander hundreds of miles away from the battlefield.

Erwin Rommel was filled with bitterness. That afternoon, he ordered a retreat to begin that night, in direct disobedience of the Fuehrer. Later, Hitler blamed a major on the staff of OKW for the disaster, stating this man had failed to awaken him and inform him of the true situation. The major, a scapegoat, was disgraced, broken to the rank of private, and sent to a labor battalion. He only barely escaped a firing squad.[17] Hitler, however, should never have issued the order in the first place, as the Desert Fox knew. For the first time, he was disappointed and disillusioned with the Fuehrer: a pregnant moment in the history of Nazi Germany. Meanwhile, the remnants of Panzer Army Afrika fell back to the west. After blowing up more than 40 tanks in the repair shops that they could not take with them, Rommel's army had only 12 tanks left. A dozen tanks in the whole army. A far cry from the proud legions that had so confidently smashed the Gazala Line, overrun Tobruk and invaded Egypt only four and a half months before.

NOTES

1. Carell, *Foxes*, pp. 238–39.
2. Mellenthin, p. 132.
3. Carell, *Foxes*, pp. 242–43.
4. Irving, *Trail*, p. 195.
5. Carell, *Foxes*, p. 247.
6. Rommel Papers, p. 287.
7. Strawson, *North Africa*, p. 132.
8. Lumsden also had the Headquarters, 8th Armoured Division under his command, but it had no subordinate troop regiments on October 23.
9. Young, *Rommel*, p. 136.
10. Ibid., p. 138.
11. Rommel Papers, p. 320; Carver, p. 173.
12. Warlimont, *Inside Hitler's Headquarters*, p. 268.
13. Carell, *Foxes*, p. 295.
14. Rommel Papers, p. 322.

15. Irving, *Trail*, p. 233.

16. Carell, *Foxes*, p. 295.

17. Jodl's deputy, General Walter Warlimont, was relieved of his post in connection with this incident, only to be recalled two days later, when Hitler cooled off and General Schmundt intervened on his behalf. Jodl, on the other hand, did nothing for the man who had been his principal deputy for several years.

CHAPTER **XXXVII**

THE HOLOCAUST CONTINUES

THE SECOND SWEEP

While Paulus pushed to the Volga and Rommel drove almost to the gates of Cairo, the Holocaust continued in the occupied territories and in the rear areas in the East.

As we have seen, the Einsatzgruppen completed their first sweep of the Jewish communities in the former Soviet regions in late 1941. The second sweep began almost simultaneously with the end of the first. Himmler, Heydrich, and others used considerably more men in the second sweep than the first, and the Einsatzgruppen were proportionally less important. Eventually they would be absorbed into the growing machinery of the Higher SS and HSSPf. They were reinforced by police regiments, army units (especially security divisions), and battalions of indigenous collaborators and auxiliary police battalions, which were called Schutzpolizei in the urban areas and Gendarmerie in the rural areas. They were also assisted by the military police (*Feldgendarmerie*), the secret field police (*Geheime Feldpolizei*), and the *Bandenkampfverbaende*: antipartisan formations under SS General Erich von dem Bach-Zelewsky, the former HSSPf leader whom Himmler named chief of Anti-Partisan Formations in early 1942. In all, more than 250,000 men were involved in the second sweep, but fewer than 15,000 were German.[1]

The Jews who had remained behind as the Soviets retreated tried to escape the Holocaust by working. By making themselves indispensable as laborers for the Wehrmacht or a private German firm, they reasoned, they would be spared the executioner's bullet. They did not realize that Himmler had already ruled that the Fuehrer's orders had priority over economic considerations: murder was more important than production.[2]

The second sweep was characterized by frenzied violence and sadism, and it was again far too public to suit Berlin. Operations focused on the Ukraine, where one town after another was fallen on by the murderers, who employed the same pattern. First, Jewish labor detachments were ordered to dig ditches, which looked suspiciously like mass graves. Second, the Jewish community or ghetto was surrounded or corridored off. This made the Jews nervous; they approached their German employers with requests to intervene. Jewish women and girls were often propositioned by the "police" (or propositioned them, in attempts to save their own lives). Normally they were used until dawn, then taken out and shot.

The actual "action" typically began at dawn, although night operations, conducted by searchlight, were not unusual. Jewish families, often only partially dressed, were hustled out of their homes at gunpoint and herded into a central assembly area. Many times the Jews tried to lock the assassins out, but their doors were knocked down or ripped open by crowbars. Many tried to hide in cellars, beneath the houses, or under beds. These tactics almost never worked: the executioners were too experienced. They lobbed hand grenades into the cellars and rolled them under the houses, which were often set on fire. Some Jews tried to run and were shot; the police had tracer bullets, which made their jobs easier. These Jews were then doused with gasoline and set on fire—even those who had only been wounded.

Meanwhile, trucks were driven to the assembly area, where the more passive Jews were collected by trucks. They were driven to the ditch and off-loaded, a process that was accompanied by blows from rifle butts or whips. They then had to strip naked and were subjected to body searches. Finally, they were lined up in or in front of the ditch and shot.

"The Jews submitted without resistance and without protest," Hilberg wrote. "It was amazing how the Jews stepped into the graves, with only mutual condolences in order to strengthen their spirits," one German recalled.[3]

The executioners were usually drunk and occasionally a sadist would hit a pregnant woman in the stomach with his fist, and then throw her alive into the pit. Many wounded Jews remained in the ditch, on top of or under the dead, all night long. Some victims, naked and wounded, actually succeeded in escaping to neighboring towns, but most were soon captured and shot by the auxiliaries.

Operations in the Ukraine ended with the massacre of the Pinsk ghetto in November 1942, and the destruction of the Jewish community of Artemovsk on the Donetz, which was wiped out on November 22, 1942. An estimated 150,000 to 200,000 Jews were killed in the Reichskommissariat Ukraine alone. Professor Peter Seraphim of Goettingen

University reported to General Georg Thomas, the chief of the economics office at OKW, that there were still a few Jews alive in some of the larger Ukrainian cities, although they received no rations from official sources.[4]

By the beginning of 1943, the focus of operations had shifted to Reichskommissariat Ostland, where about 50,000 Jews were still at large. By the time all of the mobile killing operations were over, an estimated 1.4 million Jews had been murdered.[5]

THE CONCENTRATION CAMPS:
RISE OF THE EXTERMINATION CAMP

The extermination camps had their roots in the Nazi concentration camp system, which began almost as soon as Hitler took power in 1933. Almost all of these were "wildcat camps," run by the SA. By March 1934, most of these camps had been closed down and replaced by a handful of more permanent facilities, all of which were eventually taken over by the SS. The most prominent of these were Dachau and Oranienburg, near Munich and Berlin, respectively.

The first inspector general of concentration camps was Theodor Eicke. A major figure in the history of the SS, Charles Syndor described him as "the architect, builder and director of the pre-war German concentration camp system."[6] Eicke was born in Huedingen, in the then-German province of Alsace, on October 17, 1892, the eleventh child of a railroad stationmaster. He grew up in relative poverty, was a poor student, and dropped out of *Realschule* (high school) to enlist in the Rhineland-Palatinate 23rd Infantry Regiment in 1909. He was a member of the 22nd Bavarian Infantry Regiment in 1914, when World War I broke out. He took part in the Lorraine campaign of 1914, in the Ypres battles (1914–15), and in the trench warfare in Flanders (1914–16), serving at various times as a clerk, assistant paymaster, and frontline infantryman. In 1916, he was transferred to the 2nd Bavarian Foot Artillery Regiment, which suffered 50 percent casualties in the Battle of Verdun. From 1917 until the end of the war, he served in the II Corps' Reserve Machine Gun Company on the Western Front. He emerged from the war with the Iron Cross, First and Second Classes—high decorations for an enlisted man in the era of the Imperial Army.

When he returned to Germany after four years on the Western Front, Theodor Eicke was a violent and embittered man, and the revolutions filled him with hatred and disgust. He had no desire to serve in the "new" army of the Weimar Republic and, like Adolf Hitler and many others, he blamed the democrats, Communists, Leftists, Jews, and other "November Criminals" for the defeat of the Second Reich. To make matters worse, after 10 years of service, Eicke had no education and no career prospects whatsoever. He moved to Ilmenau, Thuringia, where he enrolled in the technical school, but soon had to drop out due to a lack of funds (apparently he hoped for financial assistance from his father-in-law, but was disappointed). Unemployment was rampant in postwar Germany, and Eicke eventually became desperate enough to accept employment as a paid police informer, but he was fired in July 1920 for political agitation against the Weimar Republic. He had, however, developed a love for police work and, for the next three years, was employed in four cities. At least twice he was hired as a policeman, only to be fired for antigovernment activities. Finally, in January 1923, he became a security officer for the I. G. Farben corporation in the small Rhineland city of Ludwigshafen. Here his fierce nationalism and hatred for the Republic did not hinder him, and he remained with I. G. Farben until he became a full-time SS man in 1932. He joined the Nazi Party and the Stormtroopers in 1928 and transferred to the more elite and highly disciplined SS in 1930. In November of that year, Himmler appointed him second lieutenant and named him commander of the 147th SS Platoon (*Sturm*) in Ludwigshafen.

Eicke threw himself into his new party job with fanatical energy. He was so successful that Himmler promoted him to SS major in early 1931 and ordered him to recruit a second battalion for the 10th SS *Standarte* (regiment), then being formed in the Rhineland-Palatine. He was so successful that Himmler promoted him to SS colonel (*SS-Standartenfuehrer*) and named him commander of the 10th Standarte on November 15, 1931. Although a relative newcomer to the party, he was climbing rapidly indeed.

By 1932, the Nazis were making their big push for power, and Eicke had embarked on a career of political violence. This led to his arrest and conviction for illegal possession of high explosives and conspiracy to commit political assassination. Fortunately for him, Dr. Guertner, the Bavarian minister of justice, was a Nazi sympathizer. Guertner granted him a temporary parole for reasons of health in July 1932, but he promptly resumed his illegal activities, and the police were soon after him again. He was forced to flee to Italy in September, using a fake passport. To console him, Himmler promoted him to SS-Oberfuehrer and named him Commandant of the SA- and SS-Refugee Camp at Bozen-Gries, Italy, but he was not able to return to Germany until after Hitler became chancellor in 1933.

While Eicke was in exile, Joseph Buerckel, the Gauleiter of the Palatinate, decided to rid himself of the unstable SS man by having him replaced as commander of the 10th Standarte. Himmler, however, stood by him, and, when Eicke returned from Italy, he acted without restraint, as usual. On March 21, 1933, he and a group of his followers stormed the Ludwigshafen party headquarters and locked Buerckel—who now held a post roughly equivalent to that of a U.S. governor—in a broom closet for more than two hours, before he could be rescued by the local police.

Once again Eicke had gone too far, and the humiliated Gauleiter extracted full revenge. He had Eicke arrested, declared mentally ill, and thrown into a psychiatric facility as a "dangerous lunatic."[7] Himmler was also furious at Eicke because this incident was a major embarrassment to the NSDAP (it must be remembered that the Nazis had not yet consolidated their power or established their dictatorship at this time). On April 3, 1933, the Reichsfuehrer-SS struck Eicke's name from the roles of the SS and approved his indefinite confinement to the mental institution. Finally humbled, Eicke managed to keep his fierce temper in check for several weeks and even succeeded in acting as if he were normal—a tremendous feat of acting. He wrote to Himmler several times and, with the help of a Wuerzburg psychiatrist, finally persuaded the former chicken farmer to have him released and restored to rank. It was out of the question, of course, for him to return to the Palatinate so, on June 26, 1934, SS-Oberfuehrer Eicke left the mental institution and went directly to his new assignment: commandant of Dachau, the first major German concentration camp for political prisoners.

Dachau, which was located about 12 miles northwest of Munich, was a mess from the Nazis' point of view in 1933. The original commandant was being prosecuted for the murder of several inmates, and the guards were corrupt, undisciplined, brutal, and prone to brag about their activities in public bars. Eicke soon discovered that the SS regional commander, Sepp Dietrich, had "dumped" his worst men (thieves, antisocial types, and so on) on Dachau. Eicke quickly dismissed or replaced about 60 out of 120 men and established the code of conduct that became the model for all concentration camps in the Third Reich. Undisciplined brutality was replaced by well-organized, disciplined brutality, based on the principle of unquestioned and absolute obedience to any and all orders from superior SS officers. Eicke subjected the inmates to close confinement, solitary confinement, beatings, and other corporal punishments, which usually amounted to 25 lashes with a whip in front of the assembled prisoners and the SS staff. The whippings were administered on a rotating basis by all officers, NCOs, and privates, and were designed to toughen them so that they could torture their prisoners impersonally, without remorse or conscience. The man administering the beatings was seldom the man who put the prisoner on report; he was simply beating him because it was his turn to do so. "Under Eicke's experienced direction," Heinz Hoehne wrote later, "anyone who still retained a shred of decency and humanity was very soon brutalized."[8] He was particularly hard on his

Jewish prisoners, whom he hated most of all. (Eicke also hated Christians but treated them better than he did Jews.) Manvell and Fraenkel called him "one of Himmler's most trusted adherents on racial matters."[9] He had *Der Stuermer* displayed on bulletin boards in both the camp and in the barracks, personally delivered violently anti-Semitic speeches, and tried to incite hatred and anti-Semitism among the non-Jewish prisoners.

Himmler was so impressed by Eicke's "success" at Dachau that he promoted him to SS major general on January 30, 1934. Less than six months later, Eicke played a major role in planning the Night of the Long Knives and was selected by Himmler to personally execute Ernst Roehm—an order which he obeyed without question on the evening of July 1. Apparently Eicke was happy to carry out this order, because he shot Roehm and then taunted him as he lay dying. For his services during the Blood Purge, Eicke was appointed first inspector general of concentration camps and commander of SS guard units on July 5. Six days later he was promoted to *SS-Gruppenfuehrer* (SS lieutenant general). Eicke initially set up shop at the headquarters of the Gestapo at 7 Prince Albrecht Street, Berlin, and spread the rules that he had established at Dachau to the entire system. Later he moved his inspectorate to offices on Friedrichstrasse in Berlin and then adjacent to the Sachsenhausen concentration camp at Oranienburg—which, along with Dachau, was the main camp in the embryonic system. In the summer of 1937, Eicke added the third major concentration camp at Buchenwald (near Weimar). Later he added the Gross-Rosen camp near Striegau, Silesia; Flossenburg, near Weiden, in the Upper Palatinate in Bavaria; and a women's camp at Ravensbruck in Mecklenburg. When Austria was annexed, the Mauthausen camp was established near Linz. "By 1937," Snydor wrote, "Eicke had a formidable reputation among his SS colleagues as a tough and vicious figure. Ever suspicious, quarrelsome, cruel, humorless, and afflicted with a cancerous ambition, Eicke was a genuinely fanatic Nazi who had embraced the movement's political and racial liturgy with the zeal of a late convert."[10]

Once he had the new camp system fully operational, Eicke turned his attention to converting his SS Death's Head guard units (the *SS Totenkopfverbaende* or SS-TV) into Nazi Party paramilitary formations. His guards spent one week a month guarding prisoners and three weeks in military training, which involved rigorous physical exercise, maneuvers, weapons familiarization, and political indoctrination, aimed at making them insensitive and unquestioning political soldiers for the Fuehrer. In this aim he certainly succeeded. By 1943, the main SS-TV units had become the 3rd SS Panzer Division "Totenkopf."

Eicke had no tolerance for indolence or resistance to his orders, even among his own men. While his unit was on maneuvers, for example, one SS man declared that he had not volunteered for military service when he joined the SS and demanded that he be returned to the concentration camp. Eicke promptly obliged and sent the man back—but as an inmate, not as a guard. There were no further protests.

In 1939, Eicke went to the field with his Death's Head units, never to return. He commanded an Einsatzgruppen in Poland in 1939, and led his division in France and on the Eastern Front, where he distinguished himself during the Demyansk battles (1941–42). He was killed in action in Russia on February 26, 1943.

Eicke was replaced as inspector general of concentration camps in 1939 by SS Lieutenant General Heinrich Gluecks, who held the post until the last weeks of the war, when he was replaced by Rudolf Hoess. It was subordinate to the SS Main Office for Economics, which grew into the SS Main Economic and Administrative Office (*Hauptamt Verwaltung und Wirtschaft*); known as the YWHA, it was headed by General of SS Oswald Pohl, a harsh disciplinarian well suited to run a bureaucracy of death. After an internal struggle of several years, he emerged as the dominant power in the concentration camp hierarchy.

Pohl's office divided the concentration camps into three classes. Class I camps were labor camps and were relatively mild. Although subordinate to them for administrative purposes, they were separate from the concentration camps proper, and the inmates were normally released after 6 to 12 weeks. Class II camps were harsher and had lower living standings and working conditions. Inmates seldom left Class III camps alive.

By 1939, there were about 100 camps of various types (including labor camps). They were inhabited by several major groups of people: criminals, political opponents, members of inferior races, and "asocial" elements (vagrants, clergymen, and so on) All prisoners wore zebra-striped uniforms, which were marked with serial numbers and colored triangles sewn to the left breast of their shirts and the right leg of their trousers. At Auschwitz, the prisoner's serial number was tattooed on his left forearm. The ones who had the worst lot were the homosexuals, who were characterized by pink triangles. Ostracized and despised by SS and other inmates alike, they were maltreated by the guards and shunned by the prisoners, who considered them moral scum. When the mass murders began, the homosexuals were among the first transferred to the death camps, because they were considered the most worthless caste. Almost none of them survived.

The yellow, six-pointed Star of David was worn by the Jews, as well as by "race defilers"—that is, non-Jews who had violated the Nuremberg Laws. The race defiler's Star of David was outlined or surrounded by a black border. Foreigners had a letter imprinted on their triangles ("P" for Poland, "N" for Netherlands, "F" for France, and so on). The green triangles denoted criminals, red was the color used for political prisoners, Jehovah's Witnesses wore purple triangles, Gypsies wore brown, the "shiftless" wore black, and "labor disciplinary prisoners" wore a white A on their black triangles (A for *Arbeit* or work). Prisoners were identified by their color: greens, purples, reds, and so on. Members of penal companies had a black dot between the point of their triangles and their serial numbers. Feeble-minded prisoners wore an armband with the word *Bloed* (stupid) on it, and were often forced to wear a sign around their necks, stating "I am a Moron!" Prisoners who had tried or were suspected of trying to escape wore red-and-white targets sewn or painted on their backs and chests.[11] The implication was obvious.

The SS made no attempt to segregate the prisoners: quite the opposite, in fact. They wanted to degrade the political prisoners—the enemies of the regime—by placing them on an equal level with thugs, homosexuals, rapists, thieves, murderers, child molesters, and the rest of the scum of German society. They also mixed the prisoners to practice the age-old principle of "divide and rule." In addition, the criminals made excellent informers.

From the beginning the camps were overcrowded. Buchenwald, for example, had 17 barracks, each of which was designed to accommodate a maximum of 500 prisoners. By early 1942, each barrack held 1,500 to 2,000 inmates.[12] The triple layer wooden bunks (which were ordinarily without mattresses or blankets) were designed for five inmates. They frequently held 15 or more. Sanitary conditions were indescribably poor. The camp's day began between 4 A.M. and 5 A.M. in the summer (or around 6 A.M. in the winter) by a whistle. The inmates were given 30 minutes to wash, dress, make their beds, and eat breakfast. This meal consisted of a piece of bread and a pint of thin soup or thin black coffee. Then came the morning roll call, which usually took an hour, until it was light enough to work. The work details marched off at the double time, singing, while the camp band played lively tunes, even if it was winter, when they were so cold they could barely feel their fingers.

Work day at the camps usually lasted 14 hours, from 6 A.M. to 8 P.M. or later, Sunday included. Sunday was a day the inmates almost always went without food, although they were still required to work. Six days a week, lunch was the only hot meal the prisoners received. It usually consisted of a thin soup which, like all of their meals, had little nutritional value. The last ordeal of the prisoners' day was evening roll call. It filled the inmates with terror. They had to stand in ranks for hours, often in rain or snow, while the SS established that no prisoners had escaped during the day. If there were 20,000 inmates and one were missing, the others were kept on their feet for hours, until he was recaptured. Eugen Kogon, a Buchenwald inmate, recalled that two convicts once escaped from Buchenwald. All of the other prisoners were kept standing in ranks all night. By morning 25 of them were dead. By noon, the number had risen to 70. The health and strength of hundreds of others was seriously undermined by the experience. Naturally, the inmates were not allowed to eat or even break ranks throughout the ordeal. If they relieved themselves, they did so in their pants. And this was in 1938, months before the war broke out. Even when no one was missing, the roll call usually took at least an hour and a half.[13]

There were countless other harassments that the prisoners had to endure, such as morning calisthenics, pushups in the mud, standing on their heads in the snow, or crawling through puddles into which the guards had just urinated, but these varied from time to time, camp to camp, and barracks to barracks. At Dachau, the SS installed "dog cells," where prisoners had to lie huddled together and were forced to bark for their food. Other prisoners were placed in unlighted cells without windows and kept there until they almost went blind. Master Sergeant Sommer of Buchenwald, a confederate of camp Commandant Karl Koch, was particularly notorious. He enjoyed torturing prisoners, especially by stripping them and alternately immersing their private parts in ice water and boiling water, and then painting the testicles with iodine. He beat prisoners to death for such infractions as reading the small strips of newspaper they were given for use in the toilet. He beat at least 100 Jews to death in 1940 and 1941 alone. Isle Koch, the wife of the Buchenwald commandant, was also fond of torture. Any prisoner who happened to glance up as she entered a room was subject to being reported for having "stared shamelessly" at the Commandant's wife. The best such an unfortunate could hope for was a quick death.[14]

Work in the camps usually meant armaments work, although up to 40 percent of all inmates were engaged in internal camp jobs, including carpenter work, barber, laundry, clothing and equipment room jobs, machine shop, supply distribution, prison hospital and post office work, maintenance, gardening, sewing, tailoring, lumber yard work, and latrine details. Other prisoners who had technical specialties made luxury items, including paintings, sculptures, and others. The quarry and gardening details were the most feared assignments. In the rock quarries, prisoners often collapsed under their burdens and drunken SS men would beat them or turn dogs loose on them. Death was common in the quarries. This made Mauthausen the most dangerous concentration camp, because it consisted predominantly of quarries.

As time passed and the German war effort required more and more slave labor, the number of subsidiary camps grew. The SS, of course, did not control all of the slave laborers or even the majority of them, but they did control tens of thousands of them. Buchenwald construction detachments, for example, worked on the defenses of the Channel Islands. In 1944, Dachau had about 50 subsidiary camps, Auschwitz around 40, and Buchenwald more than 70. Sachsenhausen also had dozens. By renting out their prisoners to German business and industrial concerns, the SS was able collect 1.5 million Reichsmarks a month. Many of those on such details never returned. Conditions were incredibly bad at most of the subsidiary camps; food was poor and in short supply, and people were not able to change their clothes for six weeks at a time.

Punishment in the camps was severe and was administered for any number of minor and petty infractions, such as failing to salute, turning up one's coat collar in the rain, having a speck of dirt on one's shirt, or a "sloppy posture." Sometimes they were punished for having mud on their shoes, even though the mud was almost knee deep; other times they would be punished for having their shoes shined too well—indicating to the SS men that they were shirking work. The punishments were highly varied. Perhaps the most common was the block. Prisoners, either men or women, were tied to a wooden rack, heads down and legs forward, exposing the buttocks. They were then struck 5 to 25 times with a cane, whip or horsewhip. Theoretically, this punishment could only be given after approval had been attained from Berlin. In practice, the prisoner was beaten immediately; then, about three weeks later, when approval came from Pohl's office, he or she was beaten again. After the beating, the prisoner was often required to do 50 to 150 deep knee bends.

Being hoisted up a tree was an even more painful punishment. The victim's hands were tied behind his back and then hoisted up by the arms, so that the entire weight of the body rested on the shoulder joints, resulting in severely dislocated shoulders or rotator cuff tears. Usually the SS would also beat the screaming prisoner in the face or the sexual organs. Inmates who lost consciousness were revived with cold water. The punishment lasted 30 minutes to four hours; permanent injuries were inevitable and many died. Even more begged for death before they were hoisted down.

Food in the camps was, of course, terrible. Even in 1937, the authorized cost of the food for prisoner per month was 55 pfenning—less than $7 per month. Much of this did not reach the prisoners because of SS corruption; prisoners detailed to the supply rooms and messes also got more than their share. Then, in August 1939, rationing was imposed on the German public, and the diet of the concentration camp inmate grew worse. Table 37.1 shows the weekly ration of a Class II concentration camp inmate from 1940 to 1945.

Under this ration, prisoners frequently lost 40 to 50 pounds or more in their first two or three months in the camps. Many long-time inmates weighed 125 pounds or less, and malnutrition was a major

Table 37.1
Weekly Rations for Inmates in Class II Concentration Camps

	Aug 40 to May 42 lb.oz.	May 42 to Apr 44 lb.oz.	Apr 44 to Feb 45 lb.oz.	March 1, 1945 lb.oz.
Meat and Processed meat[a]	14.1	9.9	7.0	8.7
Fat	7.0	6.0		
Margarine	5.2	4.5		
Lard	1.8	1.5		
Cottage cheese or skimmed milk cheese	1.6	1.6		
Bread	6.0	5.6	5.12	3.14
Sugar	2.8	2.8	2.8	
Marmalade	3.5	3.5	3.5	8.5
Cereals	5.1	5.1	8.8	
Flour or flour mixture	7.9	4.4	4.4	
Skimmed milk.			0.5 pints daily	0.5 pints daily
Coffee substitute	2.7	2.2	2.2	1.1
Potatoes	7.12	1.1	6.3	7.12
Fresh vegetables[b]	6.3	5.12	8.13	13.2
SUPPLEMENTARY DIET FOR HEAVY MANUAL WORKERS				
Meat and Processed meat[a]	14.1	9.9	9.9	13.3
Fat	3.5	3.5	3.5	1.9
Bread	3.0	3.0	3.0	2.7

Notes:
[a]Low-grade beef or horse meat. Reduced to 11 lbs., 2 oz. on October 1, 1941, and to 9 lbs., 9 oz. on January 1, 1942.
[b]Mainly turnips, turnip greens, and discarded cabbage leaves and stalks.
Source:
Kogon, The Theory and Practice of Hell, pp.114–15.

contributing factor to epidemics and fatal diseases. The poor sanitation conditions and chronic shortage of water within the camps, however, seem to have been the major factors in many deaths. By the thousands, prisoners fell victim to typhus, typhoid fever, dysentery, scarlet fever, and other epidemics and diseases.

In late 1941, the SS Medical Branch started medical experiments at Dachau, Buchenwald, Sachsenhausen, Ravensbrueck, and Auschwitz, using prisoners as guinea pigs. To their shame, the Medical Science Corps of the Army and Luftwaffe also became involved in some of these experiments. These inhuman and sinister efforts did not advance medical science one step, but they did result in the deaths of thousands of prisoners, and included typhus, malaria, and altitude experiments.

In 1942, for example, Dr. Ernst Grawitz, the Reich Physician of the SS, had women inmates at Ravensbrueck infected with staphylococci, gas bacilli, tetanus bacilli, and other germ cultures to test the healing effects of certain drugs. Some of the women went untreated so the physicians could observe the course of the disease. Even for those who received treatment, it did no good, since the drugs did not work. Only a handful of the patients survived; the rest died in terrible agony. And there were at least half a dozen series in this one experiment. Another set of experiments involved warming people who had almost been frozen to death, while sterilization experiments were also conducted, as were yellow fever, smallpox, artificially induced abscesses, jaundice, diphtheria, poison gas, mustard gas, and other experiments on living human beings. There were experiments involving blood transfusions, using blood that had been stored too long; another involved deadly X-rays; another involved wounding Russian prisoners of war with poisoned bullets and then seeing if they could be saved. Muscle regeneration and bone transplants were also tried. Again, almost all of the "donors" died. Dr. Joseph Mengele, a physician at Auschwitz, involved himself in the study of twins, in an effort to help the German population grow more rapidly. Like all of the other inhuman medical experiments, this one led to dozens of deaths, but nothing in the way of scientific advancements.

Although Mengele has received the most publicity in recent years because he managed to escape human justice (it was finally determined that he drowned in South America in 1979), he was "small fry" in the SS medical hierarchy. After the war, a "Doctors' Trial" was held in Nuremberg before the American Military Tribunal. The verdicts were announced on August 20, 1947. Sixteen of the 23 defendants were pronounced guilty; seven were sentenced to death by hanging, five to life imprisonment, and four to prison terms ranging from 10 to 25 years. Those sentenced to death included SS Colonel Victor Brack, the chief administrative officer in the Reich Chancellery; SS Major General Dr. Karl Brandt, personal physician to Hitler and Reich Commissioner for Health and Sanitation; Professor Karl Gebhardt, Himmler's personal physician and president of the German Red Cross; and SS Colonel Wolfram Sievers, chief of the Institute for Military Scientific Research. General of Medical Services Dr. Siegfried Handloser, chief of Medical Services for the Armed Forces and Medical Inspector of the Army, received a life sentence, as did General of Medical Services Dr. Oskar Schroeder, the chief of Medical Services for the Luftwaffe.

Prior to the fall of 1938, the majority of the concentration camp occupants were not Jews; in fact, they made up only about 20 to 25 percent of all occupants before Crystal Night. After that, the proportion of Jews continued to increase until 1942, when the organized, assembly-line type of extermination campaign began.

CONCENTRATION AND FATEFUL DECISIONS

The Holocaust was not something Hitler and the Nazis had in mind when they took power in 1933; rather, it was an idea that evolved. In his masterpiece, *The Destruction of the European Jews*, Raul Hilberg identified six subprocesses within the destruction process: (1) definition of who and who was not a Jew; (2) expropriation of Jewish property; (3) concentration of Jews in specific areas; (4) mobile killing (Einsatzgruppen) operations; (5) deportations; and (6) killing center (death camp) operations.[15]

After the Nazis defined who the Jews were, they expropriated the bulk of their property and, beginning in September 1941, forced the German Jews to wear Stars of David, to make them easily identifiable. In 1942, the Jews were ordered to paste the Star of David on their doors. In Poland, Heydrich and the SS employed the Einsatzgruppen for the first time in 1939. This phase was short-lived, however; the Einsatzgruppen did not come into their own until the invasion of the Soviet Union in 1941. More important, in the long run, Heydrich began the progress of concentrating Jews into specific areas in November 1939. He arranged to have the *Ostbahn*, entire railroad network of the General Government, placed at his disposal for the purpose of concentrating the Jews. They were "resettled" in ghettos that resembled something out of the Middle Ages. This process was an on again, off again affair. After two months (during which Heydrich had relocated 200,000 people), Hans Frank, the General Governor, became alarmed and began putting pressure on Himmler and Goering to have the shipments of Jews halted. Goering finally gave the stop order on March 23, 1940.

Frank could not prevent some "dumping" of Jews into his domain (largely from the Vienna area), although massive deportations did not begin until September 1941, after the Holocaust began. For these Jews, however, the Polish ghettos were merely way stations; they were only kept here until the construction of the death camps could be completed.

Except for the domiciles of a small percentage of Jews who cooperated with the Germans and helped administer and police the ghettos, these places were tremendously overcrowded areas of poverty, filth, and misery. The Warsaw ghetto, for example, featured 445,000 people crowded into 1.3 square miles and, in March 1941, had a population density of 7.2 persons per room.[16] This led to the rapid spread of epidemics, especially typhus. All of these Jews, of course, had been forced to leave behind virtually all of their valuables and property. They were compelled to work as forced manual laborers and were fed only the minimum amount of food necessary to stay alive; some did not get even that. By the fall of 1941, the Jews were getting 33 ounces of bread per week (as opposed to 45 for Aryan Poles), 10 ounces of sugar per month, 3.5 ounces of marmalade per month, and less than two ounces of fat per month, excluding rare special food distributions.[17] In Warsaw, around 5,000 people per month were dying (mostly of malnutrition or the indirect effects thereof), and the first isolated cases of cannibalism were reported. Had it not been for such organizations as the American Joint Distribution Committee and others the death toll would certainly have been higher.

By the summer of 1941, when the Einsatzgruppen operations were already in full swing in the East, Heydrich received full authority to carry out the "final solution." Under this plan, Jews from the Reich and points would be deported to the East to be exterminated. To oversee these operations, Heydrich selected a then-unknown SS major named Karl Adolf Eichmann.

Eichmann was the head of the small Jewish section (IV-B-4) of Heydrich's RSHA. Eichmann's immediate superiors were SS Gruppenfuehrer Heinrich Mueller, the head of Amt IV (the Gestapo); and SS Colonel Albert Hartl, chief of IV-B (Sects). Born in Solingen, Germany in March 1906, Eichmann had spent his formative years in Linz, Austria, the hometown of Adolf Hitler, where his father owned an electrical construction company. In secondary school, his history instructor was Dr. Leopold Poetsch, the same teacher who had so influenced young Hitler. Eichmann, however, wanted to follow in his father's footsteps and train as an electrical engineer. He was only able to complete two years of study, however, before his father's business failed in 1925, and Eichmann returned to an Austria characterized by inflation, widespread unemployment and economic stagnation. He managed to get a job as a traveling salesman for an electrical firm and later for Vacuum Oil A.G., but he was a very unhappy and disappointed young man. In 1931, he joined the Austrian Nazi Party and, two years later, fled to Germany, became a Storm Trooper, and joined the Austrian *Freikorps*, where he rose to the rank of sergeant.

Slender and somewhat shy—even affable—Eichmann seemed very much out of place with the Neanderthal Brownshirts. Except for an affinity for horseback riding, Eichmann was not a bit athletic and very much looked like what he was—a future bureaucrat. On the other hand, he had an undeniable talent for organization. He joined the SD in September 1934, was transferred from Bavaria to Berlin, and was ordered to put together a card index file on Freemasonry. Later placed in charge of the office museum, he became interested in Zionism and learned a little Yiddish and Hebrew. Here he was promoted to second lieutenant, but his first major career break came shortly after the Anschluss, when he was placed in charge of the Vienna Jewish emigration office. He succeeded so well that he was promoted to captain and placed in charge of both the Central Emigration Office and the Jewish Section of the Gestapo (Section IV-A-4b of the Reich Main Security Office). In 1941, emigration turned to extermination. Eichmann's humble office at 116 Kurfurstenstrasse became the center of the destruction process, directing the deportation of the Jews to the east and coordinating mass murder. Eichmann himself worked largely behind the scenes. Only in 1944, during the massacre of the Hungarian Jews, did he enter the public limelight, and he never did rise above the rank of lieutenant colonel of SS.

The deportations of Jews from the Reich did not begin until mid-October 1941. Then 30,000 were deported to Minsk and Riga, where Eichmann expected they would be gassed. This plan miscarried, however. The Wehrmacht ordered that all Jewish deportation trains to Russia be stopped—not for humanitarian reasons, but because they needed the trains for the shipment of supplies and ammunition. This time Hitler backed the army, and the planned extermination camps at Riga and Minsk were never constructed. Many of the Jews sent to Riga were executed en masse by SS Colonel Rudolf Lange, the commander of the Gestapo and SD in Latvia, on November 29—the first mass murder of German Jews.[18] Almost all of the rest of this 30,000 eventually met their deaths at the hands of the Einsatzgruppen.

On January 20, 1942, one of the most important meetings in the history of the Holocaust was held at Gross Wannsee, in the office of the International Criminal Police Commission. Fourteen men were present, six of whom were SS: Heydrich, the chief of RSHA, was the chair. The other SS men were Heinrich Mueller and Adolf Eichmann of the Gestapo; SS Oberfuehrer Dr. Karl Schoengarth of the Gestapo in Poland; SS Colonel Dr. Rudolf Lange of the Gestapo's Latvian branch; and General of SS (*Obergruppenfuehrer*) Otto Hoffmann of the SS Race and Resettlement Office. The civilians present at the meeting included Gauleiter Dr. Alfred Meyer of Rosenburg's East Ministry and his assistant, Dr. Georg Leibbrandt; Dr. Wilhelm Stuckart, state secretary of the interior ministry; Erich Neumann, state secretary to the Office of the Four Year Plan; Dr. Roland Freisler, state secretary of the ministry of justice; Dr. Joseph Buehler, state secretary of Frank's General Government; Martin Luther, undersecretary of state in the foreign ministry; Gerhard Klopfer, State Secretary of the Party Chancellery, representing Bormann; and Ministerial Director Wilhelm Kritzinger of the Reich Chancellery.

Heydrich opened the meeting by announcing that he was the plenipotentiary for the preparation of the "final solution" of the Jewish problem. After reviewing the emigration statistics, he informed his listeners that, instead of emigration, the Fuehrer had now decided on a policy of resettlement. The Jews would be formed into huge labor columns. Many of the Jews, he said, would "fall away through natural decline." Those who survived this "natural selection" process would represent the hard core of Jewry and would have to be "treated accordingly." Everyone present knew that he meant they would have to be killed. No one raised any objections except Martin Luther, and he did not object in principle. Speaking for the foreign office, he wanted the evacuation of Jews from Denmark and Norway postponed for the time being. He saw no problem in beginning the resettlement in the Balkans and Western Europe at once.[19] After a discussion of the treatment of Jews in mixed marriages and *Mischlinge* (people with both Jewish and "Aryan" grandparents), State Secretary Buehler urged that the implementation of the Final Solution begin immediately in the General Government. Everyone agreed to cooperate in the matter and everyone did. Even the residents of Theresienstadt, the model ghetto in Czechoslovakia (consisting of German Jews over 65 years of age and severely disabled Jewish war veterans or those holding the Iron Cross First Class or better) eventually ended up in the death camp at Auschwitz.

OPERATION REINHARD

As we have seen, Heinrich Himmler was not satisfied with the mass murders of the Einsatzgruppen for a number of reasons. First of all, progress was too slow. It addition, the shootings had to be conducted at hundreds of locations and it was thus impossible to keep them secret; it would be impossible to conduct such murders in western Europe. Finally, the cumulative psychological effect on his SS men was devastating. Another method of mass murder would thus have to be found. Fortunately—from Himmler's point of view—men with experience in other forms of mass murder were readily available in the Third Reich in 1941.

In September 1941, Artur Nebe, the commander of Einsatzgruppe B, carried out an experimental mass murder using explosives. Twenty-five mentally ill persons were locked inside two bunkers in a forest outside Minsk and blown up; however, it took two attempts and a great deal of trouble to finish them off, and the experiment was judged a failure.

A few days later, Nebe and Dr. Albert Widmann of the Criminal Police tried a poison gas experiment against 20 to 30 lunatics in Mogilev. Two pipes were driven into a wall, the victims were placed inside, and the rooms were hermetically closed. The exhausts of two cars were hooked up to the pipes, and carbon monoxide killed all of the prisoners within a few minutes. As a result, Nebe came up with the idea of constructing a death van. Acting upon this recommendation, the Technical Department of the RSHA[20] developed two types of special vehicles designed for mass murder. The larger of these vans could gas 130 to 150 people, while 80 to 100 people could be exterminated in the smaller van. The entire gassing process took only 15 to 30 minutes, during which time the van was driven from the loading point to the grave site.[21] At this time, the highest concentration of Jews in Hitler's empire was in the General Government. This made occupied Poland the logical place to start the death camp (killing center) operations. The man Himmler placed in direct charge of the extermination program was SS Major General (*SS Brigadefuehrer*) Odilo Globocnik, the Higher SS and Police Leader for Lublin Province. A longtime Nazi and a veteran of the Austrian Freikorps movement in Carinthia, he was a self-indulgent drunkard who had been sent to prison in 1933 for his part in the murder of a Jewish jeweler in Vienna. A major conspirator during the Anschluss, he was rewarded by being named Gauleiter of Vienna in January 1939, but lost the post when he was caught engaging in illegal foreign currency transactions. After a period of disgrace, during which Globocnik was consigned to the ranks as an enlisted man, Himmler pardoned his friend and made him HSSPf Lublin in November 1939.[22] By 1940, Globocnik wanted to set up a "Lublinland Reserve" for Jews and Poles, who would be deported here from the Reich (or, more accurately, areas recently incorporated into the Reich). Himmler liked the idea and arranged for the transport of tens of thousands of Jews to the ghettos of the General Government, but Hitler carried the process to its ultimate extreme and, in the spring or early summer of 1941, ordered Himmler to begin the "final solution" process. Accordingly, it was Globocnik who set up the first permanent dead facility at Chelmno (Kulmhof) in the Warthegau, near the Warsaw-Posen-Berlin railroad line, using death vans sent to him by Nebe. Delays were caused due to jurisdictional disputes with Hans Frank, the Governor General, and his Landeskommissars, and the first murders at Chelmno did not take place until December 8, 1941. Chelmno, however, lacked the capacity of future death camps, and because its mass graves were reportedly causing a typhus epidemic, its operations were suspended in September 1942. In all, an estimated 66 transports left Lodz for Chelmno, carrying 55,000 victims.[23]

The Fuehrer Chancellery had been directly involved in the planning of the Holocaust since October 1941, when Victor Brack, the chief administrative officer of the Chancellery, offered to send his chemical expert to Riga, to select sites for death camps in Ostland. In December 1941, Brack ordered SS Captain Christian Wirth, a veteran of Hitler's "mercy killing" program, to go to Lublin to set up a new "euthanasia institute" under the direction of SS Major General Globocnik.[24]

(Between September 1939, and August 1941, the Fuehrer's euthanasia experts had put more than 70,000 people to death, before Hitler yielded to pressure from the religious right and ordered the mercy killings suspended. The project had been called T 4, because the organization's headquarters was located at 4 Tiergartenstrasse in Berlin; its director had been Reichsleiter Philipp Bouhler, Hitler's chief of Chancellery.)

In Poland, Wirth and his crew constructed gas chambers into which they piped carbon monoxide from diesel engines. They also employed mobile gas vans, but these were considered too slow and were seldom used after the Lodz ghetto was cleared in September 1942. Working with Globocnik, who was quite enthusiastic about his assignment, Wirth superseded SS Sergeant Joseph Oberhauser, another former euthanasia man, as commandant of the Belzec death camp in mid-December 1941.

Belzec was a small town in the southeastern part of the Lublin district, conveniently located on the Lublin-Lvov Railroad. Despite its small size (roughly 300 square yards), the camp itself had been a labor camp for thousands of Jews from January to autumn 1940, when it was closed. Now it was reopened and converted into a death camp. On March 16, 1942, they started the second permanent gas chambers at the Belzec camp. For the first time, the principles of the assembly line had been applied to the process of mass murder. The result would shock the world. Eleven days later, Joseph Goebbels wrote in his diary:

Beginning with Lublin, the Jews in the General Government are now being evacuated eastward. The procedure is a pretty barbaric one and not to be described here more definitely. Not much will remain of the Jews. On the whole it can be said that about 60 per cent of them will have to be liquidated whereas only about 40 per cent can be used for forced labor.

The former Gauleiter of Vienna, who is to carry this measure through, is doing it with considerable circumspection and according to a method that does not attract too much attention. A judgment is being visited upon the Jews that, while barbaric, is fully deserved by them. The prophesy which the Fuehrer made about them for having brought on a new world war is beginning to come true in a most terrible manner. One must not be sentimental in these matters.[25]

Sentimental they were not. When Goebbels wrote these lines, another death camp was nearing completion at Sobibor. In mid-April, about 250 Jews were brought down from the Krychow labor camp and executed in a trial run. The experiment was successful, and soon the third of the death camps was opened. Even before this occurred, a special SS team was in the process of selecting a site for yet another extermination camp. By early May, they had found one—at Treblinka.

To exterminate the 2,284,000 Jews in the General Government (including the Warsaw, Krakow, Lublin, Lvov, and Radom districts),

Globocnik had 153 SS men and policemen from the Lublin district; 205 members of SS or police staffs or units from other districts; and 92 men from the T 4 program. The latter were most important, because they had experience in setting up and operating mass murder facilities. In fact, the connection between the euthanasia people and the Holocaust has never been fully investigated, but they set up and commanded the death camps of Belzec, Sobibor, and Treblinka. To support these camps, Globocnik set up a training camp at Trawniki. Its main purpose was to train Ukrainian volunteers to work in the camps and to serve as guards and executioners. Over the next two and a half years, 2,000 to 3,000 easterners (mainly Ukrainians) were trained at Trawniki. They formed the bulk of the men running the death camps. On average, only 20 to 35 German SS men were stationed at each camp. Each camp was normally commanded by an SS captain, with perhaps one lieutenant present as a deputy commandant. All of the other SS men were sergeants; there were no SS privates in the camps.

On May 27, Reinhard Heydrich was shot in Prague and died a few days later. Globocnik's extermination program was then officially renamed Operation Reinhard in his honor. By then the "action" was well under way, and construction had begun on Treblinka, the most efficient of the death camps under Globocnik's command. It was located on the Bug River, in the northeast section of the General Government, near Malkinia, a town on the main Warsaw-Bialystok railway and near the Malkinia-Siedlce railroad. The camp was surrounded by woods and naturally concealed. Although construction was directed by SS Lieutenant Colonel Richard Thomalla, an engineer, most of the work was done by Jews under SS supervision. The SS guards would sometimes amuse themselves by forcing Jews to stand under trees that were about to fall down. Several Jews were crushed to death in this manner, but all of the Jewish construction crews were murdered when construction was completed. The first Jews to be gassed at Treblinka were murdered on July 23, 1942, although the camp was only partially completed and construction continued for months. Another major death camp was eventually erected at Maidenek (Majdanek), about two miles from Lublin, but it was a Polish and Russian prisoner-of-war camp from 1939 to 1942, when it was converted into a concentration camp. It apparently was not used for mass murders until the summer of 1943 and never rivaled Auschwitz or Treblinka. The findings of a Russian court of inquiry—that 1.5 million people were gassed here— are, to quote Reitlinger, "thoroughly suspect."[26]

Even before Treblinka was operational, the forced deportations from the ghettos began. Lublin was cleared first, because Globocnik was HSSPf Lublin, and he wanted to get rid of all the Jews from his district as quickly as possible. Late on the evening of March 16, the Jewish ghetto (which was already fenced off) was surrounded by Order Police and Ukrainian auxiliaries from Trawniki. The inhabitants were awakened by shouting and shooting, and were ordered to leave their apartments at once, or they would be shot. The Ukrainians were drunk and firing indiscriminately, causing panic among the Jews. Without regard for age or sex, they were lined up and marched under escort to the synagogue, where they were forced to wait until dawn. Then they were forced to march to the transfer station, where they were put on trains and shipped to the Belzec extermination camp.

The Lublin deportations continued for weeks. The SS men told the Jews that they were being sent to Russia as laborers, and the victims believed them. By the end of the summer, only a few Jews remained in Lublin. They were placed in a small ghetto in Majdan-Tatarsk. Later they were deported and murdered.

The deportations from the Warsaw ghetto began on July 22. Accompanied by several SS and government officials, SS Major Herman Hoefle arrived at the offices of the *Judenrat* (Jewish Council) in Warsaw that morning and informed the chairman, Adam Czerniakow, that the Jews were to be resettled to the east. The Council was ordered to supply 6,000 Jews a day, beginning that very afternoon. The exceptions to the deportation order were the Jewish workers in the German factories with valid work permits, Judenrat employees, members of the Jewish Order Service (the ghetto police), members of the hospital staff, hospitalized patients, and the families of the exempt. The deportees were permitted to carry 15 kilograms (33 pounds) of luggage, food for three days, money, gold, and other valuables. Privately, Hoefle told Czerniakow that his wife was a hostage and would be shot if the "action" were impeded in any way.

Adam Czerniakow committed suicide the next day, but the evacuations continued for weeks. The SS cut off the food supply to the ghetto, but offered Jews who volunteered for resettlement six pounds of bread and a half a pound of marmalade per person. Many were so hungry that this tactic enjoyed some success.[27] According to SS Major General Juergen Stroop, 310,332 Warsaw Jews had been "resettled" as of October 3. At least 66 percent of these were sent to Treblinka in a 10-week period—perhaps as many as three-quarters. In all, according to Stroop, 500,000 Jews were killed in 10 weeks.[28]

Between 5,000 and 6,000 Jews left Warsaw each day, accompanied by brutal beatings. But what they found when they boarded the trains was worse than the beatings.

The deportation trains were run by the Directorate General of the Eastern Railroads (Gedob), an organization headed by Dr. Adolf Gerteis. It supervised and operated the expropriated Polish railroads under the *Reichsbahn*, the German railroad service, which was part of the ministry of transportation. Gedob's employees included 9,000 Germans, 145,000 Poles, and a few thousand Ukrainians. It cooperated with the SS to the fullest extent.

The deportation trains were classified as "special trains" (*Sonderzuege*) and usually consisted of closed freight cars. Only on rare occasions did Jews travel in open cars. The freight cars were designed to carry cargo or cattle, not humans, but could have carried 60 to 70 people with a reasonable margin of comfort and safety. The SS and Ukrainian or Lithuanian guards packed each car with 150 Jews or more. As soon as they were inside, the Germans poured chlorine on top of them. "Inside the freight cars it was so dense that it was impossible to move," Ada Lichtman recalled. "There was not enough air, many people fainted, others became hysterical."[29] At each stop they were robbed by their Ukrainian guards, who occasionally cut off fingers in order to steal rings.

Abraham Kszepicki, another survivor who was deported in July or early August 1942, recalled that more than 100 people were packed into his car. "It is impossible to describe the tragic situation in our airless, closed freight car," he commented later. "It was one big toilet. Everyone tried to push his way to a small air aperture.... The stink in the car was unbearable. People were defecating in all four corners." Everyone lay down and took off most or all of their clothes. At a stop, Kszepicki paid a Lithuanian volunteer 500 zlotys (more than half of his money) for a small cup of water. Many paid 1,000 zlotys. By 7 A.M. the next morning, the sun was already heating the car. "People lay on the floor, gasping and shuddering as if feverish, their heads lolling, laboring to get some air into their lungs," Kszepicki recalled. "Some were in complete despair and no longer moved." The trip to Treblinka took 20 hours, instead of the four or five it should have taken. "If the trip had taken another half day, the number of dead would have been much higher. We would all have died of heat and asphyxiation." Often trains did take longer. Abraham Goldfarb later testified that 135 of the 150 people in his freight car died before it arrived in Treblinka in late August.[30]

When the Jews arrived at the death camps, they looked deceptively peaceful, as if they were really transit camps. There were no visible pits, graves, or gas chambers. The SS strengthened this impression by announcing that the Jews should undress; they were being sent to showers for cleaning and disinfecting, to prevent the spread of diseases and epidemics. Afterward they would receive clean clothes and be sent to work camps. The SS man making these announcements often wore a white coat, to give the impression that he was a physician. The Jews were then segregated by sex and the women were given haircuts, helping further convince them that they were going to the baths.

Everything was done at double time (that is, on the run), so that the victims would not have much time to observe and reflect; had they time to do so, they might have noticed something amiss and concluded that they were not really in a transit camp. Men were gassed first, before they could grasp what was really happening. The gas chambers themselves were camouflaged as showers; the deception was maintained until the door was shut and sealed. The Jews were also forced into the "showers" at the utmost speed by Ukrainian guards, who were equipped with whips, iron bars, and dogs. Women and children were killed last—they were much easier to murder. Death normally occurred within 15 to 30 minutes when carbon monoxide was used. To drown out the victims' screams, the SS arranged an orchestra. Elderly people and those who were unable to walk were told that they would be taken to an infirmary, where they would receive medical treatment. They were placed on carts (pulled by horses or Jewish men) and taken directly to the pits, where they were shot.

After the Jews were gassed, their bodies were dragged out and inspected. A dentist removed gold teeth and their finger rings were also removed, if they had not been taken already.

Jews did all of the physical labor at the camps. Out of each transit group, a few dozen young men were selected to remove the corpses from the gas chambers and bury them. They also collected and arranged the clothes and other goods left by the dead Jews. After working for a day or so, they were also murdered. Jewish carpenters, tailors, and other skilled workers (called *Hofjuden* or "house Jews") were allowed to live longer, but they also were also frequently gassed and replaced.

No doubt about it—the death camps were horribly efficient. About 75,000 Jews were murdered in Belzec during its first four weeks of operation. In just five weeks (July 23 to August 28, 1942), an estimated 312,500 Jews (mostly from the Warsaw ghetto) were gassed at Treblinka alone. By the time the first phase of Action Reinhard ended on October 28, 1942, approximately 40 percent of all the Jews in occupied Poland had been gassed with carbon monoxide. Hitler and Himmler were obviously quite pleased with Globocnik's "progress." They promoted him to SS lieutenant general on November 9.

Hans Frank, the ruler of the General Government, had initially opposed the mass murders—not because of any humanitarian motivations, but because he did not want his rival Himmler encroaching on his empire. By mid-1942, however, it was clear to him that the Reichsfuehrer-SS had the full support of the Fuehrer in this matter, and that was all important. On June 3, therefore, he issued a directive transferring all Jewish affairs in the General Government to the SS and the Security Police. Sixteen days later, during a visit to Lublin, Himmler issued an order to complete the deportation of all Jews from the

General Government to the death camps by December 31, 1942. He quickly met opposition from Max Frauendorfer, the chief of the labor department of the General Government; Lieutenant General Max Schindler, the armaments inspector for Wehrkreis General Government; and General of Cavalry Baron Curt Ludwig von Gienanth, the military governor. According to Frauendorfer, the armaments industry of occupied Poland was "entirely dependent on Jewish labor."[31]

On September 18, General von Gienanth sent a memo to OKH, stating that slightly more than 1 million Polish industrial laborers were working for Germany. Of these, 300,000 were Jews, 100,000 of whom were skilled laborers. Poland was short of skilled laborers and the Jews were temporarily irreplaceable. In the enterprises essential to the Wehrmacht, Jews made up 25 percent to 100 percent of the workers. Virtually all of the workers in the textile industry were Jews, he said, and they were busy making winter clothing for the armed forces. He therefore asked that the removal of Jews from industry be postponed until they could be eliminated without significantly reducing industrial output. OKH forwarded the memo to Himmler.

The Reichsfuehrer-SS did not bother to respond to the Gienanth memo until October 9. In the meantime, the more Nazi-oriented General Zeitzler had replaced the conservative General Halder as chief of the General Staff, and (probably to further intimidate the generals) Himmler had used his influence at Fuehrer Headquarters to force Baron von Gienanth into retirement for the second and final time within two weeks of sending his memo.[32] In his reply, the Reichsfuehrer-SS basically rejected all of Gienanth's recommendations and made it clear that the Final Solution had priority over military considerations. He also stated that he had no sympathy for those who tried to shield or protect Jews under the disguise of military need and implied that he suspected von Gienanth of attempting to do just that. (To his credit, the old cavalry officer seems to have been doing exactly what Himmler accused him of.) In any case, that ended the matter. Gienanth was replaced by a more politically correct officer and Himmler met no further opposition from the Wehrkreis General Government. The Holocaust continued.

In August 1942, Odilo Globocnik appointed Christian Wirth inspector (commander) of all four death camps (Chelmno, Belzec, Sobibor, and Treblinka). He was succeeded as commandant of Belzec by SS Captain Gottlieb Hering.

Wirth was born in Oberbalzheim, Wuerttemberg, in November 1885. As an NCO in World War I, he distinguished himself in combat on the Western Front, where he was highly decorated. After the war, he joined the police and, by 1939, had attained the rank of criminal inspector in the Stuttgart police. At the end of that year, he was assigned to the euthanasia program at the Grafeneck Psychiatric Clinic in Wuerttemberg; shortly thereafter, he was transferred to the euthanasia institution at Brandenburg an der Havel in Prussia. The medical director here was Dr. Irmfried Eberl, who became the first commandant of Treblinka in 1942. By mid-1940, Wirth had become a sort of roving inspector/director of the dozen or so euthanasia institutes located throughout the Third Reich. By mid-1941, he was active in the euthanasia program in western Poland.

Christian Wirth's character belied his name. He was brutal, inhumane, sadistic, and ruthless. He showed no remorse for the sick and insane he helped murder—in fact, he called them "useless mouths." Jews he viewed as subhuman "garbage" and their lives had no meaning or value to him. He savagely beat both prisoners and his Ukrainian guards with his whip when they displeased him, and even his brutal guards were afraid of him. He was, however, infrequently seen by most prisoners; instead, he allowed his men—even the most perverted and sadistic—a free hand with them.[33]

The gassing system introduced by Wirth was only partially satisfactory, but he successfully resisted the introduction of Zyklon-B into his camps because this more efficient poison gas had been developed by his rival, Rudolf Hoess, the commandant of Auschwitz. Wirth concentrated instead on expanding his camp system and working it at maximum possible capacity. By the end of April 1943, there were 13 operational gas chambers at Treblinka, 763,000 Jews from the General Government had been murdered at Treblinka alone, and another 600,000 Polish Jews had been exterminated at Belzec. This camp, however, ceased its killing operations toward the end of December 1942, when the plan to deport 200,000 Romanian Jews fell through. Belzec was obsolete; after less than a year of operation, the SS already had more efficient death camps.

Like Wirth, most of the SS men in the death camps were brutal murderers or inhuman, robotic bureaucrats who considered murder just part of a day's work. They obeyed orders, and what those orders entailed did not concern them. Franz Stangl, the commandant of Treblinka, for example, had very little contact with his prisoners, whom he looked upon as cargo of which he had to dispose. Like Wirth, he gave his men free reign in dealing with Jews, which usually resulted in their deaths. Years later, under interrogation, he admitted he enjoyed his job. As incredible as it may seem, however, there was a small minority of humane SS men who surviving Jews spoke well of years after the event. Treblinka survivor Jacob Wiernik later wrote that SS 2nd Lieutenant Erwin Herman Lambert—

was humane and likeable. He ... was considerate to us. When he first entered the camp) and saw the piles of bodies that had been suffocated by gas, he was stunned. He turned pale and a frightened look of suffering fell over his face.... With regard to us, the workers, he treated us very well. Frequently he would bring us food on the side from the German kitchen. In his eyes one could see his good-heartedness ... but he feared his friends. All of his deeds and movements expressed his gentle soul.[34]

Joe Siedlecki later testified that SS Sergeant Karl Ludwig "was a good man. If I would meet him today, I would give him everything he might need. I cannot even count the times he brought me all kinds of things and helped me, or the number of people he saved." Another SS man, Sergeant Kliehr, who was in charge of the bakery at Sobibor, also managed to keep his decency, in spite of his uniform and his surroundings. When he was arrested and put on trial in Berlin in 1950, several surviving victims of the Holocaust flocked to his defense and testified on his behalf, and he was acquitted.[35]

These men, of course, were rare exceptions. Viciousness, sadism, rabid racism, and senseless hatred were the rule. The Ukrainians were particularly brutal. Ivan Demaniuk of Treblinka and his assistant, Nikolai, were especially infamous for their harshness. They supervised the gas chambers and worked on the motors that produced the carbon monoxide for the chambers. One survivor later testified that Demaniuk took special pleasure in hurting women. "He stabbed the women's naked thighs and genitals with a sword before they entered the gas chambers and also raped young women and girls." He also cut off the noses or ears of Jews whose appearance he disliked. When a Jewish laborer's work did not please him, he often beat his skull in with an iron pipe. He especially enjoyed entwining people's heads between two strands of barbed wire; then he would beat them in the head. As the prisoner struggled, he would strangle himself on the wire.[36]

Another Jew recalled that most of the Ukrainian guards were little better.

Between Camp I and II were living quarters of the Ukrainians, who were always drunk. Everything they could get their hands on they stole from the camp and sold in exchange for vodka. They would pick out the prettiest Jewish girls, drag them to their rooms, rape them, and then lead their victims to the gas chambers.[37]

The Sobibor death camp was put out of business for several weeks in 1942 while repairs on the Lublin-Chelm Railroad were completed. Gassing resumed in early October, but at a slower pace. From the first of October until the beginning of May 1943, "only" 70,000 to 80,000 Jews were killed at Sobibor. Meanwhile, the focus of the murders shifted to the Bialystok District, an independent administrative unit under the authority of Erich Koch, the Gauleiter of East Prussia and

Reichskommissar of the Ukraine. The Einsatzgruppen had already killed 31,000 Jews (mostly men) in the Bialystok area between July and September 1941, but then the mass murders had been suspended. By autumn 1942, there were approximately 210,000 Jews in the district, largely concentrated in the Bialystok and Grodno ghettos.

On October 15, 1942, the deportations from Bialystok to Treblinka began, while other trains were sent to Auschwitz. These ghetto-clearing operations were brought to an abrupt halt in early December due to a lack of trains. They were all working overtime for the Wehrmacht, which was in the middle of the Stalingrad crisis. On January 23, 1943, Himmler made a personal appeal to Dr. Theodor Ganzenmueller, the state secretary for transportation, to make trains available for the Final Solution. Whether out of Nazi political conviction or fear of the Reichsfuehrer-SS, Ganzenmueller relented and supplied the trains. Once again the needs of the Final Solution took precedence over the needs of the military. By February 19, more than 110,000 Bialystok Jews had been murdered at Treblinka alone.

In the summer of 1943, the army and German civil authorities in Bialystok appealed that the Jews there were vital to the war effort. Himmler again rejected this argument and sent Globocnik to Bialystok to personally coordinate the final solution of the ghetto. In spite of resistance from the Jewish underground, the Bialystok ghetto was liquidated on August 18 and 19, 1943. Meanwhile, on June 21, Himmler ordered the liquidation of the Ostland ghettos, including Riga, Minsk, Vilna, Kovno, Shavli, and Lida. Most of the Jews who had lived there were already dead or gone. The Jewish population of Minsk, for example, was now only about 7,000. It had been 75,000 in June 1941. The Jewish population of Vilna fell from 57,000 to 11,500 over the same period.

The Ostland ghettos were exterminated in the fall of 1943, while another 135,000 Jews were sent to the Reinhard death camps from Germany, the Protectorate, Holland, France, Greece, and Yugoslavia. Himmler, however, had already decided to close Belzec, Sobibor, and Treblinka and bring Operation Reinhard to an end. The reason was simple: they were no longer needed. The annihilation of the Polish Jewry was virtually an accomplished fact, and the Auschwitz-Birkenau death mill had increased its killing capacity by constructing more and larger gas chambers and crematoria, and it was now able to meet all of the demands of the Nazi extermination system. In addition, Himmler was now interested in erasing the evidence of his crimes. In March 1942, he delegated this task to SS Colonel Paul Blobel, the former leader of Einsatzkommando 4a, who had carried out the mass murders at Kiev in 1941. His formal appointment was made by "Gestapo" Mueller in June 1942. Blobel's job was top secret and went by the codename "Sonderaktion 1005"; his unit was called Commando 1005. He was ordered not to put anything in writing.

Blobel carried out his first experiments at Chelmno, using incendiary bombs. They did not work well and set the neighboring woods on fire. He then tried cremation by placing the bodies on wood in open piles. The remaining skeletons were deposed of by a special bone-crushing machine, and the ashes were dumped back in the pits. This simple but effective method was soon tried at Sobibor, where the buried corpses had swelled and caused the mass graves to push above the surrounding terrain, resulting in a terrible stench, massive vermin infestations, and the danger of contamination of the drinking water. Although it took months, Blobel's crews cleaned up Sobibor. As a result of this success, crematoriums were added to all of the death camps and most of the concentration camps.

The Jews initially met the Holocaust with an understandable sense of disbelief. After they heard about the Einsatzgruppen and the rumors of death camps, many of them worked hard for the Wehrmacht, in an effort to make themselves indispensable. They logically deducted that they would be safe if they were badly needed by the German war effort. Their would-be murderers, however, did not think logically. The Jews did not realize that Himmler had already ruled that the Final Solution was more important than the Wehrmacht's war effort. This information was not common knowledge, of course, and the facts dawned on the Jews only slowly. Gradually, however, there were more and more incidents of individual escapes from the trains; acts of spontaneous resistance began to take place, the frequency of which increased with the passage of time, as more and more Jews heard about what was really happening in the camps. The first spontaneous revolt reportedly took place at Belzec on June 13, 1942. A group of Jews who had been sent to remove the corpses of murdered women and children were so revolted by the horrible sight that they threw themselves at the throats of their surprised guards. They killed four to six guards with their bare hands before they were subdued. They were all put to death.[38]

On August 2, 1943, the first uprising occurred at Treblinka. About 750 prisoners took part; 100 refused to do so. The hundred who made no effort to resist were nevertheless summarily executed by the SS the next day. Of the 750 Jews who turned on their tormentors, about half were shot in the camp and killed on or near the fences. During the night of August 2–3, about 200 prisoners were caught and shot, leaving 150 to 200 at large. They received little help from the Polish population, which was largely indifferent to their fate. Most of them did not survive the war. No more than 70 Treblinka inmates were still alive when Berlin fell.

On October 14, another uprising took place at Sobibor. About 700 tried to break out and another 150 refused to make the attempt. All 150 who "played it safe" were shot the next day. Between 230 and 270 prisoners were killed inside the camp or on the fences and in the minefields which surrounded the camp. Three hundred prisoners escaped the compound, but 100 of these were soon captured and shot. Of the 200 who escaped, only between 50 and 70 survived the war.

The Treblinka and Sobibor Uprisings shook Heinrich Himmler, who decided to act quickly, before the spirit of Sobibor could spread. He ordered General of SS Friedrich Krueger, the HSSPf Warsaw, to liquidate the remaining labor camps at once. Krueger delegated this task to SS Lieutenant General Jacob Sporrenberg, who had just replaced Odilo Globocnik as HSSPf Lublin.

The "action" took place on November 3. About 15,000 Jews, including women and children, were put to death in the Poniatowa labor camp. The Jewish underground group tried to resist but was trapped in the barracks and burned to death. After the fighting ended, wounded Jews were thrown into the burning barracks.

The Trawniki labor camp was also liquidated, at the cost of 8,000 to 10,000 Jewish lives. Another 18,000 Jews were murdered at Majdanek. All totaled, about 42,000 Jews were killed in the action, which was known as Operation *Erntefest* (Harvest Festival).

The Belzec death camp, meanwhile, was closed at the end of July, and the workers transferred to Sobibor. Some realized what that really meant and resisted but were quickly shot. The last camp commandant, SS Captain Hering, became commander of the Poniatowa labor camp.

Treblinka received its last major shipment of human cargo—25,000 Bialystok Jews—at the end of August, when the last large-scale murders took place. In September, in spite of charges of corruption that seemed to have been well founded, Globocnik was sent to Italy as Higher SS and Police Leader, Trieste—which must have been a prized appointment for him, since Trieste was his home town. His transfer was partially due to his strained relationship with Hans Frank. He was soon followed by most of the Reinhard staff, including Wirth, Stangl, Hering, and others. Treblinka was blown up and abandoned in November 1943.

Sobibor, the last of Reinhard death camps, was closed in late November 1943, and its Jewish workers were murdered. It was converted to a depot for captured ammunition under Oswald Pohl's SS Main Economic and Administrative Office. Operation Reinhard was finally over. Yitzhak Arad, who wrote perhaps the best book on the subject, called it the "largest single massacre action of the Holocaust" and estimated that 1.7 million Jews had been murdered.[39] But the Holocaust was not over—it had merely shifted its focus elsewhere.

So had the war.

NOTES

1. Hilberg, pp. 243–44.
2. Koch, *Aspects*, pp. 379–80.
3. Hilberg, pp. 248–49.
4. Reitlinger, p. 239.
5. Hilberg, p. 256.
6. Charles W. Snydor, Jr., *Soldiers of Destruction* (1977), p. 3 (hereafter cited as Syndor).
7. Heinz Hoehne, *The Order of the Death's Head*, Richard Berry, trans. (1971), p. 228 (hereafter cited as Hoehne).
8. Kogon, pp. 106–7; Hoehne, p. 229. Among Eicke's guards at this time were Adolf Eichmann, Rudolf Hoess, the future commandant of the Auschwitz concentration camp, and Helmut Becker, the future commander of the Death's Head SS Panzer Division.
9. Roger Manvell and Heinrich Fraenkel, *Himmler* (1965; reprint ed., 1968), p. 45.
10. Snydor, pp. 22–23.
11. Kogon, pp. 35–36.
12. Ibid., p. 48.
13. Ibid., pp. 79–80.
14. Kogon, pp. 233–26.
15. Hilberg, p. 39.
16. Ibid., p. 152.
17. Reitlinger, p. 61.
18. SS Colonel Rudolf Lange was directly responsible for the murder of 70,000 to 100,000 Jews during World War II. He was apparently killed in action near Posen (Poznan) on February 23, 1945, although at least one source states that he committed suicide.
19. Hilberg, pp. 264–65.
20. SS Lieutenant Colonel Walter Rauff was the head of the RSHA's Technical Department.
21. In the summer of 1941, Himmler asked SS Lieutenant General Dr. Ernst Grawitz, the chief of the Medical Services Branch of the SS, what was the best way to conduct mass killings. Grawitz suggested the use of gas chambers.
22. Globocnik was directly subordinate to Himmler for Operation Reinhard; otherwise he was subordinate to the HSSPf Warsaw, Friedrich Krueger.
23. Reitlinger, pp. 246–48.
24. Ibid., pp. 246–47.
25. Goebbels Diaries, March 27, 1942.
26. Reitlinger, p. 295.
27. Kogon, p. 193
28. Reitlinger, pp. 262–64.
29. Yitzhak Arad, *Belzec, Sobibor, Treblinka: The Operation Reinhard Death Camps* (1987), p. 63 (hereafter cited as Arad).
30. Ibid., p. 379.
31. Ibid., p. 46.

32. Baron von Gienanth was born in Eisenberg, Upper Bavaria, in 1876. He entered the service as a Fahnenjunker in 1896 and was commissioned into the 23rd Dragoons the following year. He underwent General Staff training from 1904 to 1908 and served in General Staff positions during World War I, mainly with cavalry divisions. He was chief of staff to the German Military Mission to Constantinople in 1918. During the Reichswehr era he alternated between cavalry and General Staff positions, and ended up as commander of the 3rd Cavalry Division (1929–31) and 4th Infantry Division (1931–33). He retired in 1933 as an honorary general of cavalry but was recalled to active duty in 1936. He was commander of Frontier Guard Command Breslau when World War II began. This headquarters later became the XXXIV Corps Command. He briefly served as OB East before becoming military governor of the General Government in 1940. After Himmler forced him into retirement, Gienanth settled in Heidelberg. He died in 1961 (Keilig, pp. 106–7).

33. Arad, pp. 163–64.

34. Ibid., p. 196.

35. Ibid.

36. Ibid., p. 197.

37. Ibid.

38. Ibid., p. 257.

39. Ibid.

CHAPTER XXXVIII

THE BATTLE OF THE NORTH ATLANTIC, 1941–42

THE U-BOAT WAR: SPRING 1941

At the beginning of 1941, optimism was high at OKM and in Admiral Doenitz's headquarters, and the possibility of defeating the United Kingdom seemed real. In January 1941, the U-boats sank almost 100,000 tons of Allied shipping, and in February sank more than 200,000 tons (42 ships). In January 1941, British imports amounted to less than half their totals for January 1940. With the Luftwaffe now sinking almost 100,000 tons of shipping per month, the OKM estimated that their combined forces would soon be capable of sinking 750,000 tons per month—enough to knock Britain out of the war if they could maintain it for a year. British losses already totaled 400,000 tons per month (according to OKM estimates), and they were only capable of building 200,000 tons of shipping per month; therefore, barring a fundamental change in the situation, the defeat of Britain could be predicted with mathematical certainty.[1]

At the beginning of March, Convoy OB-293 sailed outbound from Liverpool to Halifax and reached a position well south of Iceland. On the evening of March 6, it was intercepted by *U-47*, under the command of Guenther Prien, the famous "Bull of Scapa Flow." Prien immediately attacked the convoy, and Doenitz, from his headquarters at Kerneval, a chateau near Lorient, dispatched several submarines to the area. The U-boats sank two merchantmen and damaged two others, but their own losses were disastrous.

The British escort vessels were directed by Commander James Rowland, the commander of the old World War I destroyer *Wolverine*. First,

he depth-charged and severely damaged *UA-45*. Its commander, Lieutenant Commander Hans Eckermann, was able to pull it out of the battle in the general confusion and successfully nursed it back to Lorrient,
but others were not so lucky. *U-70* under Lieutenant Commander
Joachim Matz was driven to the surface by the corvettes *Camellia* and
Arbutus. Matz set off demolition charges in the hull and gave the order
to abandon ship. Even *U-99*, under "Silent Otto" Kretschmer, was
driven off before it could fire half of its torpedoes. But the redoubtable
Prien persisted in the attack. He sank his 28th merchantman but, at
dusk on March 8, depth charges blew Germany's most famous U-boat
apart. There were no survivors.

U-boat losses continued to mount. On March 15, Convoy HX-112,
with more than 50 heavily loaded merchant ships, came under attack,
and a 10,000-ton tanker erupted in a huge explosion.

The escorts for HX-112 were controlled by Commander Donald Macintyre and included his own destroyer, the *Walker*, four other destroyers, and two corvettes. During the daylight hours of March 16, the
escorts and U-boats maneuvered against each other but without effect.
Then, at 10 P.M., another merchant ship erupted. Within the next
60 minutes, the convoy was rocked by four more explosions. Macintyre
was near despair, when suddenly he saw a tell-tale white line in the
water: the wake of a U-boat. The *Walker* immediately gave chase and
forced the submarine to dive. Macintyre pounded the area with depth
charges for a half an hour but did not know for sure whether his target
had eluded him until the convoy again came under attack from the
determined U-boat commander. The *Walker* and the *Vanoc* now teamed
up and launched more depth-charge attacks; then, suddenly, the *Vanoc*
broke contact and headed into the darkness at full speed. She rammed
the surfaced submarine, *U-100*, crushing its commander, Joachim
Schepke, to death on the conning tower and sinking the U-boat. There
were only five survivors.

U-100 had been "sighted" by a new type of radar that allowed its
operators to detect a surfaced submarine at night, well beyond the
range of the human eye. It was a turning point in the Battle of the
North Atlantic, because, with asdic (sonar) and radar working in tandem, escorts could now move in on U-boats whether they were sub-
merged or surfaced. The Battle of Convoy HX-11Z was not over,
however. The *Walker*'s asdic operator was sure he had detected another
U-boat, so the destroyer fired another spread of seven depth charges,
forcing *U-99* to the surface, where it was blasted by the guns of the
Walker and *Vanoc*. The submarine signaled that it was sinking, and one
by one the crewmen jumped into the water. All but three survived.
The last of the half-frozen men to be pulled into the Walker wore the
distinctive, white captain's cap. He was Lieutenant Commander Otto

Kretschmer, a holder of the Knight's Cross with Oak Leaves and the top U-boat ace of World War II, despite the fact that he would spend the last four years of the conflict in a prison camp. He had sunk 44 ships, totaling 266,629 tons.[2]

Within the next few days, two more U-boats were destroyed. These heavy losses led an alarmed Admiral Doenitz to order his submarines further out to sea, in case the British had developed new anti-submarine devices. He could now deploy up to 19 submarines in the Atlantic at the same time (the highest total since September 1939), and in March 1941, the Allies lost 206,000 tons of shipping to U-boats. But spring brought no relief. British losses in April totaled 232,000 tons and May was worse. Doenitz put more than 20 U-boats to sea and shifted the focus of his offensive to the South Atlantic, mostly off Freetown on the West African coast. Freetown was the assembly point for shipping from South America, south Africa, and India. The U-boats sank 66 ships in May alone.

The losses of the British tankers created serious fuel shortages in the United Kingdom. The average Briton's mileage ration was now only 35 miles per week, but the government projected the country would need to have an additional 100 million gallons a year. As a result, industrial allocations were arbitrarily cut 10 percent, and rations for farmers and fishermen were reduced.

Despite these successes, the mood of optimism at OKM faded in May. The Luftwaffe left for Barbarossa, which was a major factor in the Battle of the Atlantic. The loss of the *Bismarck* also ended the day of the surface raider, and the glory days of the auxiliary surface raider were clearly over. From here on, the U-boats would have to face the Royal Navy alone. In addition, the British continued to win the technology war. Their ability to use radar and sonar in tandem certainly increased the vulnerability of the U-boat. This development was followed by the perfection of the shipborne, high-frequency direction finder, which was called the "Huff-Duff." This invention enabled British operators to tune into high-frequency coded messages from Doenitz to his captains. If two operators picked up the same signal, they could cross-reference and obtain the approximate location of the submarine. As the tracking teams received more practice and became more skillful, they were able to obtain a remarkably accurate picture of U-boat dispositions.

In May 1941, the Royal Navy scored another major victory when it captured *U-110* off the coast of Greenland. In it, they found an intact German electronic coding machine. The ULTRA crypto-analysts used the captured device to break "Hydra"—the U-boat code, as well as its successor, "Triton." From mid-1941 on, the British were able to decipher many of Doenitz's most secret dispatches.

Another major British victory was won in one of the backrooms of the Admiralty in London, where Operational Research, a little-known office, analyzed data on sinkings by U-boat and determined that the number of vessels lost per convoy was a function of the number of attacking submarines and the number of escort vessels available. The number of merchant ships in the convoy, they concluded, had little to do with it. As a result, the Admiralty increased the size of a typical convoy from about 30 to 60 ships or more. This meant that more escort vessels could be assigned to each convoy, and there would be fewer convoys for the U-boats to ambush.

The increasing size of the Canadian Navy was another contributing factor to the growing Allied control of the seas. When the war broke out, it had only six destroyers, five minesweepers, and a few auxiliary vessels, and a total strength of only 3,000 men. Prime Minister Mackenzie King, however, launched an ambitious ship construction program, and, by 1941, Canada was ready to take full responsibility for guarding the western leg of the Atlantic convoy run. By the end of the war, the Canadian Navy would have 400 ships and 90,000 men at sea.[3]

Finally, the British began to use the airplane as an anti-submarine weapon—a development that would ultimately seal the fate of the Wolf Packs. Although the Royal Air Force used airplanes against the U-boats from the beginning, the British were slow to employ its full potential against the German submarines. Airborne anti-submarine weapons were initially poor and British naval air tactics were too aggressive. Instead of overflying the convoys and coordinating their operations with those of the ships, they flew independent patrol missions, looking for U-boats. They thus spent by far the majority of their flight time on wide sweeps over empty ocean. Even when they spotted a U-boat, it was usually able to crash-dive and escape. Forcing a submarine not engaged in an attack against a convoy to dive was an insignificant incident. If the same U-boat had been on the verge of firing its torpedoes into a merchant ship, forcing it into a crash-dive would have been an important event.

British naval air tactics did not begin to improve until the spring of 1941, when operational control of Coastal Command was turned over to the Royal Navy. About the same time, Coastal Command was given about 30 American-built Catalina flying boats, which could stay airborne from 17 to 25 hours at a time. With the addition of long-range fighters and bases in Iceland, only 400 miles of ocean in the mid-Atlantic were beyond the range of protective aircraft. In addition, early airborne radar known as the ASV (air-to-surface vessel) became available in 1941. This radar had one serious drawback: it lost contact with the submarine if the airplane came too close to it (that is, if it came within a mile of it). At night, therefore, submarines could escape, until the British began attaching a powerful searchlight to each airplane. This searchlight was perfected and reaching the squadrons by August 1941. Then the British developed the tactic of making long-range contact by radar and cutting their engines, so they could glide silently toward their target; then, by cutting on their searchlight at the last minute, they were usually able to take the submarine by surprise and sink it with their improved airborne depth charges.

In the summer of 1941, the Royal Navy introduced yet another anti-submarine innovation: the Catapult Aircraft Merchantman (CAM). These ships were equipped with Hurricane fighters that could be launched by catapults, thus giving their convoys aerial protection. The CAM ship was the forerunner of an even more formidable opponent: the small escort carrier. The first of these were converted freighters or passenger ships on top of which a flight deck had been superimposed. Later, better designed escort carriers were built from scratch. Each could carry several airplanes and, when they and the new, faster escorts joined the convoys in sufficient numbers, the doom of the U-boat was sealed.

THE U-BOAT WAR, SUMMER AND FALL 1941

While British defenses grew notably stronger, so did Doenitz's forces. In June 1941, the construction yards delivered 25 U-boats in a month for the first time. Between June and the end of August, the submariners sank 96 ships (447,000 tons). This brought the total Allied shipping loss from all causes to 7,459,000 tons (one-third of Britain's prewar tonnage). Of this, 818 ships, totaling 4,034,000 tons (or 54 percent) had been sunk by U-boats. Aircraft accounted for 433 ships (1,369,000 tons).[4]

Meanwhile, the unneutral acts of the Americans made them an unofficial co-belligerent in the Battle of the Atlantic. On September 1, 1941, Admiral Ernest King, the chief of Naval Operations, ordered U.S. naval forces to convoy merchant ships in the Atlantic—a clear violation of international law. Berlin protested the decision but without success. Grand Admiral Raeder urged Hitler to lift restrictions on attacks within the American neutrality zone, but Hitler refused to do so, recalling that submarine warfare was the main reason the United States entered World War I on the side of the Allies. Nevertheless, King's convoy orders put the U.S. Navy on a collision course with the U-boats, and it was only a matter of time before a major incident occurred. It took place on October 31, when the U.S. destroyer *Reuben James*, which was escorting Convoy HX 156, turned to investigate a suspicious direction-finding bearing. As it did so, it cut in front of Erich Topp's *U-552*, which fired a torpedo into her side. It must have struck the forward magazine, judging from the violence of the explosion, which blew away the entire forward part of the ship. The vessel sank within five minutes. As it went under, its depth charges detonated, killing several men in the water. Of the 160 man crew, only 45 survived. All of the officers were killed. Four destroyers quickly sailed to the scene, but the skillful Topp made good his escape. The incident outraged American opinion and U.S. President Franklin D. Roosevelt delivered a speech in which he called the U-boats "the rattlesnakes of the sea." He "forgot" to mention that the *Reuben James* was escorting a British convoy and was engaged in a depth-charge run against a U-boat when it was struck. In any event, the incident and the speech brought the U.S. considerably closer to war.

Despite the new American escorts, September 1941, was another good month for the U-boats. Total British losses that month were 54 ships (208,822 tons). Even more disturbing to London was the fact that 40 of the sunken ships had been traveling in convoy.

THE SECOND "HAPPY TIME"

October and November 1941 were not good months for the U-boats. Some of Doenitz's best commanders were now in the Mediterranean (on Hitler's orders), where British defenses were excellent, and total Allied losses were 31 ships in October (151,000 tons) and 12 ships in November (62,000 tons). "[I]t was almost as though death had declared a holiday in the North Atlantic," Edwin P. Hoyt wrote later.[5]

The holiday ended on December 7, 1941, when the Japanese attacked the American Pacific Fleet base at Pearl Harbor. The following day, Grand Admiral Raeder told Doenitz that Hitler had rescinded his restrictions on sinking American shipping; however, due to the fact that the Germans had less prior warning about the Pearl Harbor attack than did the Americans, Doenitz was not prepared to do anything about it.

On December 8, Doenitz had 91 U-boats in his fleet, but the standard Type VII U-boat was not suitable to make the long voyage to the United States. Only the 740-ton Type IX C could stay out six full weeks, which would give it a combat patrol of about two weeks off the American coast. It would be the third week of December before the first Type IX C was ready to make the two-week trip to American waters, but Doenitz wanted a more concentrated effort. This was not achieved until the first week in January 1942, when he had 16 U-boats en route to Canada, the United States, and the Caribbean to begin the next phase of the war. Doenitz called it Operation *Paukenschlag* (Drum Beat).

The United States was utterly unprepared to participate in the Battle of the North Atlantic, but only Rear Admiral Adolphus Andrews, the commander of the Eastern Sea Frontier, seemed worried. Since December 7, he had gathered a strange collection of 20 ships and 100 obsolete airplanes to guard a coastline of 1,500 miles. Most of his ships were tugs, yachts, and fishing boats that could not even mount a depth-charge apparatus. Not one of his ships had enough firepower to challenge the four-inch deck gun found on each U-boat. Admiral Andrews appealed to Admiral King for help. King sent him a handful of mine-layers, but, in general, ignored his appeal.

The first attack came on January 12, 1942, when Lieutenant Reinhard Hardegen in *U-123* torpedoed the British passenger steamer Cyclops (9,000 tons) 300 miles off the coast of Cape Cod. The next day, Commander Ernst Kals in *U-130* sank two steamers in the Gulf of St. Lawrence. Hardegen scored again on January 14, when he sank the tanker *Norness* 60 miles off of Montauk Point, Long Island. The next day he sank the tanker *Coimbra*, followed on the 17th by the steamer *San Jose*. On January 18, Commander Richard Zapp (*U-66*) sank the tanker *Allan Jackson*, and the following day Lieutenant Hardegen sank three more ships (including the tanker *Malay*) and damaged a fourth with his last torpedo. Kals "beat the drum" again on January 21, when he sank the tanker *Alexander Hoegh* south of Cape Breton. Hardegen, meanwhile, surfaced and sank the 3,000-ton freighter *Culebra* with his deck gun. He then returned to Lorient and told Admiral Doenitz that he should rush submarines and minelayers to U.S. waters to take advantage of the unprepared Americans.

Kals, meanwhile, sank six ships (four of them tankers) on his first American patrol and damaged a fifth tanker with his deck gun. After sinking the *Allan Jackson*, Commander Zapp sank another tanker and three freighters. Lieutenant Heinrich Bleichrodt followed and sank three freighters and the Canadian tanker *Montrolite* (11,000 tons), and Lieutenant Ulrich Folker (*U-125*) sank a steamer and damaged the tanker *Olney*. All totaled, the first five U-boats to enter American waters sank more than 150,000 tons of shipping, including several vital tankers. From a loss of 23 ships (102,000 tons) in December 1941, Allied losses jumped to 50 ships (288,000 tons) in January 1942.

Admiral Andrews attempted to confuse the next wave of U-boats by rerouting the shipping lanes, but it did not work: *U-106* (Lieutenant Hermann Rasch) sank five ships, *U-103* (Lieutenant Commander Werner Winter) downed four, and *U-107* (Lieutenant Harald Gelhaus) accounted for three. Andrews still did not have enough ships to provide escorts for even two convoys, so the carnage continued. Only one U-boat was sunk in the Atlantic in January, and it was destroyed by a British ship. Losses were not strictly limited to American waters, however. Erich Topp and Lieutenant Johannes Oesterman (*U-552* and *U-754*, respectively) sank four ships in the Gulf of St. Lawrence area, and Captain Wolfgang Lueth in *U-43* sank four ships (21,307 tons) in three days of the Irish coast.[6] Meanwhile, Doenitz discovered that Type VII U-boats could operate briefly off of the U.S. coast if they were stripped of amenities and given additional fuel. At the end of January 1942, however, Hitler's intuition acted up again, and he ordered that all U-boats be stationed off of the coast of Norway, to meet an anticipated Allied invasion. Doenitz managed to get him to reduce the number to eight, which left him 20 operational U-boats for the North Atlantic.

Admiral King was extremely slow—almost criminally slow—in providing Admiral Andrews with warships to serve as convoy escorts. As of March, he only had two destroyers *on loan*, at a time when the U.S. Atlantic Fleet alone had 73 destroyers available. With the greatest diplomacy, the British advised their American cousins that the solution to their losses was the convoy system, but their advice and long experience in anti-submarine warfare was lost on Admiral King, who hated the British intensely. He ignored their suggestions. Of the 50 Allied ships sunk in January, only two were traveling in convoy. Still King refused to adopt the convoy system. American politicians were also of no help, as usual. When Admiral Andrews recommended that a blackout be imposed on the cities along the Atlantic coast, he reaped a storm of protest and criticism, especially from Miami and Atlantic City. The lights of the cities continued to burn brightly, clearly outlining the silhouettes of unescorted ships for the eager U-boat commanders. As a result, in February, Doenitz's captains, supplemented by a few Italian submarines, sank 71 ships—384,000 tons of shipping—including 23 of the vital tankers.

Typically, Admiral King tried to shift the blame for the losses to the British and accused the Royal Air Force of making insufficient efforts to destroy the U-boat bases along the Bay of Biscay. With superhuman diplomacy, Churchill swallowed this insult and ordered the Bomber Command to attack Doenitz's bases. During the past year, however, the Todt Organization had been building remarkable "U-boat pens" at Lorient, La Pallice, and other harbors. Earlier, the Royal Navy had suggested that the pens be destroyed while they were being constructed, but Bomber Command resisted the idea; now that they were finished, it was too late. Their walls and roofs were made of reinforced concrete and were 20-feet thick. Over the next three years, British and American bombers would drop hundreds of tons of bombs on the submarine pens, but to no avail: they were completely bombproof. They continued to provide shelter for the submariners until they were physically occupied by American infantrymen in 1944.

Meanwhile, the Axis submarine aces continued to sink American ships. Lieutenant Hardegen made another foray in March, sank seven more ships, and damaged three. Lieutenant Ernst Bauer also sank seven ships and damaged three more. Commander Feeia di Cossato, captain of the Italian submarine *Tazzoli*, sank six ships in March. By now, too many oil slicks and dead bodies had washed up on American beaches, and so many surviving sailors had reported that their ships had been silhouetted by lights from cities, that Lieutenant General Hugh Drum, the commander of the U.S. Army's Eastern Defense Command, ordered a blackout. In the meantime, Franklin D. Roosevelt had finally gotten enough of Admiral King's stubbornness, so he summoned the naval chief to the White House and ordered him to adopt the convoy system. On March 16, King relayed the order to his subordinates but only furnished Andrews with three destroyers. Andrews was thus forced to convoy without escorts, which defeated the purpose of having a convoy in the first place.

On March 17, five U.S. tankers and several merchant ships steamed up the American Atlantic coast. That night, near Cape Hatteras, they were ambushed by Lieutenant Commander Johann Mohr in *U-124*, who quickly torpedoed and sank four of them. By now, Admiral Andrews was virtually begging King for help, and the U.S. Petroleum Industry War Council estimated that the United States would be out of oil in six months unless something were done to improve the situation. Still Admiral King refused to give Andrews any more destroyers.

In March 1942, the U-boats sank 79 ships. The amount of tonnage sunk in American waters exceeded that of January and February combined. Allied shipping losses in the first quarter of the year totaled an astonishing 1.2 million tons—and half of the losses were tankers. Things did not get any better during the first week of April, when seven more tankers were sent to the bottom of the sea. The situation was gradually improving, however. The first British anti-submarine trawlers arrived in U.S. waters that week, finally giving Admiral Andrews a reasonably effective anti-submarine weapon. Most important, however, was the fact that the Americans finally adopted the convoy system in April—and these convoys were closely escorted by destroyers and patrol vessels and covered by airplanes. As a result of these measures, shipping losses off the American coast fell to 400,000 tons in April—100,000 less than the previous month. This figure is somewhat deceiving, however, because the overwhelming majority of the losses occurred in the first two weeks of the month. After the armed convoy system was adopted, shipping losses off of the U.S. coast fell dramatically.

Not only were American losses down—they were beginning to attack the U-boats with effectiveness. In June and July, Doenitz lost three U-boats to American escorts. This represented one-third of the U-boats operating between Halifax and Cape Hatteras. As a result, Doenitz shifted the focus of his operations to the Caribbean, where the Allies still did not have enough escorts to adopt the convoy system. Doenitz's strategic and operational concepts remained the same: the key to naval victory lay in tonnage sunk, no matter where. This could best be accomplished by finding "soft spots," where Allied merchant ships sailed unescorted or without air cover. This pattern would continue until Allied skill and technology eliminated *all* of the soft spots and finally defused the U-boat threat.

NOTES

1. Porten, pp. 175–76.
2. Kretschmer later became an admiral in the West German Navy.
3. Barrie Pitt and the editors of Time-Life Books, *The Battle of the Atlantic* (1980), p. 125 (hereafter cited as Pitt et al.).
4. Hoyt, *U-Boat Wars*, pp. 120–21.
5. Ibid., p. 132.
6. Juergen Rohwer, *Axis Submarine Successes, 1939–1945* (1983), pp. 74–75.

CHAPTER XXXIX

THE BOMBINGS BEGIN, 1942

While the bulk of the Luftwaffe was engaged on the Russian Front, the Royal Air Force recovered from the Battle of Britain. It began to bomb Germany in earnest in the fall of 1941, but it lacked the strength to make a real dent in the German war economy. British bomber losses were also high. In August 1941, it lost 107 airplanes in 18 nights. It lost another 153 in September and 108 more in October. Despite these losses, the British raids were of little more than nuisance value. Frequently, the British bombers missed their target cities altogether. There were actually cases in which the German civilians came out into the streets to watch the free fireworks displays, as the Royal Air Force dropped bombs all over the countryside. From October to December 1941, almost half of the British bombs dropped against Germany fell on open ground and another 17 percent struck dummy installations.[1]

Five events fundamentally changed the air war in the West. First, the Americans entered the war and supplied Bomber Command with Lockhead Venturas and Douglas Bostons, allowing them to replace the obsolete and disliked Bristol Blenheims. Second, British industry began to manufacture Avro Lancasters, which replaced the twin-engine Manchesters and Handley Page Halifaxes. Third, the British developed "Gee"—a navigation system that used radio pulses from three transmitting stations to guide bombers to their targets at night. Fourth, the Royal Air Force abandoned the concept of pinpoint bombing in favor of area bombing. Finally, on February 20, 1942, Air Marshal Sir Arthur Harris replaced Air Marshal Sir Richard Peirse as commander-in-chief of Bomber Command. "Bomber" Harris was a tough, blunt, and uncompromising advocate of strategic bombing. His stated objective was to create a large bomber force and to pulverize the cities of

Figure 39.1
German Cities, 1942

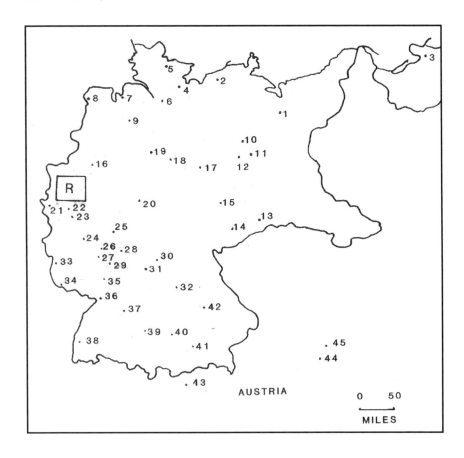

Germany until German morale collapsed and the Third Reich capitulated. His first target was Luebeck, which Harris chose because it was "built more like a fire-lighter than a human habitation."[2] Its wooden buildings were built close together, especially in the *Altstadt*, the medieval center of the town. Also, the city was known to be lightly defended.

On the night of March 28–29, 1942, 234 airplanes from Bomber Command dropped 144 tons of HE and 160 tons of incendiaries on the town. In 90 minutes, 320 people were killed and 791 were wounded, and some 200 acres of buildings were destroyed—about half of the old city. In the suburbs, another 2,000 homes were destroyed or damaged beyond repair.[3] "The British have completely destroyed Luebeck," one woman wrote to her brother, a private on the Eastern Front. She

GERMAN CITIES, 1942

1. Stettin	26. Wiesbaden
2. Rostock	27. Mainz
3. Koenigsberg	28. Frankfurt/Main
4. Luebeck	29. Darmstad
5. Kiel	30. Schweinfurt
6. Hamburg	31. Wursburg
7. Bremerhaven	32. Nuremberg
8. Wilhelmshaven	33. Trier
9. Bremen	34. Saarbruecken
10. Oranienburg	35. Mannheim
11. Berlin	36. Karlsruhe
12. Potsdam	37. Stuttgart
13. Dresden	38. Freiburg
14. Chemnitz	39. Ulm
15. Leipzig	40. Augsburg
16. Muenster	41. Munich
17. Magdeburg	42. Regensburg
18. Brunswick	43. Innsbruck
19. Hanover	44. Wiener-Neustadt
20. Kassel	45. Vienna
21. Aachen	R. The Ruhr (including Essen,
22. Cologne	Bochum, Geisenkirchen, Dortmund,
23. Bonn	Oberhausen, Wuppertal, Elberfeld,
24. Koblenz (Coblenz)	Duesseldorf and others)
25. Gieseen	

informed him that she had evacuated their parents to another city and added, "We are lucky to still be alive. I simply can't tell you how it all happened. Everywhere there was groaning and moaning.... The whole city was one mass of flame. There is not a single street left in Luebeck, no water, no light, no gas. Everybody is grief-stricken."[4]

Harris lost only a dozen bombers in the attack. Figure 39.1 shows the location of Luebeck and most of the other major cities that were subjected to major aerial bombardments in 1942, 1943, 1944, and 1945.

The raid on Luebeck was followed by raids against the Baltic Sea port of Rostock on four consecutive nights, from April 23 to 27. Also an ancient city and lightly defended, Rostock was devastated. The Royal Air Force employed 468 bombers, many of which were new Lancasters (carrying six tons of bombs). Sixty percent of all houses in the town were destroyed, 100,000 of Rostock's 140,000 residents were left homeless, the center of the city was reduced to rubble, and the Heinkel plant was severely damaged.[5] Two hundred four people were killed and 89 were seriously injuried.[6] Goebbels called the raid "terror bombing."

The *Terrorangriffen* (terror attacks) reached new heights on the night of May 30–31, when the Royal Air Force conducted its first thousand-bomber raid of the war. The attackers reached Cologne shortly after midnight and dropped 1,500 tons of bombs on the city—including 8,300 small incendiary ("stick") bombs, plus HE, phosphorus, fire bomb canisters, and heavy mine bombs. Their targets were not the Rhine River port facilities or the armaments factories in the area, nor the military bases nearby. They aimed for the heart of the city. Entire streets were wiped out and about 12,000 fires were started. The mixture of bombs was devastating. The high-explosive bombs blocked streets, so fire engines could not get to many of the burning buildings. Some 18,500 buildings were destroyed, 9,500 heavily damaged, and 31,000 partially damaged; 36 factories were destroyed and 70 more were seriously damaged. Four hundred eighty-six civilians were killed, 5,000 wounded, and 100,000 left homeless—more than 59,000 of them permanently so.[7] The entire raid had taken only 90 minutes. As at Luebeck and Rostock, the Luftwaffe's air defense had proven inadequate at Cologne. Of the 1,046 bombers involved, only 40 were shot down: 3.8 percent of the total. Bomber Command did not consider this loss excessive,[8] so the raids continued.

General Karl Bodenschatz, the Reichsmarschall's liaison officer to Fuehrer Headquarters, later testified at Nuremberg that the Cologne raid caused Goering's first serious loss of prestige with Hitler. He said:

From that moment on there were differences of opinion between Hitler and Goering which became more serious as time went on. The outward symptoms of this waning influence were as follows: first, the Fuehrer criticized Goering most severely; second, the endless conversations between Adolf Hitler and Hermann Goering became shorter, less frequent, and finally ceased altogether.[9]

Hitler did not react to the bombings by significantly strengthening the defenses of the Reich; he ordered reprisal raids against Great Britain instead. He brought the He-111 Pathfinder bomber wing (KG 100) back from the Eastern Front and two bomber groups from Sicily (weakening the effort against Malta) and assigned them to Major General Joachim Coeler's IX Air Corps, which was ordered to conduct vengeance raids, in addition to its regular mine-laying duties. Some 39 reprisal raids were conducted against Britain in the seven months after Rostock, but with little result.

The air defense of the Reich from March 21, 1942, to December 23, 1943, was the responsibility of Luftwaffe Colonel General Hubert Weise, an anti-aircraft artillery expert who had commanded a flak corps on the Western Front in 1940. His Luftwaffe Command Center (later redesignated Air Fleet Reich) included the fighter units stationed in Germany and the flak units in the Luftgaue. The Flak gun (*Fliegerabwehrkanone* or anti-aircraft cannon) was not a particularly effective weapon against aircraft. To hit its target, a flak gun crew had to know (or correctly guess) the exact altitude, speed, and direction of its target. Since one cubic mile of airspace contains 5.5 million cubic yards, and the killing zone of an 88-millimeter shell burst covered only a few thousand yards for one-fiftieth of a second, it took a well-trained and experienced gun crew to bring down an enemy bomber. The vast majority of these crews were heavily engaged on the Russian Front. Many of the flak guns in the Reich were manned by inexperienced 15, 16, and 17 year olds. As a result, German anti-aircraft fire was not accurate. During the war, it took an average of 3,400 heavy anti-aircraft shells to bring down a single enemy airplane.[10] Enemy bomber formations were decimated only when they ran into the heaviest concentrations. General Weise's main weapon against the Allied bombers was Joseph Kammhuber's XII Air Corps: the night fighters. With the bulk of the Luftwaffe's Me-109s and Me-110s engaged in Russia, however, few fighters could be spared for the defense of the Reich, so the Royal Air Force continued to press home its attacks against limited opposition.

The bombs continued to fall on Germany throughout 1942, although only two more thousand-bomber raids were launched that year. A major attack on Essen, the home of the Krupp works, was unsuccessful. Another massive raid, this one featuring 1,046 airplanes, was flown on the night of June 25–26. Its target was Bremen, especially the Focke-Wulf aircraft factory there. The plant was hit by a 4,000-pound bomb and suffered considerable damage, but because of an abrupt change in wind direction, the cloud cover did not clear as British meteorologists expected, the bombs were scattered, and the raid was not very successful.[11]

After Bremen, 32 more major raids were launched against 19 different targets, including Bremen (five raids), Duisburg (four raids), and Essen, Hamburg, and Emden (two raids each).[12] Although several fighter groups had been transferred from Russia (where they were badly needed) to the Reich, Bomber Command's impact on the German war effort had been minimal. Estimates of the total loss of the Reich's economic output due to the bombings vary from 0.7 percent to 2.5 percent of the total for 1942. Britain, on the other hand, had committed roughly 33 percent of her war economy to the prosecution of the air offensive.

Kammhuber's night fighters continued to expand (by the end of the year, he had 477 aircraft in three night fighter divisions) and began to enjoy success. By the end of 1942, the Royal Air Force had lost 2,859 aircraft in night operations and 627 British bombers had been lost in day-time raids over occupied Europe. In the last three months of the year, Bomber Command's losses exceeded 5 percent of its strength—the figure calculated as the maximum it could lose and still remain operational. Jeschonnek went so far as to say, "Every four-engine bomber the Western Allies build makes me happy, for we will bring these ... down just as we brought down the two-engine ones, and the destruction of a four-engine bomber constitutes a much greater loss to the enemy."[13]

Field Marshal Milch was worried, however. As the former head of Lufthansa, the German national airline, he had a much more international background than the typical air force general and a much greater appreciation of the capabilities of other nations. He understood that the military and industrial resources of the United States were about to come into full play in the air war and that, when combined with those of the British, it would overwhelm Germany's defenses. He could not get Goering or Hitler to listen to him on this vital issue, however. (As far as I know, Adolf Hitler only commented favorably on four things American: the sky scraper, the Indian reservation, Prohibition, and the Ku Klux Klan. Goering added a fifth item: the safety razor.) All Hitler did was place the Gauleiters (now under the general supervision of Martin Bormann) in charge of the civil defense, and on November 16 named them senior Reich Defense Commissioners.

Reichsmarschall Goering was especially militant in refusing to believe that the United States was manufacturing a fraction of the aircraft that it was, in fact, producing. In 1942, he forbade his people to even mention the American production figures, which he considered to be a colossal bluff.[14] That same year Walter Schellenberg, the head of the SS Foreign Intelligence Service, presented him with a special (and accurate) report on American war production. "Everything you have written is utter nonsense," Goering told him. "You should have a psychiatrist examine your mental condition."[15]

Meanwhile, pregnant events were occurring in Western Europe. On June 15, 1942, U.S. Air Force General Carl Spaatz arrived in England to take charge of the U.S. 8th Air Force, which would direct the American heavy (strategic) bombers in the air war against the Third Reich. On August 17, 1942, 18 American Boeing B-17E "Flying Fortresses," personally led by General Ira Eaker, bombed Rouen-Sotteville, France, and returned to England without loss. It was the modest beginning of the U.S. Air Force's daylight bombing operations in Europe. Convinced that unescorted daylight bombing could be successful if the bombers were sufficiently well armed, the American four-engine bombers "bristled" with 0.50-caliber heavy machine guns and flew a formation designed for mutual defense and maximum combined firepower.[16] Although the Rouen raid was insignificant in itself, it argued ill for the future of the Luftwaffe in the West.

By the end of 1942, the Luftwaffe was in dire straits. Largely because of Udet's mismanagement and high losses on the Eastern Front, it was short 43 percent of its establishment in combat aircraft. It had started the war with 3,356 frontline combat aircraft, and by mid-1942 it had 4,800 frontline combat airplanes; by the end of the year, however, it had only 3,950 left. In addition (unlike the Allies), the Luftwaffe had failed to equip its units with aircraft significantly better than those with which they had entered the war. Only three new models had been introduced in appreciable numbers: the disappointing Ju-88, the FW-189 (a good short-range reconnaissance plane) and the FW-190 fighter—also a bit of a disappointment, because its performance deteriorated rapidly above 20,000 feet (that is, the altitudes at which bombers operated). The FW-190 also had teething problems and its air-cooling system problems were never fully solved. It was thus decided to employ the FW-190 on the Eastern Front and keep the old Me-109s in production; indeed, more Me-109s would be manufactured than any other aircraft in World War II.

In short, most of the warplanes of the Luftwaffe were obsolete by the end of 1942, and the combined air armaments industries of the United States, the United Kingdom, and the Soviet Union were vastly outproducing that of Nazi Germany. Most of the Luftwaffe's senior officers did not realize it yet, but they were on the brink of disaster. They were in for a shock in 1943 and 1944.

NOTES

1. Cooper, *GAF*, p. 185.
2. Sir Charles Webster and Noble Frankland, *The Strategic Air Offensive Against Germany, 1939–1945* (1961), vol. 2, pp. 392–93 (hereafter cited as Webster and Noble).
3. Ibid; Noble Frankland, *Bomber Offensive: The Devastation of Europe* (1970), pp. 42–43 (hereafter cited as Frankland).
4. *True to Type*, p. 131.
5. Goebbels *Diaries*, April 27, 1942.
6. Martin K. Sorge, *The Other Price of Hitler's War* (1986), p. 91.
7. Cooper, *GAF*, pp. 185–86; Earl R. Beck, *Under the Bombs* (1986), pp. 1–2 (hereafter cited as Beck, *Under the Bombs*).
8. Webster and Frankland, vol. 2, pp. 406–8.
9. Brett-Smith, p. 138.
10. Cooper, *GAF*, pp. 58 and 191.
11. Webster and Frankland, vol. 2, pp. 414–15.

12. Beck, *Under the Bombs*, p. 9.
13. Suchenwirth, "Command."
14. Galland, pp. 134–35.
15. Roger Manvell, *Goering* (1962), pp. 266–67.
16. Musciano, p. 57.

CHAPTER XL

HITLER'S SUMMER OFFENSIVE, 1942

IZYUM AND KHAKOV

Despite the terrible losses he suffered in the winter offensive of 1941–42, Stalin stubbornly refused to believe that he had lost the initiative and wanted to resume his attacks as soon as the water from the thaw had dried. He ordered offensives along the entire Eastern Front, from the Barents to the Black Seas, to take place between April and June. For his main effort, Stalin placed the Southwest Theater under the personal command of Marshal Timoshenko and ordered him to advance north, out of the Izyum Bulge, as soon as possible. The objectives of this operation would be the recapture of Kharkov and the defeat of the German 6th Army. Timoshenko's forces consisted of six armies and the Bobkin Armored Group, of which 23 rifle divisions, two cavalry divisions, and two cavalry corps were hurled against the 11 divisions of Paulus's 6th Army. Timoshenko had 640,000 men and 560 tanks, with some 700 in reserve, and more than 2,500 guns.

While the Russians completed their preparations, Field Marshal von Bock prepared to launch an offensive against the southern flank of the Izyum Bulge with the 1st Panzer and 17th Armies, both under the command of Ewald von Kleist, whose headquarters was temporarily designated *Armeegruppe* Kleist. Simultaneously, Paulus was to attack from the north, completing a double envelopment against the Red forces in the Izyum Bulge. This offensive, dubbed Operation Fridericus, was scheduled to begin on May 18. Timoshenko, however, struck first, launching his offensive on May 12. By May 14, Paulus had committed all of his reserves, and the entire 6th Army was falling back in the direction of Kharkov.

Bock wanted to commit all of the Fridericus forces against the Soviet spearheads, but Hitler boldly held back his reserves until Kleist was ready to launch a general offensive from the south. The Soviets were within 12 miles of Kharkov on May 17, when Kleist struck (24 hours ahead of his original schedule) with eight German infantry divisions, four Romanian infantry divisions, two panzer divisions, and a German motorized division. To everyone's surprise, the Soviet 9th Army collapsed immediately. Then, well supported by the IV Air Corps, III Panzer Corps and XXXXIV Corps broke through and marched 15 miles or more, covering two-thirds of the distance to Izyum on the first day of the attack. During the next two days, Kleist tore a 50-mile gap in the Soviet line and narrowed the neck of the Izyum Bulge to 15 miles, forcing even Stalin to react by withdrawing forces from the north and ordering them to the threatened sector—thus immediately taking the pressure off of the hard-pressed 6th Army. It was too late for the Russians to stave off disaster, however. On May 22, Kleist linked up with the 44th Infantry Division of 6th Army, sealing the Izyum Pocket and surrounding three Soviet armies and the Bobkin Group. The Reds launched a powerful breakout attempt on May 25. Primed with vodka, thousands of Soviet troops hurled themselves at the Germans, sometimes with their arms linked, screaming "Urra! Urra!" ("Hurrah! Hurrah!" or "Kill! Kill!"). They were mowed down in windrows. The pocket collapsed on the morning of May 28. Between them, Paulus and Kleist captured 240,000 men and destroyed or captured more than 1,200 tanks and 2,600 artillery pieces. General Fedor I. Kostenko, the commander of the Southwest Front, was among the dead, as were the commanders of the 6th and 57th Armies. The Germans suffered 20,000 casualties and Friedrich Paulus, the product of a lower-middle-class family and the ideal National Socialist general, was decorated with the Knight's Cross and hailed as a national hero for the first time.

THE BATTLES OF KERCH AND SEVASTOPOL

During February 1942, an ice bridge formed over the Kerch Strait, enabling the Soviets to transport a third army into the Kerch Peninsula, bringing the strength of General Dmitri T. Kozlov's Transcaucasus Front to more than 300,000 men, excluding the Sevastopol garrison, which was more than 106,000 strong. Clearing the Crimea was a major priority for the High Command of the Army, because its conquest would free an entire army for operations elsewhere. Bock felt that the 11th Army should conquer Sevastopol first and then clear the Kerch Peninsula; Manstein, however, believed that the stronger enemy should be dealt with first, so he would not be a threat to his rear during the assault on Sevastopol. Hitler agreed with the army commander, and, on March 31, Manstein issued his preliminary plans for Operation Trappenjagd ("Bustard Hunt"), the reconquest of the Kerch. As usual, Manstein was proven correct.

Colonel General von Manstein planned to commit five German infantry divisions and a panzer division to Operation Bustard Hunt, as well as three Romanian divisions. That left three German infantry divisions and two Romanian divisions to continue the siege of Sevastopol, against eight Soviet divisions and three brigades. In the Kerch, Manstein faced 17 rifle and two cavalry divisions, plus three rifle and four tank brigades.

Over the protests of the High Command of the Luftwaffe, Hitler ordered Richthofen's VIII Air Corps to the Crimea, to support Bustard Hunt. Since an air corps was normally used to support an army or an army group, Manstein's two corps (the XXXXII and XXX) were extremely well supported in this operation; in fact, air power made all the difference.

During the period just before the start of the battle, Manstein concentrated five of his six German divisions on the southern flank, under the command of General of Artillery Maximilian Fretter-Pico's XXX Corps, leaving the XXXXII Corps to screen the rest of the line with only one German and three Romanian divisions of marginal quality. This deployment was a bit of a gamble, but it worked out well for Manstein. The attack began at 3:15 A.M. on May 8, and was closely supported by dive-bombers and fighters. By 4 P.M., the Russians had been pushed back six miles; then Fretter-Pico committed his armor. The tanks of the 22nd Panzer Division quickly turned north, and, by nightfall on May 9, had reached the Sea of Azov and closed the pocket around two Soviet armies.

The German advance east was slowed by rain, but the completely disorganized Soviets put up only sporadic resistance. The port of Kerch fell during the afternoon of the 14th, and the last resistance was crushed on May 20. Manstein had destroyed three Soviet armies and taken 176,000 prisoners. About 120,000 disorganized Russian troops had escaped into the Kuban before Kerch was captured. Manstein then turned back toward Sevastopol—this time with his entire army.

For its final assault on Sevastopol, 11th Army was heavily reinforced with artillery. Its guns were directed by Harko 306 (*Hoeheres Artillerie Kommando* or the 306th Higher Artillery Command) and included a dozen 11-inch (280-millimeter) coastal howitzers, six Gamma and three Karl weapons, plus Dora. The Gammas, like the Karls, were superheavy mortars. They had a 17-inch (420-mililmeter) bore and fired a one-ton shell. The Karls fired a 1.5-ton shell and had to be assembled or disassembled with a special 75-ton crane, but they were small compared with Dora, which weighed 1,345 tons and needed a 60-car railroad train to move. It had a 107-foot-long barrel, a 31.5-inch (800-millimeter) bore and could lob a seven-ton shell up to 30 miles.[1] Dora was the most powerful piece of artillery in the world, and, including maintenance crews and security troops, it took 4,120 men to fire her. More conventionally, Manstein had more than 1,000 pieces of field artillery and was also given the 300th Panzer Battalion, which was equipped with Goliaths (remote-controlled demolition vehicles that could knock out a tank 50 yards away). Perhaps even more important than his artillery, however, was Manstein's air support: three Stukas, four fighter, and seven bomber wings of Richthofen's VIII Air Corps.

Manstein attacked at dawn on June 7, with Eric Hansen's LIV Corps (four divisions) on the north launching the main attack. The Sevastopol fighting was savage. Temperatures climbed to above 100° F, and the Germans suffered appalling casualties as the assault battalions slowly scratched their way forward against Red Army troops, Black Sea marines, and thousands of *Komsomols*—the teenage boys and girls of the Communist Union of Youth. The heavy artillery blasted the major fortresses, but the smaller positions—natural and manmade caves and bunkers—had to be taken by the infantry. After five days, 11th Army had already suffered more than 10,000 casualties, and Bock considered recalling the VIII Air Corps, but he did not. Finally, on June 17, Russian resistance suddenly began to deteriorate; six Soviet forts fell, and Hansen drove to the north shore of Severnaya Bay. The next day, while the LIV Corps battled against North Fort, XXX Corps pushed to Sapun Heights and faced the inner defenses of the fortress. Manstein wanted to stop and regroup, but Bock said that he had no time to do so: he needed VIII Air for the major offensives to the north (see section below).

Because of the weakened condition of his army, Manstein decided to gamble: after nightfall on June 28, his engineers silently eased 100 assault boats into Severnaya Bay. They were boarded by the men of the 22nd Air Landing and 24th Infantry Divisions, who rapidly crossed the 1,000 yards of water and landed in the enemy's rear, just east of the city. The Soviets, who were taken by surprise, were unable to counter the new threat, and many of the defending units collapsed entirely. Elsewhere, the fighting continued to be brutal, especially in the gun positions and in the caves under the cliffs overlooking the Black Sea. Rather than surrender, several commissars blew themselves up, along with their caves, their troops, and many women and children, who had taken refuge there. In other cases, soldiers, civilians, women, and children linked arms (so that no one could hold back) and rushed the German infantry, which mowed them down with their machine guns. Manstein, who had already lost 24,000 men, cleared the built-up areas in the city and the port by artillery and air attack, killing thousands of civilians but conserving his infantry strength. The remnants of the Soviet forces surrendered on July 4. Many of the last-ditch defenders refused to surrender and took to the caves, where they were buried alive by 11th Army engineers. In all, Manstein took more than 90,000 prisoners, and some Soviet sources place their total casualties as high as 150,000. Four hundred sixty-seven guns were captured or destroyed, along with 758 mortars, 26 tanks, 141 airplanes, and 155 anti-tank guns. Hitler was so delighted by this victory that he promoted Manstein to the rank of field marshal.[2]

After Sevastopol, Hitler abandoned his original plan to send the 11th Army into the Kuban; instead, he scattered it to the four winds. The 22nd Air Landing Division was sent to Crete, while other divisions were sent to Army Groups Center or South. The XXXXII Corps remained in the Crimea. Manstein and his headquarters were sent to Army Group North for an attack against Leningrad, but only four infantry divisions accompanied him. This needless loss of a complete army formation would be sorely felt in the days ahead.

THE WEHRMACHT IN 1942

Although it had lost relatively little territory during the winter battles of 1941–42, the German Army of 1942 was a far cry from the one that had crossed into the Soviet Union so confidently in June 1941. Its losses in men and equipment had been tremendous, and its civilian-based industry was insufficient to replace its losses. It had lost more than 2,000 panzers and assault guns since Barbarossa began, but less than one-third of these had been replaced. Losses in trucks and motorized vehicles totaled almost 75,000, but only 7,500 had been replaced. The deficit was so great that Halder had almost completely demotorized the infantry divisions. More than 179,000 horses had died, but only 20,000 replacements could be secured. The Wehrmacht had lost nearly 7,000 artillery pieces on the Eastern Front, and only a fraction of them could be replaced. Virtually the entire class of 1922 had been drafted, and the armies on the Eastern Front had received 1.1 million replacements since June 22, 1941, but they were still short 625,000 men as of May 1, 1942. As of July 1, 1942, the German Army had 2,847,000 men in the East, as compared with 3,206,000 on June 22, 1941.[3] The shortages were especially serious in the infantry. Army Groups North and Center had only 35 percent of their original infantry strength, and Army Group South had only 50 percent of its June 21, 1941 infantry strength. In the spring of 1942, therefore, Hitler could only hope to launch a major offensive in only one sector, and he chose to attack in the south. Halder proposed disbanding 11 divisions to bring the others up to strength, but Hitler refused to do so, on the grounds that such a move would have a bad effect on the morale of the German soldiers and their allies and would encourage the enemy. The flaw in this reasoning was that the understrength divisions were now completely out of balance. They had full strength or nearly full strength staffs, headquarters, support units, and service units, but the infantry regiments—which naturally had suffered the majority of the casualties—had few riflemen left. After the failure of Stalin's winter offensive of 1941–42, the strength of the average German infantry company was reduced from 180 to 80. (The combat value of the typical German infantry company, however, did not decline by a corresponding percentage because of the effective organizational structures of the smaller companies and because the number of automatic weapons and machine guns in the smaller units were markedly increased.) Many of the veteran divisions, however, were forced to reorganize their infantry regiments, which were reduced from nine to six infantry battalions each. By July 1942, there were 29 more divisions on the Eastern Front than in June 1941, but the German strength in Russia had fallen by 359,000 men.[4] As a result, the German divisions earmarked for Operation Blue (as Hitler's summer offensive of 1942 was codenamed) could be brought up to strength in terms of manpower only by reducing the divisions of Army Groups North and Center to 50 percent of their authorized establishment or less; the training time for the replacements sent to these army groups was reduced from six to two months. The panzer divisions of Army Group South were brought up to a strength of three tank battalions each, but the panzer divisions of the other army groups were cut to a strength of only one or two tank battalions. Even so, the spearhead divisions of Army Group South would attack with only 85 percent of their authorized vehicle strength and only 80 percent of their authorized tank strength.[5] The artillery battalions of Army Group South could only be brought up to strength via similar measures; the artillery batteries of Army Groups North and Center had to be reduced from four to three guns, and many of these were obsolete or captured pieces. In short, the number of divisions in the German Wehrmacht was now a misleading statistic because the combat power of many of them (and eventually almost all of them) no longer warranted the term. In addition, the divisions created after the spring of 1942 would be much weaker than divisions formed previously.[6]

To make matters worse, as Milward wrote, "The whole mechanism of distributing arms at the front was faulty."[7] Newly formed divisions got 90 percent of all the newly manufactured (and best) weapons and equipment; the veteran divisions got 10 percent. Naturally, the new divisions suffered heavier losses in their first battle than the experienced units, resulting in an unnecessarily high loss of new weapons and equipment, while the veteran infantry regiments struggled along with worn-out and outmoded guns, equipment, and vehicles.

One potential source of manpower shunned by Hitler and the Nazis was the Eastern volunteer. Some enterprising German generals were recruiting and forming ad hoc Eastern battalions as early as the summer of 1941. By the spring of 1942, German forces had "absorbed" an estimated 700,000 former Red Army soldiers into their ranks, including 4,000 officers. Ultimately, more than 1 million Eastern volunteers (many of them former Soviet soldiers) joined the German Army, mostly as "Hiwis" (*Hilfsfreiwillige* or auxiliary volunteers).[8] Hitler disapproved of recruiting these "racially inferior" volunteers and, on February 10, 1942, issued an order forbidding further recruitment. This order was not strictly observed in some places and other commands ignored it altogether. By the summer of 1942, Soviet prisoners of war and volunteers made up 15 percent of the personnel of some divisions. Many were used only as auxiliaries at first (that is, as cooks, mess hall helpers, drivers, stretcher bearers, and so on) but were later used more and more as combat troops. As a result, Hitler issued another order in June 1942, stating that no further units of this type were to be formed after August 1.[9] Again his order was largely ignored, especially by Colonel General Ewald von Kleist (the Prussian ex-cavalryman who now commanded the 1st Panzer Army), who continued to form large numbers of Cossack cavalry battalions and to use them most effectively.

Despite the continued "illegal" recruitment of Hiwis, the Axis forces in the East had a strength of only 3,010,370 men as of September 20, 1942. They were opposed by 4,255,840 Soviet troops, even after the Red Army suffered appalling losses in 1941 and 1942 (see Table 40.1). In

Table 40.1
The Odds on the Eastern Front, September 20, 1942

Unit	Axis Forces	Soviet Forces
Army Group North	708,400	1,001,610
Army Group Center	1,012,070	1,356,340
Army Group B[b]	818,250	1,379,300
Army Group A[b]	266,350	518,590
TOTALS	3,013,370[a]	4,255,840

Notes:
[a]Ration Strength only. Ration strength was an estimated 250,000 men higher than actual combat strength.
[b]Formed when Army Group South was divided on July 7, 1943.
Source:
Earl F. Ziemke, *Stalingrad to Berlin* (1968), pp. 34–35.

addition, the Russians would receive 1.4 million men from its recruiting class of 1925—three times the number Germany would receive. Quantitatively, the odds against the Wehrmacht on the Eastern Front were already growing long.[10] Morale in the Wehrmacht, however, remained quite high. Having held off the Soviet threat in the winter, the Germans felt that they had proven that they could defeat the enemy at its best.

On the other side of the line, Stalin was much less hesitant than Hitler to convert to a total war economy. During the first half of 1942, the Soviet industry turned out more than 53,000 pieces of artillery, compared with 30,000 in the last six months of 1941. Airplane output remained steady at 8,300, but tank production increased to 11,200 during the first half of 1942—almost four times the German output of 3,000 over the same period. By the spring of 1942, Stalin had 5.6 million men in his armed forces and could field 348 rifle or cavalry divisions, 239 rifle or independent tank brigades, and 329 independent regiments (excluding 10 armies in Stavka reserve). By the time the spring offensive began, he had 6,000 tanks, 55,600 guns, and about 3,000 modern combat aircraft. Hitler, on the other hand, had 3.9 million men in the ground forces (excluding Allies), of which 2.6 million were on the Eastern Front; 212,000 in occupied Russia; 150,000 in Finland; and 1.3 million in the Replacement Army, in occupied Europe, or in North Africa. These figures exclude allied forces, which were as follows: Finnish, 300,000; Romanian, 330,000; Hungarian, 70,000; Italian, 68,000; Slovakian, 28,000; and Spanish volunteers, 14,000.[11] Most of the allied formations, however, were of limited value at best, except for the Finns and Spaniards.

Meanwhile, the Luftwaffe was also having serious problems. First, it had lost its numerical parity. From July to December 1941 alone, Russian factories turned out 5,173 fighters, British factories produced 4,408 fighters, and the Americans manufactured even more, but German factories could produce only 1,619 fighters for the Luftwaffe.[12]

Second, it had lost its technical advantage and was waging war with obsolete airplanes. Seeing the writing on the wall, Ernst Udet, the chief of air armaments, drank two bottles of cognac on November 17, 1941. He then telephoned his mistress in a state of hysteria. "I can't stand it any longer!" he cried, and shot himself. (The fact that he had learned about the Holocaust three days before was a major contributing factor to his despair; Ernst Udet may have been incompetent, but he was no monster.) He was officially reported as having been killed in a crash while testing a new airplane. Goering cried like a small child at Udet's funeral, but later blamed him for the destruction of the Luftwaffe.

Erhard Milch succeeded Udet in all of his offices and took energetic measures to restore the Luftwaffe to its former position, but he could not make good on four years lost to mismanagement and neglect. For the air force, the future looked grim indeed. In mid-1942, for example, as it prepared for the summer offensive, the Luftwaffe's strength in the East stood at 2,750 combat airplanes, out of a total of 4,262 in the entire air force. More than 64 percent of the Luftwaffe's combat aircraft were now on the Eastern Front, and the Red Air Force still outnumbered it at least three to one.[13]

Even to reach this strength, General Jeschonnek, the chief of the General Staff of the Luftwaffe, had to dip into the training establishment once more. This time he sent fighter training units and their instructor pilots to the front. Adolf Galland, who had succeeded the late Werner Moelders as the general of fighter forces,[14] protested this decision and called on the chief of the Air General Staff to increase the number of fighter training units, instead of decreasing them. "If you reduce them now instead of forcing them up, you are sawing off the branch on which you are sitting," he warned. General Jeschonnek listened quietly, without interrupting. He did not question the validity of Galland's arguments. When he had finished, Jeshonnek spoke "without vehemence, presumption, or demagogy." He told the new general of fighters that he understood the seriousness of his decision, but the rapid annihilation of the Soviet Union was an essential prerequisite for the continuation of the war. This was the Fuehrer's goal for the summer offensive of 1942, and all forces, including the Luftwaffe, now had to be concentrated for this decisive blow. "He was fully aware of the deathly crisis in which the Luftwaffe stood because of the war in the East," Galland recalled.[15] He also realized that, if the gamble failed, the Luftwaffe training branch probably would not be able to furnish enough replacement fighter pilots for the Western Front—or for the defense of the Reich. He sent the fighter squadrons east just the same. Victory over the Soviet Union in the summer offensive of 1942 had priority over all other considerations.

THE PLAN

In the meantime, Hitler, OKH, and Army Group South made the final plan for the decisive summer offensive of 1942, and it was complicated. Codenamed Operation Blue, (*Blau*), it would be carried out in four phases. Prior to its beginning, two preliminary operations, Operations Wilhelm and Fridericus II, would be executed. Wilhelm called for the 6th Army to cut off and destroy the Soviet 28th Army in what was left of the Volchansk salient. In Fridericus II, 1st Panzer Army was suppose to surround two Soviet armies north and east of Izyum. It would move 1st Panzer's front 30 miles further east, into its

Figure 40.1
Operation Blue: The Plan for the Summer Campaign of 1942

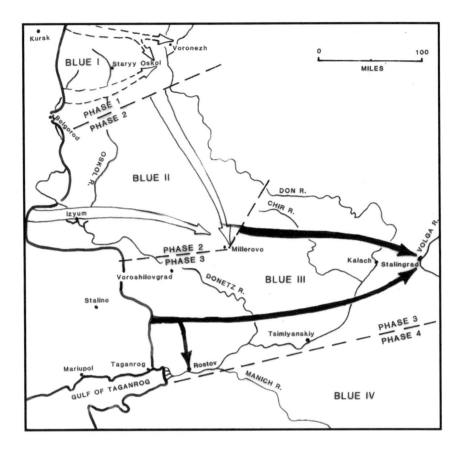

jump-off area for Blue. The plans for Blue I–III are shown on Figure 40.1. Just before Blue II began, Army Group A was to be activated under the command of Field Marshal List, and Bock's Army Group South would become Army Group B. Blue III was to conclude with the capture of Stalingrad. In Blue IV, the final phase of the offensive, Army Group A (lst Panzer, 4th Panzer, and 17th Armies) was to advance southeast, taking the Caucasus oil districts of Maikop and Grozny, and even seizing Baku, the oil city on the western shore of the Caspian Sea, which produced more than 70 percent of Russia's oil. This would secure Germany's oil resources and, according to Hitler, cripple the Soviet Union's war economy. The Caucasus was important because it produced valuable quantities of corn, manganese, and natural gas.

The Blue operations had two major objectives: the Caucasus oil districts and Stalingrad, a major industrial city on the Volga. Hitler, however, could not decide which had priority, or even which to take first. As the campaign developed, he decided to go for both, simultaneously. This would cause both advances immense difficulties and would eventually cause both to fail.

Operations Wilhelm and Fridericus II were both disappointing. Instead of stubbornly holding at all costs, as in previous battles, the Russians retreated rapidly, and most of them managed to escape before the Germans could close the jaws of the pockets. In Wilhelm, for example, 6th Army only captured a mere 24,800 prisoners, and Fridericus II yielded only 22,800 prisoners. The new Soviet tactics, which enabled them to avoid the costly defeats of 1941, were not properly appreciated by many of the German officers at the time. Sixth Army, for example, concluded that the Russian capacity for resistance had declined considerably, and Bock thought that the Soviets were going to avoid the risk of big defeats until the Americans intervened.[16]

OPERATION BLUE

Misfortune seemed to dog Operation Blue from the beginning. In direct violation of Hitler's standing orders, Major Joachim Reichel, the Ia (operations officer) of the 23rd Panzer Division, boarded a Fieseler Storch with a copy of the plan for the attack. The Storch strayed off course to the east, was fired on, and crashed two miles behind Russian lines. Several hours later, a German patrol found the airplane with a bullet hole in the fuel tank. Reichel and the pilot were missing. Two days later, another patrol found a grave containing two unidentified bodies. Reichel's papers had disappeared without a trace.

Furious over this incident, Hitler relieved Georg Stumme, the commander of the XXXX Panzer Corps; Lieutenant Colonel Gerhard Franz, his chief of staff; and Major General Baron Hans von Boineburg-Lengsfeld, the commander of the 23rd Panzer Division, of their posts. Bock protested against relieving commanders in critical posts on the eve of a great offensive, but to no avail. Baron Leo Geyr von Schweppenburg was named commander of the XXXX. Stumme and Franz were both court-martialed. Hermann Goering presided and was impressed with the pair; they were given minimal sentences of five and two years' fortress imprisonment, respectively.

Operation Blue began at 2:15 A.M. on June 28. By noon, Hoth's spearhead, General of Panzer Troops Werner Kempf's XXXXVIII Panzer Corps, had gained 10 miles. It gained another 10 that afternoon and crossed the Kshen the next day. By this time, however, the Soviets were retreating rapidly. Meanwhile, on June 30, Paulus began his offensive (Blue II). By the end of the day, his spearheads had reached the Korocha River—20 miles behind the Russian front. By July 1, the Soviets were in full retreat. The next day, the 4th Panzer Army linked up with the 6th Army near Staryy Oskol, but the pockets yielded only a few thousand prisoners.

By July 4, Hoth (who had traded places with Ruoff and was now commander of the 4th Panzer Army) had crossed the Don, and the 24th Panzer Division seized Voronezh by coup de main on July 6, taking 28,000 prisoners and capturing 1,000 tanks.[17] Hitler and Halder, however, were both unhappy with Bock's conduct of the operation. Hitler had intended that the infantry of the 2nd Army should occupy the Don River line, while the armored units pushed rapidly southward—not toward Voronezh, which lay almost due east. Hitler felt that Bock and Hoth had concentrated too much armor on their northern flank and were engaging in a mindless "stampede" toward the city, and Halder agreed with the dictator.[18] On the 5th, the Fuehrer signaled Bock and asked why the XXXX Panzer Corps had not yet reached the Don. The field marshal tactlessly (and untruthfully) replied that it was behind schedule largely because its two best generals had been fired in the Reichel affair. Meanwhile, the divisions of the Soviet Southwest Front were retreating all along 6th Army's front, and Bock's armor, instead of being in position to cut them off as planned, was far to the north.

It does seem that Field Marshal von Bock was obsessed with Voronezh and a possible threat to his left flank, and he was not reassured on July 6, when the Soviet 5th Tank Army counterattacked near the city. The Russian frontal attacks were conducted without skill, and the 9th Panzer Division destroyed two Soviet tank brigades in a single battle. Even so, the Reds committed nine rifle divisions, four rifle brigades, and seven tank brigades to the fighting. The Voronezh sector was not secure until July 13.

Because the German armor piled up around Voronezh, two Soviet armies escaped and Blue I produced a disappointing total of only 70,000 prisoners. Meanwhile, Blue II was also progressing unsatisfactorily, because the Russians were retreating almost everywhere, avoiding the German pincer movements. As early as the afternoon of July 8, Bock signaled Halder that Blue II was "dead," and if the armies advanced in accordance with their existing orders, they would "most likely strike into thin air."[19] In the meantime, an impatient Hitler ordered 1st Panzer and 4th Panzer Armies to encircle Millerovo. Bock was right: the encirclement yielded only about 40,000 prisoners. The most remarkable (and prophetic) catch was 22 trainloads of American and British lend-lease tanks and other supplies. In the meantime, 2nd and 6th Armies were also experiencing a lack of success. By mid-July, they had taken only 30,000 prisoners.[20]

On July 7, Army Group A was activated, but it was too late to cut off the Russian forces west of the Don. Even so, Hitler desperately ordered a giant encirclement north of Rostov and the mouth of the Don, disregarding Halder's advise and his own previous plans to advance on Stalingrad. On July 13, Hoth's 4th Panzer Army was transferred to the newly activated Army Group A, which was charged with conducting the Don encirclement. At the same time, Field Marshal Keitel telephoned von Bock and sacked him, on the grounds that his mobile divisions had been too slow in coming down from Voronezh, because of poor fuel arrangements. Bock protested, correctly pointing out that fuel supplies were an OKH responsibility, but Keitel informed him that the decision had been Hitler's, and discussion at the moment was out of the question. He suggested that Bock retire quietly and implied that he might be employed again. (He never was.) Bock was succeeded by Colonel General Baron Maximilian von Weichs, and General of Infantry Hans von Salmuth took over 2nd Army.

On the night of July 13–14, Army Groups A and B received their new orders, which were aimed at preventing the Soviets from escaping south and east of the Don. Stalingrad, the original Blue III objective, was not even mentioned. It was already too late, however, and all Hitler accomplished was the recapture of Rostov (on July 23), the capture of 83,000 prisoners (an insufficient number, compared with the hauls of 1941), and a giant pileup of German forces along the lower Don. On July 19, therefore, Hitler ordered 1st Panzer and 4th Panzer Armies to cross the lower Don between Rostov and Zimlyanskaya on a front 125 miles wide. Army Group A was ordered to pursue and destroy the Russian armies and to occupy the Black Sea coast (an entirely new strategic objective), to eliminate the bases and ports of the Soviet Black Sea Fleet. List's armies were to simultaneously seize the Maikop and Grozny oilfields, and prepare to continue on to Baku—700 miles southeast of Rostov. Hoth's 4th Panzer Army also received a new task: cover the gap between Army Group A (advancing south) and Army Group B (slowly advancing east)—a gap of several hundred miles and growing, since the two army groups were advancing on divergent axes. Hoth was assigned to Army Group B at this time. Meanwhile, to direct the campaign in southern Russia, Hitler moved his headquarters from East Prussia to Vinnitsa in the western Ukraine on July 14.

THE CAUCASUS CAMPAIGN

While Hitler was driving south, the Russians rallied for the defense of Stalingrad. Tens of thousands of civilian workers prepared Stalingrad for defense by constructing three lines of defensive works around the western half of the city; the outer line was almost 300 miles in length. More than 80 home guard and workers' battalions were organized and sent to the front.

All of this feverish Soviet activity was, for the moment at least, unnecessary. Paulus's 6th Army was the only German formation within striking distance of the city, and, since Army Group A had absolute priority for supply, it was soon so short of fuel and ammunition that Paulus pulled back his spearheads on July 26. The change of focus did not please Field Marshal List, the commander-in-chief of Army Group A. He was more than 700 miles from his final objective, and the width of his frontage was 800 miles long. In addition, the elevation of the Caucasus ranges extended up to 18,000 feet and could only be reached by crossing a series of east-west running rivers, which made good natural defensive positions. The plains just south of the Don were covered by huge cornfields, but, as the troops marched south, they gradually gave way to a hot, dry steppe. List's supply lines were already overextended and every step his spearheads took to the south only made the situation worse. Soviet resistance was weak, but Army Group A's motorized and panzer formations were often restricted or immobilized by lack of fuel; they could not overtake the Red Army, which fell back deeper into the interior.

Despite his difficulties, the capable and experienced field marshal was determined to do what he could; however, as his divisions marched south, Hitler shifted his strategy again. On July 20, Jodl announced that the fate of the Caucasus would be decided at Stalingrad and that some of Army Group A's strength should be moved to 6th Army. Halder sarcastically confided in his diary that he was glad that this thought had finally arisen in "the brilliant society of the OKW." In the meantime, List's infantry was pushing forward at a rate of up to 30 miles a day, and 1st Panzer Army breached the Russian defenses to a depth of 50 miles along a 100-mile front. The daily temperatures in the steppe now reached 100° F, and the men were tormented by sand storms and thirst. Fuel had to be flown in to Kleist's spearheads, but the rapid advance continued. Three Soviet armies proved unable to halt Kleist's advance, so, during the first days of August, the Maikop oilfields were turned over to the demolition squads. The panzer army pursued on to the foothills of the Caucasus, but the supply and logistical problems, the terrain, and Army Group A's lack of supply priority combined to slow Kleist's advance to around five miles per day after August 15. Air support was also a problem. Hitler's change of focus forced Richthofen (now the commander-in-chief, 4th Air Fleet) to reinforce the VIII Air Corps (supporting Army Group B) at the expense of IV Air Corps (supporting Army Group A). Stalin, meanwhile, reinforced his Caucasus front to a strength of two full air armies. By late August, the Red Air Force had air superiority in almost every sector and, by the second half of August, Army Group A's momentum was failing off everywhere. The German armies in the south had simply outrun their supply lines.

Kleist was now 60 miles from the Grozny oilfields and 350 miles from Baku. By August 20, he was opposed by about Soviet 40 divisions and brigades. His own army had eight divisions. Despite his many difficulties, the Prussian cavalry general pushed on and reached the Terek and Baksan Rivers. On August 25, he thrust across the Terek on both sides of Mozdok and struggled southward, against fierce resistance. Meanwhile, the Soviet 4th Kuban Guards Cavalry Corps rounded his open left flank and tried to seize Mozdok. Kleist had no choice but to stop his advance on September 1 and send troops to the rear, to defend his line of communications. The German advance on the oilfields was stalled. List's other army, Ruoff's 17th, was also checked near Novorossisk and in the Caucasus.

List, meanwhile, visited Hitler's headquarters at Vinnitsa on August 31, carrying with him an unmarked, small-scale map. Although quite polite while List was present, Hitler flew into a tirade against him as soon as he left, because he felt that the marshal should have brought detailed aerial photographs, showing why XXXXIX Mountain Corps was stalled. In throwing his fit, Hitler ignored the fact that, by Fuehrer Order, commanders were forbidden to carry large-scale maps showing troop dispositions. Later that week, Hitler sent Jodl to Army Group A Headquarters at Stalino, to investigate List's failures. Here, on September 7, List and General of Mountain Troops Rudolf Konrad, commander of the XXXXIX Mountain and a close personal friend of Jodl's since their cadet days in Bavaria, convinced the OKW officer that further advances in that sector were impossible. When Jodl returned the following day and presented these views to Hitler, the dictator exploded. How dare Jodl take a position diametrically opposed to his own. To the Fuehrer's surprise, Jodl rounded on him with some heat and even suggested that Hitler's own orders, which had been faithfully followed, were responsible for the stalemate in the Caucasus. Hitler was momentarily taken aback; he then ranted and roared at the unfortunate general and accused him of letting his fellow Bavarians hoodwink him. He accused Jodl of betraying him, stormed out of the room, and refused to shake hands with either Jodl or Keitel until January 1943. At noon that day, Hitler announced that henceforth he would take his midday meal in his quarters, ending his tradition of eating with Jodl and other members of his entourage. He left no one in any doubt as to his hatred of and distrust of his generals—even those of OKW.

The Hitler-Jodl confrontation resulted in a number of changes. First to go was Field Marshal List, who was sacked on September 9. Fuehrer interference in the details of the army's business reached a new peak when Hitler personally assumed command of Army Group A. The day-to-day administrative business was left to Lieutenant General Hans von Greiffenberg, the group's chief of staff. Kleist and Ruoff were ordered to submit situation reports (down to battalion level) to Hitler every other day, through OKH. Hitler also considered replacing Keitel with Kesselring and decided to replace Jodl with Paulus as soon as Stalingrad had been captured. Walter Warlimont, Jodl's deputy, was also earmarked for professional exile. Bodewin Keitel was relieved of his duties as chief of personnel and, after five months of involuntary retirement, was exiled to a territorial command in Poland (Wehrkreis XX). He was replaced by Rudolf Schmundt, Hitler's own adjutant. Finally, on September 17, Hitler decided to replace Halder with Major General Kurt Zeitzler as chief of the General Staff of the Army, a change that took effect on September 24. Keitel suggested that either Manstein or Paulus would be a better choice, but he was ignored by the Fuehrer. Halder was dismissed on the afternoon of September 23, and he left weeping. As one general put it, Halder had been kicked out like a dog piddling on the carpet. The OKW generals rejoiced at his departure, and at least one of them proclaimed that the German Army could now be steeped throughout with the true spirit of National Socialism.[22]

Kurt Zeitzler, the former chief of staff of the 1st Panzer Army and a personal friend of Rudolf Schmundt's, was known throughout the army as "Thunderball" because of his incredible energy, which belied his rotund figure. He was jovial except with his direct subordinates, with whom he was often arbitrary and overly harsh. In the late 1930s, as a lieutenant colonel on Jodl's staff, he was primarily responsible for drafting Fall Gruen, the plan for the occupation of Czechoslovakia. He had been Kleist's chief of staff in Poland, Belgium, France, and Russia, until he was promoted to chief of staff of Rundstedt's Army Group D in April, 1942. Here he had played a credible part in repulsing the British-Canadian raid on Dieppe in August. He further advanced his standing with Hitler by suggesting that these landings were not a raid at all, but an attempted Anglo-Saxon invasion of the European mainland. Upon his arrival at Fuehrer Headquarters, he was promoted to general of infantry, bypassing the rank of lieutenant general altogether. The Fuehrer's first orders to him were to replace the older army commanders and to scrap the traditional red-striped trousers and insignias of the General Staff. Zeitzler refused. Hitler had by no means appointed the subservient "yes-man" that he wanted, but he had weakened the army and the General Staff. The 47-year-old Zeitzler was junior to dozens of officers and had been promoted over the heads of hundreds of others. This naturally invoked the jealously of many and weakened his position. Zeitzler's appointment simultaneously weakened the position of the chief of the General Staff. By giving the post to such a junior officer, Hitler deprived it of the advantages of seniority, command experience, and authority in the eyes of the army and army group commanders. Hitler had, in fact, debased the office, and thus made his position even stronger in the process.

Zeitzler further undercut his own position with the senior generals of the army by publicly declaring that henceforth loyalty to and confidence in the Fuehrer was now the order of the day at OKH. In accordance with this order, Zeitzler accepted the decision to create the Luftwaffe Field divisions (air force ground combat divisions) without protest. Lieutenant Colonel Burkhart Mueller-Hillebrand, the highly capable chief of the Organizations Branch of OKH, did object and was quickly sacked by Zeitzler. He ended up on the Eastern Front.

The fact that he at first acted as little more than Hitler's mouthpiece to the army group commanders further undercut Zeitzler's standing in the eyes of the generals, but strengthened it with Hitler. Keitel and Jodl hoped that, with OKH under Zeitzler, they would at last be able to establish a unified army command under OKW—including control of the Eastern Front. Zeitzler, however, promptly dissociated himself from Keitel and Jodl and used Jodl's temporary disgrace to win back some of the ground Halder had lost to OKW. Zeitzler's standing with Hitler would not begin to fall until he began to show too much backbone and questioned too many of the Fuehrer's orders—but that lay in the future.

THE DRIVE TO STALINGRAD

While Army Group A was driving south toward the Caucasus, Weichs's Army Group B advanced east, against Stalingrad. In late July, the Italian 8th Army (six infantry divisions) took over the Don front between Pavlovsk and the Khoper, freeing Paulus to move more of his divisions to the east. Due to fuel shortages, however, 6th Army was immobilized on the Don for almost two weeks. Meanwhile, on July 31, 4th Panzer Army was split in half. Hoth was ordered to drive north against Stalingrad with three of his corps (which controlled only four German and four Romanian divisions). His fourth corps, Geyr's XXXX Panzer, was assigned to the 1st Panzer Army and was ordered to advance south, finalizing the gap between the two army groups. Hoth's advance toward Stalingrad was slow, however, due to the same fuel shortages that immobilized 6th Army altogether.

It was not until August 7 that Paulus had accumulated enough fuel to resume the advance. His attacks that day were immensely successful, however, thanks primarily to an order Stalin issued forbidding the Red forces west of the Don to take one step back. Before the day was out, XIV Panzer and XXIV Panzer Corps had broken the Soviet lines and linked up in the Soviet rear, surrounding the bulk of the 62nd Army. Along with the infantry of the LI Corps, they spent the next four days clearing the Kalach Pocket, which yielded nearly 50,000 prisoners, as well as some 270 tanks and 600 guns.

After crossing the Don, 6th Army advanced out of the Vertyachiy bridgehead at dawn on August 23 and drove toward the Volga on a narrow front. Heavily supported by the VIII Air Corps, XIV Panzer Corps slashed through the 62nd Army and gained 50 miles before dark. Hube's 16th Panzer Division reached the river north of the city about nightfall, while Richthofen pounded Stalingrad with his bombers. It all, 1,000 tons of bombs fell on the city on August 23 alone. That night, Stalingrad was described as a sea of flames. It was later reported that one could read a newspaper 20 miles away by the light of the fires. An estimated 40,000 civilians were killed in this attack and a second raid the following day, and the city was left without water. Hube's troops pushed to the outskirts of the city that evening, but could advance no further. By August 25, XIV Panzer Corps, which occupied a salient nearly 30 miles long and only two miles wide, was under heavy attack from all sides. Wietersheim had to bring up fuel and ammunition by night, via armored convoy. Paulus signaled him not to retreat; LI and VIII Corps would extend their lines to the east, to close up with XIV Panzer.

Meanwhile, Hoth was checked by stubborn Russian resistance and minefields north of Tinguta. He had to break off his offensive, regroup, and attack again, 20 miles to the west. It was not until August 31 that his vanguards cut the railroad south of Pitomnik, less than 20 miles from Stalingrad. The Soviet 62nd and 64th Armies, which had been pinning down 6th Army and putting up a desperate resistance, suddenly retired to the east, into the inner defenses of Stalingrad, immediately taking the pressure off of the hard-pressed XIV Panzer Corps. While VIII Air Corps launched around-the-clock bombing raids (terror attacks) on the city, 4th Panzer and 6th Army linked up at Gonchary, seven miles north of Voroponovo Station on September 3–4. The stage was set for the decisive Battle of Stalingrad.

NOTES

1. Rudolf Lusar, *German Secret Weapons of World War II* (1959), pp. 15–16.

2. Erich von Manstein, *Lost Victories*, Anthony G. Powell, trans. (1958; reprint ed., 1982), p. 259 (hereafter cited as Manstein); Plocher MS 1943;

O'Neill, pp. 504–11; John Shaw and the editors of Time-Life Books, *Red Army Resurgent* (1979), pp. 36–39 (hereafter cited as Shaw et al.).

3. Burkhart Mueller-Hillebrand, Burkhart. *Das Heer, 1933–1945* (1954–69), vol. 3, table 38.

4. Seaton, *German Army*, p. 90.

5. Kramarz, p. 95.

6. Carell, *Hitler Moves East*.

7. Alan S. Milward, *The German Economy at War* (1965), p. 17.

8. Juergen Thorwald, *The Illusion: Soviet Soldiers in Hitler's Armies*, Richard and Clara Winston, trans. (1975), pp. xiv–xv.

9. Kramarz, p. 98.

10. Earl F. Ziemke, "The German Northern Theater of Operations, 1940–1945," United States Department of the Army, Pamphlet 20-271 (1959), p. 34 (hereafter cited as Ziemke).

11. Ziemke and Bauer, pp. 283–303; *Kriegstagebuch des Oberkommando des Wehrmacht* (1961; reprint ed., 1982), June 28, 1942 (hereafter cited as *Kriegstagebuch des OKW*).

12. Plocher MS 1941; Overy, *Air War*, p. 62.

13. Cooper, *GAF*, p. 245.

14. Werner Moelders had been killed in an air accident near Breslau on November 22, 1941. He was returning to the Eastern Front after attending the funeral of Ernst Udet.

15. Galland, pp. 87–88.

16. Ziemke and Bauer, pp. 316–19.

17. Irving, *Hitler's War*, p. 401.

18. Ziemke and Bauer, p. 339.

19. Ibid., p. 344.

20. Ibid.

21. According to Ziemke and Bauer (p. 349). Seaton (*Russo-German War*, pp. 275–76) put the total number of prisoners at 14,000.

22. Ziemke and Bauer, p. 364; Halder Diaries, September 24, 1942.

23. Irving, *Hitler's War*, p. 465.

CHAPTER XLI

THE BATTLE
OF STALINGRAD

RATTENKRIEG

In 1942, Stalingrad was one of the most important industrial cities in the Soviet Union, producing approximately a quarter of Russia's tanks and other mechanized vehicles. It was a narrow, ribbon-like city of 600,000 people, stretching almost 20 miles along the Volga, which was a mile wide at this point. Most of its buildings had been reduced to ruins by Richthofen's air raids of August 23 and 24, when more than 100 blocks of downtown Stalingrad were destroyed. The ruins, however, provided excellent defensive positions for the Soviets. In addition, the entire district was cross-cut by a series of deep ravines, carved out of the soil by small west-east running Volga tributaries. These ravines would make good anti-tank ditches in the days ahead.

To Stalin, this city became the focal point of the war. He believed that its loss would give Hitler the option of wheeling north against Moscow or south to the Caucasus and might convince the Western Allies that the Soviet Union was doomed. "Not one step backward," he ordered his commanders in Stalingrad. "The Volga now has only one bank." Hitler also became obsessed with the City of Stalin. "You may rest assured that nobody will ever drive us out of Stalingrad," he told the German people. From that point on, a retreat from the Volga became psychologically impossible for the Nazi dictator. Stalingrad became a kind of giant magnet, drawing in dozens of units from both armies into a lethal vortex of house-to-house fighting, in which superior German maneuverability was neutralized and all of the advantages accrued to the defense. It was exactly the kind of fighting the Soviet soldiers, with less tactical skill than their opponents but with grim stubbornness, incredible tenacity, and an infinite capacity for suffering, naturally excelled.

Sixth Army began the battle with 250,000 men, 500 tanks, 7,000 guns and mortars, and 25,000 horses. It was commanded by Friedrich Wilhelm Paulus, a Hessian and the son of a bookkeeper in the civil service. Born in 1890, he joined the Imperial Army in 1910 and was commissioned in 1911. During World War I, Paulus fought on both the Eastern and Western Fronts and in Romania, and emerged from the war as a captain and staff officer with a reputation for attention to detail. During the interwar years, he accumulated a number of revealing efficiency reports. One declared, "He is slow, but very methodical ... is inclined to spend overmuch time on his appreciation, before issuing his orders." The report also commented that he was too fond of working all night, sustaining himself on coffee and cigarettes. Another evaluator commented, "This officer lacks decisiveness."[1] He nevertheless advanced to the rank of major general by 1939, because of his personal charm, his ability to get along with his superiors, and his capacity for hard General Staff work. On August 26, 1939, just five days before the war began, he was named chief of staff of Walter von Reichenau's 10th (later 6th) Army, which was the main German assault force in the invasion of Poland. The two men were perfectly matched: the dashing, energetic, and often-harsh Reichenau hated paperwork and the details of running a headquarters, while Paulus might have been chained to his desk. They performed effectively in Poland, Belgium, and France, before Paulus was promoted to lieutenant general and became deputy chief of the General Staff of the Army and chief of the operations branch in September 1940. In this post, he first came to the attention of Adolf Hitler, who was impressed by his bearing, charm, and background; like Hitler, Paulus was a "commoner," and the Fuehrer hated aristocratic General Staff officers.

Reichenau, meanwhile, was placed in charge of the southern sector of the Eastern Front on December 1, 1941, and persuaded Hitler to give Paulus command of the 6th Army. He received a special promotion to general of panzer troops on January 1, 1942, and assumed command of the army on January 5.

Field Marshal von Reichenau was a powerful and dominating figure who no doubt intended to guide his former chief of staff and teach him what it took to command an army in combat. Reichenau, however, suffered a major heart attack on January 12, 1942, and died on January 17. He was succeeded by the less able Fedor von Bock, who was eventually replaced by the equally mediocre Colonel General Baron von Weichs.

It would be difficult to imagine a general less suited to command a field army than Friedrich Paulus in 1942. He was a solid and technically proficient General Staff officer but had never held a command higher than that of an experimental motorized battalion. He was a desk soldier from his head to his toes. Tall, slim, and fastidious, he habitually wore gloves because he hated dirt. He bathed and changed clothes twice a day and was sarcastically nicknamed "Our Most Elegant Gentleman" and "The Noble Lord" by many of his combat-hardened peers.[2] (It must be recalled that most Europeans do not bathe daily, as is the custom with Americans.) Worse than his lack of experience, however, was his lack of decisiveness, his slowness, and the fact that he had convinced himself that Adolf Hitler was an infallible military genius whose judgment was far superior to his own. This was to be a fatal combination in the weeks ahead.

The Battle of Stalingrad began on September 2, 1942, when General Vasili Chuikov's rebuilt 62nd Army withdrew into the city. It would be heavily reinforced throughout the battle by the Volga Flotilla, which ferried men, supplies, ammunition, and equipment across the river.

On the German side, Weichs, the commander-in-chief of Army Group B and Paulus's immediate superior, felt that it was essential to attack the city immediately, before the Soviets had time to fully organize their defenses, but Paulus was tied down for several days by hastily launched counterattacks from the Russian forces on his northern flank. While these ill-coordinated attacks were in progress, he was reluctant to launch an assault on the city. This hesitation and his cautious attitude cost him thousands of casualties later on and perhaps the battle itself, for Stalin used the delay to pour thousands of reinforcements into the ruins. Finally, on September 7, Paulus began his advance. His drive was methodical; he had to clear a block at a time, because the Russians fought for every building and launched dozens of local counterattacks. Casualties on both sides were extremely heavy, but Paulus finally penetrated to the Volga on September 20, cutting the 62nd Army in two. Meanwhile, five miles to the south, General Werner Kempf's XXXXVIII Panzer Corps of the 4th Panzer Army was handed over to Paulus, who used it to clear the southern district of Stalingrad—a mission for which it was totally unsuited. Paulus, in fact, wasted his mobile units in street fighting—a job that foot soldiers should have handled.

The Battle of Stalingrad was fought in rubble. The Russians used the bomb craters and ruined buildings as positions for platoons, squads, sections, and individual snipers—hundreds of snipers. The fighting deteriorated into dozens of local actions against individual positions and buildings, all fought under the most savage conditions, with little quarter asked for or given. The German infantry called it *Rattenkrieg*: the war of the rats.

Back at his command post at Golubinsky, west of Stalingrad, General Paulus was showing signs of strain. He developed an uncontrollable tic in his left eye and became increasingly nervous. Unwilling or unable to see that he was stuck, he brought almost his entire army eastward into the cauldron, leaving Weichs to cover his rear with "allied" divisions: Italians, Romanians, and Hungarians. Victor von Schwelder, the veteran commander of the IV Corps, expressed concern that 6th Army was at the apex of a giant bulge, which was covered by unreliable foreign allies. He questioned the advisability of this strategy and thus indirectly questioned the strategic genius of the Fuehrer himself. Hitler sacked him immediately. General von Wietersheim, the highly competent commander of the XIV Panzer Corps, objected to the way Paulus was conducting the battle. He was relieved of his command by Paulus on September 15 and was replaced by the tough Lieutenant General Hans Valentin Hube. Wietersheim ended the war as a private in the Volkssturm. Baron Wolfram von Richthofen, who had replaced Loehr as commander-in-chief of the 4th Air Fleet, was highly critical of Paulus's conduct of the battle, but, as a Luftwaffe general known to be pro-Nazi, nothing was done to him. But no changes were made at 6th Army, either.

Paulus resumed his frontal assaults on October 2, but they had to be cancelled on October 6, because of declining infantry strength. He struck again on October 14 and, by October 23, 90 percent of Stalingrad was in German hands, but Paulus's units were depleted and he was almost out of ammunition. As had been the case the previous year, the "General Mud" had taken over in the German rear, strangling 6th Army's supply lines. Stalin, meanwhile, threw more troops into the fighting, no doubt delighted that Hitler had allowed himself to be lured into a battle of attrition in an urban area, where all of the advantages were with the defense. By early October, he had already reinforced Chuikov with nine infantry divisions, two tank brigades, and an independent rifle brigade. When these were gone, he simply threw in more. Meanwhile, the foot battalions of one German division fell to an average strength of three officers and 73 NCOs and enlisted men.[3]

Paulus, meanwhile, regrouped and attacked again on November 10. His assault forces consisted of four fresh engineer battalions (about 2,400 men), which had been specially trained for urban combat and flown in from Germany. Within 48 hours, all four battalions had been pinned down and cut to ribbons. Paulus's offensive had failed. It turned out to be his last.

THE TRAP IS SPRUNG

In the fall of 1942, Weichs's Army Group B included the German 4th Panzer and 6th Armies, as well as the Hungarian 2nd, Italian 8th, and the Romanian 3rd and 4th Armies, the last of which was in the process of forming. While the 4th Panzer and 6th Armies drove on

Stalingrad, Weichs used the Italian 8th and Romanian 3rd armies to cover the northern flank of the 6th Army and, by mid-November, was in the process of committing the Romanian 4th Army to cover Paulus's southern flank, along with the 4th Panzer Army (Figure 41.1 shows these dispositions and the situation on the Eastern Front as of November 15.) By this time, however, Hitler had dissipated the strength of the 4th Panzer, sending its best units to Stalingrad, the Caucasus, and even to France, leaving Hoth with only four German divisions (including only one panzer and one motorized division) and the Romanian VI Corps (two Romanian divisions).

Weichs was not insensitive to the threat posed to the 6th Army by using unreliable and ill-equipped allies to cover his flanks and rear, and he pointed out the dangers to OKH. Even Hitler became concerned. On November 9, he said, "If only this front were held by German formations, I would not lose a moment's sleep over it. But this is different. The 6th Army really must make an end of this business and take the remaining parts of Stalingrad quickly."[4]

By the second week in November, Weichs had concluded that there would definitely be a major offensive in the zone of the Romanian 3rd Army and probably against the 4th Panzer Army as well. Since all of his German reserves had been committed at Stalingrad, Weichs created a new one, under Headquarters, XXXXVIII Panzer Corps, which was now commanded by Lieutenant General Ferdinand Heim, the former chief of staff of the 6th Army. Weichs moved Heim's corps headquarters to the rear of the Romanian 3rd Army but could give him only the weak 22nd Panzer Division and the Romanian 1st Armored Division. The latter amounted to little, however, since it had only 122 tanks—mostly obsolete Czech T-38s, which weighed only nine tons, and a few old PzKw IIIs, armed with outmoded 50-millimeter guns.

On November 10, an increasingly nervous Adolf Hitler ordered the 22nd Panzer Division to move 150 miles to the north, to support General Petre Dumitrescu's 3rd Romanian Army. This division, however, had been in reserve and had dug in its tanks and covered them with straw, because of the increasing cold. Of its 104 tanks, 39 would not start, and most of the rest fell out during the road march. Mice had nested in the straw that covered the panzers and had eaten the rubber insulation off the wiring, causing massive electrical failures. Only 42 tanks would be in place on November 19.

The Romanians were ill-prepared for an attack of any sort. Their divisions had only one 37-millimeter anti-tank gun per company, and this weapon was practically useless against all but the lightest Soviet tanks. Even so, they failed to do what could have been done to improve their forward positions.

Figure 41.1
The Eastern Front, November 15, 1942

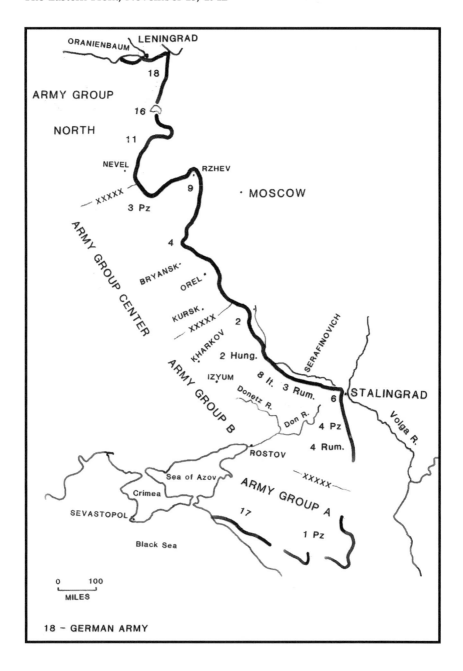

Meanwhile, the Russians concentrated 10 armies against the Romanian 3rd. On November 19, they struck this 40-mile sector with a million men, supported by 900 new T-34 tanks, 1,115 airplanes, and more than 13,500 guns—the greatest concentration of firepower yet achieved on the Eastern Front. As soon as the Reds committed their armor, the Romanians were seized with "tank fright." Major Hans-Ulrich Rudel, the Stuka pilot, led his group in support of the Romanians, and remembered the scene:

Masses in brown uniforms—are they Russians? No. Romanians. Some of them are even throwing away their rifles in order to be able to run the faster: a shocking sight.... [We reach] our allies' artillery emplacements. The guns are abandoned, not destroyed. We have passed some distance beyond them before we sight the first Soviet troops.

We find all the Romanian positions in front of them deserted. We attack with bomb and gun-fire—but how much use is that when there is no resistance on the ground?

We are seized with a blind fury.... Relentlessly I drop my bombs on the enemy and spray bursts of M.G. fire into these shoreless yellow-green waves of oncoming troops that surge up against us out of Asia and the Mongolian hinterland. I haven't a bullet left ...

On the return flight we again observe the fleeing Romanians; it is a good thing for them I have run out of ammunition.[5]

By nightfall on November 19, the Reds had ripped a 50-mile gap in the Romanian front and had committed their pursuit forces. The following day, they attacked Weichs's southern flank. Once again the Romanian elements ran away, allowing the Soviets to split the 4th Panzer Army in two. The 29th Motorized Division and Headquarters, IV Corps escaped to the north, into the Stalingrad pocket, along with two infantry divisions. Hoth fell back to the south; all he had left was his own headquarters, two disintegrating Romanian divisions, and the 16th Motorized Division, which had to cut its way out of an encirclement to reach the 4th Panzer Army.

November 20 was the decisive day of the battle. General Heim counterattacked desperately with his little corps, but it ran straight into the 2nd Guards Tank Army and was soon crushed and swept aside; in the end, it only narrowly managed to escape across the Chir with the remnants of the 22nd Panzer. Hitler was so furious at this weak performance that he ordered Heim arrested, and he was held in prison without trial until August 1943.

Paulus, meanwhile, could do nothing to prevent the impending encirclement. Sixth Army had three panzer divisions (the 14th, 16th, and 24th), but none of them had more than 60 operational tanks. In addition, 40 percent of Paulus's battalions were considered too exhausted to be battleworthy, and many of his 20 divisions could not move their artillery or heavy equipment because their horses had been taken west of the Don, where they would find fodder—an item in short supply on the Volga Steppe.[6]

On November 21, both Russian spearheads pivoted 90 degrees into the Paulus's rear and scattered his command post. On the afternoon of November 22, the Russian 21st and 51st Armies linked up, completing the encirclement of the 6th Army. Figure 41.2 shows the encirclement and the development of the Stalingrad pocket.

THE STALINGRAD AIRLIFT

On November 21, even before the Russians could complete their encirclement, Adolf Hitler issued a fatal order: 6th Army was to stand fast in Stalingrad, despite the fact that it was in danger of being surrounded. The Luftwaffe would resupply it by air, he declared, if that became necessary.

Meanwhile, Reichsmarschall Hermann Goering thought he saw an opportunity in the disastrous situation between the Volga and the Chir. His standing at Fuehrer Headquarters had been deteriorating since the loss of the Battle of Britain, and this decline had accelerated in 1942, because of the Allied bombings of the Fatherland and the rise of Martin Bormann, who had replaced Rudolf Hess as the Fuehrer's secretary in May 1941. Before Bormann had been in office for long, he had Hitler living in virtual isolation, because "the secretary" was able to freeze out those whom he disliked from contact with the dictator. As his influence with and over the Fuehrer grew, Bormann used it to strengthen the party's position against the Wehrmacht and the SS—and against Hermann Goering and the Luftwaffe. With such an enemy constantly whispering derogatory comments in Hitler's ear, Goering's decline in the eyes of the Fuehrer was predictable, even if the Luftwaffe performed up to expectations, which it did not. By late 1942, the Reichsmarschall felt the only way he could recapture some of his lost prestige with Hitler was to score a spectacular military victory. He therefore promised Hitler that the Luftwaffe would resupply Stalingrad by air.

The military experts involved in the operation were unanimously opposed to the airlift. "Supply an entire army by air?" General of Fliers Martin Fiebig, whose VIII Air Corps was supporting 6th Army, cried when he received the order. "Impossible!"[7] That same day Fiebig's commander, Baron von Richthofen, signaled Goering, Zietzler, and Field Marshal von Manstein that it was an impossible task. He also telephoned Colonel General Hans Jeschonnek, the chief of the General Staff of the Luftwaffe, and screamed at him, "You've got to stop it [the

Figure 41.2
The Stalingrad Encirclement

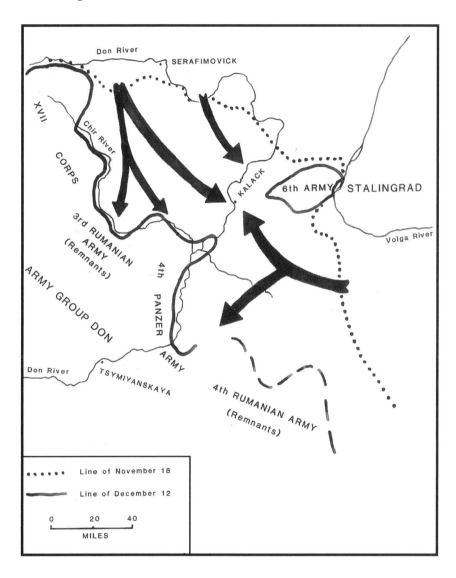

airlift]! In this miserable weather there's no way to supply an army of 250,000 men from the air. It's madness!"[8] Jeschonnek, who always listened to Richthofen, promptly revised his original estimate, which called for Paulus to stand fast, and on November 22 he strongly recommended that 6th Army break out. Like Weichs, Manstein, Richthofen, Fiebig, and others, he was ignored, both by Goering and Hitler. Only

Keitel and Jodl—OKW officers who were in no way responsible for the actual conduct of operations—backed the Fuehrer's decision, and Jodl later changed his mind. Even Dr. Goebbels opposed the airlift and almost succeeded in persuading Hitler to let 6th Army break out while there was still time.

Hitler never did ask Paulus for his opinion and only seriously discussed the airlift once, on November 24 (three days after he issued the original order), when Kurt Zeitzler, the chief of the General Staff of Army and the most outspoken critic of the plan, confronted Goering in his presence at Fuehrer Headquarters. Zeitzler began by stating in no uncertain terms that the airlift was impossible. This led to a heated conference, which went like this:

HITLER: "Goering, can you keep the 6th Army supplied by air?"
GOERING (with solemn confidence): "My Fuehrer! I assure you that the Luftwaffe can keep the 6th Army supplied."
ZEITZLER: "The Luftwaffe certainly cannot."
GOERING (scowling): "You are not in a position to give an opinion on the subject."
ZEITZLER: "My Fuehrer! May I ask the Reichsmarschall a question?"
HITLER: "Yes, you may."
ZEITZLER: "Herr Reichsmarschall, do you know what tonnage has to be flown in every day?"
GOERING (embarrassed): "I don't, but my staff officers do."
Zeitzler stated that the minimum was 300 tons per day. Allowing for bad weather, that meant 500 tons per day was the "irreducible minimum average."
GOERING: "I can do that."
ZEITZLER (losing his temper): "My Fuehrer! That is a lie!"
An icy silence descended on the conference. Zeitzler later recalled that Goering was white with fury.
HITLER: "The Reichsmarschall has made his report to me, which I have no choice but to believe. I therefore abide by my original decision [to resupply Stalingrad by air, instead of allowing the 6th Army to break out]."[9]

This was the turning point of the war.

On November 24, Hitler dispatched his famous order commanding 6th Army to stand fast, without thought of withdrawing. No breakout would be allowed. The following day, Baron von Richthofen telephoned Goering (now in Paris) and urged him to use his influence with the Fuehrer to obtain permission for 6th Army to break out to the southwest. Goering answered that he would do nothing of the sort, so Richthofen contacted the dictator directly. Hitler, however, refused to reconsider his decision, because he did not believe that the Wehrmacht would ever reach Stalingrad again if he withdrew now.

Once the decision had been made, Richthofen did his best to carry out his orders. "We have only one chance to cling to," he said. "So far the Fuehrer has always been right, even when none of us could understand his actions and most of us strongly advised against them."[10] The Red Baron's cousin said this even though he knew the results of the airlift could be predicted mathematically before it began. Sixth Army needed 500 tons of supplies per day. To provide this would require 500 operational Ju-52 transports, which could carry one ton each. Richthofen had only 298 Ju-52s, fewer than half of which were operational. In addition, the Luftwaffe in November 1942 was undergoing its greatest strain of the war, because it was also having to supply Army Group Afrika in Libya and Tunisia, in addition to its massive commitment on the Eastern Front. As a result, Richthofen had to employ He-111 bombers (which could transport a half a ton of supplies each) as emergency transports, but there were not enough of these available to make much difference. Nevertheless, the airlift began on November 29. By December 9, the Luftwaffe was delivering an average of 84.4 tons of supplies per day—less than a fifth of the amount required. To make matters worse, the Luftwaffe (ever jealous of its prerogatives) refused to let army quartermasters oversee the cargo shipments. The result, as one author put it, was a "ludicrous mess."[11] One day, four tons of jam and pepper were landed, followed by thousands of right shoes. Finally, Goering's air force delivered several million contraceptives to the starving troops of the 6th Army. The Luftwaffe never came close to delivering 500 tons of supplies to Stalingrad—not even for a single day. In fact, its maximum daily delivery was 290 tons; its average daily delivery was only 94 tons.

Kurt Zeitzler, meanwhile, never ceased to agitate for a breakout attempt. After Hitler snapped at him that the subject was closed, Zeitzler found a way to bring it up indirectly. He put his entire staff on the same diet as that of the troops in Stalingrad. They soon visibly lost weight. Meanwhile, inside the pocket, most of the generals wanted to break out at once. As we have seen, however, Friedrich Paulus could be mentally dominated by men of stronger will. Following the death of von Reichenau, Paulus allowed himself to be guided by the perceived infallibility of the Fuehrer and dominated by the strong will of his own chief of staff, Major General Arthur Schmidt.

Schmidt, a bachelor, was born in Hamburg in 1895, the son of a merchant. Like Paulus, he did not come from a military tradition, but he volunteered for the army when World War I broke out in 1914 and became a dedicated soldier. Unfortunately, the hard-working Schmidt lacked command experience and—even more seriously—was a true believer in the genius of the Fuehrer, just like his army commander. Like Paulus, he was a master of detail, but there the similarity ended, for Schmidt lacked Paulus's conscience, good breeding, and polished manners. He was an autocratic, rude, overbearing bully who was thoroughly disliked by most of the officers with whom he came into contact. Unfortunately, as the situation at Stalingrad deteriorated, Paulus's self-confidence declined, and he allowed himself (and 6th Army) to be guided more and more by his chief of staff, until Arthur Schmidt was virtually conducting the battle for the German side. Schmidt was not a man of great tactical skill, daring, or initiative; rather, he was characterized by a stubborn optimism, tenacity, and a willingness to obey the orders of his superiors without question. These characteristics of Paulus and Schmidt would prove to be fatal to the trapped garrison of Stalingrad.

At the beginning of the encirclement, Paulus favored an immediate breakout attempt (even though Schmidt did not), and sent a message to that effect to Army Group B on November 21. The next day, he and Schmidt met with Hermann Hoth and Major General Wolfgang Pickert, the commander of the 9th Flak Division. Schmidt asked Pickert, an old friend, what they should do now. "Get the hell out of here!" was Pickert's frank reply. The gifted Hoth also recommended an immediate breakout, but Schmidt replied that there was no need to panic, and nothing in the present tactical situation justified making decisions independent of Rastenburg. Paulus did not open his mouth during the entire conference, except to agree with his chief of staff.[12]

Once he received the Fuehrer's order, Paulus set aside his own professional opinion and accepted Hitler's decision with an attitude of almost detached resignation. This listless and almost lifeless obsequiousness characterized Paulus's attitude for the rest of the battle.

On November 27, the corps commanders of the 6th Army unanimously urged Paulus to order a breakout on his own initiative. General von Seydlitz-Kurzbach, commander of the LI Corps, urged him to "take the course of the Lion," a reference to General Karl von Litzmann, who made a daring breakout against orders in November 1914. "A breakout is our only chance!" General Hube, the one-armed commander of the XIV Panzer Corps, declared. "We can't just remain here and die!" cried General Karl Strecker, the commander of the XI Corps. General Walter Heitz (Commanding General [CG], VIII Corps), a strong Nazi, also called for an immediate breakout, regardless of casualties. It would be better to escape with only five divisions, he declared, than to die with 20.

"Reichenau would have brushed aside all doubts," General Erwin Jaenecke, the commander of the IV Corps, commented.

"I am no Reichenau," Paulus replied gravely.

Jaenecke, a close personal friend of Paulus's, put heavy pressure on him. Seydlitz informed the conferees that he had already ordered his corps to destroy all surplus equipment that could not be carried on a long march. He had personally set the example by burning everything he had except the uniform he was wearing. All of the corps commanders expressed their approval and advocated a breakout, in spite of Hitler's orders.

"We must obey," Schmidt said.

"I shall obey," Paulus answered.

"In spite of his intelligence," Jaenecke wrote later, "Colonel General Paulus was far too pliable to cope with Hitler. I am convinced that this is the real and deeper cause of his failure."[13]

Ironically, when he learned that Seydlitz' corps was preparing for an unauthorized breakout, Hitler assumed that Paulus was preparing to disobey him. He therefore removed LI Corps from the control of 6th Army and placed it directly under the command of OKH, in effect making Seydlitz independent of Paulus's orders. Paulus, at least, recognized the irony of this situation, but Walter von Seydlitz was too furious to see anything except red. He promptly signaled Baron von Weichs, the commander-in-chief of Army Group B: "To remain inactive is a crime from the military viewpoint, and it is a crime from the point of view of responsibility of the German people."[14]

Weichs did not reply. And 6th Army did not move.

MANSTEIN TAKES CHARGE

Almost as soon as the Soviet pincers closed around 6th Army, Hitler correctly decided that the uninspiring Baron von Weichs was not the man to rescue it. If anyone could salvage the southern sector of the Russian Front, it was Erich von Manstein.

"The general verdict among the German generals I interrogated in 1945 was that Field Marshal von Manstein had proved the ablest commander in their army, and the man they had most desired to become Commander-in-Chief," B. H. Liddell Hart recalled.[15] This was the opinion of Field Marshal Rommel (the Desert Fox), Gerd von Rundstedt, the senior German field marshal, and even Heinz Guderian, the father of the blitzkrieg and a man not easily impressed by anyone other than himself, and there were many others. Even Hitler said, "Manstein is perhaps the best brain that the General Staff Corps has produced."[16] He was universally respected and even held somewhat in awe by the German generals—a class not exactly known for its lack of personal ego. This is precisely why Hitler feared him.

Manstein was born to be a general. When he first saw the light of day, in Berlin on November 24, 1887, his name was Fritz Erich von Lewinski. His father was General of Artillery Eduard von Lewinski, the product of a distinguished Prussian military family that traced its heritage back to the Teutonic knights. Field Marshal von Hindenburg was the baby's uncle. Erich, however, was the tenth child born to the

Lewinski family, and Frau von Lewinski's sister (Frau von Manstein) was childless, so the Lewinskis gave him to her. (That was how uncontested adoptions were handled in the nineteenth century.) Erich's adopted father was a lieutenant general and he eventually took his name, becoming Fritz Erich von Lewinski gennant von Manstein—Erich von Manstein for short.

Manstein was educated in various cadet schools and entered the Imperial Army as an officer cadet in the elite 3rd Prussian Foot Guard Regiment in 1906. He distinguished himself as a General Staff officer in World War I (despite being seriously wounded) and continued his advancement during the Reichswehr and Wehrmacht eras, finally being named deputy chief of the General Staff in 1936. In this position he tried to shield Jewish servicemen from discriminatory Nazi regulations. He lost his job because of his anti-Nazi attitude in 1938, but was considered too competent to be sent into retirement, so he was given command of the 18th Infantry Division. As chief of staff of Army Group A in late 1939, he devised the plan that led to the conquest of France in six weeks. Later, he led the LVI Panzer Corps in the invasion of the Soviet Union, with a great deal of success. When Ritter von Schobert was killed in action in the fall of 1941 (when his airplane made an emergency landing in what turned out to be a Russian minefield), Manstein succeeded him as commander of the 11th Army. In 1942, he captured the Soviet naval fortress of Sevastopol, which had earned him his marshal's baton. Afterward, Hitler sent Manstein's army to Army Group North, where he severed a major Soviet penetration at its base, destroying seven infantry divisions, six infantry brigades, and four armored brigades in the process. More than 300 guns, 500 mortars, and 244 tanks were captured or destroyed. When the Russians encircled Stalingrad, his Headquarters, 11th Army, was upgraded to Headquarters, Army Group Don, and Manstein received the most critical and demanding orders of his military career: rescue 6th Army and stabilize the southern sector of the Eastern Front. He also had the task of preventing the Russians from reaching Rostov and cutting off Army Group A in the Caucasus. Unfortunately for Manstein, he had little with which to work. When he arrived, he had only (north to south) the XVII Corps on the Chir; the remnants of the Romanian 3rd Army, which was nearly useless; the weak 4th Panzer Army; and the remnants of the Romanian 4th Army. He was facing 10 Soviet combined arms armies; a tank army; four air armies; several independent cavalry, tank, and mechanized corps; and more than 100 independent tank, artillery, anti-tank, combat engineer, and other regiments—excluding the Soviet forces surrounding the 6th Army in Stalingrad.[17]

Almost as soon as Army Group Don was activated on November 27, Manstein divided it into two German Armeegruppen: Hoth and

Hollidt. The initial reinforcements all went to General Hollidt, while the Headquarters of the LVII Panzer Corps was transferred from the 17th Army in the Caucasus to organize the breakthrough to Stalingrad. By mid-December, Group Hoth had been reinforced with Kirchner's LVII Panzer, which controlled the weak 23rd Panzer Division (transferred from Army Group A) and the full-strength 6th Panzer Division (just arriving from France). The 5th SS Panzer Grenadier and 17th Panzer Divisions were added later, but the 17th Panzer amounted to little: it only had 30 operational tanks and no armored cars, and one company from each panzer grenadier battalion had to march behind the division on foot, because of a shortage of motorized vehlcles.[18]

During the last days of November and the first days of December, while his new divisions arrived, it was all Manstein could do to hold off Soviet attacks across the Chir and the Aksai. In the meantime, he planned his relief attack. The Soviets expected him to take the shortest route, from a bridgehead at Verkhnaya Chirskaya, north and east of the confluence of the Don and Chir, and less than 40 miles from the southwest corner of the Stalingrad perimeter. Manstein, however, realized that the Russians were concentrating there, so he attacked along the Kotelnikovo-Stalingrad railroad, across more than 80 miles of open, shelterless steppe. This approach was defended by only five Soviet divisions.

Due to bad weather and the low capacity of the Soviet railroads, Manstein's relief attempt, codenamed Operation Winter Storm, could not start until December 12, when Kirchner attacked with 230 tanks and assault guns, which were well supported by the IV Air Corps, just up from the Caucasus. Just as Manstein hoped, Kirchner's attack took the Soviets by surprise, and he gained 12 miles on the first day, despite atrocious weather. The Reds, however, reacted quickly, and by December 14 had committed two mechanized corps and two tank brigades from the Stalingrad area against LVII Panzer. That day a tank battle began at Verkhne-Kumski. When it ended three days later, 11th Panzer Regiment alone had destroyed about 400 Soviet tanks. Kirchner was able to push within 30 miles of Stalingrad, but was not able to break the back of the Soviet defense. In the meantime, Stalin awakened to the danger and committed the elite 2nd Guards Army against Kirchner. Meanwhile, on December 16, several Soviet armies with more than 1,000 tanks attacked the 8th Italian Army (of Weichs's Army Group B). Their objectives were to break through, then turn south into Manstein's rear and capture the airfields that were being used to resupply Stalingrad. Within a few days, the Italian Army was completely routed and fleeing to the east, having lost or abandoned almost all of its artillery and heavy equipment. By December 19, the Russian spearheads had overrun the major supply base of Kantemirovka, capturing tons of ammunition, food, and fuel. There were no German reserves in this sector, so the Soviet tanks were able to advance 150 miles in five days and, on Christmas Eve, launched a surprise attack on Tatsinkskaya, the main Ju-52 airfield, 50 miles in the rear of Group Hollidt. Many of the air and ground crews were still asleep when the Russians struck, and losses in men and material were devastating. Seventy Ju-52s were destroyed, along with irreplaceable cold weather avionics equipment. Group Hollidt was in danger of being cut off and destroyed, and there was a real possibility that a Soviet thrust might take Rostov, cutting off Army Groups A and much of Army Group Don—which is exactly what Stalin intended to do.

Manstein called on Paulus to break out on December 19, and even Hitler gave conditional approval, but Paulus hesitated. He estimated that he had only enough fuel to travel 18 miles—no more. Manstein sent his Ic (intelligence officer), Major Georg Eismann, to Stalingrad, to reason with Paulus and Schmidt; but to no avail. "What ultimately decided the attitude of 6th Army Headquarters," Manstein wrote later, "was the opinion of the chief of staff ... 'Sixth Army,' he told Eismann, 'will still be in position at Easter. All you people have to do is to supply it better'." Manstein concluded that all of Eismann's remonstrances "were like water off a duck's back."[19]

On December 26, the temperature dropped to −15° F. Inside Stalingrad, the physical condition of the soldiers deteriorated rapidly and the combat strength of 6th Army declined alarmingly. Men suddenly started dropping dead for no apparent reason. OKW flew a distinguished anatomist from Berlin into the pocket, to conduct an investigation. Autopsies revealed that death was caused by a combination of undernourishment, overwork, exhaustion, and exposure, which caused the heart to shrink, except for the right ventricle, which greatly enlarged. This condition was normally found only in the very old.[20] The troops went on one-third rations on November 23, and almost all of the horses had been eaten by mid-December. "Horse-meat is not so bad at all," Corporal Schaffstein of the 226th Infantry Regiment wrote in his diary on December 9. "It's a jolly sight worse to go hungry."[21] The troops washed their meager rations down with what they called "German tea"—which was melted snow.[22] As of December 7, 6th Army was living on one loaf of stale bread for every five soldiers.

Every day, the German ranks were depleted by wounds, dysentery, typhus, spotted fever, and frostbite. Still they gave ground only slowly and the defense continued to be stubborn, even though 6th Army was gradually crushed, one unit at a time.

On Christmas Day, 1942, Paulus authorized the slaughtering of 400 horses for food as a holiday gift for his men. Later that week, he was forced to reduce rations again, to a daily allowance of two ounces of bread, one bowl of soup (without fat) for lunch, and one can of unsalted meat for dinner per man. Often this was not available. The panzer and motorized divisions suffered worst of all, because they had no horses to eat.

THE DEATH OF AN ARMY

To meet the emergency caused by the collapse of the Italian 8th Army, Manstein had no choice but to withdraw the 6th Panzer Division from Kirchner's corps. He took this step with a heavy heart, for he knew that the loss of this division ended all chances of resuming the breakthrough to Stalingrad; however, by now, the Russians were within 75 miles of Rostov. Manstein, a commander with nerves of steel, only withdrew the 6th Panzer when it was absolutely necessary to save Rostov and to prevent the Soviets from cutting off Army Group A and the 4th Panzer Army. As it was, the Reds penetrated to within 15 miles of Rostov before they were checked by Manstein's last reserves.

The reduction of the Stalingrad pocket was left to General Andrei Ivanovich Yeremenko's Stalingrad Front and Konstantin K. Rokossovsky's Don Front: seven armies in all. They were supported by 7,000 guns and by the 16th Air Army, which established air superiority over the battle zone. Another major offensive against the trapped 6th Army began on January 10, against the western portion of the perimeter. The Soviets gained five miles the first day, decimated the 44th Infantry Division, and virtually destroyed the 29th Motorized and 376th Infantry Divisions. The fighting was heavy and bitter, in temperatures below $-20°$ F. Even so, the pocket, which originally extended 40 miles west to east and 20 miles north to south, had been reduced by half by January 17. Even more seriously, six of the seven airstrips had been lost, including Pitomnik (on January 11), the main air base, and the only one with night-landing facilities. The only airstrip left was Gumrak, but it was frequently out of commission because of enemy bombing and shelling and high snow. Air supply continued via parachute drops, but this method was inefficient and inaccurate. Even those canisters that landed in German territory were not properly collected and distributed, because 6th Army's internal organization had broken down.

The Reds launched another offensive on January 22; Gumrak fell that day, and the German defense at last began to collapse. On January 25, the Russians broke through the western perimeter and penetrated to the Tractor Works, where they linked up with Chuikov's 62nd Army, cutting the pocket in two and isolating XI Corps to the north. Paulus ordered that rations no longer be issued to the wounded. Only those who could fight were to be fed. He signaled Hitler, "Your orders are being executed. Long live Germany!"[23]

Privately, Paulus was in despair. He told a pilot that his men had nothing to eat for four days. "Can you imagine soldiers falling upon the carcass of a horse, smashing his head open and eating its brains raw?" he asked.[24] But Hitler had ordered him not to surrender, and, to Paulus, the Fuehrer had to be obeyed at all costs, so the unequal battle continued. By now, there were 20,000 unattended wounded lying in the streets.

The southern pocket was cut in half on January 28, and Paulus's headquarters was isolated in the southernmost of the three pockets, where it was guarded by the remnants of Major General Alexander von Hartmann's 71st Infantry Division.

On January 30, the 76th Infantry Division was overwhelmed. Near Railroad Station Number 1, the Headquarters, XIV Panzer Corps, was surrounded and forced to capitulate. General Hube had been flown out on Hitler's orders a few days before, and the corps was surrendered by Lieutenant General Hellmut Schloemer. In the northern pocket, a number of T-34 tanks broke through to the joint command bunker of the VIII and LI Corps. Walter von Seydlitz, Walter Heitz, and five other generals were captured.

As his command was bleeding to death, General Hartmann stood up on an embankment and deliberately exposed himself to Soviet fire. He was promptly cut down. Shortly after midnight on January 31, at the urging of General Zeitzler, Hitler—despite his personal misgivings—promoted Paulus to the rank of field marshal. Because no field marshal had been captured in German history, this was a clear invitation to Paulus to commit suicide. Paulus ignored the hint. He and his staff surrendered that morning, and fighting in the southern pocket ended. The northern pocket, under the command of General Strecker, continued to resist until February 2.

The Soviets took about 91,000 prisoners, including 24 generals and 2,500 other officers, when Stalingrad fell. Sources disagree over the total number of German casualties, but the commonly accepted figure is 230,000. This number, of course, excludes thousands killed or captured before and during the encirclement. By any measure, for the Third Reich, the disaster was enormous. It lost the headquarters and entire command organization of the 6th Army; five corps headquarters; 13 infantry divisions; three panzer divisions, three motorized divisions; and the 9th Flak Division: 20 of its best divisions. Losses in panzers and motorized vehicles were the equivalent of six months' new production. The equivalent of four months' production of artillery and two months' production of small arms and mortars were also lost.[25]

The losses suffered by Germany's allies were also terrible. Romania lost an estimated 300,000 men, Italy 130,000, and Hungary 120,000. Total Axis losses were in the neighborhood of three-quarters of a million men.

Luftwaffe losses were also devastating: 488 aircraft, including 266 Ju-52s, 165 He-111s, 42 Ju-86s, nine FW-200s, five He-177s, and a Ju-290. "There died the core of the German bomber fleet," Goering moaned later. Typically, he immediately looked for scapegoats and announced his intention to court-martial Jeschonnek and General of Fliers Hans-Georg von Seidel, the quartermaster general of the Luftwaffe, because they were responsible for the Stalingrad catastrophe.[26] Hitler, however, refused to allow Goering to proceed with his court-martial. He knew where the real blame lay.

Publicly, the ministry of propaganda announced that the heroic 6th Army, under the exemplary leadership of Field Marshal Paulus, had been overwhelmed by a numerically superior enemy. Privately, Hitler fiercely berated Paulus, declared that he had made an about-face on the threshold of history, and promised to court-martial him after the war. He also swore that he would create no more field marshals in this war—an oath that he did not keep. Ironically, von Weichs, Ewald von Kleist, and Ernst Busch all received their promotions to field marshal on February 1, 1943.

For the 91,000 prisoners, there followed an endless series of hunger marches. The thinly guarded prisoner-of-war columns were frequently attacked by bands of civilian marauders, who fell on the sick and wounded. The men who dropped out of their columns were never seen again. Even the prisoners who were put on trains or trucks were not properly fed, and only about half of the captives ever reached the prisoner-of-war camps in Siberia. There, most of them died of malnutrition or from various epidemics. Fewer than 7,000 of them ever saw Germany again.

NOTES

1. Walter Goerlitz, *Paulus and Stalingrad* (1974), pp. 10–12.
2. Shaw et al., p. 136.
3. Ziemke, p. 46.
4. Dana V. Sadarananda, *Beyond Stalingrad* (1990), p. 7 (hereafter cited as Sadarananda).
5. Hans Ulrich Rudel, *Stuka Pilot* (1958; reprint ed., 1979), p. 73.
6. Seaton, *Russo-German War*, pp. 310–14.
7. Plocher MS 1942.
8. James D. Carnes, "A Study in Courage: General Walther von Seydlitz' Opposition to Hitler," Unpublished Ph.D. Dissertation (1976), p. 147.
9. Plocher MS 1942; Kurt Zeitzler, "Stalingrad," in *The Fatal Decisions*, William Richardson and Seymour Freidon, eds. (1956), pp. 144–45.
10. Shaw et al., p. 181.
11. Plocher MS 1942.

12. Ibid.

13. Ibid.

14. F. W. von Mellenthin, *German Generals of World War II* (1977), p. 115 (hereafter cited as Mellenthin, *German Generals*).

15. B. H. Liddell Hart, "Foreword," in Manstein, p. 13.

16. Guderian, p. 241.

17. T. N. Dupuy and Paul Martell, *Great Battles on the Eastern Front* (1982), p. 69.

18. Frido von Senger und Etterlin, *Neither Fear Nor Hope*, George Malcolm, trans. (1963; reprint ed., 1989), p. 63.

19. Mellenthin, *German Generals*, p. 211.

20. Shaw et al., p. 182.

21. *True to Type*, p. 75.

22. Hanson W. Baldwin, *Battles Won and Lost* (1976), p. 174.

23. Carell, *Scorched Earth* (1991), p. 214.

24. Manstein, pp. 433–34.

25. Sadarananda, pp. 145–46.

26. Seidel (1891–1955) later commanded the 10th Air Fleet (1944–45), which was the Luftwaffe's replacement air fleet.

TABLE OF COMPARATIVE RANKS

U.S. Army	German Army and Luftwaffe
——	Reichsmarschall (Luftwaffe only)[a]
General of the Army	Field Marshal (Generalfeldmarschall)
General	Colonel General (Generaloberst)
Lieutenant General	General of (Infantry, Panzer Troops, etc.)
Major General	Lieutenant General (Generalleutnant)
Brigadier General[b]	Major General (Generalmajor)
Colonel	Colonel (Oberst)
Lieutenant Colonel	Lieutenant Colonel (Oberstleutnant)
Major	Major (Major)
Captain	Captain (Hauptmann)
First Lieutenant	First Lieutenant (Oberleutnant)
Second Lieutenant	Second Lieutenant (Leutnant)
——	Senior Officer Cadet or Ensign (Faehnrich)
Officer Candidate	Officer-Cadet (Fahnenjunker)
Master Sergeant	Sergeant Major (Stabsfeldwebel)
First Sergeant	——
Technical Sergeant	Technical Sergeant (Oberfeldwebel)
Staff Sergeant	Staff Sergeant (Feldwebel)
Sergeant	Sergeant (Unterfeldwebel)
Corporal	Corporal (Unteroffizier)
——	Lance Corporal (Gefreiter)
Private First Class	Private First Class (Obersoldat)
Private	Private (Soldat, Grenadier, Jaeger, etc.)

Appendix 1

U.S. Army	Waffen–SS
General of the Army	Reichsfuehrer-SS
General	SS Colonel General (SS-Oberstgruppenfuehrer)
Lieutenant General	SS General (SS-Obergruppenfuehrer)
Major General	SS Lieutenant General (SS-Gruppenfuehrer)
Brigadier General	SS Major General (SS-Brigadefuehrer)
——	SS Oberfuehrer (SS-Oberfuehrer)
Colonel	SS Colonel (SS-Standartenfuehrer)
Lieutenant Colonel	SS Lieutenant Colonel (SS-Obersturmbannfuehrer)
Major	SS Major (SS-Sturmbannfuehrer)
Captain	SS Captain (SS-Hauptsturmfuehrer)
First Lieutenant	SS First Lieutenant (SS-Obersturmfuehrer)
Second Lieutenant	SS Second Lieutenant (SS-Untersturmfuehrer
Officer Candidate	SS Officer-Cadet (SS Fahnenjunker)
Master Sergeant	SS Sergeant Major (SS-Sturmscharfuehrer)
First Sergeant	SS First Sergeant (SS-Hauptscharfuehrer)
Technical Sergeant	SS Technical Sergeant (SS-Oberscharfuehrer)
Staff Sergeant	SS Staff Sergeant (SS-Scharfuehrer)
Sergeant	SS Sergeant (SS-Unterscharfuehrer)
Corporal	SS Corporal (SS-Rottenfuehrer)
Private First Class	SS Private First Class (SS Sturmann)
Private	SS Private (SS-Mann)
	SS Aspirant (SS-Anwaerter)

German Army/ Luftwaffe	German Navy (Officer Ranks Only)
Reichsmarschall (Luftwaffe only)	Grand Admiral (Grossadmiral)
Field Marshal (Generalfeldmarschall)	——
Colonel General (Generaloberst)	General Admiral (Generaladmiral)
General (General der . . .)	Admiral (Admiral)
Lieutenant General (Generalleutnant)	Vice Admiral (Vizeadmiral)
Major General (Generalmajor)	Rear Admiral (Konteradmiral)
——	Commodore
Colonel (Oberst)	Captain (Kapitaen zur See)
Lieutenant Colonel (Oberstleutnant)	Commander (Fregattenkapitaen)
Major (Major)	Lieutenant Commander (Korventtenkapitaen)
Captain (Hauptmann)	Lieutenant (Kapitaenleutnant)

German Army/ Luftwaffe	German Navy (Officer Ranks Only)
First Lieutenant (Ober-leutnant)	Leutnant[c]
Second Lieutenant (Leutnant)	Leutnant zur See[d]
Officer-Cadet (Fahnen-junker)	Seekadett

[a]Held only by Hermann Goering (July 19, 1940–April 23, 1945).
[b]Brigadier in British Army.
[c]Equivalent to lieutenant (j.g.) in U.S. Navy.
[d]Equivalent to ensign in the U.S. Navy.

GERMAN STAFF POSITIONS

	Chief of Staff (Not present below the corps level)
Ia	Chief of Operations
Ib	Quartermaster (Chief Supply Officer)
Ic	Staff Officer, Intelligence (subordinate to Ia)
Id	Director of Training (Not present below army level)
IIa	Chief Personnel Officer (Adjutant)
IIb	Second Personnel Officer (subordinate to IIa)
III	Chief Judge Advocate (subordinate to IIa)
IVa	Chief Administrative Officer (subordinate to Ib)
IVb	Chief Medical Officer (subordinate to Ib)
IVc	Chief Veterinary Officer (subordinate to Ib)
IVd	Chaplain (subordinate to IIa)
V	Motor Transport Officer (subordinate to Ib)
	National Socialist Guidance Officer (added 1944)
	Special Staff Officers (Chief of Artillery, Chief of Projectors [Rocket Launchers], Chief Signal Officer, etc.

Note:

The Ia was referred to as the Generalstabsoffizier 1 (1st General Staff Officer or GSO 1); the Ib was the Generalstabsoffizier 2; the Ic was the Generalstabsoffizier 3; and the Id was the Generalstabsoffizier 4.

GERMAN ARMY CHAIN OF COMMAND: GERMAN UNITS, RANKS, AND STRENGTHS

Unit	Rank of Commander[a]	Strength
Army Group	Field Marshal	2 or more armies
Army	Colonel General	2 or more corps
Army Detachment	General	1 or more corps plus independent divisions
Corps	General	2 or more divisions
Division	Lieutenant General/Major General	10,000–18,000 men[b] and 200–350 tanks (if panzer)
Brigade[c]	Major General/Colonel	2 or more regiments
Regiment	Colonel	2–7 battalions
Battalion	Lieutenant Colonel/Major/ Captain	2 or more companies (approximately 500 men per infantry battalion; usually 50–80 tanks per panzer battalion)
Company[d]	Captain/Lieutenant	3–5 platoons
Platoon	Lieutenant/Sergeant Major	Infantry: 30–40 men; Panzer: 4 or 5 tanks
Section	Warrant Officer/Sergeant Major	2 squads (more or less)
Squad	Sergeant	Infantry: 7–10 men; Armor: 1 tank

[a]Frequently, units were commanded by lower-ranking men as the war went on.
[b]As the war progressed, the number of men and tanks in most units declined accordingly. SS units usually had more men and tanks than Army units.
[c]Brigade Headquarters were rarely used in the German Army after 1942.
[d]Called batteries in the artillery (4 or 5 guns per battery).

CHARACTERISTICS OF SELECTED TANKS

Model	Weight (in tons)	Speed (mph)	Range (miles)	Main Armament	Crew
British					
Mark IV "Churchill"	43.1	15	120	16-pounder	5
Mark VI "Crusader"	22.1	27	200	12-pounder	5
Mark VIII "Cromwell"	30.8	38	174	175mm	5
American[a]					
M3A1 "Stuart"[b]	14.3	36	60	137mm	4
M4A3 "Sherman"	37.1	30	120	176mm	5
German					
PzKw II	9.3	25	118	120mm	3
PzKw III	24.5	25	160	150mm	5
PzKw IV	19.7	26	125	175mm	5
PzKw V "Panther"	49.3	25	125	175mm	5
PzKw VI "Tiger"	62.0	23	73	188mm	5
Russian					
T34/Model 76	29.7	32	250	176mm	4
T34/Model 85	34.4	32	250	185mm	5
KV 1	52	25	208	176.2mm	5
JSII "Joseph Stalin"	45.5	23	150	122mm	4

[a]Characteristics of each tank varied somewhat from model to model.
[b]All American tanks were also in the British inventory. The British Shermans were sometimes outfitted with a heavier main battle gun. These Shermans were called "Fireflies."

APPENDIX 5

LUFTWAFFE AVIATION UNITS, STRENGTHS, AND RANKS OF COMMANDERS

Unit	Composition	Rank of Commander
OKL	all Luftwaffe units	Reichsmarschall
Air Fleet	Air Corps and Air and Flak Division(s)	General to Field Marshal
Air Corps	Air and Flak Divisions plus various miscellaneous units	Major General to General
Air Division	2 or more wings	Colonel to Major General
Wings	2 or more groups	Major to Colonel; rarely Major General
Group	2 or more squadrons, 30 to 36 aircraft	Major to Lieutenant Colonel
Squadrons	2 or more sections, 9 to 12 aircraft	Lieutenant to Captain
Section	3 or 4 aircraft	Lieutenant

BIBLIOGRAPHY

Absolom, Rudolf, comp. *Rangliste der Generale der deutschen Luftwaffe Nach dem Stand vom 20 April 1945*. 1984.

Accoce, Pierre, and Pierre Quet. *A Man Called Lucy*. 1966.

Addington, Larry. *The Blitzkrieg and the German General Staff, 1865–1941*. 1971.

Air University Files SRGG 1106 (c).

Allmayer-Beck, Baron Christoph von. *Die Geschichte der 21 (ostpr./westpr.) Infanterie-Division*. 1960.

Andres, Wladyslaw, and Antonio Munoz. "Russian Volunteers in the German Wehrmacht in World War II." Available at http://www.feldgrau.com/rvol.html.

Angolia, John R. *On the Field of Honor*. 2 vols. 1981.

Angolia, John R., and Adolf Schlicht. *Uniforms and Traditions of the German Army*. 1984.

Arad, Yitzhak. *Belzec, Sobibor, Treblinka: The Operation Reinhard Death Camps*. 1987.

Assmann, Karl. "Hitler and the German Officer Corps." *U.S. Naval Institute Proceedings* 82 (May 1956).

Badoglio, Pietro. *Italy and the Second World War*, Muriel Currey, trans. 1948. Reprint ed., 1976.

Balck, Hermann, and F. W. von Mellenthin. "Generals Balck and von Mellenthin on Tactics: Implications for NATO Military Doctrine, Dec. 19, 1980." U.S. Army Command and General Staff College, Publication M-313–5. 1981.

Baldwin, Hansen W. *Battles Won and Lost*. 1976.

———. *The Critical Years, 1939–1941*. 1976.

Bannister, Sybil. *I Lived Under Hitler*. 1957.

Barker, A. J. *Afrikakorps*. 1978.

Barnett, Correlli, ed. *Hitler's Generals*. 1989.

Bartov, Omar. *The Eastern Front, 1941–1945: German Troops and the Barbarisation of Warfare*. 1986.

Bibliography

Baumann, Hans. *Die 35 Infanterie Division im Zweiten Weltkrieg.* 1964.

Baumbach, Werner. *The Life and Death of the Luftwaffe.* 1960.

Beck, Alois. *Die 297 Infanterie-Division.* 1983.

Beck, Earl R. *Under the Bombs.* 1986.

———. *Verdict on Schacht.* 1955.

Bekker, Cajus. *Hitler's Naval War.* 1974.

———. *The Luftwaffe War Diaries.* 1969.

Benary, Albert. *Die Berliner 257 Baeran-Division.* 1957.

Benoist-Mechin, Jacques. *Sixty Days That Shook the West: The Fall of France.* 1963.

Bethell, Nicholas W. *The War Hitler Won.* 1972.

Beyersdorff, Ernst. *Geschichte der 110 Infanterie-Division.* 1965.

Bidlingmaier, Gerhard. "Exploits and End of the Battleship *Bismarck.*" *U.S. Naval Institute Proceedings* 84 (July 1958).

Bock und Polach, Berndt von, and Hans Grene. *Weg und Schicksal der bespannten 290 Infanterie-Division.* 1986.

Boehmer, Rudolf, and Werner Haupt. *Fallschirmjaeger.* 1979.

Boucsein, Heinrich. *Halten oder Sterben: Die hessisch-thueringische 129 Infanterie-Division in Russlandfeldzug und Ostpreussen, 1941–1945.* 1999.

Braake, Guenther. *Bildchronik der 126 rheinisch-westfaelischen 126 Infanterie-Division.* 1985.

Bradley, Dermot, Karl-Friedrich Hildebrand, and Markus Roevekamp. *Die Generale des Heeres, 1921–1945.* 7 vols. 1993–2006.

Braun, Julius. *Enzian und Edelweiss: Die 4 Gebirgs-Division, 1940–1945.* 1955.

Brehm, Werner. *Mein Kriegstagebuch, 1939–1945: Mit der 7 Panzer-Division 5 Jahre in West und Ost.* 1953.

Breithaupt, Hans. *Die Geschichte der 30 Infanterie-Division, 1939–1945.* 1955.

Brett-Smith, Richard. *Hitler's Generals.* 1977.

Breymayer, Helmut. *Das Wiesel–Geschichte der 125 Infanterie-Division, 1940 bis 1944.* 1982.

British Broadcasting Corporation, in Association with the Arts and Entertainment Network. "The Fatal Attraction of Adolf Hitler," Peter Graves, narrator. 1989.

Brown, Dale M., and the Editors of Time-Life Books. *The Luftwaffe.* 1982.

Bullock, Alan J. *Hitler: A Study in Tyranny.* 1964.

Burchardt, Lothar. "The Impact of the War Economy on the Civilian Population of Germany during the First and Second World Wars." In *The German Military in the Age of Total War*, Wilhelm Deist, ed., pp. 40–70. 1985.

Caidin, Martin. *The Tigers Are Burning.* 1974. Reprint ed., 1975.

Carell, Paul. *Foxes of the Desert.* 1960. Reprint ed., 1972.

———. *Hitler Moves East, 1941–1943.* 1965. Reprint ed., 1966.

Carlson, Verner R. "Portrait of a German General Staff Officer." *Military Review* 70 (April 1990).

Carnes, James D. "A Study in Courage: General Walther von Seydlitz's Opposition to Hitler." Unpublished Ph.D. Dissertation, Florida State University. 1976.

Carter, Kit C., and Robert Mueller, comp. *The Army Air Force in World War II: A Combat Chronology, 1941–1945.* 1973.

Carver, Michael. *El Alamein.* 1962.

Chant, Christopher, et al. *Hitler's Generals and Their Battles.* 1979.

———. *The Marshall Cavendish Illustrated History of World War II.* 25 vols. 1979.

Chapman, Guy. *Why France Fell: The Defeat of the French Army in 1940.* 1968.

Charman, Terry C. *The German Home Front, 1939–1945.* 1989.

Choltitz, Dietrich von. *Soldat unter Soldaten.* 1951.

Churchill, Winston S. *Closing the Ring.* 1951

Ciano, Galeazzo. *The Ciano Diaries, 1939–1943*, Hugh Gibson, ed. 1946.

Clark, Alan. *Barbarossa: The Russian-German Conflict, 1941–1945.* 1965.

Collier, Richard L., and the Editors of Time-Life Books. *War in the Desert.* 1979.

Constable, Trevor J., and Raymond F. Toliver. *Horrido!* 1968.

Conze, Werner. *Die Geschichte der 291 Infanterie-Division, 1940–1945.* 1953.

Cooper, Matthew. *The German Air Force.* 1978.

———. *The German Army, 1933–1945.* 1978.

Cooper, Matthew, and James Lucas. *Panzer: The Armored Force of the Third Reich.* 1976.

Craig, William. *Politics of the Prussian Army.* 1956.

Cruickshank, Charles. *Greece, 1940–1941.* 1976.

Czarnomski, F. B., ed. *The Fight for Poland.* 1941.

Dallin, Alexander. *German Rule in Russia.* 1957.

Davin, Daniel M. *Official History of New Zealand in the Second World War, 1939–1945: Crete.* 1953.

Deighton, Len. *Blitzkrieg: From the Rise of Hitler to the Fall of Dunkirk.* 1979.

Deist, Wilhelm, ed. *The German Military in the Age of Total War.* 1985.

Deist, Wilhelm. *The Wehrmacht and German Rearmament.* 1980.

Deist, Wilhelm, Manfred Messerschmidt, Hans-Erich Volkmann, and Wolfram Wette. "Causes and Preconditions of German Aggression." In *The German Military in the Age of Total War*, Wilhelm Deist, ed., pp. 336–53. 1985.

Denniston, Peter. "Jaeger Kopold." Available at www.gebirgsjaeger.4mg.com.

Denzel, Egon. *Die Luftwaffen-Felddivision, 1942–1945.* 3rd ed. 1976.

Desch, John. "The 1941 German Army/The 1944–1945 U.S. Army: A Comparative Analysis of Two Forces in Their Primes." In *Hitler's Army: The Evolution and Structure of the German Forces.* 1995.

Detlev von Plato, Anton. *Die Geschichte der 5 Panzer-Division, 1939–1945.* 1978.

Deulffer, Jost. "Determinants of German Naval Policy, 1920–1939." In *The German Military in the Age of Total War*, Wilhelm Deist, ed. 1985.

Deutsch, Harold C. *The Conspiracy Against Hitler in the Twilight War.* 1978.

———. *Hitler and His Generals: The Hidden Crisis, January–June 1938.* 1978.

Dieckhoff, Gerhard. *3 Infanterie-Division, 3 Infanterie-Division (mot.), 3 Panzergrenadier-Division.* 1960.

DiNardo, Richard L. *Mechanized Juggernaut or Military Anachronism? Horses and the German Army of World War II.* 1991.

Dobson, Christopher, John Miller, and Ronald Payne. *The Cruelist Night.* 1979.

Documents on German Foreign Policy. Series D. German Foreign Office. 1949.

Doenitz, Karl. *Ten Years and Twenty Days.* 1959.

Drum, Karl. "The German Air Force in the Spanish Civil War." U.S. Air Force Historical Studies, no. 150. Aerospace Studies Institute. 1965.

Bibliography

Dulles, Allen W., and Peter Hoffmann. *Germany's Underground*. 1947.

Dupuy, T. N. *A Genius for War*. 1984.

Dupuy, T. N., and Paul Martell. *Great Battles on the Eastern Front*. 1982.

Dwonchya, Wayne M. "Armored Onslaught Frozen." *World War II* 4 (May 1989).

Edwards, Roger. *German Airborne Troops, 1936–1945*. 1974.

———. *Panzer: A Revolution in Warfare, 1939–1945*. 1989.

Eisenhower, Dwight D. *Crusade in Europe*. 1949.

Eisenhower, John S. D. *The Bitter Woods*. 1969.

Ellis, L. E. *The War in France and Flanders, 1939–1940*. 1953.

Emmerson, James T. *The Rhineland Crisis*. 1977.

Engelmann, Joachim. *Die 18 Infanterie- und Panzergrenadier-Division, 1934–1945*. 1984.

Esteban-Infantes, Emilio. *Die Blaue Division*. 1958.

Farrar-Hockley, A. H. *Student*. 1973.

Finnegan, Jack. "A Man Called Lucy." *World War II* 3 (January 1989).

Fleming, Gerald. *Hitler and the Final Solution*. 1986.

Fletcher, Harry R. "Legion Condor: Hitler's Military Aid to Franco." Unpublished Master's Thesis, University of Wisconsin. 1961.

Foerster, Juergen E. "The Dynamics of Volkegemeinschaft: The Effectiveness of German Military Establishment in the Second World War." In *Military Effectiveness*, Allan R. Millett and Williamson Murray, eds., vol. 3, *The Second World War*. 1988.

Foster, Tony. *Meeting of the Generals*. 1986.

Frank, Wolfgang. *The Sea Wolves*, R. O. B. Long, trans. 1958.

Frankland, Noble. *Bomber Offensive: The Devastation of Europe*. 1970.

Fraser, David. *Knight's Cross: A Life of Field Marshal Erwin Rommel*. 1994.

Frischauer, Willi. *Reichsmarschall Hermann Goering*. 1951.

Fuerbringer, Herbert. *9 SS-Panzer-Division "Hohenstaufen."* 1984.

Fuller, J. F. C. *The Second World War*. 1949.

Gackenholz, Herman. "The Collapse of Army Group Center." In *Decisive Battles of World War II*, H. A. Jacobsen and J. Rohwer, eds., pp. 355–83. 1965.

Galante, Pierre. *Operation Valkyrie: The German Generals' Plot Against Hitler*. 1981.

Galland, Adolf. *The First and the Last*. 1954. Reprint ed., 1987.

Gallo, Max. *The Night of the Long Knives*, Lily Emmet, trans. 1972. Reprint ed., 1973.

Gisevius, Hans Bernd. *To the Bitter End*, Richard Winston and Clara Winston, trans. 1947. Reprint ed., 1975.

Goebbels, Paul Joseph. *The Goebbels Diaries*, Louis P. Lochner, ed. and trans. 1948. Reprint ed., 1971.

Goerlitz, Walter. *The German General Staff, 1657–1945*. 1953. Reprint ed., 1957.

———. *Paulus and Stalingrad*. 1974.

———. *Walter Model: Strategie der Defensives*. 2nd ed. 1975.

Goodspeed, D. J. *The German Wars, 1914–1945*. 1977.

Goralski, Robert. *World War II Almanac, 1931–1945*. 1981.

Gordon, Harold J., Jr. *The Reichswehr and the German Republic, 1919–1926.* 1957.

Gouhard, A. *The Battle of France, 1940.* 1959.

Graber, G. S. *Stauffenberg.* 1973.

Grams, Rolf. *Die 14 Panzer-Division, 1940–1945.* 1957.

Graser, Gerhard. *Zwischen Kattegat und Kaukasus: Weg und Kaempfe der 198 Infanterie-Division, 1939–1945.* 1961.

Grossmann, Horst. *Geschichte der rheinisch-westfaelischen 6 Infanterie-Division, 1939–1945.* 1958.

Grube, Rudolf. *Unternehmen Erinnerung: Eine Chronik ueber den Weg und den Einsatz des Grenadier-Regiment 317 in der 211 Infanterie-Division, 1935–1945.* 1961.

Grunberger, Richard. *The Twelve-Year Reich.* 1971.

Gschoepf, Rudolf. *Mein Weg mit der 45 Infanterie-Division.* 1955.

Guderian, Heinz. *Panzer Leader*, Constantine Fitzgibbon, trans. 1957. Reprint ed., 1967.

Gundelack, Karl. "The Battle for Crete, 1941." In Hans-Adolf Jacobsen and J. Rohwer, *Decisive Battles of World War II*, Edward Fitzgerald, trans. 1965.

Gundlack, Georg. *Wolchow-Kesselschlacht der 291 Infanterie-Division (Bildband).* 1995.

Guttman, Jon. "Bid for Roman Empire." *World War II* 5 (November 1990).

Haape, Heinrich. *Moscow Tram Stop.* 1957.

Hake, Friedrich von. *Der Schicksalsweg der 13 Panzer-Division, 1939–1945.* 1971.

Halder, Franz. *The Halder Diaries*, Arnold Lissance, ed., and Office of the Chief of Counsel for War Crimes, Office of the Military Government, U.S., trans. 2 vols. 1948. Reprint ed., 1976.

———. *The Halder War Diary, 1939–1942*, Charles Burdick and Hans-Adolf Jacobsen, eds. 1988.

Hamilton, Nigel. *Master of the Battlefield: Monty's War Years, 1942–1944.* 1983.

Hanser, Richard. *True Tales of Hitler's Reich.* 1962.

Hart, B. H. Liddell. *History of the Second World War.* 2 vols. 1972.

Hart, W. E. *Hitler's Generals.* 1944.

Hartmann, Theodor. *Wehrmacht Divisional Signs, 1938–1945.* 1970.

Haslob, Gevert. *Ein Blich zurueck im die Eifel–Schicksalsweg der 89 Infanterie-Division.* 2000.

Hassell, Ulrich von. *The Von Hassell Diaries, 1938–1944.* 1979.

Hastings, Max. *Das Reich.* 1981.

Haupt, Werner. *Das Buch der Panzertruppe, 1916–1945.* 1989.

———. *Geschichte der 134 Infanterie-Division.* 1971.

———. *Heeresgruppe Nord, 1941–1945.* 1966.

———. *A History of the Panzer Troops*, Edward Force, trans. 1990.

———. *Der springende Reiter—1 Kavallerie-Division—24 Panzer-Division im Bild.* 1962.

———. *Die 260 Infanterie-Division, 1940–1944.* 1970.

Hermann, Carl Hans. *Die 9 Panzerdivision, 1939–1945.* N.d.

———. *68 Kriegsmonate: Der Weg der 9 Panzerdivision durch zweiten Weltkrieg.* 1975.

Hertlein, Wilhelm. *Chronik der 7 Infanterie-Division.* 1984.

Hilberg, Raul. *The Destruction of the European Jews.* 1961.

Bibliography

Hildebrand, Hans-Friedrich. *Die Generale der deutschen Luftwaffe, 1935–1945.* 3 vols. 1990–92.

Hildebrand, Hans H., and Ernst Henriot. *Deutschland Admirale, 1849–1945.* 3 vols. 1990.

Hinze, Rolf. *Geschichte der 31 Infanterie-Division.* 1997.

Hoehne, Heinz. *Canaris*, J. Maxwell Brownjohn, trans. 1979.

———. *The Order of the Death's Head*, Richard Berry, trans. 1971.

Hoerner, Helmut. *A German Odyssey*, Allan K. Powell, ed. and trans. 1991.

Hoffmann, Dieter. *Die Magdeburger Division—Zur Geschichte der 13 Infanterie— und 13 Panzer-Division, 1935–1945.* 1999.

Hoffmann, Peter. *The History of the German Resistance, 1933–1945.* 1977.

Hoppe, Harry. *Die 278 Infanterie-Division in Italien, 1944–1945.* 1953.

Horne, Alister. *To Lose a Battle: France, 1940.* 1969.

Hossbach, Friedrich. *Infanterie im Ostfeldzug, 1941–1942 (31 Infanterie-Division).* 1951.

Howe, George F. *Northwest Africa: Seizing the Initiative in the West.* 1957.

Hoyt, Edwin P. *The U-Boat Wars.* 1984. Reprint ed., 1986.

Hubatsch, Walter. *Geschichte der 61 Infanterie-Division.* 2nd ed. 1961.

International Military Tribunal. *Trial of the Major War Criminals Before the International Military Tribunal.* 42 vols. 1946–48.

Irving, David. *Hitler's War.* 2 vols. 1977.

———. *The Rise and Fall of the Luftwaffe: The Life of Field Marshal Erhard Milch.* 1973.

———. *The Trail of the Fox.* 1977.

———. *The War Path: Hitler's Germany, 1933–1939.* 1979.

Jackson, W. G. F. *The Battle for North Africa, 1940–1943.* 1975.

Jacobsen, Hans-Adolf. "Dunkirk, 1940." In Hans-Adolf Jacobsen and J. Rohwer. *Decisive Battles of World War II*, Edward Fitzgerald, trans. 1965.

Jacobsen, Hans-Adolf, and J. Rohwer. *Decisive Battles of World War II*, Edward Fitzgerald, trans. 1965.

Jenner, Martin. *Die 216/272 niedersaechsische Infanterie-Division, 1939–1945.* 1964.

Jukes, Geoffrey. *Kursk.* 1968.

Kaltenegger, Roland. *Kampf der Gebirgsjaeger um die Westalpen und den Semmering: Die Kriegschroniken der 8 und 9 Gebirgs-Division "Kampfgruppe Semmering."* 1987.

Kamenestsky, Ihor. *Hitler's Occupation of the Ukraine.* 1956.

Kameradschaftsbund 8. Jaeger-Division. *Die Geschichte der 8 (Oberschlesisch-sudetendeutschen) Infanterie-Jaeger-Division.* 1979.

Kameradschaftsbund 16. Panzer-und Infanterie-Division. *Bildband der 16 Panzer-Division.* 1956.

Kameradschaftsdienst 35. Infanterie-Division. *Die 35 Infanterie-Division, 1935–1945, Deutsche Infanterie-Divisionen im Bild.* 1980.

Kardel, Hennecke. *Die Geschichte der 179 Infanterie-Division.* 1953.

Kardorff, Ursula von. *Diary of a Nightmare: Berlin, 1942–1945*, Ewan Butler, trans. 1965. Reprint ed., 1966.

Keegan, John. *Waffen SS: The Asphalt Soldiers.* 1970.

Keilig, Wolf. *Die Generale des Heeres.* 1983.

Keitel, Wilhelm. *In the Service of the Reich*, Walter Goerlitz, ed. 1966.

Kennedy, Robert M. "The German Campaign in Poland." U.S. Department of the Army Pamphlet 20-255. 1956.

Kersten, Felix. *The Memoirs of Doctor Felix Kersten*. 1947.

Kesselring, Albert. *A Soldier's Record*. 1954. Reprint ed., 1970.

Kilgast, Emil. *Rueckblick auf die Geschichte der 302 Infanterie-Division*. 1976.

Kimche, Jon. *The Unfought Battle*. 1968.

Kiriakopoulos, G. C. *Ten Days to Destiny*. 1985. Reprint ed., 1986.

Klatt, Paul. *Die 3 Gebirgs-Division*. 1958.

Knappe, Siegfried. *Soldat*. 1992.

Knappe, Siegfried, and Ted Brusaw. "At What Cost!" Manuscript in possession of the author. N.d.

Knobelsdorf, Otto von. *Geschichte der niedersaechsischen 19 Panzer-Division*. 1958.

Knoblauch, K. *Kampf und Untergang einer Infanterie-Division: Die 95 Infanterie-Division*. 2 vols. 1991.

Koch, H. W., ed. *Aspects of the Third Reich*. 1985.

Koch, H. W. "Hitler's 'Programme' and the Genesis of Operation "Barbarossa." In *Aspects of the Third Reich*, H. W. Koch, ed., pp. 39–61. 1985.

Koch, Horst-Adalbert. *Die Geschichte der deutschen Flakartillerie, 1935–1945*. 1955.

Kraeutler, Matthias and Karl Springenschmid. *Schichsal und Weg der 2 Gebirgs-Division*. N.d.

Kramarz, Joachim. *Stauffenberg*. 1967.

Krancke, Theodor, and H. J. Brennecke. *Pocket Battleships*. 1958.

Kriegstagebuch des Oberkommando der Wehrmacht (Wehrmachtfuehungsstab). 4 vols. 1961.

Kroener, Bernard R. "Squaring the Circle: The Blitzkreig Strategy and Manpower Shortage, 1939–1942." In *The German Military in the Age of Total War*, William Deist, ed., pp. 282–303. 1985.

Krueger, Heinz F. *Bildband der rheinisch-pfaelzischen 263 Infanterie-Division, 1939–1945*. 1962.

Kueppers, F. W. *Taten und Schicksal der mittelrheinisch-hessisch-saarpfaelzischen 197 Infanterie-Division*. 1969.

Kurowski, Frank. *Panzer Aces*, David Johnston, trans. 1992.

Kursiestis, Andris J. *Wehrmacht at War, 1939–1945*. 1998.

Kuznetsov, Anatoli A. *Babi Yar*, David Floyd, trans. 2nd ed. 1970.

Lamey, Hubert. *Der Weg der 118 Jaeger-Division*. 1954.

Landwehr, Richard. "Budapest: The Stalingrad of the Waffen-SS." *Siegrunen*, no. 37 (1985).

Lang, Joachim von. *Bormann: The Man Who Manipulated Hitler*, Christa Armstrong and Peter White, trans. 1979. Reprint ed., 1981.

Lanz, Hubert. *Gebirgsjaeger Die 1 Gebirgsdivision, 1935–1945*. 1954.

Law, Richard D., and Craig W. H. Luther. *Rommel*. 1980.

Lehmann, Rudolf. *The Leibstandarte*, Nick Olcott, trans. 4 vols. 1987–98.

Lemelsen, Joachim. *29 Division*. 1955.

Lewin, Ronald. *Rommel as a Military Commander*. 1970.

Loeser, Jochen. *Bittere Pflicht: Kampf und Untergang der 76 Berlin-Brandenburgischen Infanterie-Division*. 1986.

Bibliography

Lohse, Gerhard. *Geschichte der rheinisch-westfaelischen 126 Infanterie-Division.* 1957.

Lucas, James. *Alpine Elite: German Mountain Troops in World War II.* 1980.

———. *Germany's Elite Panzer Force: Grossdeutschland.* 1978.

———. *Hitler's Enforcers.* 1996.

———. *War on the Eastern Front, 1941–1945.* 1979.

Luck, Hans von. *Panzer Commander.* 1989.

Lusar, Rudolf. *German Secret Weapons of World War II.* 1959.

Luther, Craig W. H. *Blood and Honor: The History of the 12th SS Panzer Division "Hitler Youth," 1943–1945.* 1987.

MacDonald, Charles B. "The Fall of the Low Countries and France." In *A Concise History of World War II,* Vincent J. Esposito, ed. 1964.

Macksey, Kenneth. *Kesselring.* 1978.

MacLean, French L. "German General Officer Casualties in World War II: Lessons for Future War." *Military Review* 70 (April 1990).

Maier, Klaus A. "Total War and German Air Force Doctrine Before the Second World War." In *The German Military in the Age of Total War,* Wilhelm Deist, ed., pp. 210–19. 1985.

Manstein, Erich von. *Lost Victories,* Anthony G. Powell, trans. 1958. Reprint ed. 1982.

Manteuffel, Hasso von. *Die 7 Panzer-Division im Zweiten Weltkrieg.* 1986.

Manvell, Roger. *Goering.* 1962.

Manvell, Roger, and Heinrich Fraenkel. *Himmler.* 1965. Reprint ed., 1968.

March, Cyril, ed. *The Rise and Fall of the German Air Force, 1933–1945.* 1948. Reprint ed., 1983.

Markovna, Nina. *Nina's Journey.* 1989.

Mason, Herbert M., Jr. *The Rise of the Luftwaffe.* 1973.

Mayrhofer, Franz. *Geschichte des Grenadier-Regiment 315 der bayrischen 167 Infanterie-Division—Almhuetten-Division, 1939–1945.* 1975.

Mehner, Kurt, ed. *Die Geheimen Tagesberichte der deutschen Wehrmachtfuehrung im Zweiten Weltkrieg, 1939–1945.* 12 vols. 1984–1995.

Mehrle, Hans, and Walter Schelm. *Von den Kaempfen der 215 wuerttembergisch-badischen Infanterie-Division.* 1954.

Meier-Welcker, Hans. *Seeckt.* 1967.

Mellenthin, F. W. von. *German Generals of World War II.* 1977.

———. *Panzer Battles.* 1956.

Melzer, Walter. *Geschichte der 252 Infanterie-Division, 1939–1945.* 1960.

Memminger, Fritz. *Die Kriegsgeschichte der Windhund-Division, 16 Infanterie-Division (mot.), 16 Panzergrenadier-Division, 116 Panzer-Division.* 3 vols. 1962.

Messerschmidt, Manfred. "German Military Effectiveness Between 1919 and 1939." In *Military Effectiveness,* Alan R. Millet and Williamson Murray, eds. Vol. 2, *The Interwar Period.* 1988.

Metzsch, Friedrich-August. *Die Geschichte der 22 Infanterie-Division, 1939–1945.* 1952.

Metzsch, Walther. *Geschichte der 252 Infanterie-Division, 1939–1945.* 1960

Meyer, Franz. *Tapfere Schlesier: Mit der 102 Infanterie-Division im Russland.* 1983.

Meyer-Detring, Wilhelm. *Die 137 Infanterie-Division im Mittelabschnitt der Ostfront.* 1962.

Miehe, Walter. *Der Weg der 225 Infanterie-Division*. 1980.

Military Intelligence Division, U.S. War Department. "The German Replacement Army (Ersatzheer)." On file at the U.S. Army War College, Carlisle Barracks, Pennsylvania. 1945.

Millett, Allan R., and Williamson Murray, eds. *Military Effectiveness*. Vol. 2, *The Interwar Period*. 1988.

Milward, Alan S. *The German Economy at War*. 1965.

Mitcham, Samuel W., Jr. *Order of Battle of the German Army in World War II*. 3 vols. 2007.

———. *Panzer Legions*. 2001.

———. *Rommel's Desert Commanders*. 2007.

Mitcham, Samuel W., Jr., and Gene Mueller. *Hitler's Commanders*. 1992.

Mitchell, Ruth. *The Serbs Chose War*. 1941.

Moll, Otto E. *Die deutschen Generalfeldmarshaelle, 1939–1945*. 1961.

Morison, Samuel Eliot. *History of the United States Naval Operations in World War II*. Vol. 9, *Sicily-Salerno-Anzio*. 1962.

Mosley, Leonard. *The Reich Marshal*. 1974.

Mosley, Leonard, and the Editors of Time-Life Books. *The Battle of Britain*. 1977.

Mueller-Hillebrand, Burkhart. *Germany and Its Allies*. 1980.

———. *Das Heer*. 3 vols. 1954–69.

Munoz, Antonio J. *The Kaminski Brigade: A History, 1941–1945*. 1996.

Munzel, Oskar. *Die deutschen Panzer Truppen bis 1945*. 1965.

Murray, Williamson. *Strategy for Defeat: The Luftwaffe, 1933–1945*. 1983.

Musciano, Walter A. *Messerschmitt Aces*. 1982.

Nafziger, George F. *The German Order of Battle: Infantry in World War II*. 2000.

———. *The German Order of Battle: Panzers and Artillery in World War II*. 1999.

Neidhardt, Hanns. *Mit Tanne und Eichenlaub: Kriegschronik der 100 Jaeger-Division, vormals 100 leichte Infanterie-Division*. 1981.

Neumann, Peter. *The Black March*. 1960.

Newland, Samuel J. *Cossacks in the German Army*. 1991.

Nitz, Guenther. *Die 292 Infanterie-Division*. 1957.

Noelke, Hans, ed. *Die 71 Infanterie-Division im Zweiten Weltkrieg, 1939–1945*. 1984.

Nogueres, Henri. *Munich*, Patrick O'Brian, trans. 1965.

Oberkommando des Wehrmacht. *Kriegstagebuch des Oberkommando des Wehrmacht*. 4 vols. 1961. Reprint ed., 1982.

O'Neill, Robert J. *The German Army and the Nazi Party, 1919–1933*. 1966.

Ott, Ernst-Ludwig. *Jaeger und Feind: Geschichte und Opfergang der 97 Jaeger-Division*. 1982.

———. *Die Spielhahnjaeger, 1940–1945: Bilddokumentation der 97 Jaeger-Division, 1940–1945*. 1982.

Overy, R. J. *The Air War, 1939–1945*. 1980.

Pabst, Helmut. *The Outermost Frontier*. 1957.

Packard, Reynolds, and Eleanor Packard. *Balcony Empire*. 1942.

Padfield, Peter. *Doenitz: The Last Fuehrer*. 1984.

Paul, Wolfgang. *Geschichte der 18 Panzer-Division, 1940–1943*. N.d.

———. *Die Truppengeschichte der 18 Panzer-Division, 1940–1943 (mit 18 Artillerie-Division, 1943–1944, und Heeres-Artillerie Brigade 88, 1944–1945*. 1988.

Bibliography

Pauley, Bruce F. *Hitler and the Forgotten Nazis: A History of the Austrian National Socialism*. 1989.

Payk, Ernst. *Die Geschichte der 206 Infanterie-Division, 1939–1944*. 1952.

Payne, Robert. *The Life and Death of Adolf Hitler*. 1973.

Perrett, Bryan. *Knights of the Black Cross: The Panzerwaffe and Its Leaders*. 1986.

Pertinax [André Géraud]. *The Gravediggers of France*. 1944.

Pesch, Franz, Hans May, Matthias Roth, and Jupp Steffen. *Die 72 Infanterie-Division, 1939–1945*. 1982.

Pfannes, Charles E., and Victor A. Salamone. *The Great Admirals of World War II*. Vol. 2, *The Germans*. 1984.

Pirnie, Bruce R. "First Test of the War Machine." *World War II* 1 (January 1987).

Pitt, Barrie, and the Editors of Time-Life Books. *The Battle of the Atlantic*. 1980.

Playfair, I. S. O. *The Mediterranean and Middle East*. Vol. 3, *British Fortunes Reach Their Lowest Ebb*. 1960.

Plocher, Hermann. "The German Air Force Versus Russia, 1941." U.S. Air Force Historical Studies, no. 153. U.S. Air Force Historical Division, Aerospace Studies Institute, Maxwell Air Force Base, Alabama. 1965.

———. "The German Air Force Versus Russia, 1942." U.S. Air Force Historical Studies, no. 154. U.S. Air Force Historical Division, Aerospace Studies Institute, Maxwell Air Force Base, Alabama. 1965.

———. "The German Air Force Versus Russia, 1943." U.S. Air Force Historical Studies, no. 155. U.S. Air Force Historical Division, Aerospace Studies Institute, Maxwell Air Force Base, Alabama. 1965.

Podzun, H. H. *Weg und Schicksal der 21 Infanterie-Division*. 1951.

Pohlmann, Hartwig. *Geschichte der 96 Infanterie-Division, 1939–1945*. 1959.

Porten, Edward P. von der. *The German Navy in World War II*. 1969.

Preradovich, Nikolaus von. *Die Generale der Waffen-SS*. 1985.

Proctor, Raymond L. *Hitler's Luftwaffe in the Spanish Civil War*. 1983.

Quarrie, Bruce. *Panzer-Grenadier-Division "Grossdeutschland."* 1977.

Quinett, Robert L. "The German Army Confronts the NSFO." *Journal of Contemporary History* 13 (January 1978).

Raeder, Erich. *My Life*, Henry W. Drexel, trans. 1960.

Rebentisch, Ernst. *Zum Kaukasus und zu den Tauern: Die Geschichte der 23 Panzer-Division, 1941–1945*. 1963.

Reck-Malleczemen, Friedrich. *Diary of a Man in Despair*. 1970.

Rehm, W. *Jassy*. 1959.

Reinicke, Adolf. *Die 5 Jaeger Division, 1939–1945*. 1962.

Reinicke, Adolf, H. G. Hermann, and Friedrich Kittel. *Die 62 Infanterie-Division, 1938–1944—Die 62 Volks-Grenadier-Division, 1944–1945*. 1968.

Reitlinger, Gerald. *The Final Solution*. 1961.

———. *The SS: Alibi of a Nation, 1922–1945*. 1968.

Rendulic, Lothar. *Gekaempft Gesiegt*. 1957.

Reynolds, Nicholas. *Treason Was No Crime*. 1976.

Riebenstahl, Horst. *The 1st Panzer Division*, Edward Force, trans. 1990.

Riedel, Hermann. *Aasen/Schicksal einer Division (352 Volks-Grenadier Division)*. 1969.

Ringel, Julius. *Hurra die Gams: Ein Gedenkbuch fuer die Solaten der 5 Gebirgsdivision.* N.d.

Ritgen, Helmut. *Die Geschichte der Panzer-Lehr-Division im Westen, 1944–1945.* 1979.

———. *The 6th Panzer Division, 1937–1945.* 1982. Reprint ed., 1985.

Roemhild, Helmut. *Geschichte der 269 Infanterie-Division.* 1967.

Rohwer, Juergen. *Axis Submarine Successes, 1939–1945.* 1983.

Rommel, Erwin. *The Rommel Papers,* B. H. Liddell Hart, ed. 1953.

Rowe, Vivian. *The Great Wall of France: The Triumph of the Maginot Line.* 1967.

Rudel, Hans Ulrich. *Stuka Pilot.* 1958. Reprint ed., 1979.

Ruef, Karl. *Gebirgsjaeger zwischen Kreta und Murmansk: Die 6 Gebirgs-Division im Einsatz.* N.d.

Ruge, Friedrich. *Der Seekrieg.* 1977.

Ruhland, Paul John von. *As the World Churns.* N.d.

Sadarananda, Dana V. *Beyond Stalingrad.* 1990.

Sajer, Guy. *The Forgotten Soldier,* Lily Emmet Sajer, trans. 1965.

Salisbury, Harrison E. *The 900 Days: The Siege of Leningrad.* 1969.

Scheibert, Horst. *Bildband der 6 Panzer-Division, 1939–1945.* 1958.

———. *Die Traeger des deutschen Kreuzes in Gold.* N.d.

Scheiderbauer, Armin. *Adventures in My Youth: A German Soldier on the Eastern Front, 1941–1945,* C. F. Colton, trans. 2003.

Schick, Albert. *Die Geschichte der 10 Panzer-Division, 1939–1943.* 1993.

Schimak, Anton, Karl Lamprecht, and Friedrich Dettmer. *Die 44 Infanterie-Division: Tagebuch der Hoch- und Deutschmeister.* 1969.

Schlabendorff, Fabian von. *Revolt Against Hitler,* Gero V. S. Gaevernitz, ed. 1948.

Schmidt, August. *Geschichte der 10 Division, 10 Infanterie-Division (mot.), 10 Panzergrenadier-Division, 1935–1945.* 1963.

Schmidt, Paul. *Hitler's Interpreter.* 1951.

Schmitz, Peter, Klaus-Juergen Thies, Guenter Wegmann, and Christian Zweng. *Die deutschen Divisionen, 1939–1945.* 3 vols. 1993–97.

Schnabel, Ernst. *Weg und Schicksal der 183 Infanterie-Division: Geschichte der fraenkisch-sudetendeutschen 183 Infanterie-Division, Divisiongruppe 183 in der Korps-Abteilung C, 183 Volks-Grenadier-Division, 1939–1945.* 1988.

Schraml, Franz. *Kriegsschauplatz Kroatien: Die deutsch-kroatischen Legionaers-Divisionen 369, 373, 392, Infanterie-Division (kroat.).* 1962.

Schreiber, Gerhard. "The Mediterranean in Hitler's Strategy in 1940, 'Programme' and Military Planning." In *The German Military in the Age of Total War,* Wilhelm Deist, ed. 1985.

Schrodek, G. W. *Die 11 Panzer-Division "Gespenster-Division"–Bilddokumente, 1940–1945.* 1984.

Schroeder, Juergen, and Joachim Schultz-Naumann. *Die Geschichte der pommerschen 32 Infanterie-Division, 1935–1945.* 1962.

Schuschnigg, Kurt von. *Austrian Requiem,* Franz von Hildebrand, trans. 1946.

Seaton, Albert. *The Battle of Moscow.* 1980. Reprint ed., 1981.

———. *The Fall of Fortress Europe, 1943–1945.* 1981.

———. *The German Army, 1933–1945.* 1981. Reprint ed., 1982.

———. *The Russo-German War, 1941–1945.* 1970.

Bibliography

Seemen, Gerhard von. *Die Ritterkreuztraeger, 1938–1945.* 1976.

Senger und Etterlin, Frido von. *Neither Fear Nor Hope*, George Malcolm, trans. 1963. Reprint ed., 1989.

———. *Die 24 Panzer-Division, vormals 1 Kavallerie-Division, 1939–1945.* 1962.

Shachtman, Tom. *The Phony War, 1939–1940.* 1982.

Shaw, John, and the Editors of Time-Life Books. *Red Army Resurgent.* 1979.

Shirer, William L. *The Rise and Fall of the Third Reich.* 1960.

Shoemaker, John O. "Sichelschnitt." *Military Review* 42 (March 1962).

Snyder, Louis L. *Encyclopedia of the Third Reich.* 1976.

———. *Hitler's Elite.* 1989.

———. *Hitler's German Enemies.* 1990. Reprint ed., 1992.

Snydor, Charles W., Jr. *Soldiers of Destruction: The SS Death's Head Division, 1939–1945.* 1977.

Sokol, A. E. "German Attacks on the Murmansk Run." *U.S. Naval Institute Proceedings* 88 (December 1952).

Sorge, Martin K. *The Other Price of Hitler's War.* 1986.

Spaeter, Helmuth. *Panzerkorps Grossdeutschland Bilddokumentation.* 1984.

Speer, Albert. *Inside the Third Reich.* 1970.

Speidel, Wilhelm. "The Luftwaffe in the Polish Campaign." U.S. Air Force Historical Studies, no. 151. 1956.

Stahl, Friedrich Christian, et al. *Geschichte der 121 Ostpreussischen Infanterie-Division, 1940–1945.* 1970.

Stahlberg, Alexander. *Bounden Duty*, Patricia Crampton, trans. 1990.

Staiger, Georg. *26 Panzer-Division: Ihr Werden und Einsatz, 1942–1945.* 1957.

Stauffenberg, Friedrich von. "Panzer Commanders of the Western Front." Unpublished manuscript in the possession of the author.

———. "Papers." Unpublished papers in the possession of the author.

Stein, George. *Waffen-SS.* 1966.

Steinhoff, Johannes, Peter Pechel, and Dennis Showalter. *Voices From the Third Reich.* 1989.

Stoeber, Hans. *Die Eiserne Faust–Bildband der 17 SS-Panzergrenadier-Division "Goetz von Berlichingen."* 1966.

Stoves, Rolf O. G. *Die 1 Panzerdivision, 1935–1945: Die deutschen Panzerdivision in Bild.* N.d.

———. *Die Gepanzerten und Motorisierten deutschen Grossverbaende (Divisionen und selbstaendige Brigaden 1935–1945.* 1986.

———. *Die 22 Panzer-Division, 25 Panzer-Division, 27 Panzer-Division, und 233 Reserve-Panzer-Division.* 1985.

Strassner, Peter. *Europaeische Freiwillige: Die Geschichte der 5 SS-Panzer-Division "Wiking."* 1968.

Strawson, John. *The Battle for North Africa.* 1969.

———. *Hitler's Battles for Europe.* 1971.

Studnitz, Hans-Georg von. *While Berlin Burns.* 1964.

Suchenwirth, Richard. "Command and Leadership in the German Air Force." U.S. Air Force Historical Studies, no. 174. 1969.

———. "The Development of the German Air Force." U.S. Air Force Historical Studies, no. 160, Harry R. Fletcher, ed. 1968.

——. "Historical Turning Points in the German Air Force War Effort." U.S. Air Force Historical Studies, no. 189. 1969.

Taylor, Telford. *The Breaking Wave.* 1967.

——. *March of Conquest.* 1958.

——. *Munich.* 1979. Reprint ed., 1980.

——. *Sword and Swastika.* 1952. Reprint ed., 1969.

Tessin, Georg. *Formationgeschichte der Wehrmacht, 1933–1939.* 1974.

——. *Formationsgeschichte der Wehrmacht, 1933–1939: Stabe und Truppenteile des Heeres und der Luftwaffe.* 1959.

——. *Verbaende und Truppen der deutschen Wehrmacht und Waffen-SS im Zweiten Weltkrieg, 1939–1945.* 16 vols. 1973–81.

Tettau, Hans von, and Kurt Versock. *Geschichte der 24 Infanterie-Division, 1935–1945.* 1956.

Thomas, Franz. *Die Eichenlaubtraeger, 1940–1945.* 2 vols. 1997–98.

Thorwald, Juergen. *The Illusion: Soviet Soldiers in Hitler's Armies,* Richard and Clara Winston, trans. 1975.

Thumm, Helmut. *Der Weg der 5 Infanterie-und-Jaeger Division, 1921–1945.* 1976.

Tiemann, Reinhard. *Geschichte der 83 Infanterie-Division, 1939–1945.* 1960.

Toland, John. *Adolf Hitler.* 1976. Reprint ed., 1977.

Treffer, Rudolf. *Geschichte des Artillerie-Regiment 193 im Verband der 93 Infanterie-Division, 1939–1945.* 1988.

Trevor-Roper, Hugh R. *The Last Days of Hitler.* 1947. Reprint ed., 1973.

True to Type: A Selection from Letters and Diaries of German Soldiers and Civilians Collected on the Soviet-German Front. 1945.

Ullrich, Kar. *Wie ein Fels im Meer: Kriegsgeschichte der 3 SS-Panzer-Division "Totenkopf."* 2 vols. 1984, 1987.

U.S. Army Office of Military History. *Command Decisions.* 1959.

U.S. Chief Counsel for the Prosecution of Axis Criminality. *Nazi Conspiracy and Aggression.* 7 vols. 1946.

U.S. Department of the Army. "The German Campaign in the Balkans (Spring 1941)." U.S. Department of the Army Pamphlet 20-260. 1953.

——. "The German Campaign in Russia–Planning and Operations (1940–1942)." U.S. Department of the Army Pamphlet 20-261a. 1955.

U.S. Military Intelligence Service. "Order of Battle of the German Army, 1942." 1942.

——. "Order of Battle of the German Army, 1943." 1943.

U.S. War Department. *Technical Manual TM-E 30-451,* "Handbook on German Military Forces." 1945.

Vassiltchikov, Marie. *The Berlin Diaries, 1940–1945.* 1985. Reprint ed., 1987.

Velten, Wilhelm. *Vom Kugelbaum zur Handgranate: Der Weg der 65 Infanterie-Division.* 1974.

Vetter, Fritz. *Die 78 Infanterie- und Sturmdivision, 1938–1945: Eine Dokumentation in Bildern.* 1981.

Waite, Robert G. L. *Vanguard of Nazism: The Free Corps Movement in Postwar Germany, 1918–1923.* 1952.

Warlimont, Walter. "German Estimate of the United States, Russia, and Dakar." ETHINT 8, August 9, 1945.

Bibliography

————. *Inside Hitler's Headquarters*, R. H. Barry, trans. 1964. Reprint ed., n.d.

Watt, D. C. "German Plans for the Reoccupation of the Rhineland: A Note." *Journal of Contemporary History* 1 (October 1966).

Webster, Charles, and Noble Frankland. *The Strategic Air Offensive Against Germany, 1939–1945*. 4 vols. 1961.

Wedemeyer, Albert C. *Wedemeyer Reports*. 1958.

Wegner, Bernd. "The 'Aristocracy of National Socialism': The Role of the SS in National Socialist Germany." In *Aspects of the Third Reich*, H. W. Koch, ed. (1985).

Weizsaecker, Ernst von. *Memoirs*, John Andrews, trans. 1951. Reprint ed., 1951.

Werbaneth, James P. "Helpful Conduct by the Enemy." *World War II* 7 (May 1992).

Werthen, Wolfgang. *Geschichte der 16 Panzer-Division, 1939–1945*. 1958.

Wheeler-Bennett, John W. *Knaves, Fools, and Heroes*. 1974.

————. *The Nemesis of Power: The German Army in Politics, 1918–1945*. 1964. Reprint ed., 1967.

Whiting, Charles. *Hunters From the Sky: The German Parachute Corps, 1940–1945*. 1974.

Williamson, Gordon. *Infantry Aces of the Third Reich*. 1991.

Wilmot, Chester. *The Struggle for Europe*. 1981.

Windrow, Martin. *The Panzer Divisions*. 1985.

Wiskemann, Elizabeth. *The Rome-Berlin Axis*. 1949.

Wistrich, Robert. *Who's Who in Nazi Germany*. 1982.

Witte, Hans Joachim, and Peter Offermann. *Die Boeselagerschen Reiter: Das Kavallerie-Regiment Mitte und die aus ihm hervorgegangene 3 Kavallerie-Brigade/Division*. 1998.

Wood, Tony, and Bill Gunston. *Hitler's Luftwaffe*. N.d. Reprint ed., 1984.

Yerger, Mark C. *SS-Oberst-Gruppenfuehrer und Generaloberst der Waffen-SS Paul Hausser*. 1986.

————. *Waffen-SS Commanders: The Army, Corps and Divisional Leaders of a Legend*. Vol. 1, *Augsberger to Kreutz*; vol. 2, *Krueger to Zimmermann*. 1997–99.

Young, Desmond. *Rommel: The Desert Fox*. 1950. Reprint ed., 1965.

Young, Peter, ed. *The Marshall Cavendish Illustrated Encyclopedia of World War Two*. 20 vols. 1981.

Zaloga, Steven, and Victor Madej. *The Polish Campaign, 1939*. 1985.

Zeitzler, Kurt. "Men and Space in War: A German Problem in World War II." *Military Review* 42 (April 1962).

————. "Stalingrad." In *The Fatal Decisions*, William Richardson and Seymour Freidon, eds., pp. 115–65. 1956.

Zeller, Konrad, Hans Mehrle, and Theodor Glauner. *Weg und Schicksal der 215 wuerttembergisch-badischen Infanterie-Division, 1936–1945: Eine Dokumentation im Bildern*. 1980.

Ziemke, Earl F. "The German Northern Theater of Operations, 1940–1945." U.S. Department of the Army Pamphlet 20-271. 1959.

————. *Stalingrad to Berlin*. Office of the Chief of Military History, U.S. Department of the Army. 1968.

———. *Stalingrad to Berlin: The German Defeat in the East*. Office of the Chief of Military History, U.S. Department of the Army. 1966.

Ziemke, Earl F. and Magna E. Bauer. *Moscow to Stalingrad: Decision in the East*. 1975.

INTERNET SOURCES

http://en.wikipedia.org/wiki/Koszalin

http://50-infanterie-division.de

http://philosophy.elte.hu

http://spearhead1944.com/toe1.htm

http://www.das-ritterkreuz.de

http://www.diedeutschewehrmacht.de

http://www.feldgrau.com

http://www.forum.axishistory.com

http://www.gebirgsjaeger.4mg.com

http://www.lexikon.com

http://www.ritterkreuztraeger-1939-45.de

INDEX OF GERMAN MILITARY UNITS

Oberkommando des Wehrmacht (High Command of the Armed Forces or OKW), 108–9, 113–14, 119, 122, 157, 177–78, 187, 236, 246, 248, 263, 318, 326, 327, 346, 356, 376, 379, 441, 445, 447, 457, 462, 476, 480–81, 489–90, 554, 581, 585, 644, 646–47, 660, 666

**German Army
(including Waffen-SS units):**
Higher Commands
    Army Command, The, 11, 13
    OB East (*Oberbefehlshaber Ost*), 213, 215, 229, 612
    Oberkommando des Heeres (High Command of the Army or OKH), 109, 132, 137, 142, 145–46, 157, 173, 177, 179, 183, 185, 187, 209, 211, 215–16, 219, 227–28, 231, 248, 263, 273, 278–79, 286, 316, 318, 326–27, 333–34, 338, 346, 350, 352, 356, 385, 392, 397, 402, 432, 439, 444–47, 455–56, 465, 476, 479–80, 486–87, 494, 509, 520, 537, 543, 554, 605, 632, 639, 643, 647, 655, 663
    OB South (*Oberbefehlshaber Sued*), 547

Army Groups
    1, 11, 13, 14, 70, 144
    2, 11, 13, 70, 111, 112, 145, 155
    3, 69, 70, 120, 155
    4, 102, 109, 119, 144
    5, 124, 144
    6, 155
    A (1939–40), 273–76, 278–80, 285–86, 301, 303, 316, 324, 326, 328, 333–34, 339, 376
    A (1942), 638, 640, 643, 644, 645, 646, 647, 664, 667
    Afrika, 661
    B (1939–40), 273, 274, 277, 279, 280, 285, 301, 326, 333, 334, 335, 338, 339
    B (1942), 638, 640, 643, 644, 647, 653, 654, 663, 665
    C, 183, 187, 191, 225, 228, 273, 286, 334, 341, 350
    Center, 402, 440, 444–45, 447–48, 464–65, 474, 477–81, 484, 487, 492, 495, 498–99, 502, 506, 510–12, 514–15, 531, 635, 636–37
    D, 646
    Don, 664
    North, 187–88, 190, 213, 273, 440, 444–45, 447, 462, 474, 476, 478, 487, 513, 519–21, 523, 531, 536, 635–37, 664

South, 187–88, 190, 199, 203–5, 440, 444–45, 447, 474, 481–82, 492, 515, 519, 531, 537–38, 635–37, 639

Armies
  1st, 145, 183, 190, 214, 225, 226, 286
  1st Panzer, 389–90, 392, 395, 444–45, 471, 481–84, 486, 515, 517, 537, 631, 639–40, 642–43, 647
  2nd, 144–46, 183, 187–88, 225, 334, 339, 390–92, 395–96, 445, 471, 474, 480, 487, 491–92, 498, 502, 642–43
  2nd Panzer, 437, 444–45, 464–66, 471, 473–74, 481, 484, 487, 490–92, 499, 503, 505, 514
  3rd, 145, 183, 188, 190, 197, 201, 202, 205, 209, 213, 215, 225
  3rd Panzer, 444–45, 464, 465–66, 471, 478, 487–89, 491–92, 494, 497–99, 503, 508, 510, 512–13
  4th, 115, 145, 183, 188, 190, 197–98, 201–2, 213, 225, 324, 328, 333, 337, 444–45, 465–66, 471, 486–87, 491–92, 505–6, 509–12, 514
  4th Panzer, 444–45, 462, 471, 475–76, 478, 487–88, 492, 499, 503, 506, 508, 510, 512, 537, 640, 642–43, 647–48, 653–54, 655, 657, 664, 667
  5th, 145, 183, 225
  6th, 225, 274, 280, 285–86, 291, 293, 300–301, 303, 327, 329, 333, 338, 444–45, 481, 483, 516, 539, 631–32, 639, 641–42, 644, 647–48, 652, 654–55, 658–61, 663–64, 666–67
  7th, 145, 155, 183, 190, 225, 286
  8th, 120, 144, 145, 183, 188, 190, 203, 207, 211, 214, 225
  9th, 334, 337–38, 444–45, 462, 466, 486–87, 489, 491–92, 497, 499–502, 506, 510–14
  10th, 144, 145, 146, 183, 188, 190, 203, 204, 225, 652
  11th, 444, 445, 481, 483, 517, 531, 537, 632, 633, 634, 635, 664

12th, 144–46, 183, 188, 225, 285, 307, 313, 318, 334, 339, 389–92, 396, 401
14th, 144, 145, 214, 183, 188, 189, 190, 203, 204, 208, 225,
16th, 280, 285, 334, 339, 444, 445, 475, 476, 477, 479, 513, 521
17th, 444, 445, 481, 483, 484, 489, 537, 631, 640, 665
18th, 280, 285, 294, 296–99, 303, 334, 339, 341, 439, 444–45, 475–77, 479, 519, 521–22, 536
20th Mountain, 445
Lapland, 445, 479
Norway, 445, 479
Panzer Group (later Army) Afrika, 548, 549, 552, 555, 557, 559, 571, 572, 573, 574, 581
Replacement (Home), 115, 185, 219, 220, 225, 229, 230, 282, 437, 442, 443, 489, 638

Panzer Groups
  1st. *See* Armies, 1st Panzer
  2nd. *See* Armies, 2nd Panzer
  3rd. *See* Armies, 3rd Panzer
  4th. *See* Armies, 4th Panzer
  Guderian, 279, 334, 339, 341
  Kleist, 279, 285, 286, 303, 312, 327, 338, 340, 341

Corps
  I, 173, 190, 197, 209, 225, 504, 520, 523, 524
  I SS Panzer, 541
  II, 145, 190, 225, 337, 521, 524
  II SS, 16
  III, later III Panzer, 115, 190, 207, 225, 483, 484, 515, 632
  III (germ.) SS Panzer, 541
  IV, 145, 190, 208, 225, 301, 654, 657, 662
  V, 79, 145, 225, 502, 506, 510, 514
  VI, 145, 225, 510, 513
  VII, 120, 190, 209, 225, 473
  VIII, 134, 145, 190, 225, 226, 462, 662, 668
  IX, 145, 190, 225, 336, 460
  X, 145, 190, 207, 225, 327, 476, 477, 524

XI, 145, 190, 225, 392, 662, 667
XII, 145, 225
XIII, 120, 190, 207, 225
XIV Motorized, later Panzer, 101,
    145, 190, 208, 225, 279, 285,
    313, 333, 392, 395, 483, 654,
    662, 668
XV Motorized, 101, 190, 208, 225,
    279, 285, 304, 329, 333
XVI Motorized, later Panzer, 101,
    111, 120, 146, 174, 190, 208, 225,
    285, 301, 316, 336–37, 648
XVII, 125, 145, 190, 225, 664
XVIII, later XVIII Mountain, 125,
    145, 190, 209, 225, 342
XIX Motorized (later Panzer Group
    Guderian), 124, 174, 190, 198,
    202, 213, 225, 279–80, 285, 303–
    7, 315, 324
XX, 462, 509, 646
XXI, 190, 201, 202, 225, 247, 249
XXII, 190, 225
XXIII, 191, 513
XXIV Panzer, 191, 459, 473, 474,
    480, 484, 648
XXV, 191
XXVI, 216, 296, 297, 477
XXVII, 225, 301
XXVIII, 478
XXX, 225, 392, 398, 517, 538, 633,
    634
XXXVIII, 278, 337, 523
XXXIX Panzer, 298, 334, 339, 343,
    344, 478, 479, 480, 519, 520
XXXX Panzer, 392, 396, 398, 399,
    400, 512, 641, 642, 647
XXXXI Panzer, 278–79, 285, 303–4,
    306, 317, 334, 343, 392, 395, 397,
    462, 475, 478, 489, 513
XXXXII, 517, 633, 635
XXXXIII, 504, 505, 512
XXXXIV, 340, 504, 632
XXXXVI Panzer, 391, 392, 395, 396,
    481, 502, 513, 514
XXXXVII Panzer, 481, 484
XXXXVIII Panzer, 483, 641, 653, 655
XXXXIX Mountain, 392, 397
L, 392

LI, 392, 397, 648, 662, 663, 668
LII, 216, 392, 504
LIV, 517, 634
LVI Panzer, 80, 115, 463, 475, 477,
    499, 664
LVII (later LVII Panzer), 478, 512,
    665
LXVI, 79
Afrika (DAK), 385, 387, 423, 431–32,
    435–36, 543–44, 547, 550–53,
    557, 559, 561–62, 564, 567–68,
    571–74, 576–78
Cavalry, 34
Norway, 445
Wodrig, 190, 197, 201, 209
Corps Commands
    XXXI, 214, 225
    XXXII, 214, 225
    XXXII, 214, 225
    XXXIV, 214, 225, 612
    XXXV, 214, 225
    XXXVI, 214, 225
    XXXVII, 225
    XXXXV, 225
Frontier Guard Commands
    I, 190, 202
    XI, 190
    Eifel, 184, 191
    Guard Command Center, 225
    Saarpflaz, 184, 191
    Upper Rhine, 184, 190, 191
Wehrkreis
    I, 11, 22, 34, 70, 110, 216, 221
    II, 11, 34, 70, 125, 221, 351
    III, 11, 34, 70, 138, 152, 155, 221
    IV, 11, 34, 70, 221, 229, 351
    V, 11, 34, 69, 70, 153, 221
    VI, 11, 34, 62, 69, 70, 153, 221, 351
    VII, 11, 34, 70, 119, 221, 351
    VIII, 33, 34, 70, 111, 221, 351
    IX, 34, 62, 69, 70, 221, 351
    X, 70, 79, 221
    XI, 69, 221, 351
    XII, 69, 111, 222
    XIII, 222
    XVII, 124, 222
    XVIII, 124, 222
    XX, 214, 222

XXI, 214, 216, 222, 248, 249, 262, 267. *See also* Armies, Norway
Bohemia and Moravia, 168, 222
General Gouvernement, 222, 605
Divisions
1st Cavalry, 13, 34, 57, 296
1st Infantry, 34, 190
1st Light. *See* Divisions, 6th Panzer
1st Mountain, 102, 190, 392, 397
1st Panzer, 34, 57, 146, 186–87, 190, 204, 207, 283, 285, 306–8, 310–13, 315, 320, 325, 334, 339, 343–44, 462–63, 478, 513
1st SS Panzer, 120, 140, 296, 298, 325, 333, 515
2nd Cavalry, 13, 33, 34
2nd Infantry (later Motorized), 34, 53, 101, 146, 190, 285, 333, 336, 351, 352
2nd Light. *See* Divisions, 7th Panzer
2nd Mountain, 124, 190, 263, 264, 267, 268
2nd Panzer, 57, 120, 122, 124, 186–87, 190, 209, 283, 285, 306, 308, 310–13, 320, 324–25, 334, 341, 392, 401, 493
2nd SS Panzer "Das Reich," 42, 226, 297, 298, 336, 392, 396, 513, 535, 541
3rd Cavalry, 13, 33, 34
3rd Infantry (later Motorized), 34, 55, 190, 216, 352, 477
3rd Light. *See* Divisions, 8th Panzer
3rd Mountain, 124, 190, 257, 266
3rd Panzer, 57, 186, 187, 190, 198, 199, 201, 229, 283, 285, 329, 333, 336, 466, 484
3rd SS Panzer "Totenkopf," 16, 42, 285, 329, 333, 477, 541, 588
4th Infantry, 34, 190, 351
4th Light. *See* Divisions, 9th Panzer
4th Mountain, 392, 443
4th Panzer, 133, 186, 187, 190, 204, 207, 213, 274, 283, 285, 328, 333, 336, 466
4th SS Panzer Grenadier "Police," 523
5th Infantry, 34, 190

5th Mountain, 392, 408, 414, 443
5th Panzer, 186–87, 190, 283, 285, 303, 306, 317, 328, 333, 344–45, 392, 396, 400–402, 408, 514
5th Parachute, 16
5th SS Panzer Grenadier "Viking," 665
6th Infantry, 34, 191, 499–500
6th Mountain, 392, 408, 443
6th Panzer, 140, 186, 187, 190, 283, 285, 313, 334, 344, 352, 462, 478, 665, 667
6th Parachute, 96
7th Infantry, 34, 190
7th Panzer, 186–87, 190, 279, 283, 285, 303–5, 315, 317, 323–24, 328, 333, 337–38, 344, 352, 385, 481, 492, 568
8th Infantry, 34, 190, 305
8th Panzer, 186, 187, 190, 207, 283, 285, 320, 334, 352, 392, 397, 463, 525
9th Infantry, 34, 191
9th Panzer, 124, 186, 187, 190, 205, 209, 283, 296, 297, 298, 333, 392, 400
10th Infantry (later Motorized), 34, 33, 190, 352
10th Panzer, 186–87, 190, 201, 209, 216, 283, 285, 306–8, 311–13, 324–25, 333, 488
11th Infantry, 34, 190
11th Panzer, 351, 392, 481, 546
12th Infantry, 34, 190
12th Panzer, 351, 352, 479
13th Infantry (later Motorized), 34, 101, 146, 190, 285, 333, 351
13th Panzer, 351, 352, 515
14th Infantry (later Motorized), 34, 190, 351, 352, 397, 481
14th Landwehr, 190
14th Panzer, 351, 392, 515, 657
15th Infantry, 34, 191
15th Panzer, 351, 385, 431, 436, 544, 546, 550, 552, 557, 559, 562–65, 567, 571, 575–76, 578–79
16th Infantry, 34, 191, 351, 352
16th Motorized, 352, 392, 437, 657

16th Panzer, 351, 352, 387, 392, 485, 648, 657
17th Infantry, 34, 190, 339
17th Panzer, 351, 484, 488, 665
18th Infantry, 505, 664
18th Infantry (later Motorized), 34, 80, 107, 114, 120, 190, 207, 352, 466, 520
18th Panzer, 351, 466
19th Infantry, 34, 190, 351
19th Panzer, 351, 352, 466
20th Infantry (later Motorized), 34, 101, 146, 190, 198, 209, 334, 352
20th Panzer, 351, 352
21st Infantry, 34, 190
21st Panzer, 385, 431, 433–34, 436, 544, 546, 550, 552, 557, 559, 563–64, 566–67, 574–76, 578
22nd Panzer, 633, 655, 657
22nd Infantry (later Air Landing), 107, 247, 294, 296, 302, 517, 634, 635
23rd Infantry, 139, 190, 503
23rd Panzer, 641, 665
24th Infantry, 125, 190, 207, 634
24th Panzer, 642, 657
25th Infantry (later Motorized), 190, 352
26th Infantry, 191
27th Infantry, 190, 351
28th Infantry, 190
29th Infantry (later Motorized), 101, 190, 285, 334, 344, 466, 473, 657, 667
30th Infantry, 190, 216
31st Infantry, 190
32nd Infantry, 190, 305
33rd Infantry, 190
34th Infantry, 113, 115, 191
35th Infantry, 190, 503
36th Infantry (later Motorized), 191, 352, 463, 478
44th Infantry, 124, 190, 632, 667
45th Infantry, 124, 190, 498
46th Infantry, 190, 392, 504, 517, 518
50th Infantry, 190, 392
52nd Infantry, 191
58th Infantry, 191, 478, 523

60th Infantry (later Motorized), 321, 352, 392, 515
61st Infantry, 190, 327, 504
62nd Infantry, 190
65th Infantry, 342
68th Infantry, 190
69th Infantry, 191, 256, 257, 265
71st Infantry, 190, 668
72nd Infantry, 392
73rd Infantry, 190, 392
75th Infantry, 191
76th Infantry, 392, 668
78th Infantry, 191
79th Infantry, 191, 392
81st Infantry, 216, 504
82nd Infantry, 115, 216
83rd Infantry, 216
86th Infantry, 191
87th Infantry, 191, 341
88th Infantry, 216
90th Light, 443, 546–47, 550, 552, 559, 562–64, 567–68, 570–71, 574–75, 577–79
93rd Infantry, 220
94th Infantry, 220
95th Infantry, 220, 498
96th Infantry, 220
97th Jaeger, 442
98th Infantry, 220
99th Jaeger, 442
100th Jaeger, 442
101st Jaeger, 392, 442
102nd Infantry, 442
103rd Infantry, 442
104th Jaeger, 442
105th Infantry, 442
106th Infantry, 442
107th Infantry, 442
108th Infantry, 442
109th Infantry, 442
110th Infantry, 442
111th Infantry, 442
112th Infantry, 442, 494
113th Infantry, 442
114th Jaeger, 457
117th Jaeger, 457
118th Jaeger, 457
125th Infantry, 392

129th Infantry, 508
132nd Infantry, 392
134th Infantry, 499
137th Infantry, 504
162nd Infantry, 505
163rd Infantry, 258, 259, 262
164th Infantry (later Light Afrika),
    392, 571, 572, 575, 576, 577, 578,
    580
170th Infantry, 256
181st Infantry, 265
183rd Infantry, 392
196th Infantry, 259, 262, 264
198th Infantry, 256, 392
201st Security, 443
203rd Security, 443
205th Infantry, 191
206th Infantry, 190
207th Infantry, 190
208th Infantry, 190, 296
209th Infantry, 191, 350
211th Infantry, 191
212th Infantry, 190
213th Infantry, 190, 207
214th Infantry, 191, 249, 265
215th Infantry, 190
216th Infantry, 191
217th Infantry, 190
218th Infantry, 190, 354
221st Infantry, 190, 207
223rd Infantry, 191
225th Infantry, 296
227th Infantry, 191, 296
228th Infantry, 190, 350
231st Infantry, 191, 350
239th Infantry, 190
246th Infantry, 191
250th Infantry (Spanish Blue
    Division), 479
254th Infantry, 298
256th Infantry, 297, 298
258th Infantry, 494
267th Infantry, 58, 504
268th Infantry, 191
269th Infantry, 463
281st Security, 521
291st Infantry, 478
292nd Infantry, 491

294th Infantry, 392, 504
295th Infantry, 504
296th Infantry, 505
311th Infantry, 350
319th Infantry, 442
329th Infantry, 504, 505
332nd Infantry, 442
333rd, Infantry, 442
335th Infantry, 442
336th Infantry, 442
337th Infantry, 442
339th Infantry, 442, 504
340th Infantry, 442
342nd Infantry, 442
376th Infantry, 667
538th Frontier Guard, 392
554th Infantry, 220, 350
555th Infantry, 220, 350
556th Infantry, 220, 350
557th Infantry, 220, 350
707th Infantry, 538
Das Reich SS Division. *See* Divi-
    sions, 2nd SS Panzer "Das
    Reich"
Division Bardia, 553
Leibstandarte SS Adolf Hitler
    (LSSAH). *See* Divisions, 1st SS
    Panzer
Panzer Division Kempf, 186, 201
Replacement Divisions, 221–22
Spanish Blue Division, 479
Special Administrative Division
    Staffs, 221–22
SS Division "Nord," 541
SS-Totenkopfverbaende (SS-TV). *See*
    Divisions, 3rd SS Panzer
    "Totenkopf"
SS-Verfuegungstruppe (SS-VT). *See*
    Divisions, 2nd SS Panzer "Das
    Reich"
Artillery Commands (Arkos)
    3rd Artillery Command, 216
    104th Artillery Command, 550, 577
    306th Higher Artillery Command,
        633
Brigades
    1st Cavalry, 53, 190
    1st Panzer, 187, 311

2nd Panzer, 187, 321
3rd Panzer, 187
4th Panzer, 133, 153, 186, 187
5th Panzer, 133, 153, 187
6th Panzer, 153, 187
8th Panzer, 133, 153, 187
10th Rifle, 504
11th Motorized, 247, 249, 256, 263, 286, 351
15th Rifle, 559
201st Security, 443
202nd Security, 443
203rd Security, 443
204th Security, 443
Eberhardt, 188, 197
Regiments
1st Danziger Infantry, 188
1st Infantry, 33
1st Rifle, later Panzer Grenadier, 310, 320, 341
1st Panzer, 187
1st SS Panzer Grenadier, 392, 399, 400
1st SS Totenkopf, 323
2nd Danziger Infantry, 188
2nd Infantry, 33
2nd Panzer, 52, 187, 351
2nd Panzer Artillery, 308
2nd SS Totenkopf, 328
3rd Artillery, 229
3rd Panzer, 52, 187, 204
4th Artillery, 87
4th Cavalry, 52, 187
4th Panzer, 187, 351, 352
5th Motorized, later Panzer Grenadier, 351
5th Panzer, 187, 434, 559, 561
6th Panzer, 52, 187
6th Rifle, later Panzer Grenadier, 304, 323, 336
7th Cavalry. *See* Regiments, 2nd Panzer
7th Panzer, 187
7th Rifle, later Panzer Grenadier, 321, 323
8th Cavalry, 163
8th Panzer, 187, 351, 545, 559, 578, 579

9th Infantry, 19, 54, 229
10th Infantry, 33
10th Panzer Artillery, 308
11th Cavalry, 52
11th Panzer, 187
12th Cavalry. *See* Regiments, 3rd Panzer
15th Panzer, 187, 229, 351, 554
16th Infantry, 296
16th Panzer, 52
18th Artillery, 504
18th Panzer, 351
21st Panzer, 351
22nd Infantry, 33
23rd Infantry, 33
23rd Panzer, 187
24th Artillery, 77, 80
25th Motorized, later Panzer Grenadier, 351
25th Panzer, 187, 305, 324, 336
26th Artillery, 457
26th Infantry, 207
27th Panzer, 351
29th Panzer, 351, 352
33rd Panzer Artillery, 435, 559, 579
35th Panzer, 187
36th Panzer, 187, 351
38th Infantry, 62
39th Infantry, 62, 351
40th Motorized, later Panzer Grenadier, 351
47th Infantry, 294
50th Infantry, 140
52nd Motorized, later Panzer Grenadier, 351
63rd Motorized, later Panzer Grenadier, 351
64th Motorized, later Panzer Grenadier, 351
65th Infantry, 294
66th Motorized, later Panzer Grenadier, 351
69th Infantry, 216
73rd Motorized, later Panzer Grenadier, 351
74th Motorized, later Panzer Grenadier, 351
78th Motorized Artillery, 324

Index of German Military Units

79th Motorized, later Panzer Grenadier, 351
82nd Infantry, 115
93rd Motorized, later Panzer Grenadier, 351
98th Mountain, 163
100th Mountain, 414
101st Motorized, later Panzer Grenadier, 351
103rd Motorized, later Panzer Grenadier, 351
104th Motorized, later Panzer Grenadier, 351, 435, 545, 553, 559
108th Motorized, later Panzer Grenadier, 351
110th Motorized, later Panzer Grenadier, 351
111th Motorized, later Panzer Grenadier, 351
112th Motorized, later Panzer Grenadier, 351
115th Motorized, later Panzer Grenadier, 351, 559, 563
125th Infantry, later Motorized, 392, 577, 578
138th Mountain, 257
139th Mountain, 266, 267
155th Panzer Artillery, 559
185th Infantry, 499–500
190th Infantry, 504
190th Motorized Artillery, 559
200th Special Purposes (later Motorized), 435
226th Infantry, 666
292nd Artillery, 491
308th Infantry, 255
329th Infantry, 505
340th Infantry, 264
361st Motorized, 559
382nd Grenadier, later Motorized, 572, 577
413th Infantry, 504
433rd Motorized, 577
504th Infantry, 504
Grossdeutschland Fusilier, 79
Grossdeutschland Motorized, later Panzer Grenadier, 285, 306, 310, 313, 333, 392

Hermann Goering Panzer, 392
Panzer Lehr, 187
SS Artillery Regiment, 186
SS Motorized Infantry Regiment "Deutschland," 186
SS Motorized Infantry Regiment "Der Fuehrer," 541
SS Motorized Division "Police," 523

Battalions
1st Panzer Engineer, 311
3rd Motorized Transport, 55
3rd Panzer Reconnaissance, 432, 433, 434, 559
3rd SS Engineer, 506
7th Motorcycle, 304, 321
7th Motorized Transport, 53
8th Machine Gun, 433, 434, 435, 437
15th Motorcycle, 434
33rd Panzer, 187
33rd Panzer Engineer, 559, 563
33rd Panzer Reconnaissance, 559
40th Panzer, 262
51st Engineer, 293
65th Panzer, 187
66th Panzer, 187
67th Panzer, 187
86th Light Anti-Tank, 324
200th Panzer Engineer, 437, 559, 563
300th Oasis Reserve, 553
300th Panzer, 634
580th Reconnaissance, 559
605th Anti-Tank, 433
900th Engineer, 559, 563
Brandenburg Lehr z.b.V., 297
Panzer Lehr, 187

Miscellaneous
1st Oasis Company, 545
Army Detachment A, 226
Armeegruppe Hoth, 664, 665
Armeegruppe Hollidt, 664
Frontier Guard Command Center, 215
Frontier Guard Command North, 215
Group XXI. See Corps, XXI; Armies, Norway

Luftwaffe:
High Command of the Luftwaffe
(OKL), 82, 89, 93, 211, 248, 249,
359, 447, 490
Groups/Air Fleets
1st, 120, 133, 146, 188, 199, 277, 444,
447, 461, 478
2nd, 133, 146, 158, 277, 286, 298,
334, 359, 360, 444, 447, 462, 487,
547, 553
3rd, 133, 146, 201, 286, 334, 359,
360, 363, 364, 447
4th, 188, 199, 201, 391, 406, 408, 416,
444, 447, 644, 654
5th, 265, 359, 360, 364, 445, 447
10th, 670
Reich, 626
Luftwaffe Commands
Afrika, 447, 548
Austria, 124, 146
Center, 626
Kirkenes, 445
Corps
I Air, 360, 461
I Flak, 286, 448
II Air, 97, 286, 360, 361, 547, 573
II Flak, 286, 448
IV Air, 286, 360, 632, 644, 665
V Air, 286, 360
VIII Air, 96, 286, 308–9, 360–61, 389,
394, 400, 408, 410–12, 414, 416,
462, 478, 633–34, 644, 648, 659
IX Air, 286, 360, 626
X Air, 249, 258, 360, 447, 547
XI Air, 406, 408, 409, 411, 417
XII Air, 626
Air Landing, 294
Luftkrieskommando
I, 82
II, 82
III, 82
IV, 82
V, 82
VI, 82
VII, 82
Divisions
1st Air, 146
1st Night Fighter, 360

2nd Air, 146, 199, 200, 203
2nd Night Fighter, 360
3rd Air, 146
3rd Fighter Command, 361
4th Air, 146
5th Air, 146
7th Air, 146, 247, 267, 276, 277, 356,
408, 410
9th Flak, 662, 668
Wings
1st Bomber (KG 1), 360
1st Lehr (LG 1), 360
1st Stuka (StG 1), 360
2nd Bomber, 360
2nd Destroyer, 361
2nd Fighter, 361, 447
2nd Lehr, 200
2nd Stuka, 360, 415
3rd Bomber, 360
3rd Fighter (JG 3), 360
3rd Stuka, 360
4th Bomber, 360
26th Bomber, 360
26th Destroyer (ZG 26), 360
26th Fighter, 360, 447
27th Bomber, 360
27th Fighter, 360
38th Bomber, 360
40th Bomber, 360, 374
51st Bomber, 360
51st Fighter, 360
52nd Fighter, 360
53rd Bomber, 360
53rd Fighter, 361
54th Bomber, 299, 360
54th Fighter, 360
55th Bomber, 360
76th Bomber, 360
76th Destroyer (ZG 76), 360
77th Bomber, 200, 211, 360
77th Fighter, 358
77th Stuka, 360
100th Bomber, 360, 626
Regiments
1st Parachute, 296, 298, 412
2nd Parachute, 296, 401, 412
3rd Parachute, 410, 411, 506–7
23rd Anti-Aircraft, 324

Index of German Military Units

59th Anti-Aircraft, 324
Assault, 408, 411, 412, 413
Miscellaneous
2nd Parachute Brigade, 571
Air Command East Prussia, 146
Condor Legion, 94, 95, 96, 98, 97, 100
Group 210 (Gruppe 210), 360
Regiment "General Goering," 262
Special Purposes Air Command,
    199, 200, 211

German Navy:
Naval Operations Staff (SKL). *See*
    Oberkommando der Marine
Oberkommando der Marine (High
    Command of the Navy or
    OKM), 109, 235, 245, 261–62,
    356, 422–23, 430, 613, 615
Naval Groups
Baltic, 271
East, 240
South, 271
West, 240
Battleships
Bismarck, 160, 423, 424, 425, 426,
    427, 428, 429, 430
Gneisenau, 160, 250, 255, 268, 269,
    422, 423
Scharnhorst, 160, 250, 255, 268, 269,
    422, 423
Schleswig-Holstein, 197, 430
Tirpitz, 160, 423, 424
Heavy Cruisers
Bluecher, 160, 258
Hipper, 160, 250, 255, 260, 268, 423
Prinz Eugen, 160, 422–23, 424, 425, 426
Seydlitz, 160
Panzerschiffen (armored/heavy cruisers or pocket battleships)
Admiral Scheer, 246, 422, 423
Graf Spee, 179, 237, 238–39, 246, 247

Deutschland. See *Luetzow*
Luetzow, 160, 179, 237, 239–40, 250,
    258
Light Cruisers
Emden, 250
Karlsrule, 250, 260
Koeln, 250, 260
Koenigsberg, 250, 257, 260
Destroyers
Berndt von Arnim, 254–55, 257
Submarines
U-25, 261
U-28, 375
U-29, 235
U-30, 235
U-38, 375
U-43, 620
U-46, 375
U-47, 236, 237, 613
U-48, 261, 375
U-56, 261
U-66, 619
U-70, 614
U-99, 375, 614–15
U-100, 375, 614
U-101, 375
U-103, 375, 619
U-106, 619
U-107, 619
U-110, 615
U-123, 375, 619
U-124, 621
U-125, 619
U-126, 421
U-130, 619
U-552, 617–18, 620
U-754, 620
Miscellaneous
Altmark (supply ship), 247
Atlantis (commerce raider), 421
Python (commerce raider), 421

GENERAL INDEX

Rank listed is the highest attained by that individual during World War II.

Abernetty, Colonel Otto, 343

Abwehr, 137, 297, 362, 396

Adam, Colonel General Wilhelm, 19, 73, 112, 133, 135, 143, 155, 163, 203

Albrecht, Generaladmiral Conrad, 176

Alexander, British Field Marshal Sir Harold, 573

Altmayer, French Lieutenant General Marie-Robert, 335, 336, 344

Amann, Max, 347

Ambrosio, Italian General Vittorio, 391, 392

Andrew, New Zealand Lieutenant Colonel, 412, 413

Andrews, U.S. Vice Admiral Adolphus, 619, 620, 621

Anschluss, 48, 117, 129, 148, 596

Antonescu, Romanian Marshal and dictator Ion, 538

Aosta, Duke of, 418

Apanasenko, Soviet General Iosif, 490

Arnim, GO Juergen von, 519, 520

Attolico, Italian Ambassador Bernardo, 148

Auchinleck, British Field Marshal Claude J. E., 267, 547, 551, 554, 564, 567, 569, 571, 572, 573

Audet, French Lieutenant General Sylvestre, 335

Auftragstaktik Doctrine, 464, 503

Baade, Lieutenant General Ernst, 563

Bach, Major Reverend Wilhelm "Papa," 545, 553

Bach-Zelewski, SS General and General of Police Erich von dem, 535, 536, 540, 583

Badoglio, Italian Marshal Pietro, 340, 342, 345, 381

Balbo, Italian Marshal Italo, 340

Balck, General of Panzer Troops Hermann, 310, 311, 320, 340, 341, 464

Baldwin, Stanley, 48

Baltasar, Luftwaffe Major Wilhelm, 358

Baudouin, French Minister of Foreign Affairs Paul, 343

Bauer, Naval Lieutenant Ernst, 621

Bayerlein, Lieutenant General Fritz, 546, 578

Beaverbrook, British Minister of Aircraft Production Lord, 357

Bechtoldsheim, Major General Baron Gustav von Mauchenheim gennant, 538

Beck, Polish Foreign Minister Colonel Jozef, 172, 173, 174, 210

Beck, GO Ludwig, 31, 41, 47, 56, 62, 64–65, 69–70, 72–74, 104–6, 109, 112, 114, 120, 128, 130–38, 140, 143–45, 148, 152, 155–57, 188, 229, 352, 456, 529

Becker, SS Major General Helmuth, 16, 611

Becker, General of Artillery Dr. Karl, 228

Becker, Lieutenant Rudi, 505

Behlendorff, General of Artillery Hans, 111

Below, Luftwaffe Colonel Nicolaus von, 176

Beresford-Peirse, British Lieutenant General Sir Noel, 543, 545

Bergmann, Lieutenant General Friedrich, 504

Benes, Czechoslovakian President Eduard, 141, 142, 151, 154, 168

Berger, Colonel Hans, 504

Berthold, Major General Gerhard, 504

Berti, Italian General Mario, 383

Besson, French General Antoine, 288, 335, 342

Beust, General of Bombers Baron Hans-Henning, 97

Bey, Rear Admiral Erich, 260

Beyer, General of Infantry Eugen, 124, 125, 145

Bieneck, General of Fliers Helmuth, 146

Billotte, French General Gaston-Henri, 233, 281, 286, 301, 305

Bismarck, Lieutenant General Georg von, 323, 557, 566, 568, 574

Bismarck, Chancellor Otto von, 6, 117

Bittrich, General of Waffen SS Wilhelm, 16

Blagrove, British Rear Admiral H. F. C., 237

Blanchard, French General Georges, 286, 327

Blaskowitz, GO Johannes von, 70, 145, 155, 168, 190, 203, 206, 207, 208, 212, 214, 215

Bleichrodt, Lieutenant Commander Heinrich, 375, 619

Blobel, SS Colonel Paul, 539, 608, 609

Blomberg, Eva Gruhn von, 105

Blomberg, Field Marshal Werner von, 19, 21–22, 24–31, 38–43, 47, 54, 56, 61, 64–65, 69, 72–73, 102–9, 113, 128, 139, 157

Blood Purge, 28–30, 139, 588

Blumenkrieg (Flower Wars), 59

Blumentritt, General of Infantry Guenther, 177

Bock, Field Marshal Fedor von, 70, 112, 115, 120, 123, 145, 150, 187, 190, 201, 203, 209, 227–29, 273–74, 276, 279, 285, 301, 326–27, 333, 336, 338, 354, 440–41, 444–5, 464–66, 471, 474, 479–82, 486–87, 489, 492, 494–95, 497–98, 500–501, 519, 631–32, 634, 640–43

Bock, General of Infantry Max, 214

Bodenschatz, General of Fliers Karl, 112, 176, 181, 625

Boehm, Generaladmiral Hermann, 239–40, 423

Boehme, General of Mountain Troops Franz, 342, 392, 398

Boehm-Tettelbach, General of Infantry Alfred, 224

Boettcher, Lieutenant General Karl, 550, 552

Boineburg-Lengsfeld, Lieutenant General Baron Hans von, 641

Bonhoeffer, Pastor Dietrich, 136

Bonhoeffer, Professor Dr. Karl, 141

Bonte, Commodore Friedrich, 255, 257, 260, 262

Boris, Bulgarian King, 387

Bormann, State Secretary Martin, 468, 627, 658

Borne, Colonel Claus von dem, 435–36

Bortnowski, Polish Major General Wladyslaw, 208, 216

Bouffet, French Lieutenant General Jean-Gabriel, 303, 321

Bouhler, Reichsleiter Philipp, 530, 600

Bourret, French General Victor, 335, 341
Brack, Victor, 599
Braeuer, Luftwaffe Lieutenant General Bruno, 410, 412, 416
Brandenberger, General of Panzer Troops Erich, 463
Brandt, General of Cavalry Georg, 224
Brauchitsch, Luftwaffe Colonel Bernd von, 93
Brauchitsch, Charlotte Rueffer Schmidt von, 110, 111
Brauchitsch, Field Marshal Walter von, 70, 102, 106, 109–10, 112, 114–15, 130–35, 143–48, 166, 173, 176, 178, 180, 188, 214, 225, 227–28, 230–31, 248, 261, 273–76, 278–79, 318–19, 326, 330, 335, 338, 353–54, 356, 377, 390, 392, 431–32, 440, 465–66, 475, 480–81, 487, 489, 494, 497, 501–2, 515, 520, 530
Braun, Luftwaffe Major, 411, 412, 413, 419
Breith, General of Panzer Troops Hermann, 55
Brelow, Major General Kurt von, 24, 29, 138
Briesen, General of Infantry Kurt von, 206, 207, 215, 216, 392, 504
Brink, South African Lieutenant General George L. 549
Brinkmann, Vice Admiral Helmuth, 424
Brockdorff-Ahlefeldt, General of Infantry Walter von, 139, 224, 521, 524
Brook, British Field Marshal Sir Alan (1st Viscount Alanbrooke), 328, 342
Brownshirts. See SA
Bruche, French Brigadier General Albert, 313–14, 315
Budenny, Soviet Marshal Semen M., 466, 483, 484, 486
Buechting, Colonel Andreas, 577
Buehler, State Secretary Dr. Joseph, 597, 598

Buelow, Major General Cord von, 504
Buelow, State Secretary Wilhelm von, 64, 113
Buerckel, Gauleiter Joseph, 586, 587
Buisson, French Major General Louis, 335
Busch, Field Marshal Ernst, 58, 112, 134, 145, 215, 280, 285, 334, 339, 354, 444–45, 475–76, 478–79, 523, 669
Buschenhagen, General of Infantry Erich, 250
Bussche, Major Alex von der, 530

Canaris, Admiral Wilhelm, 41, 94, 113, 116, 137, 141, 153, 173, 174, 229, 408, 409, 455
Carls, Generaladmiral Rolf, 250
Carol, Yugoslavian King, 389
Cavallero, Italian Marshal Ugo, 381–82, 573
Chales de Beaulieu, Lieutenant General Walter, 55
Chamberlain, British Prime Minister Sir Neville, 122, 147–48, 150, 154, 165, 167, 169, 174–75, 180, 219, 227, 232, 247, 288
Chappel, British Major General Brian H., 407
Choltitz, General of Infantry Dietrich von, 296, 298, 300
Christian X, Danish King, 256
Chuikov, Soviet General Vasili, 653, 654
Churchill, Winston, 150, 154, 165, 219, 246–47, 254, 261–62, 288, 339, 349, 353, 367, 372, 374, 377, 387, 389, 405, 407, 416, 433, 547, 564–65, 573, 581, 620
Chvalkovsky, Czechoslovakian Foreign Minister Frantisek, 167, 168
Ciano, Italian Foreign Minister Galeazzo, 151, 175, 345, 346, 389
Cincar-Marcovic, Yugoslavian Foreign Minister Aleksander, 390
Ciuperca, Romanian General Nicolae, 444, 445

General Index

Clausewitz, Prussian General Karl von, 3, 75
Cochenhausen, Lieutenant General Conrad, 499
Coeler, General of Fliers Joachim, 360, 626
Conde, French General Charles, 286, 335, 341, 347
Cooper, British First Lord of the Admirality Duff, 147, 150, 153–54, 165
Corap, French General Andre, 286, 293, 303, 304, 305, 310, 312, 313
Cossato, Italian Commander Feeia di, 621
Craigie, Sir Robert, 48
Cranz, Lieutenant General Friedrich-Karl, 330
Crasemann, Lieutenant General Eduard, 563, 575
Cruewell, General of Panzer Troops Ludwig, 546, 549, 550, 557, 559, 560, 561, 562
Crystal Night, 152
Cunningham, British General Alan G., 405, 547, 548, 549, 551
Cunningham, British Admiral of the Fleet Sir Andrew B., 383, 415, 416, 417, 418
Cvetkovic, Yugoslavian Prime Minister Dragisha, 390
Czerniakow, Adam, 602

Dab-Biernacki, Polish General Stefan, 204
Daladier, French Prime Minister Edouard, 150, 254, 288, 320
Darlan, French Admiral Francois, 345
Deichmann, General of Fliers Paul, 89
Demaniuk, Ivan, 607
Denis, Belgian Defense Minister Henri, 316
Desrousseaux, Belgian General Olivier-Jules, 329
Dessloch, Luftwaffe GO Otto, 286
Dietl, GO Eduard, 250, 257, 260, 263, 266, 267, 354, 445, 479

Dietrich, SS GO Joseph "Sepp," 42, 120, 229, 325, 327, 399, 517, 587
Dirksen, Ambassador Herbert, 113
Djugashvili, Yakov, 470
Doenitz, Grand Admiral Karl, 161, 188, 235–37, 261–62, 373–75, 613, 615, 618, 620–22
Doering, Kurt-Bertram von, 360
Dohnanyi, Judge Advocate Dr. Hans von, 140–41
Dollmann, GO Friedrich, 34, 62, 70, 145, 190, 286, 334, 354
Douhet, Italian General Emilio, 36, 84
Dowding, British Air Chief Marshal Sir Hugh C. T., 359, 365, 367
Drum, U.S. Lieutenant General Hugh, 621
Drum, General of Fliers Karl, 98–99, 100
Dumitrescu, Romanian General Petre, 444, 445, 655
Durcansky, Deputy Provincial Premier of Slovakia Ferdinand, 166

Eaker, U.S. Air Force General Ira C., 628
Eberhard, Major General Kurt, 539
Eberhardt, Lieutenant General Friedrich-Georg, 188
Eberl, Dr. Irmfried, 606
Ebert, President Friedrich, 14
Eberth, General of Fliers Karl, 82, 83
Eckermann, Lieutenant Commander Hans, 614
Eden, British Foreign Secretary Anthony, 63, 150, 384
Ehlers, Major, 435
Eichmann, SS Lieutenant Colonel Adolf, 596, 597, 611
Eichstaedt, Colonel Max, 435
Eicke, General of Waffen SS, 28, 42, 324, 541, 585–87, 588, 589, 611
Einsatzgruppen (SS murder squads), 214, 356, 441, 467, 531–32, 534–40, 583, 589, 595–98, 608–9
Eismann, Major Georg, 666
Ellis, British Major, 329

Endrass, Naval Lieutenant Englebert, 374

Engel, Lieutenant General Gerhard, 176

Engelbrecht, General of Artillery Erwin, 250, 258

Epp, Major General Ritter von, 26,

Ernst, General of SA Karl, 27

Esebeck, General of Panzer Troops Baron Hans-Karl, 436

Falck, Luftwaffe Colonel Wolfgang, 63, 67

Falkenhausen, General of Infantry Alexander von, 229

Falkenhayn, General Erich von, 8

Falkenhorst, GO Nikolaus von, 197, 202, 247–48, 249, 256, 259, 264, 265, 267, 354, 445, 479

Fegelein, SS Lieutenant General Hermann, 510

Fehn, General of Panzer Troops Gustav, 400, 514

Feige, General of Infantry Hans, 224

Fellgiebel, General of Signal Troops Fritz, 55, 490

Felmy, General of Fliers Helmuth, 82, 92, 95, 112, 146, 158, 277

Fessmann, General of Panzer Troops Ernst, 57, 58

Feurstein, General of Mountain Troops Valentin, 250, 267, 268, 269

Fiebig, General of Fliers Martin, 658, 659

Fink, General of Fliers Johannes, 362

Fischboeck, Austrian Finance Minister Dr. Hans, 118, 121

Fischer, Lieutenant General Hermann, 264

Fischer, Major General Karl, 504

Flavigny, French Lieutenant General Jean, 312

Foch, French Marshal Ferdinand, 281, 345

Foerster, General of Fliers Helmuth, 461

Folker, Naval Lieutenant Ulrich, 619

Forbes, British Admiral Sir Charles, 254, 260, 261

Forster, Charge d'affairs Dirk, 63–64

Fortune, British Major General Sir Victor M., 336, 338

Franco, Spanish dictator Francisco, 94, 95

Francois-Poncet, French Ambassador Andre, 133

Frank, Hans, Governor-General of Poland, 65, 168, 214, 595, 599, 604, 610

Frantzius, Colonel Botho von, 504

Franz, Major General Gerhard, 576, 641

Frauendorfer, Max, 605

Frauenheim, Lieutenant Commander Fritz, 375

Frederick II, King (Frederick the Great), 1

Frederick Wilhelm II, King, 2

Frederick Wilhelm III, King, 3

Freikorps, 13, 14

Freisler, State Secretary (later Judge) Dr. Roland, 597

Frere, French General Aubert, 317, 335, 337

Fretter-Pico, General of Artillery Maximilian, 633

Freyberg, Lieutenant General Baron Bernard C., 407, 408, 409, 414, 416, 568

Freydenberg, French Lieutenant General Henry, 335, 341, 549

Fricke, Admiral Kurt, 161

Friedrich, Lieutenant General Rudolf, 538

Friemel, Colonel Georg, 342–43

Fritsch, GO Baron Werner von, 26, 28, 31, 33, 41, 43–44, 47, 56, 62, 64–65, 69–70, 72, 102–9, 112, 128, 134, 139–40, 156, 210, 352, 529

Fromm, GO Friedrich, 21, 22, 56, 185, 220, 229, 354, 442, 443, 447, 489

Fuchs, Colonel Egon, 343

Fuchs, Admiral Werner, 161

Fuller, British Major General J. M. C., 53, 54
Funck, General of Panzer Troops Baron Hans von, 203, 385, 492

Gabcke, Lieutenant General Otto, 504
Galland, General of Fighters Adolf, 97, 211, 362, 639
Gambler-Parry, British Major General Michael D., 433
Gamelin, General Maurice, 64, 66, 225, 226, 234, 281, 288, 293, 307, 311, 314, 320
Ganzenmueller, State Secretary Dr. Theodor, 608
Garchery, French General Jeanny, 288
Gaulle, Charles de, 53, 319, 342
Gause, Lieutenant General Alfred, 436, 546, 562
Geisler, General of Fliers Hans, 249, 256, 354, 360
Geitner, Lieutenant General Herbert, 504
Gelhaus, Naval Lieutenant Harald, 619
General Staff, 1–5, 7, 15, 17, 21, 50–52, 54–55, 72–75, 128, 131, 156, 177, 382, 456, 486, 529, 646, 663–664
George, Lloyd, 180
Georges, French General Alphonse-Joseph, 226, 234, 281, 314, 316, 336, 342
George VI, British King, 147
Gerteis, Dr. Adolf, 602
Gessler, Defense Minister Dr. Otto, 19
Gestapo, 29, 108, 139, 231, 256, 258, 356, 531, 532, 596, 597
Geyer, General of Infantry Hermann, 70, 112, 145
Geyr von Schweppenburg, General of Panzer Troops Baron Leo, 64, 198, 201, 229, 459, 484, 641, 647
Gienanth, General of Cavalry Baron Curt Ludwig von, 215, 605, 612
Giorgis, Italian Major General Fedele de, 553
Giraud, French General Henri, 286, 297, 316

Gisevius, Dr. Hans Bernd, 136, 138, 139, 490
Glaise-Horstenau, General of Infantry Edmund von, 118, 120, 121
Glein, Major, 255, 256
Globocnik, SS Major General Odilo, 599, 601, 604, 605, 610, 611
Gluecks, SS Lieutenant General Heinrich, 589,
Gneisenau, Prussian General Neidhardt, 3
Godwin-Austen, British Lieutenant General Sir Alfred R., 547, 549
Goebbels, Propaganda Minister Dr. Paul Joseph, 32, 43, 63, 81, 91, 110, 112, 165, 199, 235, 241, 300, 446, 508, 529, 600, 624, 660
Goerdeler, Mayor Carl, 136, 137, 141, 229, 490
Goering, Frau Emmy Sonnemann, 91, 277
Goering, Reichsmarschall Hermann, 28–29, 35–36, 47, 63, 84–85, 87–94, 96, 98, 102–3, 106, 108, 110–11, 114, 121–23, 130, 146–47, 158, 167–68, 176, 178, 211, 225, 227, 229, 248–49, 265, 277, 284, 299, 325, 330, 345, 354–55, 361–63, 365–68, 371, 375, 390, 406, 440, 462, 468, 519, 530, 576, 595, 625–27, 638, 641, 658–60, 669
Goering, Frau Karin, 91, 355
Goetting, Vice Admiral Friedrich, 262
Goldfarb, Abraham, 603
Golikov, Soviet Marshal Filipp Ivanovich, 453
Goltz, General Ruediger von der, 52
Gort, British Field Marshal Lord, 286, 320, 324, 325, 328, 331
Gossler, General of Cavalry Konrad von, 112
Gott, British General William H. E., 543, 544, 545, 549, 561, 567, 568
Gottberg, SS Lieutenant General Kurt von, 469
Grandsard, French Lieutenant General Pierre, 308, 309

Grauert, Luftwaffe GO Ulrich, 146, 286, 360
Gravenreuth, Luftwaffe Colonel Baron Siegmund-Ulrich von, 97
Grawitz, SS Lieutenant General Dr. Ernst, 594, 611
Graziani, Italian Marshal Rudolfo, 383, 384, 431, 436–37
Greiff, General of Infantry Kurt von, 224
Greiffenberg, General of Infantry Hans von, 439, 646
Greim, Luftwaffe Field Marshal Ritter Robert von, 90, 93, 112, 286, 354, 359
Groener, General Wilhelm, 9, 19, 22, 31, 37
Guderian, Major General Friedrich, 51
Guderian, GO Heinz, 51–56, 58, 111–12, 120, 145–46, 155, 174, 198, 206, 209, 213, 275, 278–79, 285, 303, 306–19, 324, 326, 329–30, 335, 351–52, 354, 437, 441, 445, 456, 466, 471, 473–74, 479–81, 484, 487–89, 491, 494, 497–99, 501, 505, 663
Guertner, Bavarian Minister of Justice Dr., 586
Guse, Admiral Guenther, 132

Haase, GO Curt, 155, 207, 354
Hacha, Czechoslovakian President Dr. Emil, 151, 166, 167
Hagen, Colonel Oskar von dem, 343
Halder, GO Franz, 74, 89, 112, 114, 134–42, 144, 146–48, 152, 176, 180, 192, 215, 224–25, 227–31, 273–75, 278–79, 318–19, 326, 333, 338, 353–54, 378, 388, 390, 392, 431–32, 435–36, 440, 456, 465, 473–74, 480–82, 487, 492, 498, 501, 505, 509, 517, 523, 554, 605, 635–36, 642–44, 646
Halifax, British Foreign Secretary Lord, 122
Halm, General of Fliers Hans, 82, 111
Hammerstein-Equord, General of Infantry Baron Kurt von, 13, 19, 21, 22, 29, 143, 155, 226, 529

Hansen, General of Artillery Christian, 296, 476, 477, 524
Hansen, General of Cavalry Eric, 634
Hardegen, Naval Lieutenant Reinhard, 619, 621
Hargest, New Zealand Brigadier Janies, 412, 413
Harlinghausen, Luftwaffe Lieutenant General Martin, 97
Harpe, GO Joseph, 54
Harris, British Air Marshal Sir Arthur "Bomber," 623, 624
Hart, B. H. Liddell, 53, 54
Hartl, SS Colonel Albert, 596
Hartmann, Major General Alexander von, 668
Hartmann, General of Artillery Otto, 392
Harwood, British Commodore Henry H., 238
Hase, Lieutenant General Paul von, 140
Hasse, GO Otto, 19
Hassell, Ambassador Ulrich von, 63, 113, 136, 148, 229
Hausser, SS GO Paul, 297, 300, 336
Hausser, Lieutenant General Wolfgang, 435
Hecker, Lieutenant General Hans, 563
Heidrich, General of Paratroopers Richard, 410, 411, 416
Heilmann, Luftwaffe Major General Ludwig, 16, 411
Heim, Lieutenant General Ferdinand, 655, 656, 657
Heines, General of SA Edmund, 27
Heinkel, Ernst, 449
Heinrici, Colonel General Gotthard, 224, 512, 514
Heinz, Major Friedrich Wilhelm, 140–41
Heitz, Colonel General Walter, 662, 668
Helldorf, Count Wolf Heinrich von, Police President of Berlin, 105, 140, 153, 229
Hellmich, Lieutenant General Heinz, 503

Henderson, British Ambassador Sir
Neville, 129
Henlein, Konrad, 127, 141, 168
Hering, SS Captain Gottlieb, 605, 610
Hering, French General Pierre, 338,
339, 341
Hess, Nazi Party Chief Rudolf, 127,
345, 658
Heusinger, Lieutenant General Adolf,
327
Hewelke, Lieutenant General Georg, 504
Heydrich, SS General Reinhard, 29,
41, 108, 123, 214, 356, 529–31, 535,
539, 583, 595–97, 601
Heydte, Luftwaffe Colonel Baron Frie-
drich-August von der, 418
Heye, Vice Admiral Helmut, 132–33,
160, 161, 255, 260
Heye, Colonel General Wilhelm, 19,
22, 54
Himer, Lieutenant General Kurt, 250,
256, 504, 518, 519
Himmler, Reichsfuehrer-SS Heinrich,
27–28, 41–43, 108, 152, 168, 214,
229, 441, 468, 529–30, 535, 540–41,
586–88, 595, 598–99, 604–5, 608–11
Hindenburg, Lieutenant von, 509
Hindenburg, President Paul von, 8,
18, 19, 25, 26, 28, 29, 81, 529, 663
Hippler, Major General Bruno, 504
Hitler, Adolf, 10, 19–22, 24–25, 27–30,
32, 38–39, 42–44, 47–48, 56, 59,
63–67, 69, 72, 75, 84–85, 92, 94,
102–6, 108–11, 113–15, 117–21,
123–24, 127–38, 140–42, 144, 146–
50, 152, 155–61, 165–69, 171–80,
188, 209–15, 219, 225–31, 234,
236–37, 241–42, 245–49, 254, 263–
64, 266, 268–70, 273–74, 276–80,
288, 292–94, 299, 308, 318–19,
323–24, 326–30, 333, 335, 340, 343,
345–47, 349–51, 353–56, 363, 365,
367, 369, 372–73, 375–79, 382, 385,
387–92, 396, 400, 402–3, 406, 418,
421, 424, 428–29, 431, 440–43, 445,
451, 453–55, 457, 463, 465–68,
470–71, 474–81, 486–87, 489, 492,
494–95, 497, 499, 500–501, 503,
505–6, 508–9, 510, 512, 515, 517,
519–20, 522–23, 528–30, 537, 547,
552, 555, 557, 563, 566, 576, 578–
82, 585–86, 596, 599–600, 604,
617–18, 620, 625–27, 632–33, 635–
47, 651–55, 658–64, 666–69
Hitler, Alois, 528
Hitler Youth, 62, 157, 159, 185, 285,
508
Hoare, British Foreign Minister Sir
Samuel, 48
Hoeffle, SS Major Herman, 602
Hoehne, Luftwaffe Major General
Otto, 299
Hoenmanns, Major of Reserves Erich,
276–77
Hoepner, Colonel General Erich, 139,
174, 208, 229, 285–86, 301, 316,
333, 336, 338, 340, 354, 444–45,
475–76, 487–88, 491, 502, 506,
509–10, 537
Hoess, SS Lieutenant Colonel Rudolf,
589, 606, 611
Hoffmann, Heinrich, 530
Hoffmann, Major General Max, 8
Hoffmann, General of SS Otto, 597
Holland, British Vice Admiral Lance-
lot, 424, 425, 429
Holle, Luftwaffe Lieutenant General
Alexander, 96
Hollidt, Colonel General Karl Adolf,
665
Holmes, British Lieutenant General
Sir William G., 547, 568
Holtzendorff, Major General Hans-
Henning von, 435
Horn, Lieutenant General Max, 250
Horrocks, British Lieutenant General
Sir Brian, 573, 575, 577
Hossbach, General of Infantry
Friedrich, 64, 102
Hoth, Colonel General Hermann, 101,
145, 208, 279, 285, 303–4, 306, 333,
338, 354, 444–45, 464–66, 471, 474,
478–79, 487, 489, 492, 537, 641–43,
647–48, 655, 657, 662

Hube, Colonel General Hans Valentin, 485, 648, 654, 662, 668
Hubicki, General of Panzer Troops Dr. Ritter Alfred von, 205
Hueber, Austrian Minister of Justice Dr. Franz, 121
Huehnlein, General of SA Adolf, 57
Hull, U.S. Secretary of State Cordell, 453
Huntziger, French General Charles, 286, 293, 308–13, 335, 340, 342, 345–47

Ihlefeld, Luftwaffe Colonel Herbert, 97
Ihler, French Lieutenant General Marcel, 338
Inglis, Brigadier Lindsay M., 568
Ironside, British Field Marshal Sir Edmund, 349

Jaeger, SS Colonel Karl, 535
Jaenecke, Colonel General Erwin, 662, 663
Jeckeln, General of SS Franz, 536
Jenisch, Naval Lieutenant Hans, 374
Jeschonnek, Luftwaffe Colonel General Hans, 88, 92, 98–100, 112, 131, 146, 158, 176, 326, 354, 359, 367–68, 361, 448–50, 627, 639, 658–59
Jodl, Colonel General Alfred, 64, 73, 89, 106, 113, 123, 142, 147, 210, 236, 246, 249, 278, 326–27, 354, 377, 390, 406, 446–47, 465, 480, 554, 582, 644–47, 660
Joffre, French Marshal Joseph, 281
Jost, Major General of Police Heinz, 535
Junck, Luftwaffe Lieutenant General Werner, 361

Kageneck, Lieutenant Count Franz Joseph von, 505
Kahsnitz, Major General Erwin, 79
Kals, Commander Ernst, 619
Kalterbrunner, Head of the Reich Main Security Office Ernst, 121

Kammhuber, General of Fliers Joseph, 112, 277, 360, 626, 627
Kantzow, Thomas von, 355
Kapp, Wolfgang, 14
Kapp Putsch, 13–14
Karmasin, Franz, Brownshirt leader in Slovakia, 166
Kaupisch, General of Fliers (later General of Artillery) Leonard, 82, 111, 202, 212, 224, 249, 250
Keitel, General of Artillery Bodewin, 111, 646
Keitel, Lisa Fontaine, 106
Keitel, Field Marshal Wilhelm, 105–7, 109, 111–14, 120, 129–30, 146–48, 155, 166–67, 173, 176, 180, 190, 210, 214, 225, 227, 248, 263, 326, 340, 345, 354, 377, 390, 406, 440–41, 465, 480, 501, 520, 530, 554, 643–47, 660
Keller, Luftwaffe Colonel General Albert "Bomber," 67, 93, 159, 286, 444, 447
Kempf, General of Panzer Troops Werner, 55, 186, 205, 313, 343, 641, 653
Keppler, General of Waffen-SS Georg, 535, 541
Keppler, Wilhelm, 121
Kersten, Dr. Felix, 535
Kessel, Albrecht von, 140
Kesselring, Luftwaffe Field Marshal Albert, 87–90, 92–93, 112, 146, 188, 199, 277, 286, 299, 326, 330, 334–35, 354, 359–60, 363–65, 368, 444, 447, 460, 462, 487, 547, 553, 557, 566–67, 571, 583, 646
Kesselschlacht, 49
Keyes, Admiral Sir Roger, 328
Kienitz, General of Infantry Werner, 124, 125, 145,
King, British Rear Admiral Edward I. S., 415
King, U.S. Admiral of the Fleet Ernest J., 617, 619, 620, 621
King, Canadian Prime Minister Mackenzie, 616

Kinzel, General of Infantry Eberhard, 455
Kirchheim, Lieutenant General Heinrich, 436, 437
Kirchner, General of Panzer Troops Friedrich, 306, 325, 339, 512, 665
Kirponos, Soviet General Mikhail P., 444, 459, 461, 481, 483, 486
Kleeberg, Polish Brigadier General Franciszek, 212, 217, 482
Kleeman, General of Panzer Troops Ulrich, 574
Kleist, Field Marshal Ewald von, 70, 111–12, 163, 280, 285, 288, 292, 303, 307–9, 311, 315–19, 324–25, 330, 333, 335, 344, 389, 391–92, 395–97, 445, 471, 481, 482–84, 515, 517, 535, 631–32, 637, 645–46, 669
Kliehr, SS Sergeant, 607
Klingenberg, SS Oberfuehrer Fritz, 396
Klopfer, State Secretary Gerhard, 597
Kluge, Field Marshal Guenther von, 62, 70, 134, 145, 190, 198, 285, 324, 328, 333, 337–38, 354, 444–45, 465–66, 471, 487, 494, 501–2, 505–6, 509–10, 513–14
Knappe, Major Siegfried, 75–80
Knauss, Luftwaffe General of Fliers Dr. Robert, 36–37
Knochenhauser, General of Cavalry Wilhelm, 70, 112, 115, 145
Knoechlein, SS Lieutenant Colonel Fritz, 329
Koch, Gauleiter and Reichskommissar Erich, 110, 467–68, 531, 607–8
Koch, General of Infantry Fritz, 224
Koch, Isle, 591
Koch, SS Colonel Karl, 591
Koch, Captain Walter, 292, 411
Koenig, French General Pierre, 563
Koerner, State Secretary Paul "Pilli," 93
Kogon, Eugen, 591
Konrad, General of Mountain Troops Rudolf, 645
Kopanski, Polish Major General Stanislaw, 549

Kopets, Soviet Major General Ivan Ivanovich, 460
Koppenburg, Dr. Heinrich, 448
Korten, LW Colonel General Guenther, 363
Kortzfleisch, General of Infantry Joachim, 392
Koryzis, Greek President Alexander, 388, 401
Kostenko, Soviet General Fedor I., 632
Kozlov, Soviet General Dmitri T., 632
Krancke, Admiral Theodor, 246, 247, 248, 249, 422
Krause, Major General Fritz, 577
Krebs, Guenter von, 343
Krebs, General of Infantry Hans, 455
Kress von Kressenstein, General of Cavalry Franz, 111
Kretschmer, Commander Otto, 375, 614, 615, 622
Kries, Colonel Otto von, 504
Kritzinger, Ministerial Director Wilhelm, 597
Krueger, General of SS Friedrich, 610, 611
Krueger, General of Panzer Troops Walter, 513
Kszepicki, Abraham, 603
Kube, Reichscommissioner Wilhelm, 469, 539
Kuebler, General of Mountain Troops Ludwig, 392, 505, 506, 512
Kuechler, Field Marshal Georg von, 143, 173, 190, 197, 201, 215, 280, 285, 294, 296, 298, 334, 339, 341, 354, 444–45, 475, 477, 522–23, 536–37, 659
Kuehl, Lieutenant General Bernard, 158
Kuhnke, Lieutenant Commander Guenter, 375
Kummetz, Generaladmiral Oskar, 258
Kunto, Battle of, 208
Kuntze, General of Engineers Walter, 112
Kuntzen, General of Panzer Troops Adolf, 111

Kutrzeba, Polish Lieutenant General
  Tadeusz, 206, 207, 208, 212, 216,
  217
Kuznetsov, Soviet General Fedor I.,
  463, 475

Lackner, Luftwaffe Lieutenant Gen-
  eral Walter, 299
Lambert, SS Lieutenant Erwin Her-
  man, 606
Landsturm, 71
Landswehr, 71
Lange, SS Colonel Rudolf, 597, 611
Langsdorff, Naval Captain Hans, 238,
  239
Lanz, General of Mountain Troops
  Hubert, 397
Laure, French General Auguste, 335,
  341
Leach, British Captain John C. ''Jack,''
  425, 426, 430
League of Nations, 48
Lebensraum, 130, 135, 152, 159, 165,
  168, 176, 349, 376
Leber, labor leader Julius, 136
LeBigot, French Admiral, 344
Lebrun, French President Albert, 343
Leeb, General of Artillery Emil von,
  228
Leeb, Field Marshal Ritter Wilhelm
  von, 21–23, 70, 109, 111–13, 139,
  144–46, 150, 155, 187, 203, 225,
  227–28, 273, 286, 334, 341, 354,
  444–45, 474–79, 482, 519–21, 536–
  37
Leese, British Lieutenant General Sir
  Oliver, 577
Lemelsen, General of Panzer Troops
  Joachim, 484
Lemp, Naval Lieutenant Fritz-Lud-
  wig, 235
Leopold III, Belgian King, 301, 316,
  326, 329
Lequerica Erquiza, Spanish Ambassa-
  dor Jose Felix de, 343
Lewinski, Prussian General of Artillery Eduard, 663

Libaud, French Lieutenant General
  Emmanuel, 303
Liebbrandt, Deputy Gauleiter Dr.
  Georg, 597
Liebe, Lieutenant Commander Hein-
  rich, 375
Liebmann, General of Infantry Curt,
  72, 73, 143, 145
Liese, General Kurt, 111, 115, 191
Lindemann, Naval Captain Ernst, 426,
  428, 430
Lindemann, General of Cavalry
  Georg, 392, 522
Linke, Lieutenant Gerhardt, 499
Lipski, Polish Ambassador Jozef, 171,
  172, 173
Liss, Major General Ulrich, 455
List, Field Marshal Wilhelm, 70, 112,
  124, 144, 151, 168, 189–90, 203,
  205, 208, 273, 285, 307–8, 318, 334,
  339, 346–47, 354, 389–92, 398,
  400–401, 640, 643–45
Litvinov, Soviet Foreign Minister
  Maxim, 175
Lloyd George, British Prime Minister
  David, 180
Locarno, Treaty of, 66
Lock, General of Artillery Herbert, 339
Loefen, Colonel Max-Hermann von,
  504
Loehr, Luftwaffe Colonel General
  Alexander, 124, 146, 188, 199, 391,
  406, 408, 418, 444, 447, 654
Loerzer, Luftwaffe Colonel General
  Bruno, 93, 127, 203, 286, 354, 360,
  361, 362
London Naval Treaty, 48
Lossberg, Major General Bernhard
  von, 263, 327, 439
Lucht, Luftwaffe Lieutenant General
  Rulof, 449
Ludendorff, General Erich von, 8, 10,
  81
Ludwig, SS Sergeant Karl, 607
Lueth, Naval Captain Wolfgang, 620
Luetjens, Admiral Guenther, 254, 269,
  422, 423, 424, 425, 426, 428

Luettwitz, General Baron Walter von, 13, 14

Luetzow, Luftwaffe Colonel Guenther, 97

Lumsden, British Lieutenant General Herbert, 577, 581

Lungershausen, Lieutenant General Carl-Hans, 576

Luther, State Secretary Martin, 531, 597, 598

Lutz, General of Panzer Troops Oswald, 52, 53, 55, 57, 101, 111, 112, 115

MacDonald, British Prime Minister Ramsay, 48

Macintyre, British Commander Donald, 614

Mackensen, Field Marshal August von, 10, 29, 44, 72, 113

Mackensen, Colonel General Eberhard von, 339, 484, 515

Mackensen, State Secretary Hans-Georg von, 113, 342

Maginot Line, 63

Makeig-Jones, Captain W. T., 235

Mannerheim, Finnish Marshal Carl, 444

Manstein, Field Marshal Erich von, 41, 44, 107, 113–14, 120, 135, 139, 145, 177, 187, 189, 207, 224, 229, 274–76, 278–79, 337, 352, 354, 463, 475–77, 518, 537, 632–35, 646, 658, 663–67

Mantel, G. Le Q., 53

Manteuffel, General of Panzer Troops Hasso von, 351, 492, 494

Marcks, General of Artillery Erich, 439, 440, 456

Markovna, Nina, 507

Marquardt, Luftwaffe Engineer General, 449

Marriot, British Major General Sir John C. O., 549

Marschall, Generaladmiral Wilhelm, 240, 254, 268, 269, 271, 423

Martin, French Lieutenant General Julein, 303, 305, 306

Marx, Chancellor Dr. Wilhelm, 18

Mastelarz, Polish Colonel Kazimlerz, 198–99

Matz, Lieutenant Commander Joachim, 614

Matzky, General of Infantry Gerhard, 455

May, author Karl, 274

Mechelen Incident, 276–78

Meindl, General of Paratroopers Eugen, 409, 411, 412

Meissner, State Secretary Otto von, 29, 30

Mellenthin, Major General Friedrich Wilhelm, 436, 554, 555, 558, 571, 572

Mengele, SS Captain Dr. Joseph, 594

Messervy, British General Sir Frank W., 545

Metaxas, Greek President Joannis, 382, 388

Metz, General of Infantry Hermann, 224, 504

Meyer, Gauleiter Dr. Alfred, 597

Mieth, General of Infantry Friedrich, 214, 494

Miklas, Austrian President Wilhelm, 118, 120, 121, 123

Milch, Anton, 35–36

Milch, Luftwaffe Field Marshal Erhard, 35–36, 84–85, 87–90, 92–94, 100, 155, 265, 354, 362, 450, 627, 638

Minart, French Colonel, 314

Model, Field Marshal Walter, 352, 466, 484, 485, 489, 513

Moelders, General of Fighters Werner, 95, 97, 284, 371, 639, 649

Moessel, Rear Admiral Wilhelm, 359

Mohle, Lieutenant Commander Karl-Heinz, 375

Mohr, Lieutenant Commander Johann, 621

Molotov, Soviet Foreign Minister Vyacheslav, 175, 179, 376, 388

Moltke, Ambassador Hans-Adolf von, 173

Moltke, Count Helmuth von, 135
Moltke, Field Marshal Helmuth von (Moltke the elder), 49
Moltke, General Helmuth von (Moltke the younger), 7–8, 50
Montgomery, British Field Marshal Sir Bernard Law, 573, 575, 576, 577, 578, 579, 580, 581
Morell, Dr. Theodor, 167, 168
Morshead, Australian Major General Leslie J., 433
Moscicki, Polish President, 210, 217
Mueller, Major General Gerhard, 561
Mueller, Gestapo Chief Heinrich, 531, 596, 597, 608
Mueller-Gebhard, Lieutenant General Philip, 546
Mueller-Hillebrand, Major General Burkhart, 647
Muencheberg, Luftwaffe Major Joachim, 358
Muff, General of Infantry Wolfgang, 121, 124
Munch, Danish Foreign Minister, 256
Munich Protocols, 175
Mussolini, Benito, 69, 148, 150, 175–76, 179, 340, 342, 345–47, 379, 381–83, 385, 387, 400, 418, 544, 555

Napoleon III, Emperor, 49
National Socialist Flying Corps (NSFK), 159
National Socialist Motor Corps (Nationalsozialistisches Kraftfahrerkorps or NSKK), 57, 62, 157
Natzmer, Major General von, 53, 54
Naumann, SS Major General Erich, 532, 538, 539
Nazi Party (Nationalsozialistische Deutsche Arbeitpartei or NSDAP), 24–25, 40–41, 104, 127, 173, 241
Neame, British Lieutenant General Sir Philip, 433
Nebe, SS Lieutenant General Arthur, 229, 532, 538, 539, 540, 598, 599

Nehring, General of Panzer Troops Walter, 55, 310, 351, 466, 491, 557, 559, 561, 565, 571, 574
Neumann, State Secretary Erich, 597
Neumann-Silkow, Lieutenant General Walter, 546, 552
Neurath, Foreign Minister Baron Konstantin von, 63, 102, 103, 104, 112, 130, 168
Nicholson British Brigadier Claude N., 325, 327
Niebelschuetz, Lieutenant General Guenther von, 111
Nincic, Yugoslavian Foreign Minister Momcilo, 390
Nolden, Private Willi, 505
Norrie, British Lieutenant General Charles Willoughby Moke, 547, 548, 549, 559, 562, 564
Noske, Defense Minister Gustav, 13, 14

Obstfelder, General of Infantry Hans von, 224
O'Connor, British General Sir Richard, 383, 384, 433
Oesau, Luftwaffe Lieutenant Colonel Walter, 97
Oesterman, Naval Lieutenant Johannes, 620
Ohlendorf, SS Lieutenant General Otto, 467, 531, 532, 539, 541
Olbricht, General of Infantry Friedrich, 207, 229
Olbricht, Colonel Herbert, 434, 435
Olry, French General Rene, 345
Oster, Major General Hans, 137, 140, 151, 153, 228, 229, 231, 294, 296, 490
Oumansky, Soviet Ambassador Konstantin A., 453, 454

Pabst, Sergeant, 508
Papagos, Greek General Alexandros, 382, 400, 403
Papen, Ambassador Franz von, 120
Patzig, Admiral Conrad, 41

Paul, Prince of Yugoslavia, 389, 390
Paulewicz, Lieutenant, 545
Paulus, Field Marshal Friedrich, 57, 391, 440, 516, 631–32, 642, 644, 646–48, 652–53, 655, 657, 659, 661–63, 666–69
Pavlov, Soviet General Dmitry, 460, 465, 466
Peirse, British Air Marshal Sir Richard, 623
Pellengahr, Lieutenant General Richard, 250, 264, 265
Pendele, Luftwaffe Colonel Max, 450
Perth, Earl of, 148
Petain, French Marshal (later Premier) Henri Philippe, 320, 340, 341, 342, 345, 347, 379
Peter II, Yugoslavian King, 390
Petiet, French Lieutenant General Robert, 335, 337
Petzel, General of Artillery Walter, 209, 214, 216
Pflugbeil, General of Fliers Kurt, 89, 360
Philip, Prince of Hesse, 120
Pickert, General of Flak Artillery Wolfgang, 662
Pierlot, Belgian Prime Minister Hubert, 316
Pilsudski, Polish Marshal Jozef, 32
Piskor, Polish Major General Tadeusz, 209, 216
Plocher, Luftwaffe Lieutenant General Hermann, 96, 158
Poetsch, Dr. Leopold, 596
Pogrell, General of Cavalry Guenther von, 111
Pohl, General of SS Oswald, 540, 589, 592, 610
Pohlman, Lieutenant Colonel, 259
Ponath, Lieutenant Colonel Gustav, 434, 435
Popitz, Prussian Minister of Finance Johannes, 136
Popov, Soviet General Markian M., 475
Portes, Mademoiselle de, 314

Pound, Admiral of the Fleet Sir Dudley, 261
Pretelat, French General Andre, 286, 335, 341, 343
Prien, Naval Lieutenant Guenther, 236, 237, 374, 375, 613, 614
Prioux, French General Rene, 301, 302
Prittwitz und Gaffron, Major General Heinrich von, 433, 434
Pruetzmanni, General of Police Adolf, 535–36
Puttick, New Zealand Brigadier Edward, 407
Putzier, General of Fliers Richard, 146

Quisling, Norwegian Minister President Vidkum, 245

Radom Pocket, Battle of, 208
Raeder, Grand Admiral Erich, 21, 26, 38–39, 102–4, 114, 130, 159–60, 162, 173, 176, 178, 237, 240, 245, 249, 262, 264, 268–69, 271, 345, 356, 378–79, 422–24, 428–29, 557, 617–18
Ramcke, General of Paratroopers Hermann Bernard, 414, 537
Ramsay, British Admiral Sir Bertram H., 328
Randow, Major General Hans von, 576
Rasch, Naval Lieutenant Hermann, 619
Rasch, SS Lieutenant General Dr. Otto, 531, 539
Rauff, SS Lieutenant Colonel Walter, 611
Ravenstein, Lieutenant General Johannes von, 436, 546, 552
Reichel, Major Joachim, 641
Reichenau, Field Marshal Walter von, 23–26, 29–30, 39, 56, 65, 70, 105–6, 109, 134, 144, 146, 150, 190, 203, 228–29, 273, 280, 285, 291–93, 300–301, 316, 326, 328–29, 333, 336, 338, 340, 354, 444–45, 481–84, 515–17, 519, 536–39, 652, 661–62

Reich Labor Service (RAD), 62, 75–77, 133, 157, 185
Reichsheer, 9
Reichsmarine, 9
Reichswehr, 9, 27
Reid, British Major General Dennis, 550
Reinberger, Major Hellmuth, 276–77
Reinecke, General of Infantry Hermann, 113
Reinhardt, Colonel General Georg-Hans, 206, 224, 278–79, 285, 303–4, 306, 317, 319, 334, 341, 392, 396–97, 462–63, 476, 478, 489–90, 494, 498, 506, 508, 510, 512
Reinhardt, General of Infantry Hans, 392
Reinhardt, General Walter, 10, 13, 14
Rendulic, Colonel General Dr. Lothar, 124
Renthe-Fink, Ambassador Cecil von, 256
Requin, French General Edouard-Jean, 286, 288, 335
Reynaud, French Premier, 254, 288, 314, 317, 320, 339, 340, 341, 343
Ribbentrop, Foreign Minister Joachim von, 27, 36, 48, 66, 112, 127, 129–30, 151–52, 166–68, 171–73, 175, 178–79, 229, 345, 376–78, 389–90, 400, 531
Ribstein, Major General Hugo, 504
Richthofen, Lieutenant Baron Lothar von, 97
Richthofen, Captain Baron Manfred von (the "Red Baron"), 97, 98
Richthofen, Luftwaffe Field Marshal Baron Wolfram von, 93, 96–99, 199–200, 211–12, 286, 301, 308–10, 326, 354, 360–62, 389, 394–95, 408, 414–15, 462, 474, 633–34, 644, 648, 651, 654, 658, 660
Riege, Admiral Dr. Hans-Releff, 428
Ringel, General of Mountain Troops Julius, 410, 414, 416, 417
Rintelen, General of Infantry Enno von, 566

Ritchie, British General Sir Neil M., 551, 552, 559, 561, 562, 564, 567
Rodrique, Belgian Captain, 277
Roehm, Ernst, SA Leader, 25, 27, 28, 42, 588
Roessler, Rudolf, 490, 91
Roettig, General of Infantry Otto, 250, 256
Rogge, Vice Admiral Berhard, 421
Rokossovsky, Soviet General Konstantin K., 667
Rommel, Field Marshal Erwin, 16, 79, 189, 304–6, 315, 317, 323, 385, 405, 407, 418, 431–36, 439, 543–55, 557–73, 575–76, 578, 580–81, 663
Rommel, Polish Lieutenant General Juluisz K. W. J., 212, 213, 217
Roosevelt, Franklin D., 341, 353, 372–73, 377, 499, 618, 621
Roques, General of Infantry Karl von, 537
Rosenberg, Minister of Eastern Territories Alfred, 468
Rothenburg, Major General Karl, 305, 324, 336
Rowland, British Commander James, 613–14
Rudel, Luftwaffe Colonel Hans-Ulrich, 657
Ruedel, Luftwaffe Colonel General Guenther, 112
Ruge, Norwegian General Otto, 268, 271
Rundstedt, Field Marshal Gerd von, 64, 70, 106, 109, 112, 134, 139, 144–46, 150, 155, 163, 177, 188, 190, 203–4, 207–8, 213, 227–29, 273, 275–76, 278–79, 285, 303, 318, 326–28, 333, 339–41, 346, 354, 444–45, 474, 481, 487, 515–16, 537, 646, 663
Ruoff, Colonel General Rudolf, 501, 506, 510, 512, 642, 645
Rychagov, Soviet Lieutenant General Pavel, 460
Rydz-Smigly, Polish Marshal Edward, 193, 204, 205, 210, 216–17

General Index

SA (Sturmabteilung or Storm Troopers), 23, 24, 26, 31, 40, 62, 585

Saalwaechter, Generaladmiral Alfred, 250, 268

Salmuth, General of Infantry Hans von, 538, 643

Sassen, Corporal Bruno, 506

Schaal, General of Panzer Troops Ferdinand, 201, 202, 216, 306, 307, 314, 499, 546

Schacht, Minister of Economics Dr. Hjalmar, 84, 136, 137, 138, 188, 229, 529

Schaffstein, Corporal, 666

Scharnhorst, Prussian General Johann von, 2

Scharroo, Dutch Colonel, 298, 300

Scheel, Lieutenant, 505

Scheidies, Major General Franz, 504

Schellenberg, SS General Walter, 491, 531, 627

Schenckendorff, General of Infantry Max, 224

Schepke, Naval Lieutenant Joachim, 375, 614

Scherber, Luftwaffe Major, 411

Scherer, Lieutenant General Theodor, 521, 525

Schilhausky, Austrian General Sigmund, 124

Schindler, Lieutenant General Max, 605

Schirach, Hitler Youth Leader Baldur von, 157

Schirach, Henrietta von, 530

Schleicher, Frau Elisabeth von, 29

Schleicher, Chancellor/General of Infantry Kurt von, 19, 22, 24, 28–29, 138

Schlieffen, General Count Alfred von, 6, 7, 49, 50, 281

Schloemer, Lieutenant General Hellmut, 668

Schmid, Luftwaffe Lieutenant General Joseph "Beppo," 362, 363, 368, 456

Schmidt, Major General Arthur, 661, 662

Schmidt, Ernst, 347

Schmidt, Paul, 48, 65, 130

Schmidt, Colonel General Rudolf, 114, 204, 224, 296, 298–300, 339, 477–79, 498, 505, 514

Schmitt, Lieutenant General Artur, 553

Schmundt, General of Infantry Rudolf, 114, 131, 176, 278, 307, 500, 501, 582, 646

Schneider, Commander Adalbert, 428

Schniewind, Generaladmiral Otto, 176, 268

Schnittger, Sergeant, 500

Schobert, Colonel General Ritter Eugen von, 112, 119, 120, 145, 354, 445, 481, 483, 517, 664

Schoengarth, SS Oberfuehrer Dr. Karl, 597

Schroth, General of Infantry Walter, 112, 145

Schuetze, Naval Lieutenant Victor, 261

Schuhart, Naval Lieutenant Otto, 235

Schulenburg, Count Fritz-Dietlof von der, 140, 229

Schulenburg, Count Werner von der, 140, 178, 179, 376, 388

Schulz, Lieutenant Commander Georg-Wilhelm, 375

Schulze, Naval Lieutenant Herbert, 261

Schuschnigg, Austrian Prime Minister Kurt von, 65, 118, 120, 121

Schwartzkorp, Luftwaffe Colonel Guenther, 343

Schweickhard, Luftwaffe Major General Karl, 82

Schwelder, General of Infantry Victor von, 57, 111, 112, 145, 156, 208, 301, 654

Schwerin, General of Panzer Troops Count Gerhard, 435

Scobie, British Lieutenant General Ronald M., 548, 549

Seeckt, General Hans von, 9, 10, 13, 15, 17, 18, 19, 22, 50, 52, 81

Seidel, General of Fliers Hans-Georg von, 669, 670
Seidemann, General of Fliers Hans, 96–97
Seraphim, Professor Peter, 584–85
Seutter von Loetzen, General of Infantry Baron Hans, 143, 135, 145
Seybold, Luftwaffe Colonel, 211
Seydlitz-Kurzbach, General of Artillery Walter von, 519, 524, 662, 663, 668
Seyss-Inquart, Austrian Prime Minister Dr. Arthur, 118, 120, 121, 123
Sidor, Slovakian Provincial Premier Karol, 166, 167
Siedlecki, Joe, 607
Simon, British Foreign Secretary Sir John, 43, 44
Simovic, Yugoslavian Prime Minister and Air Force General Dusan, 390
Skubi, Dr. Michael, 120
Soddu, Italian General Ubaldo, 381
Sodenstern, General of Infantry Georg, 376
Somerville, British Vice Admiral Sir John, 426
Sommers, SS Master Sergeant, 591
Sorge, Dr. Richard, 454, 490
Spaak, Belgian Foreign Minister Paul-Henri, 278, 316
Spaatz, U.S. Air Force General Carl, 628
Speck, General of Artillery Ritter Hermann von, 224, 342
Speer, Albert, 347
Speidel, General of Fliers Wilhelm, 200, 203, 211, 277
Sperrle, Luftwaffe Field Marshal Hugo, 37, 93–96, 98, 112, 120, 146, 200, 277, 286, 309, 334, 354, 359–60, 363–65, 368, 447
Sponeck, Lieutenant General Count Hans, 294–96, 300, 517, 519
Sponeck, Lieutenant General Count Theodor, 576
Sporrenberg, SS Lieutenant General Jacob, 610

Stahlecker, SS Major General Franz, 531, 532, 535, 536, 537, 539
Stalin, Joseph, 175, 178, 376–77, 387–88, 390, 451–55, 460–61, 470, 477, 483–84, 486, 488, 490–92, 499–500, 502, 515, 522, 539, 631–32, 638, 644, 648, 651, 653–54, 665–66
Stangl, SS Captain Franz, 606, 610
Starzynski, Stefan, Mayor of Warsaw, 205
Stauffenberg, Berthold von, 136
Stauffenberg, Colonel Count Claus von, 72, 73, 519
Steinhoff, Luftwaffe Colonel Johannes, 461
Steinkeller, Major General Friedrich-Carl, 304, 321
Stemmermann, Lieutenant General Wilhelm, 505
Stentzler, Luftwaffe Major, 412
Strauch, SS Lieutenant Colonel Dr., 539
Strauss, Colonel General Adolf, 212, 334, 337, 354, 445, 465, 466, 487, 499, 506, 509
Strecker, General of Infantry Karl, 662, 668
Streich, Lieutenant General Johannes, 433, 434, 435, 437
Streicher, Gauleiter Julius, 468
Stresemann, Chancellor Gustav, 18
Stroop, SS Lieutenant General Juergen, 602
Stuckart, State Secretary Dr. Wilhelm, 123, 597
Student, Luftwaffe Colonel General Kurt, 16, 92, 144, 146, 294, 296–98, 300, 354, 406, 408, 413, 418
Studnitz, Lieutenant General Bogislav von, 341
Stuelpnagel, General of Infantry Carl-Heinrich von, 142, 229–30, 337, 348, 445, 481, 483–84, 489, 537
Stuelpnagel, General of Infantry Joachim von, 109
Stuelpnagel, General of Fliers/General of Infantry Otto von, 54, 56

Stumme, General of Panzer Troops Georg, 224, 392, 398, 400, 576, 577, 578, 641

Stumpff, Luftwaffe Colonel General Hans-Juergen, 89, 90, 92, 277, 359, 360, 364, 445

Stumpff, General of Panzer Troops Horst, 216

Stutterheim, Major General Wolf von, 342

Suemmermann, Major General Max, 546, 552

Suessmann, Luftwaffe Lieutenant General Wilhelm, 409, 410

Syrovy, Czechoslovakian General Jan, 151

Teege, Colonel Wilhelm, 579

Teske, Luftwaffe Lieutenant Colonel Werner, 93

Thiele, Vice Admiral August, 258

Thiele, Major General Fritz, 490

Thoma, General of Panzer Troops Ritter Wilhelm, 54, 204, 351, 484, 576, 577, 578, 580, 581

Thomalla, SS Lieutenant Colonel Richard, 601

Thomas, General of Infantry Georg, 113, 178, 188, 228, 229, 242, 585

Timoshenko, Soviet Marshal Semen, 451, 460, 461, 466, 473, 484, 515, 631

Tiso, Slovakian Premier Monsignor, 166, 167, 168

Tittel, General of Artillery Hermann, 250, 257

Todt, Minister of Munitions Dr. Fritz, 132–33, 178, 242

Topp, Lieutenant Commander Erich, 617, 618

Touchon, French Lieutenant General Robert, 288, 316, 317, 319, 335, 337

Toussaint, General of Infantry Rudolf, 396

Tovey, British Admiral Sir Charles, 424, 426, 427

Treschow, Major General Henning von, 229

Trotha, Admiral Alfred von, 13

Tsolakoglu, Greek Lieutenant General Georgias, 400, 403

Tyulenev, Soviet General F. V., 483

Udet, Luftwaffe Colonel General Ernst, 90, 91, 98, 99, 310, 357, 448, 449, 450, 628, 638, 649

Ulex, General of Artillery Wilhelm, 112, 145, 207

Ullrich, SS Lieutenant Colonel Karl, 506

Urbays, Lithuanian Foreign Minister Juozas, 173

Vaerst, General of Panzer Troops Gustav von, 557, 561, 562

Vasey, Australian Brigadier G. Alan., 407

Vashugin, Soviet Commissar Nikolai N., 461

Veiel, General of Panzer Troops Rudolf, 209, 306, 318, 398, 493, 494

Veith, Lieutenant General Richard, 552

Versailles, Treaty of, 9–11, 17, 18, 31, 35, 37, 47, 48, 59, 171, 227

Vian, British Admiral Philip, 247

Viebahn, Lieutenant General Max von, 113, 122

Vietinghoff, Colonel General Heinrich von, 107, 392, 396, 481, 502, 514

Villiers, South African Major General Isaac P. de, 550

Visconti-Prasca, Italian General Sebastiano, 281, 381

Vlasov, Soviet General Andrey A., 523, 525

Volkmann, General of Fliers Helmuth, 96

Vollard-Bockelberg, General of Artillery Alfred von, 54

Voroshilov, Soviet Marshal Kliment, 477

Vuillermin, General Joseph, 284

Wachenfeld, General of Fliers Edmund, 82, 111

Waeger, General of Infantry Alfred, 301

Wagner, General of Artillery Eduard, 220, 228, 530

Walsporn, Lieutenant General Maximilian von, 306, 338, 344

War Academy (Kriegsakademie), 9, 17, 40, 72, 75

Warburton-Lee, British Captain Bernard A. W., 260

Warlimont, General of Artillery Walter, 176, 249, 278, 379, 440, 456, 582, 646

Warning, Lieutenant Colonel Elmar, 580

Warsaw, Siege of, 201

Wassmuth, Colonel August-Heinrich, 504

Watkins, Major General Sir Harry R. B., 549

Wavell, British Field Marshal Sir Archibald, 384, 387, 389, 403, 405, 407, 416, 543, 547

Weckmar, Lieutenant General Baron von, 434

Wedemeyer, U.S. General Alfred C., 73–74

Wehr, Rear Admiral Oskar, 262

Weichs, Field Marshal Baron Maximilian von, 57, 120, 145, 207, 334, 339, 390, 391, 392, 396, 471, 474, 480, 487, 488, 491, 492, 498, 643, 652, 653, 654, 655, 657, 659, 663, 665, 669

Weise, Luftwaffe Colonel General Hubert, 286, 626

Weiss, Major General Wilhelm, 257

Weizsaecker, State Secretary Baron Ernst von, 130, 137, 140, 167, 173

Wenck, General of Panzer Troops Walter, 58

Weston, British Marine Major General Eric C., 407

Westphal, General of Cavalry Siegfried, 562, 580

West Wall (Siegfried Line), 132

Wetzel, General of Infantry Wilhelm, 79

Wetzell, General Wilhelm, 19

Wever, General of Fliers Walter, 81, 82, 83, 84, 85, 86–87, 89, 90, 94

Weygand, French General Maxime, 281, 320, 331, 334, 335, 336, 337, 338, 340, 341, 342, 346

Whitworth, British Vice Admiral William J., 260

Widmann, Dr. Albert, 598

Wietersheim. General of Infantry Gustav von, 101, 112, 135, 145, 208, 279, 285, 313, 316, 333, 392, 483, 648, 654

Wilberg, General of Fliers Helmut, 84, 111

Wilhelm, Crown Prince August Wilhelm "Auwi," 26

Wilhelm II, Kaiser, 1, 6

Wilson, British Brigadier A. C., 549

Wilson, British Field Marshal Sir Henry M. "Jumbo," 389, 394

Wimmer, General of Fliers Wilhelm, 84, 90, 93, 146, 200

Winkelmann, Dutch General Henri, 298, 300, 302

Winter, Lieutenant Commander Werner, 619

Wirth, SS Captain Christian, 599, 606, 610

Wittke, Lieutenant General Walter, 250

Witzig, Major Rudolf, 292

Witzleben, Field Marshal Erwin von, 44, 70, 138, 140, 152–53, 155, 190, 225–26, 229, 286, 334

Wodrig, General of Artillery Albert, 201, 209, 216, 296, 298, 299, 302, 354, 477

Wolff, General of SS Karl, 540

Wolff, General of Fliers Ludwig, 146

Woods, American Attache Sam E., 453

Woytasch, Lieutenant General Kurt, 250, 265

Yeremenko, Soviet General Andrei Ivanovich, 667

General Index

Zahn, Lieutenant Commander Wilhelm, 261

Zander, General of Fliers Konrad, 82

Zapp, Commander Richard, 619

Zehner, Austrian Minister of War General Wilhelm, 122

Zeitzler, Colonel General Kurt, 315, 517, 605, 646, 647, 658, 660, 661, 668

Zhukov, Soviet Marshal Georgi, 451, 461, 490, 492, 494, 497, 498, 512, 514

Zorn, General of Infantry Hans, 512, 524

About the Author

SAMUEL W. MITCHAM JR. is an internationally recognized authority on Nazi Germany and the Second World War and is the author twenty books on the subject, including *Panzers in Winter* (Praeger Security International, 2006), *Rommel's Lieutenants* (Praeger Security International, 2006), *Crumbling Empire* (Praeger, 2001), *Retreat to the Reich* (Praeger, 2000), and *The Desert Fox in Normandy* (Praeger, 1997). A former Army helicopter pilot and company commander, he is a graduate of the U.S. Army's Command and General Staff College. He has appeared on the History Channel and National Public Radio, among other media outlets.